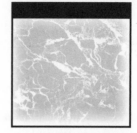

Testing Applications on the Web:
Test Planning for Mobile and Internet-Based Systems

Second Edition

Hung Q. Nguyen
Bob Johnson
Michael Hackett

WILEY

Wiley Publishing, Inc.

Executive Publisher: Robert Ipsen
Executive Editor: Carol Long
Development Editor: Scott Amerman
Editorial Manager: Kathryn A. Malm
Production Editor: Felicia Robinson
Text Design & Composition: Wiley Composition Services

Published by Wiley Publishing, Inc., Indianapolis, Indiana
Published simultaneously in Canada

For general information on our other products and services please contact our Customer Care Department within the United States at (800) 762-2974, outside the United States at (317) 572-3993 or fax (317) 572-4002.

Wiley also publishes its books in a variety of electronic formats. Some content that appears in print may not be available in electronic books.

Library of Congress Cataloging-in-Publication Data:

ISBN: 0-471-20100-6

Printed in the United States of America

10 9 8 7 6 5 4 3 2 1

To Heather, Wendy, Denny, Leilani, Jesse and Anne, whose love and friendship give me the endless source of energy and happiness.

Hung Q. Nguyen

To Victoria, for all the advice, help, support, and love she has given me.

Bob Johnson

To Ron, from whom I have stolen much time to make this book happen. Thank you for your love and support.

Michael Hackett

Contents

Preface

Testing Applications on the Web introduces the essential technologies, testing concepts, and techniques that are associated with browser-based applications. It offers advice pertaining to the testing of business-to-business applications, business-to-end-user applications, Web portals, and other Internet-based applications. The primary audience is software testers, software quality engineers, quality assurance staff, test managers, project managers, IT managers, business and system analysts, and anyone who has the responsibility of planning and managing Web-application test projects.

Testing Applications on the Web begins with an introduction to the client-server and Web system architectures. It offers an in-depth exploration of Web application technologies such as network protocols, component-based architectures, and multiple server types from the testing perspective. It then covers testing practices in the context of various test types from user interface tests to performance, load, and stress tests, and security tests. Chapters 1 and 2 present an overview of Web testing. Chapters 3 through 6 cover methodology and technology basics, including a review of software testing basics, a discussion on networking, an introduction to component-based testing, and an overview of the mobile device platform. Chapters 7 through 9 discuss testing planning fundamentals, a sample application to be used as an application under test (AUT) throughout the book, and a sample test plan. Chapters 10 through 20 discuss test types that can be applied to Web testing. Finally, Chapters 21 and 22 offer a survey of Web testing tools and suggest where to go for additional information.

Testing Applications on the Web answers testing questions such as, "How do networking hardware and software affect applications under test?" "What are Web application components, and how do they affect my testing strategies?"

"What is the role of a back-end database, and how do I test for database-related errors?" "How do I test server-side software?" "What are performance, stress, and load tests, and how do I plan for and execute them?" "What do I need to know about security testing, and what are my testing responsibilities?" "What do I need to consider in testing mobile Web applications?"

With a combination of general testing methodologies and the information contained in this book, you will have the foundation required to achieve these testing goals—maximizing productivity and minimizing quality risks in a Web application environment.

Testing Applications on the Web assumes that you already have a basic understanding of software testing methodologies, including test planning, test-case design, and bug report writing. Web applications are complex systems that involve numerous components: servers, browsers, third-party software and hardware, protocols, connectivity, and much more. This book enables you to apply your existing testing skills to the testing of Web applications.

NOTE This book is not an introduction to software testing. If you are looking for fundamental software testing practices, you will be better served by reading *Testing Computer Software*, Second Edition, by Kaner, Cem, Jack Falk, and Hung Q. Nguyen (Wiley, 1999). For additional information on Web testing and other testing techniques and resources, visit www.QAcity.com.

We have enjoyed writing this book and teaching the Web application testing techniques that we use every day to test Web-based systems. We hope that you will find here the information you need to plan for and execute a successful testing strategy that enables you to deliver high-quality applications in an increasingly distributed-computing, market-driven, and time-constrained environment in this era of new technology.

Foreword

Writing about Web testing is challenging because the field involves the interdependence of so many different technologies and systems. It's not enough to write about the client. Certainly, the client software is the part of the application that is the most visible to the customer, and it's the easiest to write about (authors can just repackage the same old stuff published about applications in general. Hung, Michael, and Bob do provide client-side guidance, but their goal is to provide information that is specific to Web applications. (For more generic material, you can read *Testing Computer Software*, Second Edition, Wiley, 1999.)

But client-side software is just the tip of the iceberg. The application displays itself to the end user as the client, but it does most of its work in conjunction with other software on the server-side, much of it written and maintained by third parties. For example, the application probably stores and retrieves data via third-party databases. If it sells products or services, it probably clears customer orders with the customer's credit card company. It might also check its distributor for available inventory and its shippers for the cost of shipping the software to the customer. The Web application communicates with these third parties through network connections written by third parties. Even the user interface is only partially under the application developer's control—the customer supplies the presentation layer: the browser, the music and video player, and perhaps various other multimedia plug-ins.

The Web application runs on a broader collection of hardware and software platforms than any other type of application in history. Attributes of these platforms can change at any time, entirely outside of the knowledge or control of the Web application developer.

In *Testing Applications on the Web,* Nguyen, Hackett, and Johnson take this complexity seriously. In their view, a competent Web application tester must learn the technical details of the systems with which the application under test interacts. To facilitate this, they survey many of those systems, explaining how applications interact with them and providing testing tips.

As a by-product of helping testers appreciate the complexity of the Web testing problem, the first edition of *Testing Applications on the Web* became the first book on gray-box testing. In so-called black-box testing, we treat the software under test as a black box. We specify the inputs, we look at the outputs, but we can't see inside the box to see how it works. The black-box tester operates at the customer's level, basing tests on knowledge of how the system *should* work. In contrast, the white-box tester knows the internals of the software, and designs tests with direct reference to the program's source code. The gray-box tester doesn't have access to the source code, but he or she knows much more about the underlying architecture and the nature of the interfaces between the application under test and the other software and the operating systems.

The second edition continues the gray-box analysis by deepening the discussions in the first edition. It also adds several new chapters to address business-critical testing issues from server-side, performance- and application-level security testing to the latest mobile Web application testing. A final strength of the book is the power of the real-world example. Hung Quoc Nguyen is the president of the company that published TRACKGEAR, a Web-based bug tracking system, enabling the authors can give us the inside story of its development and testing.

This combination of a thorough and original presentation of a style of analysis, mixed with detailed insider knowledge is a real treat to read. It teaches us about thinking through the issues involved when the software under test interacts in complex ways with many other programs, and it gives the book a value that will last well beyond the specifics of the technologies described therein.

Cem Kaner, J.D., Ph. D.
Professor of Computer Sciences
Florida Institute of Technology

Acknowledgments

While it is our names that appear on the cover, over the years, many people have helped with the development of this book. We want to particularly thank Brian Lawrence, for his dedication in providing thorough reviews and critical feedback. We all thank Cem Kaner for his guidance, friendship, and generosity, and for being there when we needed him. We thank, too, Jesse Watkins-Gibbs for his work on examples and sample code, as well as for his technical expertise and his commitment to getting our book done.

We would also like to thank our professional friends who took time out from their demanding jobs and lives to review and add comment on the book: Yannick Bertolus, George Hamblin, Elisabeth Hendrickson, Nematolah Kashanian, Pat McGee, Alberto Savoia, and Garrin Wong. We would like to thank our copyeditor Janice Borzendowski. We also want to thank the following people for their contributions (listed in alphabetical order): James L. Carr, William Coleman, Norm Hardy, Pam Hardy, Thomas Heinz, Chris Hibbert, Heather Ho, Brian Jones, Denny Nguyen, Kevin Nguyen, Wendy Nguyen, Steve Schuster, Kurt Thams, Anne Tran, Dean Tribble, and Joe Vallejo. Finally, we would like to thank our colleagues, students, and staff at LogiGear Corporation, for their discussions and evaluations of the Web testing training material, which made its way into this book. And thanks to our agent Claudette Moore of Moore Literacy Agency.

Certainly, any remaining errors in the book are ours.

About the Authors

Hung Q. Nguyen is Founder, President, and CEO of LogiGear Corporation. Nguyen has held leadership roles in business management, product development, business development, engineering, quality assurance, software testing, and information technology. Hung is an international speaker and a regular contributor to industry publications. He is the original architect of TRACK-GEAR, a Web-based defect management system. Hung also teaches software testing for the University of California at Berkeley and Santa Cruz Extension, and LogiGear University.

Hung is the author of *Testing Applications on the Web*, First Edition (Wiley 2000); and with Cem Kaner and Jack Falk, he wrote the best-selling book *Testing Computer Software* (ITP/Wiley 1993/1999). He holds a Bachelor of Science in Quality Assurance from Cogswell Polytechnical College, and is an ASQ-Certified Quality Engineer and a member of the Advisory Council for the Department of Applied Computing and Information Systems at UC Berkeley Extension.

You can reach Hung at hungn@logigear.com; or, to obtain more information about LogiGear Corporation and Hung's work, visit www.logigear.com.

Bob Johnson has been a software developer, tester, and manager of both development and testing organizations. With over 20 years of experience in software engineering, Bob has acquired key strengths in building applications on a variety of platforms. Bob's career in software development ranges from Web programming to consulting on legal aspects of e-commerce to the requirement and review process. Whether working in test automation, Web security, or back-end server testing, Bob is at the forefront of emerging technologies.

In addition to participating in the Los Altos Workshops on Software Testing (LAWST), Bob has written articles for *IEEE Software*, *Journal of Electronic Commerce*, and *Software Testing and Quality Engineering*. He can be reached at rjohnson@testingbook.com.

Michael Hackett is Vice President and a founding partner of LogiGear Corporation. He has over a decade of experience in software engineering and the testing of shrink-wrap and Internet-based applications. Michael has helped well-known companies release applications ranging from business productivity to educational multimedia titles, in English as well as a multitude of other languages. Michael has taught software testing for the University of California at Berkeley Extension, the Software Productivity Center in Vancouver, the Hong Kong Productivity Centre, and LogiGear University. Michael holds a Bachelor of Science in Engineering from Carnegie-Mellon University. He can be reached at michaelh@logigear.com.

Introduction

CHAPTER

1

Welcome to Web Testing

Why Read This Chapter?

The goal of this book is to help you effectively plan for and conduct the testing of Web-based applications developed for fixed clients, systems in fixed locations such as desktop computers, as well as for mobile clients such as mobile phones, PDAs (Personal Digital Assistants), and portable computers. This book will be more helpful to you if you understand the philosophy behind its design.

Software testing practices have been improving steadily over the past few decades. Yet, as testers, we still face many of the same challenges that we have faced for years. We are challenged by rapidly evolving technologies and the need to improve testing techniques. We are also challenged by the lack of research on how to test for and analyze software errors from their behavior, as opposed to at the source code level. We are challenged by the lack of technical information and training programs geared toward serving the growing population of the not-yet-well-defined software testing profession. Finally, we are challenged by limited executive management support as a result of management's underestimation and lack of attention to the cost of quality. Yet, in today's world of *Internet time,* the systems under test are getting more complex by the day, and resources and testing time are in short supply. The quicker we can get the information that we need, the more productive and more successful we will be at doing our job. The goal of this book is to help you do your job effectively.

TOPICS COVERED IN THIS CHAPTER

 ◆ **Introduction**

 ◆ **The Evolution of Software Testing**

 ◆ **The Gray-Box Testing Approach**

 ◆ **Real-World Software Testing**

 ◆ **Themes of This Book**

 ◆ **What's New in the Second Edition**

Introduction

This chapter offers a historical perspective on the changing objectives of software testing. It touches on the gray-box testing approach and suggests the importance of having a balance of product design, both from the designer's and the user's perspective, and system-specific technical knowledge. It also explores the value of problem analysis to determine what to test, when to test, and where to test. Finally, this chapter will discuss what assumptions this book has about the reader.

The Evolution of Software Testing

As the complexities of software development have evolved over the years, the demands placed on software engineering, information technology (IT), and software quality professionals have grown and taken on greater relevance. We are expected to check whether the software performs in accordance with its intended design and to uncover potential problems that might not have been anticipated in the design. We are expected to develop and execute more tests, faster, and more often. Test groups are expected to offer continuous assessment on the current state of the projects under development. At any given moment, we must be prepared to report explicit details of testing coverage and status, the health or stability of the current release, and all unresolved errors. Beyond that, testers are expected to act as user advocates. This often involves anticipating usability problems early in the development process so those problems can be addressed in a timely manner.

In the early years, on mainframe systems, many users were connected to a central system. Bug fixing involved patching or updating the centrally stored program. This single fix would serve the needs of hundreds or thousands of individuals who used the system.

As computing became more decentralized, minicomputers and microcomputers were run as stand-alone systems or on smaller networks. There were many independent computers or local area networks, and a patch to the code on one of these computers updated relatively fewer people. Mass-market software companies sometimes spent over a million dollars sending disks to registered customers just to fix a serious defect. Additionally, technical support costs skyrocketed.

As the market has broadened, more people use computers for more things and rely more heavily on computers, hence the consequences of software defects has risen every year. It is impossible to find all possible problems by testing, but as the cost of failure has gone up, it has become essential to do risk-based testing. In a risk-based approach, you ask questions like these:

- Which areas of the product are so significant to the customer or so prone to serious failure that they must be tested with extreme care?

- For the average area, and for the program as a whole, how much testing is enough?

- What are the risks involved in leaving a certain bug unresolved?

- Are certain components so unimportant as to not merit testing?

- At what point can a product be considered adequately tested and ready for market?

- How much longer can the product be delayed for testing and fixing bugs before the market viability diminishes the return on investment?

Tracking bugs, analyzing and assessing their significance are priorities. Management teams expect development and IT teams, testing and quality assurance staff, to provide quantitative data regarding test coverage, the status of unresolved defects, and the potential impact of deferring certain defects. To meet these needs, testers must understand the products and technologies they test. They need models to communicate assessments of how much testing has been done in a given product, how deep testing will go, and at what point the product will be considered adequately tested. Given better understanding of testing information, we make better predictions about quality risks.

In the era of the Internet, the connectivity that was lost when computing moved from the mainframe model to the personal computer (PC) model, in effect, has been reestablished. Personal computers are effectively networked over the Internet. Bug fixes and updated builds are made available—sometimes on a daily basis—for immediate download over the Internet. Product features that are not ready by ship date are made available later in *service packs*. The ability to distribute software over the Internet has brought down much of the cost that is associated with distributing some applications and their subsequent bug fixes.

Although the Internet offers connectivity for PCs, it does not offer the control over the client environment that was available in the mainframe model. The development and testing challenges with the Graphical User Interface (GUI) and event-based processing of the PC are enormous because the clients attempt remarkably complex tasks on operating systems (OSs) as different as UNIX, Macintosh OS, Linux, and the Microsoft OSs. They run countless combinations of processors, peripherals, and application software. Additionally, the testing of an enterprise client-server system may require the consideration of thousands of combinations of OSs, modems, routers, and client-server software components and packages. Web applications increase this complexity further by introducing browsers and Web servers into the mix. Furthermore, wireless networks are becoming more pervasive, and their bandwidths continue to improve. On the client-side, computer engineers continue to advance in building smaller, yet more powerful portable or mobile devices. Communication and wearable devices and Internet appliances are expanding the possible combinations of Web client environments beyond the desktop environments. On the server-side, software components that were normally located in a company's enterprise server are making their move toward the application services or Web services model. In this model, the components will be hosted outside of the corporate enterprise server, usually at the third-party ASPs (application service providers), adding more challenges to the testing of Internet-based systems.

Software testing plays a more prominent role in the software development process than ever before. Developers are paying more attention to building testability into their code, as well as coming up with more ways to improve the unit-test framework around their production code. Companies are allocating more money and resources for testing because they understand that their reputations and success rest on the quality of their products, or that their failure is more probable due to poor product and service quality. The competitiveness of the computing industry (not to mention the savvy of most computer users) has eliminated most tolerance for buggy software. Nevertheless, many companies believe that the only way to compete in *Internet time* is to develop software as rapidly as possible. Short-term competitive issues often outweigh quality issues. One consequence of today's accelerated development schedules is the industry's tendency to push software out into the marketplace as early as possible. Development teams get less and less time to design, code, test, and undertake process improvements. Market constraints and short development cycles often do not allow time for reflection on past experience and consideration of more efficient ways to produce and test software.

The Gray-Box Testing Approach

Black-box testing focuses on software's external attributes and behavior. Such testing looks at an application's expected behavior from the user's point of view. White-box testing (also known as glass-box testing), on the other end of the spectrum, tests software with knowledge of internal data structures, physical logic flow, and architecture at the source code level. White-box testing looks at testing from the developer's point of view. Both black-box and white-box testing are critically important complements of a complete testing effort. Individually, they do not allow for balanced testing. Black-box testing can be less effective at uncovering certain error types, such as data-flow errors or boundary condition errors at the source level. White-box testing does not readily highlight macro-level quality risks in operating environment, compatibility, time-related errors, and usability.

Gray-box testing incorporates elements of both black-box and white-box testing. It considers the outcome on the user end, system-specific technical knowledge, and operating environment. It evaluates application design in the context of the *interoperability* of system components. The gray-box testing approach is integral to the effective testing of Web applications because Web applications comprise numerous components, both software and hardware. These components must be tested in the context of system design to evaluate their functionality and compatibility.

In our view, gray-box testing consists of methods and tools derived from the knowledge of the application internals and the environment with which it interacts. The knowledge of the designer's intended logic can be applied in test design and bug analysis to improve the probability of finding and reproducing bugs. See Chapter 5, "Web Application Components," the section entitled "Testing Discussion," for an example of gray-box testing methods.

Here are several unofficial definitions for gray-box testing from the Los Altos Workshop on Software Testing (LAWST) IX. (For more information on LAWST, visit www.kaner.com.)

Gray-box testing—Using inferred or incomplete structural or design information to expand or focus black-box testing. —Dick Bender

Gray-box testing—Tests designed based on the knowledge of algorithms, internal states, architectures, or other high-level descriptions of program behavior. —Doug Hoffman

Gray-box testing—Tests involving inputs and outputs; but test design is educated by information about the code or the program operation of a kind that would normally be out of scope of the view of the tester. —Cem Kaner

Gray-box testing is well suited for Web application testing because it factors in high-level design, environment, and interoperability conditions. It will reveal problems that are not as easily considered by a black-box or white-box analysis, especially problems of end-to-end information flow and distributed hardware/software system configuration and compatibility. Context-specific errors that are germane to Web systems are commonly uncovered in this process.

Another point to consider is that many of the types of errors that we run into in Web applications might well be discovered by black-box testers, if only we had a better model of the types of failures for which to look and design tests. Unfortunately, we are still developing a better understanding of the risks that are associated with the new application and communication architectures. Therefore, the wisdom of traditional books on testing (e.g., *Testing Computer Software*, 2nd ed., John Wiley & Sons, Inc. (1999), by Kaner, Falk, and Nguyen and *Lessons Learned in Software Testing*, John Wiley & Sons, Inc. (2002), by Kaner, Bach, and Pettichord) will not fully prepare the black-box tester to search for these types of errors. If we are equipped with a better understanding of the system as a whole, we'll have an advantage in exploring the system for errors and in recognizing new problems or new variations of older problems.

As testers, we get ideas for test cases from a wide range of knowledge areas. This is partially because testing is much more effective when we know and model after the types of bugs we are looking for. We develop ideas of what might fail, and of how to find and recognize such a failure, from knowledge of many types of things [e.g., knowledge of the application and system architecture, the requirements and use of this type of application (domain expertise), and software development and integration]. As testers of complex systems, we should strive to attain a broad balance in our knowledge, learning enough about many aspects of the software and systems being tested to create a battery of tests that can challenge the software as deeply as it will be challenged in the rough and tumble of day-to-day use.

Finally, we are not suggesting that *every* tester in a group be a gray-box tester. We have seen a high level of success in several test teams that have a mix of different types of testers, with different skill sets (e.g., subject matter expert, database expert, security expert, API testing expert, test automation expert, etc.). The key is, within that mix, for at least some of the testers to understand the system as a collection of components that can fail in their interaction with each other, and these individuals must understand how to control and how to see those interactions in the testing and production environments.

Real-World Software Testing

Web businesses have the potential to be high-profit ventures. In the dot-com era, venture capitalists could support a number of losing companies as long as they had a few winners to make up for their losses. A CEO has three to five years to get a start-up ready for IPO (six months to prove that the prototype works, one or two years to generate some revenue—hence, justifying the business model—and the remainder of the time to show that the business can be profitable someday). It is always a challenge to find enough time and qualified personnel to develop and deliver quality products in such a fast-paced environment.

Although standard software development methodologies such as Capability Maturity Model (CMM) and ISO-9000 have been available, they are not yet well accepted by aggressive start-up companies. These standards and methods are great practices, but the fact remains that many companies will rely on the efforts of a skilled development and testing staff, rather than a process that they fear might slow them down. In that situation, no amount of improved standards and process efficiencies can make up for the efforts of a skilled development and testing staff. That is, given the time and resource constraints, they still need to figure out how to produce quality software.

The main challenge that we face in Web application testing is to learn the associated technologies in order to have a better command over the environment. We need to know how Web technologies affect the interoperability of software components, as well as Web systems as a whole. Testers also need to know how to approach the testing of Web-based applications. This requires being familiar with test types, testing issues, common software errors, and the quality-related risks that are specific to Web applications. We need to learn, and we need to learn fast. Only with a solid understanding of software testing basics and a thorough knowledge of Web technologies can we competently test Web-based systems.

The era of high-profit dot-com ventures has ended. Many businesses based on the dot-com model have closed their doors. The NASDAQ Stock Exchange within three years of March 2000, from its best performance of above 5,000 points, has dropped to as low as 1,100. We have learned many great and painful business lessons from this era, but unfortunately, not many quality-related lessons. However, the good news is, in a difficult economic time, the market demand is low, hence customers are in control. They want to pay less money for more, and demand higher-quality products and services. Bugs left in the product could mean anything from high support costs to loss of sales to contract cancellation. That is money loss that companies can normally absorb during the good economic times, but not in the bad times. We have seen many movements and initiatives in which executive staffs are paying more attention and asking more interesting quality-related questions. They are asking questions like, "How can we produce better software (higher-quality), faster (improve time-to-market) at a lower cost (lower production and quality costs)?" While this type of question has been asked before, executive staffs now have more time to listen and are more willing to support the QA effort. It also means a lot more demand is placed on testing, which requires QA staff to be more skilled in testing strategy, better educated in software engineering and technology, better equipped with testing practices, and savvier in the concept and application of software testing tools.

Themes of This Book

The objective of this book is to introduce testers into the discipline of gray-box testing, by offering readers information about the interplay of Web applications, component architectural designs, and their network systems. We expect that this will help testers develop new testing ideas, enabling them to uncover and troubleshoot new types of errors and conduct more effective root-cause analyses of software failures discovered during testing or product use. The discussions in this book focus on determining what to test, where to test, and when to test. As appropriate, real-world testing experiences and examples of errors are included.

To effectively plan and execute the testing of your Web application, you need to possess the following qualities: good software testing skill; knowledge of your application, which you will need to provide; knowledge of Web technologies; understanding of the types of tests and their applicability to Web application; knowledge of several types of Web application-specific errors (so you know what to look for); and knowledge of some of the available tools and their applicability, which this book offers you. (See Figure 1.1.)

Based on this knowledge and skill set, you can analyze the testing requirements to come up with an effective plan for your test execution. If this is what you are looking for, this book is for you. It is assumed that you have a solid grasp of standard software testing practices and procedures.

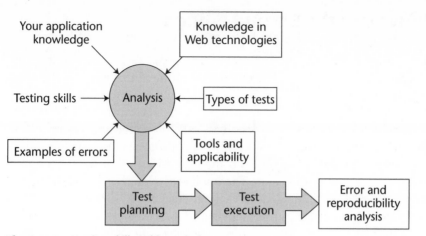

Figure 1.1 Testing skill and knowledge.

TESTER RESPONSIBILITIES

- Identifying high-risk areas that should be focused on in test planning
- Identifying, analyzing, and reproducing errors effectively within Web environments (which are prone to multiple environmental and technological variables)
- Capitalizing on existing errors to uncover more errors of the same class, or related classes

To achieve these goals, you must have high-level knowledge of Web environments and an understanding of how environmental variables affect the testing of your project. The information and examples included in this book will help you to do just that.

There is one last thing to consider before reading on. Web applications are largely platform-transparent. However, most of the testing and error examples included in this book are based on Microsoft technologies. This allows us to draw heavily on a commercial product for real examples. While Hung was writing the first edition of this book, his company was developing TRACK-GEAR, a Web-based bug-tracking solution that relies on Microsoft Web technologies. As the president of that company, Hung laid out the engineering issues that were considered in the design and testing of the product that testing authors cannot normally reveal (because of nondisclosure contracts) about software that they have developed or tested. Our expectation, however, is that the testing fundamentals should apply to technologies beyond Microsoft.

What's New in the Second Edition

Much has changed since the first edition of this book. Technology in the digital world continues to move at a fast pace. At the time of this writing, the economy has gone into a recession (at least in the United States, if not elsewhere), which has lead to the demand of less buggy products and services. Consequently, there has been a more widespread call for better and faster testing methods. The second edition of *Testing Web Applications* is our opportunity to make improvements and corrections on the first edition that have been suggested by our readers over the years. The book is also enjoying the addition of the two co-authors, Bob Johnson and Michael Hackett, who bring with them much experience in Web testing strategies and practices, as well as training expertise, which help elevate the usefulness of the contents to the next level.

New Contents and Significant Updates

- A new chapter, entitled "Mobile Web Application Platform" (Chapter 6), that covers mobile Web application model, exploring the technological similarities and differences between a desktop and a mobile Web system. The chapter provides the Web mobile technology information necessary to prepare you for developing test plans and strategies for this new mobile device platform. There will also be a more in-depth discussion in a follow-up chapter, entitled "Testing Mobile Web Applications" (Chapter 20).

- A new chapter, entitled "Testing Mobile Web Applications" (Chapter 20), covers experience-based information that you can use in the development of test strategies, test plans, and test cases for mobile Web applications. This is the companion to Chapter 6.

- A new chapter, entitled "Using Scripts to Test" (Chapter 13), covers the use of scripts to execute tests, to help you analyze your test results, and to help you set up and clean up your system and test data.

- A new chapter, entitled "Server-Side Testing" (Chapter 12), covers both the testing of the application servers and testing the server side of the applications function that may never be accessible through the client.

- The first-edition Chapter 16, entitled "Performance, Load and Stress Tests," comprising much of current Chapter 19 ("Performance Testing"), has been significantly updated with new information and tips on how to effectively design, plan for, and deploy performance related tests.

- The first-edition Chapter 15, entitled "Web Security Concerns," now entitled "Web Security Testing," and comprising much of current Chapter 18, has been significantly updated with new information on common software and Web sites vulnerabilities and tips on how to test for software-specific security bugs.

What Remains from the First Edition

- We have worked hard to keep the organizational layout that was well received by the first-edition readers intact.

- We continue our commitment to offering the technology-related information that has the most impact to testers in the clear and pleasant-to-read writing style, with plenty of visuals.

- QACity.Com will continue to be the Internet resource for busy testers, tracking all the Internet links referenced in this book. Given that the Internet changes by the minute, we expect that some of the links referenced will be outdated at some point. We are committed to updating QACity.Com on an ongoing basis to ensure that the information is there and up-to-date when you need it.

CHAPTER

2

Web Testing versus Traditional Testing

Why Read This Chapter?

Web technologies require new testing and bug analysis methods. It is assumed that you have experience in testing applications in traditional environments; what you may lack, however, is the means to apply your experience to Web environments. To effectively make such a transition, you need to understand the technology and architecture differences between traditional testing and Web testing.

TOPICS COVERED IN THIS CHAPTER

- ◆ **Introduction**
- ◆ **The Application Model**
- ◆ **Hardware and Software Differences**
- ◆ **The Differences between Web and Traditional Client-Server Systems**
- ◆ **Web Systems**
- ◆ **Bug Inheritance**

(continued)

Introduction

This chapter presents the application model and shows how it applies to mainframes, PCs, and, ultimately, Web/client-server systems. It explores the technology differences between mainframes and Web/client-server systems, as well as the technology differences between PCs and Web/client-server systems. Testing methods that are suited to Web environments are also discussed.

Although many traditional software testing practices can be applied to the testing of Web-based applications, there are numerous technical issues that are specific to Web applications that need to be considered.

The Application Model

A computer system, which consists of hardware and software, can receive *inputs* from the user, then *stores* them somewhere, whether in volatile memory such as RAM (Random Access Memory), or in nonvolatile memory, such as hard disk memory. It can execute the instructions given by software by performing *computation* using the CPU (Central Processing Unit) computing power. Finally, it can process the *outputs* back to the user. Figure 2.1 illustrates how humans interact with computers. Through a user interface (UI), users interact with an application by offering input and receiving output in many different forms: query strings, database records, text forms, and so on. Applications take input, along with requested logic rules, and store them in memory, and then manipulate data through computing; they also perform file reading and writing (more input/output and data storing). Finally, output results are passed back to the user through the UI. Results may also be sent to other output devices, such as printers.

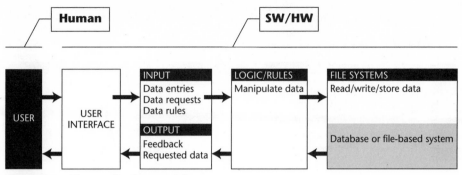

Figure 2.1   The application model.

In traditional mainframe systems, as illustrated in Figure 2.2, all of an application's processes, except for UI controls, occur on the mainframe computer. User interface controls take place on dumb terminals that simply echo text from the mainframe. Little computation or processing occurs on the terminals themselves. The network connects the dumb terminals to the mainframe. Dumb-terminal UIs are text-based or form-based (nongraphical). Users send data and commands to the system via keyboard inputs.

Desktop PC systems, as illustrated in Figure 2.3, consolidate all processes—from UI through rules to file systems—on a single physical box. No network is required for a desktop PC. Desktop PC applications can support either a text-based UI (command-line) or a Graphical User Interface (GUI). In addition to keyboard input events, GUI-based applications also support mouse input events such as click, double-click, mouse-over, drag-and-drop, and so on.

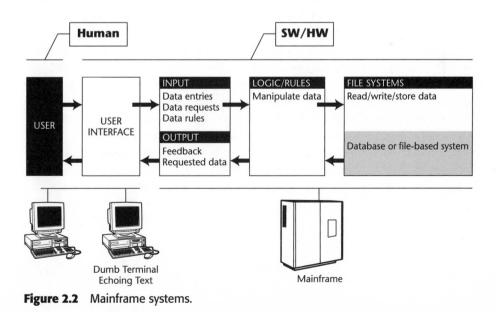

Figure 2.2   Mainframe systems.

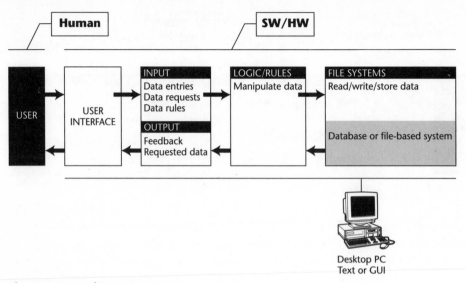

Figure 2.3   Desktop PC systems.

Client-server systems, upon which Web systems are built, require a network and at least two machines to operate: a *client* computer and a *server* computer, which serves requested data to the client computer. With the vast majority of Web applications, a Web browser serves as the UI container on the client computer.

The server receives input requests from the client and manipulates the data by applying the application's *business logic rules*. Business logic rules are the computations that an application is designed to carry out based on user input—for example, sales tax might be charged to any e-commerce customer who enters a California mailing address. Another example might be that customers over age 35 who respond to a certain online survey will be mailed a brochure automatically. This type of activity may require reading or writing to a database. Data is sent back to the client as output from the server. The results are then formatted and displayed in the client browser.

The client-server model, and consequently the Web application model, is not as neatly segmented as that of the mainframe and the desktop PC. In the client-server model, not only can either the client or the server handle some of the processing work, but server-side processes can be divided between multiple physical boxes or computers (application server, Web server, database server, etc.). Figure 2.4, one of many possible client-server models, depicts I/O and logic rules handled by an *application server* (the server in the center), while a *database server* (the server on the right) handles data storage. The dotted lines in the illustration indicate processes that may take place on either the client-side or the server-side. See Chapter 5, "Web Application Components," for information regarding server types.

A Web system may comprise any number of physical server boxes, each handling one or more service types. Later in this chapter, Table 2.1 illustrates some of the possible three-box server configurations. Note that the example is relatively a basic system. A Web system may contain multiple Web servers, application servers, and multiple database servers (such as a *server farm*, a grouping of similar server types that share workload). Web systems may also include other server types, such as e-mail servers, chat servers, e-commerce servers, and user profile servers (see Chapter 5 for more information). Understanding how your Web application-under-test is structured is invaluable for bug analysis—trying to reproduce a bug or learning how you can find more bugs similar to the one that you are seeing.

Keep in mind that it is software, not hardware, that defines clients and servers. Simply put, clients are software programs that request services from other software programs on behalf of users. Servers are software programs that offer services. Additionally, *client-server* is also an overloaded term; it is only useful from the perspective of describing a system. A server may, and often does, become a client in the chain of requests. In addition, the server-side may include many applications and systems including mainframe systems.

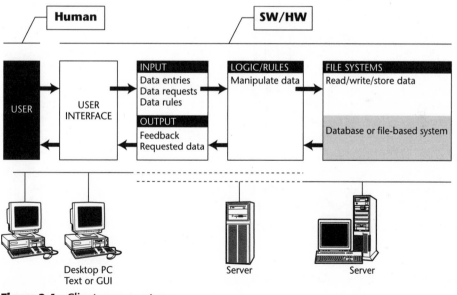

Figure 2.4   Client-server systems.

Hardware and Software Differences

Mainframe systems (Figure 2.5) are traditionally *controlled* environments, meaning that hardware and software are primarily supported (it does not necessarily mean that all the subcomponents are produced by the same company), end to end, by the same manufacturer. A mainframe with a single operating system, and applications sold and supported by the same manufacturer, can serve multiple terminals from a central location. Compatibility issues are more manageable compared to the PC and client-server systems.

A single desktop PC system consists of mixed hardware and software—multiple hardware components built and supported by different manufacturers, multiple operating systems, and nearly limitless combinations of software applications. Configuration and compatibility issues become difficult or almost impossible to manage in this environment.

A Web system consists of many clients, as well as server hosts (computers). The system's various flavors of hardware components and software applications begin to multiply. The server-side of Web systems may also support a mixture of software and hardware and, therefore, are more complex than mainframe systems, from the configuration and compatibility perspectives. See Figure 2.6 for an illustration of a client-server system running on a local area network (LAN).

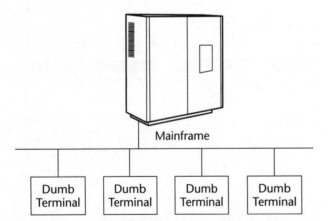

Figure 2.5   Controlled hardware and software environment.

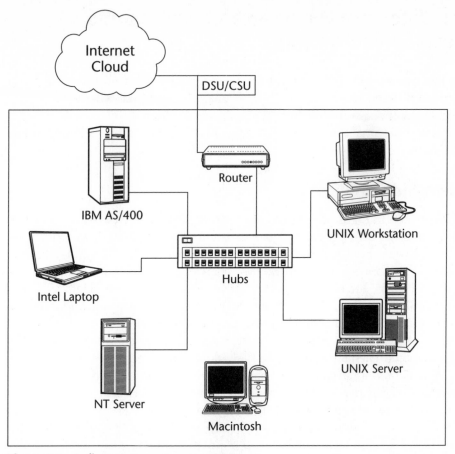

Figure 2.6   A client-server system on a LAN.

The GUI of the PC makes multiple controls available on screen at any given time (e.g., menus, pull-down lists, help screens, pictures, and command buttons.). Consequently, event-driven browsers (in event-driven model, inputs are driven by events such as a mouse click or a keypress on the keyboard) are also produced, taking advantage of the event-handling feature offered by the operating system (OS). However, event-based GUI applications (data input coupled with events) are more difficult to test. For example, each event applied to a control in a GUI may affect the behavior of other controls. Also, special dependencies can exist between GUI screens; interdependencies and constraints must be identified and tested accordingly.

The Differences between Web and Traditional Client-Server Systems

The last two sections point out the application architecture and hardware and software differences among the mainframe, PC, and Web/client-server systems. We will begin this section by exploring additional differences between Web and traditional systems so that appropriate testing considerations can be formulated.

Client-Side Applications

As illustrated in Figure 2.7, most client-server systems are data-access-driven applications. A client typically enables users, through the UI, to send input data, receive output data, and interact with the back end (for example, sending a query command). Clients of traditional client-server systems are platform-specific. That is, for each supported client operating system (e.g., Windows 16- and 32-bit, Solaris, Linux, Macintosh, etc.), a client application will be developed and tested for that target operating system.

Most Web-based systems are also data-access-driven applications. The browser-based clients are designed to handle similar activities to those supported by a traditional client. The main difference is that the Web-based client is operating within the Web browser's environment. Web browsers consist of operating system-specific client software running on a client computer. It renders HyperText Markup Language (HTML), as well as active contents, to display Web page information. Several popular browsers also support active content such as client-side scripting, Java applet, ActiveX control, eXtensible Markup Language (XML), cascading style sheet (CSS), dynamic HTML (DHTML), security features, and other goodies. To do this, browser vendors must create rendering engines and interpreters to translate and format HTML contents. In making these software components, various browsers and their releases introduce incompatibility issues. See Chapter 10, "User Interface Tests," and Chapter 17, "Configuration and Compatibility Tests," for more information.

From the Web application producer's perspective, there is no need to develop operating-system-specific clients since the browser vendors have already done that (e.g., Netscape, Microsoft, AOL, etc.). In theory, if your HTML contents are designed to conform to HTML 4 standard, your client application should run properly in any browser that supports HTML 4 standard from any vendor. But in practice, we will find ourselves working laboriously to address vendor-specific incompatibility issues introduced by each browser and its various releases. At the writing of this book, the golden rule is: "Web browsers are not created equal."

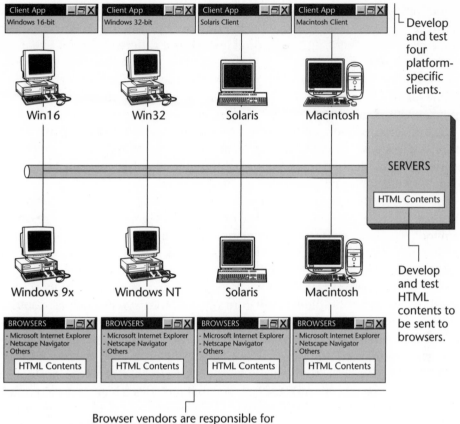

Figure 2.7 Client-server versus Web-based clients.

In addition to the desktop client computer and browser, there are new types of clients and browsers, which are a lot smaller than the desktop PC version. These clients are often battery-powered, rather than wall-electric-powered as is a desktop PC. These clients are mobile devices including PDAs (Personal Digital Assistants), smart phones, and handheld PCs. Since these devices represent another class of client computers, there are some differences in the mobile application model. For simplicity, in this chapter, we will only refer to the desktop PC in the client discussion. Read Chapter 6, "Mobile Web Application Platform," for discussions on the mobile client application model.

Event Handling

In the GUI and event-driven model, inputs, as the name implies, are driven by *events*. Events are actions taken by users, such as mouse movements and clicks, or the input of data through a keyboard. Some objects (e.g., a push button) may receive mouse-over events whenever a mouse passes over them. A mouse single-click is an event. A mouse double-click is a different kind of event. A mouse click with a modifier key, such as Ctrl, is yet another type of event. Depending on the type of event applied to a particular UI object, certain procedures or functions in an application will be executed. In an event-driven environment, this is a type of procedure referred to as *event-handling code.*

Testing event-driven applications is more complicated because it's very labor-intensive to cover the testing of many combinations and sequences of events. Simply identifying all possible combinations of events can be a challenge because some actions trigger multiple events.

Browser-based applications introduce a different flavor of event-handling support. Because Web browsers were originally designed as a data presentation tool, there was no need for interactions other than single-clicking for navigation and data submission, and mouse-over ALT attribute for an alternate description of graphic. Therefore, standard HTML controls such as form-based control and hyperlinks are limited to single-click events. Although script-based events can be implemented to recognize other events such as double-clicking and drag-and-drop, it's not natural in the Web-based user interface to do so (not to mention that those other events also cause incompatibility problems among different browsers.

In Web-based applications, users may click links that generate simulated dialog boxes (the server sends back a page that includes tables, text fields, and other UI objects). Users may interact with browser-based UI objects in the process of generating input for the application. In turn, events are generated. Some of the event-handling code is in scripts that are embedded in the HTML page and executed on the client-side. Others are in UI components (such as Java applets and ActiveX controls) embedded in the HTML page and executed on the client-side. Still others are executed on the server-side. Understanding where (client- or server-side) each event is handled enables you to develop useful test cases as well as reproduce errors effectively.

Browser-based applications offer very limited keyboard event support. You can navigate within the page using Tab and Shift-Tab keys. You can activate a hyperlink to jump to another link or push a command button by pressing the Enter key while the hyperlink text, graphic, or a button is highlighted. Supports for keyboard shortcuts and access keys, such as Alt-[key] or Ctrl-[key], are not available for the Web applications running in the browser's environment, although they are available for the browser application itself. Another event-handling implication in browser-based applications is in the one-way request and submission model. The server generally does not receive commands or data until the user explicitly clicks a button, such as Submit to submit form data; or the user may request data from the server by clicking a link.

This is referred to as the *explicit submission model.* If the user simply closes down a browser but does not explicitly click on a button to save data or to log off, data will not be saved and the user is still considered logged on (on the server-side).

TEST CASE DEVELOPMENT TIPS

Based on the knowledge about the *explicit submission model,* try the following tests against your application under test:

TEST #1

- ◆ Use your valid ID and password to log on to the system.
- ◆ After you are in, close your browser instead of logging off.
- ◆ Launch another instance of the browser and try to log in again. What happens? Does the system complain that you are already in? Does the system allow you to get in and treat it as if nothing has happened? Does the system allow you to get in as a different instance of the same user?

TEST #2

Suppose that your product has a user-license restriction: That is, if you have five concurrent-user licenses, only five users can be logged on to the system concurrently. If the sixth user tries to log on, the system will block it and inform the sixth user that the application has run out of concurrent-user licenses.

- ◆ Use your valid set of ID and password to log on to the system as six separate users. As the sixth user logs on, you may find that the system will detect the situation and block the sixth user from logging on.
- ◆ Close all five browsers that have already logged on instead of logging off.
- ◆ Launch another instance of the browser and try to log on again. Does the system still block this log on because it thinks that there are five users already on the system?

TEST #3

- ◆ Use your valid ID and password to log on to the system.
- ◆ Open an existing record as if you are going to update it.
- ◆ Close your browser instead of logging off.
- ◆ Launch another instance of the browser and try to log on again.
- ◆ Try to open the same record that you opened earlier in the previous browser. What happens? Is the record locked? Are you allowed to update the record anyway?

By the way, there is no right or wrong answer for the three preceding tests because we don't know how your system is designed to handle user session, user authentication, and record locking. The main idea is to present you with some of the possible interesting scenarios that might affect your application under test due to the nature of the explicit submission model in Web-based applications.

Application Instance and Windows Handling

Standard event-based applications may support multiple instances, meaning that the same application can be loaded into memory many times as separate processes. Figure 2.8 shows two instances of Microsoft Word application. Similarly, multiple instances of a browser can run simultaneously. With multiple browser instances, users may be able to log in to the same Web-based application and access the same data table—on behalf of the same user or different users. Figure 2.9 illustrates two browser instances, each accessing the same application and data using the same or different user ID and password.

From the application's perspective, keeping track of multiple instances, the data, and the users who belong to each instance can be problematic. For example, a regular user has logged in using one instance of the browser. An Admin user has also logged in to the same system using another instance for the browser. It's common that the application server may mistakenly receive data from and send data to one user thinking that the data belongs to the other users. Test cases that uncover errors surrounding multiple-instance handling should be thoroughly designed and executed.

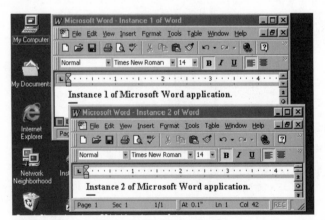

Figure 2.8   Multiple application instances.

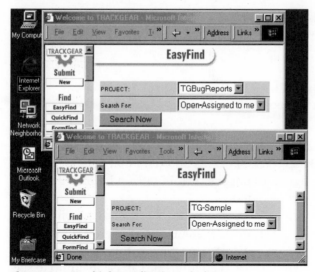

Figure 2.9 Multiple application windows.

Within the same instance of a standard event-based application, multiple windows may be opened simultaneously. Data altered in one of an application's windows may affect data in another of the application's windows. Such applications are referred to as *multiple document interface (MDI)* applications (Figure 2.10). Applications that allow only one active window at a time are known as *single document interface (SDI)* applications (Figure 2.11). SDI applications allow users to work with only one document at a time. Microsoft Word (Figure 2.10) is an example of an MDI application. Notepad (Figure 2.11) is an example of an SDI application.

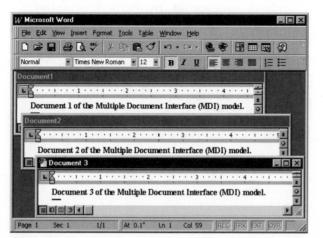

Figure 2.10 Multiple document interface (MDI) application.

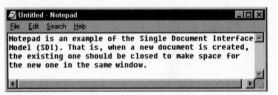

Figure 2.11   Single document interface (SDI) application.

Multiple document interface applications are more interesting to test because they might fail to keep track of events and data that belong to multiple windows. Test cases designed to uncover errors caused by the support of multiple windows should be considered.

Multiple document interface or multiple windows interface are only available for clients in a traditional client-server system. The Web browser interface is considered *flat* because it can only display one page at the time. There is no hierarchical structure for the Web pages, therefore, one can easily jump to several links and quickly lose track of the original position.

UI Controls

In essence, an HTML page that is displayed by a Web browser consists of text, hyperlinks, graphics, frames, tables, forms, and balloon help text (ALT tag). Basic browser-based applications do not support dialog boxes, toolbars, status bars, and other common UI controls. Extra effort can be made to take advantage of Java applets, ActiveX controls, scripts, CSS, and other helper applications to go beyond the basic functionality. However, there will be compatibility issues among different browsers.

Web Systems

The complexities of the PC model are multiplied exponentially in Web systems (Figure 2.12). In addition to the testing challenges that are presented by multiple client PCs and mobile devices, the server-side of Web systems involves hardware of varying types and a software mix of OSs, service processes, server packages, and databases.

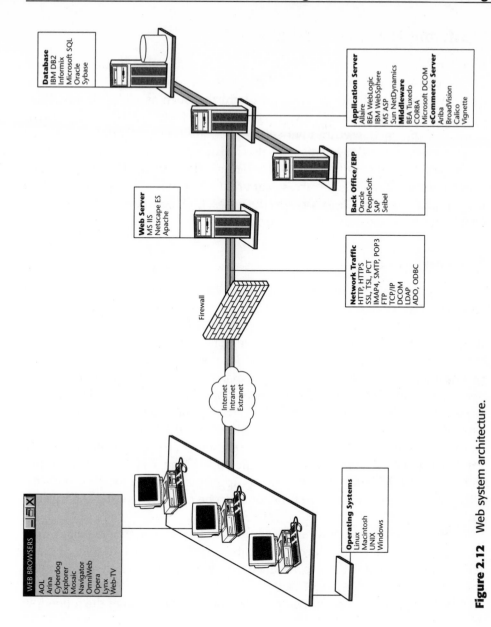

Figure 2.12 Web system architecture.

Hardware Mix

With Web systems and their mixture of many brands of hardware to support, the environment can become very difficult to control. Web systems have the capacity to use machines of different platforms, such as UNIX, Linux, Windows, and Macintosh boxes. A Web system might include a UNIX server that is used in conjunction with other servers that are Linux, Windows-based, or Macintosh-based. Web systems may also include mixtures of models from the same platform (on both the client- and server-sides). Such hardware mixtures present testing challenges because different computers in the same system may employ different OSs, CPU speeds, buses, I/O interfaces, and more. Each combination has the potential to cause problems.

Software Mix

At the highest level, as illustrated in Figure 2.12, Web systems may consist of various OSs, Web servers, application servers, middleware, e-commerce servers, database servers, major enterprise resource planning (ERP) suites, firewalls, and browsers. Application development teams often have little control over the kind of environment into which their applications are installed. In producing software for mainframe systems, development was tailored to one specific system. Today, for Web systems, software is often designed to run on a wide range of hardware and OS combinations, and risks of software incompatibility are always present. An example is that different applications may not share the same version of a database server. On the Microsoft platform, a missing or incompatible DLL (dynamic link library) is another example. (Dynamic link libraries are software components that can exist on both the client- and server-sides whose functions can be called by multiple programs on demand.)

Another problem inherent in the simultaneous use of software from multiple vendors is that when each application undergoes a periodic upgrade (client- or server-side), there is a chance that the upgrades will not be compatible with preexisting software.

A Web system software mix may include any combination of the following:

- Multiple operating systems
- Multiple software packages
- Multiple software components
- Multiple server types, brands, and models
- Multiple browser brands and versions

Server-Based Applications

Server-based applications are different from client applications in two ways. First, server-based applications are programs that don't have a UI with which the end users of the system interact. End users only interact with the client-side application. In turn, the client interacts with server-based applications to access functionality and data via communication protocols, application programming interface (API), and other interfacing standards. Second, server-based applications run unattended; that is, when a server-based application is started, it's intended to stay up, waiting to provide services to client applications whether there is any client out there requesting services. In contrast, to use a client application, an end user must explicitly launch the client application and interact with it via a UI. Therefore, to black-box testers, server-based applications are black boxes.

You may ask: "So it is with desktop applications. What's the big deal?" Here is an example: When a failure is caused by an error in a client-side or desktop application, the users or testers can provide essential information that helps reproduce or analyze the failure because they are right in front of the application. Server-based applications or systems are often isolated from the end users. When a server-based application fails, as testers or users from the client-side, we often don't know when it failed, what happened before it failed, who was or how many users were on the system at the time it failed, and so on. This makes reproducing bugs even more challenging for us. In testing Web systems, we need a better way to track what goes on with applications on the server-side.

One of the techniques used to enhance our failure reproducibility capability is _event logging_. With event logging, server-based applications can record activities to a file that might not be normally seen by an end user. When an application uses event logging, the recorded information that is saved can be read in a reliable way. Operating systems often include logging utilities. For example, Microsoft Windows 2000 includes the Event Viewer, which enables users to monitor events logged in the Application (the most interesting for testing), Security, and System logs. The Application log allows you to track events generated by a specific application. For example, you might want the log file to read and write errors generated by your application. The Application log will allow you to do so. You can create and include additional logging capabilities to your application under test to facilitate the defect analysis and debugging process, should your developers and your test teams find value in them. (Refer to the "Server-Side Testing Tips" section of Chapter 12, "Server-Side Testing," for more information on using log files.) Have discussions with your developers to determine how event logging can be incorporated into or created to support the testing process.

Distributed Server Configurations

Server software can be distributed among any number of physical server boxes, which further complicates testing. Table 2.1 illustrates several possible server configurations that a Web application may support. You should identify the configurations that the application under test claims to support. Matrices of all possible combinations should be developed. Especially for commercial-off-the-shelf server applications, testing should be executed on each configuration to ensure that application features are intact. Realistically, this might not be possible due to resource and time constraints. For more information on testing strategies, see Chapter 17.

Table 2.1   Distributed Server Configurations

	BOX 1	BOX 2	BOX 3
One-box model	NT-based Web server		
	NT-based application server		
	NT-based database server		
Two-box model	NT-based Web server	NT-based database server	
	NT-based application server		
Three-box model	NT-based Web server	NT-based Web server	UNIX-based database server
	NT-based application server	NT-based application server	
One-box model	UNIX-based Web server		
	UNIX-based application server		
	UNIX-based database server		
Two-box model	UNIX-based Web server	UNIX-based database server	
	UNIX-based application server		

(continued)

Table 2.1   *(continued)*

	BOX 1	BOX 2	BOX 3
Three-box model	NT-based Web server	NT-based Web server	NT-based database server
	NT-based application server	NT-based application server	

The Network

The network is the glue that holds Web systems together. It connects clients to servers and servers to servers. This variable introduces new testing issues, including reliability, accessibility, performance, security, configuration, and compatibility. As illustrated in Figure 2.12, the network traffic may consist of several protocols supported by the TCP/IP network. It's also possible to have several networks using different net OSs connecting to each other by gateways. Testing issues related to the network can be a challenge or beyond the reach of black-box testing. However, understanding the testing-related issues surrounding the network enables us to better define testing problems and ask for appropriate help. (See Chapter 4, "Networking Basics," for more information.) In addition, with the proliferation of mobile devices, wireless networks are becoming more popular. It is useful to also have a good understanding of how a wireless network may affect your Web applications, especially mobile Web applications. (See Chapter 6, "Mobile Web Application Platform," for an overview of wireless network.)

Bug Inheritance

It is common for Web applications to rely on preexisting objects or components. Therefore, the newly created systems inherit not just the features but also the bugs that existed in the original objects.

One of the important benefits of both *object-oriented programming* (OOP) and *component-based programming* is reusability. Rather than writing the code from scratch, a developer can take advantage of preexisting features created by other developers (with use of the application programming interface or the API and proper permission) by incorporating those features into his or her own application. In effect, code is recycled, eliminating the need to rewrite existing code. This model helps accelerate development time, reduces the amount of code that needs to be written, and maintains consistency between applications.

The potential problem with this shared model is that bugs are passed along with components. Web applications, due to their component-based architecture, are particularly vulnerable to the sharing of bugs.

At the lowest level, the problem has two major impacts on testing. First, existing objects or components must be tested thoroughly before other applications or objects can use their functionality. Second, regression testing must be executed comprehensively (see "Regression Testing" in Chapter 3, "Software Testing Basics," for more information). Even a small change in a parent object can alter the functionality of an application or object that uses it.

This problem is not new. Object-oriented programming and component-based software have long been used in PCs. With the Web system architecture, however, the problem is multiplied due to the fact that components are shared across servers on a network. The problem is exacerbated by the demand that software be developed in an increasingly shorter time.

At the higher level, bugs in server packages, such as Web servers and database servers, and bugs in Web browsers themselves, will also have an effect on the software under test (see Chapter 5 "Web Application Component," for more information). This problem has a greater impact on security risks. Chapter 18, "Web Security Testing," contains an example of a Buffer Overflow error.

Back-End Data Accessing

Data in a Web system is often distributed; that is, it resides on one or more (server) computers rather than the client computer. There are several methods of storing data on a back-end server. For example, data can be stored in flat files, in a nonrelational database, in a relational database, or in an object-oriented database. In a typical Web application system, it's common that a relational database is employed so that data accessing and manipulation can be more efficient compared to a flat-file database.

In a flat-file system, when a query is initiated, the results of that query are dumped into files on a storage device. An application then opens, reads, and manipulates data from these files and generates reports on behalf of the user. To get to the data, the applications need to know exactly where files are located and what their names are. Access security is usually imposed at the application level and file level.

In contrast, a database, such as a relational database, stores data in tables of records. Through the database engine, applications access data by getting a set of records without knowing where the physical data files are located or what they are named. Data in relational databases are accessed via database names (not to be mistaken with file names) and table names. Relational database files can be stored on multiple servers. Web systems using a relational database can impose security at the application server level, the database server level, as well as at table and user-based privilege level. All of this means that testing back-end data accessing by itself is a big challenge to testers, especially black-box testers because they do not see the activities on the back end. It makes reproducing errors more difficult and capturing test coverage more complicated. See Chapter 14, "Database Tests," for more information on testing back-end database accessing.

Thin-Client versus Thick-Client Processing

Thin-client versus thick-client processing is concerned with where applications and components reside and execute. Components may reside on a client machine and on one or more server machines. The two possibilities are:

Thin client. With thin-client systems, the client PC or mobile device does very little processing. Business logic rules are executed on the server side. Some simple HTML Web-based applications and handheld devices utilize this model. This approach centralizes processing on the server and eliminates most client-side incompatibility concerns. (See Table 2.2.)

Thick client. The client machine runs the UI portion of the application as well as the execution of some or all of the business logic. In this case, the browser not only has to format the HTML page, but it also has to execute other components such as Java applet and ActiveX. The server machine houses the database that processes data requests from the client. Processing is shared between client and server. (See Table 2.3.)

Table 2.2   Thin Client

DESKTOP PC THIN CLIENT	SERVER
UI	Application rules
	Database

Table 2.3   Thick Client

DESKTOP PC THICK CLIENT	SERVER
UI	Database
Application rules	

The client doing much of a system's work (e.g., executing business logic rules, DHTML, Java applets, ActiveX controls, or style sheets on the client-side) is referred to as *thick-client processing*. Thick-client processing relieves processing strain on the server and takes full advantage of the client's processor. With thick-client processing, there are likely to be more incompatibility problems on the client-side.

Thin-client versus thick-client application testing issues revolve around the compromises among feature, compatibility, and performance issues. For more information regarding thin-client versus thick-client application, please see Chapter 5.

Interoperability Issues

Interoperability is the ability of a system or components within a system to interact and work seamlessly with other systems or other components. This is normally achieved by adhering to certain APIs, communication protocol standards, or to interface-converting technology such as Common Object Request Broker Architecture (CORBA) or Distributed Common Object Model (DCOM). There are many hardware and software interoperability dependencies associated with Web systems, so it is essential that our test-planning process include study of the system architectural design.

Interoperability issues—it is possible that information will be lost or misinterpreted in communication between components. Figure 2.13 shows a simplified Web system that includes three box servers and a client machine. In this example, the client requests all database records from the server-side. The application server in turn queries the database server. Now, if the database server fails to execute the query, what will happen? Will the database server tell the application server that the query has failed? If the application server gets no response from the database server, will it resend the query? Possibly, the application server will receive an error message that it does not understand. Consequently, what message will be passed back to the client? Will the application server simply notify the client that the request must be resent? Or will it neglect to inform the client of anything at all? All of these scenarios need to be investigated in the study of the system architectural design.

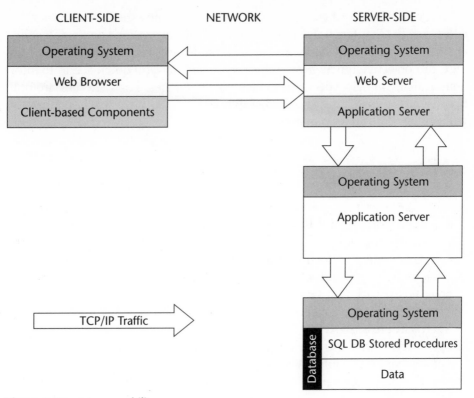

Figure 2.13   Interoperability.

Testing Considerations

The key areas of testing for Web applications beyond traditional testing include:

- Web UI implementation
- System integration
- Server and client installation
- Web-based help
- Configuration and compatibility
- Database
- Security
- Performance, load, and stress

For definitions for these tests, see Chapter 3, "Software Testing Basics." In addition, see Chapters 9 through 19 for in-depth discussions on these tests.

Now that we have established the fact that testing Web applications is complex, our objective for the rest of the book is to offer you quick access to information that can help you meet the testing challenges. The materials are built upon some of the testing knowledge that you already have. We hope that you will find the information useful.

Bibliography

Kaner, Cem, Jack Falk, Hung Q. Nguyen *Testing Computer Software,* 2nd edition. New York: John Wiley & Sons, Inc., 1999.

LogiGear Corporation. *QA Training Handbook: Testing Web Applications.* Foster City, CA: LogiGear Corporation, 2002.

————*QA Training Handbook: Testing Windows Desktop and Server-Based Applications.* Foster City, CA: LogiGear Corporation, 2002.

Microsoft Corporation. *Microsoft SQL Server 2000 Resource Kit.* Redmond, WA: Microsoft Press, 2001.

Orfali, Robert, Dan Harkey, Jeri Edwards, *Client/Server Survival Guide, Third Edition.* New York: John Wiley & Sons, 1999.

Reilly, Douglas J. *Designing Microsoft ASP.NET Applications.* Redmond, WA: Microsoft Press, 2001.

————*Inside Server-Based Applications.* Redmond, WA: Microsoft Press, 2000.

Methodology
and Technology

Software Testing Basics

Why Read This Chapter?

In general, the software testing techniques that are applied to other applications are the same as those that are applied to Web-based applications. Both cases require basic test types such as functionality tests, forced-error tests, boundary condition and equivalence class analysis, and so forth. Some differences between the two are that the technology variables in the Web environment multiply, and the additional focus on security- and performance-related tests, which are very different from feature-based testing. Having the basic understanding in testing methodologies, combined with a domain expertise in Web technology, will enable you to effectively test Web applications.

TOPICS COVERED IN THIS CHAPTER

- ◆ **Introduction**
- ◆ **Basic Planning and Documentation**
- ◆ **Common Terminology and Concepts**
- ◆ **Test-Case Development**
- ◆ **Bibliography**

Introduction

This chapter includes a review of some of the more elemental software testing principles upon which this book is based. Basic testing terminology, practices, and test-case development techniques are covered. However, a full analysis of the theories and practices that are required for effective software testing is not a goal of this book. For more detailed information on the basics of software testing, please refer to *Testing Computer Software* (Kaner, Falk, and Nguyen, John Wiley & Sons, Inc., 1999). Another useful book that we reecommend is *Lessons Learned in Software Testing* (Kaner, Bach, and Pettichord, John Wiley & Sons, Inc., 2002).

Basic Planning and Documentation

Methodical record-keeping builds credibility for the testing team and focuses testing efforts. Records should be kept for all testing. Complete test-case lists, tables, and matrices should be collected and saved. Chapter 7, "Test Planning Fundamentals," details many practical reporting and planning processes.

There are always limits to the amount of time and money that can be invested in testing. There are often scheduling and budgetary constraints on development projects that severely restrict testing—for example, adequate hardware configurations may be unaffordable. For this reason, it is important that cost justification, including potential technical support and outsourcing, be factored into all test planning.

To be as efficient as possible, look for redundant test cases and eliminate them. Reuse test suites and locate preexisting test suites when appropriate. Become as knowledgeable as possible about the application under test and the technologies supporting that application. With knowledge of the application's technologies, you can avoid wasted time and identify the most effective testing methods available. You can also keep the development team informed about areas of possible risk.

Early planning is key to the efficiency and cost savings that can be brought to the testing effort. Time invested early in core functionality testing, for example, can make for big cost savings down the road. Identifying functionality errors early reduces the frequency that developers will have to make risky fixes to core functionality late in the development process when the stakes are higher.

Test coverage (an assessment of the breadth and depth of testing that a given product will undergo) is a balance of risk and other project concerns, such as resources and scheduling (complete coverage is virtually impossible). The extent of coverage is a negotiable concept for which the product team will be required to give input.

Common Terminology and Concepts

Following are some essential software testing terms and concepts.

Test Conditions

Test conditions are critically important factors in Web application testing. The test conditions are the circumstances in which an application under test operates. There are two categories of test conditions, *application-specific* and *environment-specific,* which are described in the following text.

1. *Application-specific conditions.* An example of an application-specific condition includes running the same word processor spell-checking test while in Normal View and then again when in Page View mode. If one of the tests generates an error and the other does not, then you can deduce that there is a condition that is specific to the application that is causing the error.
2. *Environment-specific conditions.* When an error is generated by conditions outside of an application under test, the conditions are considered to be environment-specific.

In general, we find it useful to think in terms of two classes of operating environments, each having its own unique testing implications:

1. *Static environments (configuration and compatibility errors).* An operating environment in which incompatibility issues may exist, regardless of variable conditions such as processing speed and available memory.
2. *Dynamic environments (RAM, disc space, memory, network bandwidth, etc.).* An operating environment in which otherwise compatible components may exhibit errors due to memory-related errors or latency conditions.

Static Operating Environments

The compatibility differences between Netscape Navigator and Internet Explorer illustrate a static environment.

Configuration and *compatibility* issues may occur at any point within a Web system: client, server, or network. Configuration issues involve various server software and hardware setups, browser settings, network connections, and TCP/IP stack setups. Figures 3.1 and 3.2 illustrate two of the many possible physical server configurations, one-box and two-box, respectively.

Dynamic Operating Environments

When the value of a specific environment attribute does not stay constant each time a test procedure is executed, it causes the operating environment to become dynamic. The attribute can be anything from resource-specific (available RAM, disk space, etc.) to timing-specific (network latency, the order of transactions being submitted, etc.).

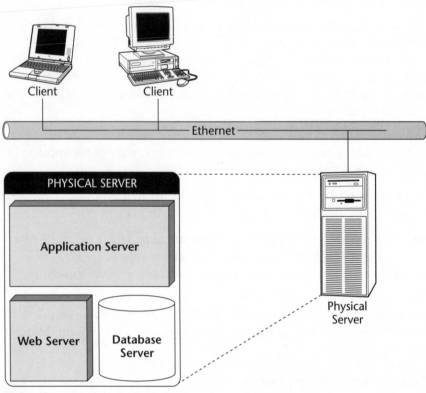

Figure 3.1 One-box configuration.

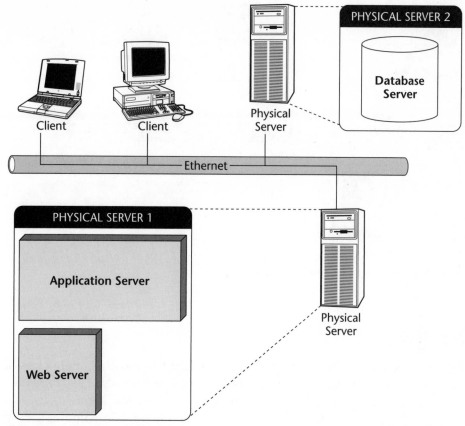

Figure 3.2   Two-box configuration.

Resource Contention Example

Figure 3.3 and Table 3.1 illustrate an example of a dynamic environment condition that involves three workstations and a shared temp space. Workstation C has 400Mb of temporary memory space on it. Workstation A asks Workstation C if it has 200Mb of memory available. Workstation C responds in the affirmative. What happens though if, before Workstation A receives an answer to its request, Workstation B writes 300Mb of data to the temp space on Workstation C? When Workstation A finally receives the response to its request, it will begin writing 200Mb of data to Workstation C—even though there will be only 100Mb of memory available. An error condition will result.

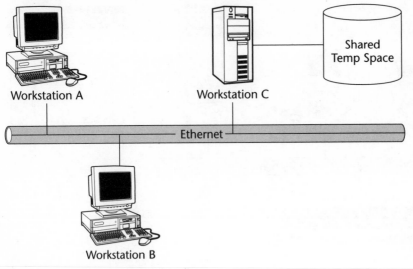

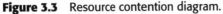

Figure 3.3   Resource contention diagram.

Test Types

Test types are categories of tests that are designed to expose a certain class of error or verify the accuracy of related behaviors. The analysis of test types is a good way to divide the testing of an application methodically into logical and manageable groups of tasks. Test types are also helpful in communicating required testing time and resources to other members of the product team.

Following are a number of common test types. See Chapter 7, "Test Planning Fundamentals," and Chapter 9, "Sample Test Plan," for information regarding the selection of test types.

Acceptance Testing

The two common types of acceptance tests are *development acceptance tests* and *deployment acceptance tests*.

Development Acceptance Test

Release acceptance tests and functional acceptance simple tests are two common classes of test used during the development process. There are subtle differences in the application of these two classes of tests.

Table 3.1 Resource Contention Process

STEP	WORKSTATION A	WORKSTATION B	BEFORE WORKSTATION C: SHARED TEMP SPACE AVAILABLE MEMORY	AFTER WORKSTATION C: SHARED SPACE AVAILABLE MEMORY
1	Workstation A needs to write 200Mb of data to the shared temp space on Workstation C. Workstation A asks Workstation C if the needed space is available. Workstation C tells Workstation A that it has the available memory space. Note that Workstation A did not reserve the space.		400Mb	400Mb
2		Workstation B needs to write 300Mb of data to the shared temp space on Workstation C. Workstation B asks Workstation C to give it the needed space. Workstation C tells Workstation B that it has the available memory space, and it reserves the space for Workstation B. Workstation B writes the data to Workstation C.	400Mb	100Mb
3	Workstation A finally gets its response from Workstation C and begins to write 200Mb of data. Workstation C, however, now has only 100Mb of temp space left. Without proper error handling, Workstation A crashes.			0Mb

Release Acceptance Test

The *release acceptance test* (RAT), also referred to as a *build acceptance* or *smoke test*, is run on each development release to check that each build is stable enough for further testing. Typically, this test suite consists of entrance and exit test cases, plus test cases that check mainstream functions of the program with mainstream data. Copies of the RAT can be distributed to developers so that they can run the tests before submitting builds to the testing group. If a build does not pass a RAT test, it is reasonable to do the following:

- Suspend testing on the new build and resume testing on the prior build until another build is received.
- Report the failing criteria to the development team.
- Request a new build.

TESTING THE SAMPLE APPLICATION

STATIC OPERATING ENVIRONMENT EXAMPLE

This sample application illustrates incompatibility between a version of Netscape Navigator and a version of Microsoft Internet Explorer. (See Chapter 8, "Sample Application," for more information.) The application has charting functionality that enables users to generate metrics reports, such as bar charts and line charts. When a user requests a metrics report, the application server pseudocode runs as follows:

1. Connects to the database server and runs the query.
2. Writes the query result to a file named c:\temp\chart.val.
3. Executes the chart Java applet. Reads and draws a graph using data from c:\temp\chart.val.
4. Sends the Java applet to the browser.

During testing of the sample application, it was discovered that the charting feature works on one of the preceding configurations but not the other. The problem occurred only in the two-box configuration. After examining the code, it was learned that the problem was in steps 2 and 3. In step 2, the query result is written to c:\temp\chart.val of the database server local drive. In step 3, the chart Java applet is running on the application server, which is not in the same box as the database server. When the database server attempts to open the file c:\temp\chart.val on the application server local drive, the file is not found.

It should not be inferred from this example that you should read the code every time you come across an error—leave the debugging work for the developers. It is essential, however, to identify which server configurations are problematic and include such information in bug reports. You should consider running a cursory suite of test cases on all distributed configurations that are supported by the application server under test. You should also consider replicating every bug on at least two configurations that are extremely different from each other when configuration dependency is suspect.

Consider the compatibility issues involved in the following example:

◆ The home directory path for the Web server on the host myserver is mapped to C:\INETPUB\WWWROOT\.

◆ When a page is requested from http://myserver/, data is pulled from C:\INETPUB\WWWROOT\.

◆ A file name, mychart.jar, is stored at C:\INETPUB\WWWROOT \MYAPP\BIN.

◆ The application session path (*relative path*) points to C:\INETPUB \WWWROOT\MYAPP\BIN, and a file is requested from .\LIB.

Using a version of Internet Explorer, the Web server looks for the file in C:\INETPUB\WWWROOT\MYAPP\BIN\LIB, because the browser understands relative paths. This is the desired behavior, and the file will be found in this scenario.

Using a version of Netscape Navigator, which uses absolute paths, the Web server looks for the file in C:\INETPUB\WWWROOT\LIB. This is a problem because the file (mychart.jar) will not be found. The feature does not work with this old version of Netscape Navigator (which some people still use).

Bringing up the Java Console, you can see the following, which confirms the finding: #Unable to load archive http://myserver/lib/mychart.jar:java.io. IOException:<null>.

This is not to say that Internet Explorer is better than Netscape Navigator. It simply means that there are incompatibility issues between browsers. Code should not assume that relative paths work with all browsers.

Functional Acceptance Simple Test

The *functional acceptance simple test (FAST)* is run on each development release to check that key features of the program are appropriately accessible and functioning properly on at least one test configuration (preferably the minimum or common configuration). This test suite consists of simple test cases that check the lowest level of functionality for each command to ensure that task-oriented functional tests (TOFTs) can be performed on the program. The objective is to decompose the functionality of a program down to the command level and then apply test cases to check that each command works as intended. No attention is paid to the combination of these basic commands, the context of the feature that is formed by these combined commands, or the end result of the overall feature. For example, FAST for a File/Save As menu command checks that the Save As dialog box displays. However, it does not validate that the overall file-saving feature works, nor does it validate the integrity of saved files.

Typically, errors encountered during the execution of FAST are reported through the standard issue-tracking process. Suspending testing during FAST is not recommended.

Note that it depends on the organization for which you work. Each might have different rules in terms of which test cases should belong to RAT versus FAST, and when to suspend testing or to reject a build.

Deployment Acceptance Test

The configurations on which the Web system will be deployed will often be much different from develop-and-test configurations. Testers must consider this in the preparation and writing of test cases for installation time acceptance tests. This type of test usually includes the full installation of the applications to the targeted environments or configurations. Then FASTs and TOFTs are executed to validate the system functionality.

Feature-Level Testing

This is where we begin to do some serious testing, including boundary testing and other difficult but valid test circumstances.

BUG ANALYZING AND REPRODUCTION TIPS

To reproduce an *environment-dependent* error, you must replicate both the exact sequence of activities and the environment conditions (e.g., operating system, browser version, add-on components, database server, Web server, third-party components, client-server resources, network bandwidth, and traffic, etc.) in which the application operates.

Environment-independent errors are easier to reproduce, as they do not require replicating the operating environment. With environment-independent errors, all that need to be replicated are the steps that generate the error.

BROWSER BUG ANALYZING TIPS

- ◆ Check if the client operating system (OS) version and patches meet system requirements.
- ◆ Check if the correct version of the browser is installed on the client machine.
- ◆ Check if the browser is properly installed on the machine.
- ◆ Check the browser settings.
- ◆ Check if the bug is reproducible in different browsers (e.g., Netscape Navigator versus Internet Explorer).
- ◆ Check with different supported versions of the same browsers (e.g., Internet Explored version 4.1, 4.2, 5.0, 5.5, etc.).

Task-Oriented Functional Test

The task-oriented functional test (TOFT) consists of positive test cases that are designed to verify program features by checking that each feature performs as expected against specifications, user guides, requirements, and design documents. Usually, features are organized into list or test matrix format. Each feature is tested for:

- The validity of the task it performs with supported data conditions under supported operating conditions.
- The integrity of the task's end result.
- The feature's integrity when used in conjunction with related features.

Forced-Error Test

The *forced-error test (FET)* consists of negative test cases that are designed to force a program into error conditions. A list of all error messages that the program issues should be generated. The list is used as a baseline for developing test cases. An attempt is made to generate each error message in the list. Obviously, tests to validate error-handling schemes cannot be performed until all the handling and error messages have been coded. However, FETs should be thought through as early as possible.

Sometimes, the error messages are not available. Nevertheless, error cases can still be considered by walking through the program and deciding how the program might fail in a given user interface (UI), such as a dialog or in the course of executing a given task or printing a given report. Test cases should be created for each condition to determine what error message is generated (if any).

USEFUL FET EXECUTION GUIDELINES

- Check that the error-handling design and the error communication methods are consistent.
- Check that all common error conditions are detected and handled correctly.
- Check that the program recovers gracefully from each error condition.
- Check that the unstable states of the program (e.g., an open file that needs to be closed, a variable that needs to be reinitialized, etc.) caused by the error are also corrected.
- Check each error message to ensure that:
  - Message matches the type of error detected.
  - Description of the error is clear and concise.
  - Message does not contain spelling or grammatical errors.
  - User is offered reasonable options for getting around or recovering from the error condition.

Boundary Test

Boundary tests are designed to check a program's response to extreme input values. Extreme output values are generated by the input values. It is important to check that a program handles input values and output results correctly at the lower and upper boundaries. Keep in mind that you can create extreme boundary results from nonextreme input values. It is essential to analyze how to generate extremes of both types. In addition, sometimes you know that there is an intermediate variable involved in processing. If so, it is useful to determine how to drive that one through the extremes and special conditions such as zero or overflow condition.

System-Level Test

System-level tests consist of batteries of tests that are designed to fully exercise a program as a whole and check that all elements of the integrated system function properly. System-level test suites also validate the usefulness of a program and compare end results against requirements.

Real-World User-Level Test

These tests simulate the actions customers may take with a program. Real-world user-level testing often detects errors that are otherwise missed by formal test types.

Exploratory Test

Exploratory tests do not necessarily involve a test plan, checklists, or assigned tasks. The strategy here is to use past testing experience to make educated guesses about places and functionality that may be problematic. Testing is then focused on those areas. Exploratory testing can be scheduled. It can also be reserved for unforeseen downtime that presents itself during the testing process.

Load/Volume Test

Load/volume tests study how a program handles large amounts of data, excessive calculations, and excessive processing, often over a long period of time. These tests do not necessarily have to push or exceed upper functional limits. Load/volume tests can, and usually must be, automated.

FOCUS OF LOAD/VOLUME TESTING

- Pushing through large amounts of data with extreme processing demands
- Requesting many processes simultaneously
- Repeating tasks over a long period of time

Load/volume tests, which involve extreme conditions, are normally run after the execution of feature-level tests, which prove that a program functions correctly under normal conditions. See Chapter 19, "Performance Testing," for more information on planning for these tests.

Stress Test

Stress tests force programs to operate under limited resource conditions. The goal is to push the upper functional limits of a program to ensure that it can function correctly and handle error conditions gracefully. Examples of resources that may be artificially manipulated to create stressful conditions include memory, disk space, and network bandwidth. If other memory-oriented tests are also planned, they should be performed here as part of the stress test suite. Stress tests can be automated. See Chapter 19 for more information on planning for these tests.

Performance Test

The primary goal of performance testing is to develop effective enhancement strategies for maintaining acceptable system performance. Performance testing is a capacity analysis and planning process in which measurement data are used to predict when load levels will exhaust system resources.

The testing team should work with the development team to identify tasks to be measured and to determine acceptable performance criteria. The marketing group may even insist on meeting a competitor's standards of performance. Test suites can be developed to measure how long it takes to perform relevant tasks. See Chapter 19 for more information on planning for these tests.

Fail-over Test

Fail-over testing involves putting the system under test in a state of failure to trigger the predesigned system-level error handling and recovering processes. These processes might be automatic recovery through a restart, or redirection to a back-up system or another server.

Availability Test

Availability testing measures the probability to which a system or component is operational and accessible, sometimes known as *uptime*. This testing involves not only putting the system under a certain load or condition but also analyzing the components that may fail and developing test scenarios that may cause them to fail. In availability testing you may devise a scenario of running transactions to bring down the server and make it unavailable, thereby initiating the built-in recovery and standby systems.

Reliability Test

Reliability testing is similar to availability testing, but reliability infers operational availability under certain conditions, over some fixed duration of time, for example, 48 or 72 hours. Reliability testing is sometimes known as *soak testing*. Here you are testing the continuous running of transactions, looking for memory leaks, locks, or race condition errors. If the system stays up or properly initiates the fail-over process, it passes the test. Reliability testing would mean running those low system resource tests over, perhaps, 72 hours, looking not for the system response time when the low resource condition is detected but what happens if it stays in that condition for a long time.

Scalability Testing

Testing how well the system will scale or continue to function with growth, without having to switch to a new system or redesigning, is the goal of scalability testing. Client-server systems such as Web systems often will grow to support more users, more activities, or both. The idea is to support the growth by adding processors and memory to the system or server-side hardware, without changing system software, which can be expensive.

API Test

An application program interface (API) is a set of input interfaces for functions and procedures that are made available by application or operating system components that export them, and for other application and operating system components that use or import them. Where the graphical user interface (GUI) receives requests from the user, the API receives requests from software components.

Because there is no direct access to the API though GUI, a *harness application* must be built to provide the necessary access and implementation of test-case execution needed for API testing. These harnesses are most often built by developers. Exercising the API involves designing test cases that call the function with certain selected parameters, calling the function with many possible combinations of parameters, and designing the sequences in which the function is called to test functionality and error conditions. In addition, due to the labor-intensive nature of API testing, caused by the vast number of possible test cases, you should consider test automation architecture and methods to effectively test the software at the API level.

Regression Test

Regression testing is used to confirm that fixed bugs have, in fact, been fixed, that new bugs have not been introduced in the process, and that features that were proven correctly functional are intact. Depending on the size of a project, cycles of regression testing may be performed once per milestone or once per build. Some bug regression testing may also be performed during each acceptance test cycle, focusing on only the most important bugs. Regression tests can be automated.

CONDITIONS DURING WHICH REGRESSION TESTS MAY BE RUN

Issue-fixing cycle. Once the development team has fixed issues, a regression test can be run to validate the fixes. Tests are based on the step-by-step test cases that were originally reported.

- If an issue is confirmed as fixed, then the issue report status should be changed to *Closed*.

- If an issue is confirmed as fixed, but with side effects, then the issue report status should be changed to *Closed*. However, a new issue should be filed to report the side effect.

- If an issue is only partially fixed, then the issue report resolution should be changed back to *Unfixed*, supplemented with comments outlining the outstanding problems.

  Note: Your company might be using different terminology other than *Closed* or *Unfixed*.

Open-status regression cycle. Periodic regression tests may be run on all open issues in the issue-tracking database. During this cycle, issue status is confirmed as one of the following: the report is reproducible as-is with no modification; the report is reproducible with additional comments or modifications; or the report is no longer reproducible.

Closed-fixed regression cycle. In the final phase of testing, a full-regression test cycle should be run to confirm the status of all fixed-closed issues.

Feature regression cycle. Each time a new build is cut or is in the final phase of testing, depending on the organizational procedure, a full-regression test cycle should be run to confirm that the proven correctly functional features are still working as expected.

Compatibility and Configuration Test

Compatibility and configuration testing is performed to check that an application functions properly across various hardware and software environments. Often, the strategy is to run FASTs or a subset of TOFTs on a range of software and hardware configurations. Sometimes, another strategy is to create a specific test that takes into account the error risks associated with configuration differences. For example, you might design an extensive series of tests to check for browser compatibility issues. You might not run these tests as part of your normal RATs, FASTs, or TOFTs.

Software compatibility configurations include variances in OS versions, input/output (I/O) devices, extensions, network software, concurrent applications, online services, and firewalls. Hardware configurations include variances in manufacturers, CPU types, RAM, graphic display cards, video capture cards, sound cards, monitors, network cards, and connection types (e.g., T1, DSL, modem, etc.).

Documentation Test

Testing of reference guides and user guides check that all features are reasonably documented. Every page of documentation should be keystroke-tested for the following errors:

- Accuracy of every statement of fact.
- Accuracy of every screen shot, figure, and illustration.
- Accuracy of placement of figures and illustrations.
- Accuracy of every tutorial, tip, and instruction.
- Accuracy of marketing collateral (claims, system requirements, and screen shots).
- Accuracy of downloadable documentation (PDFs, HTML, or text files).

Online Help Test

Online help tests check the accuracy of help contents, correctness of features in the help system, and functionality of the help system. See Chapter 15 "Help Tests," for more information.

Utilities/Toolkits and Collateral Test

If there are utilities and software collateral items to be tested, appropriate analysis should be done to ensure that suitable and adequate testing strategies are in place.

Install/Uninstall Test

Web systems often require both client-side and server-side installs. Testing of the installer checks that installed features function properly—including icons, support documentation, the README file, configuration files, and registry keys (in Windows operating systems). The test verifies that the correct directories have been created and that the correct system files have been copied to the appropriate directories. The test also confirms that various error conditions have been detected and handled gracefully.

Testing of the uninstaller checks that the installed directories and files have been appropriately removed, that configuration and system-related files have also been appropriately removed or modified, and that the operating environment has been recovered in its original state. See Chapter 16, "Installation Tests," for more information.

User Interface Tests

Ease-of-use UI testing evaluates how intuitive a system is. Issues pertaining to navigation, usability, commands, and accessibility are considered. User interface *functionality* testing examines how well a UI operates to specifications.

AREAS COVERED IN UI TESTING

- Usability
- Look and feel
- Navigation controls/navigation bar
- Instructional and technical information style
- Images
- Tables
- Navigation branching
- Accessibility

Usability Tests

Usability testing consists of a variety of methods for setting up the product, assigning the users tasks to carry out, having the users to carry out the tasks, and observing users interacting and collecting information to measure ease of use or satisfaction. See the "Usability and Accessibility Testing" section in Chapter 11, "Functional Tests," for more information.

Accessibility Tests

In producing a Web site for accessibility, the designer must take into consideration that the Web content must be available to and accessible by everyone, including people with disabilities. Accessibility testing is done to verify that the application meets the accessibility standards and practices. The goal of accessibility is similar to that of usability: that is, to ensure the end user will get the best experience in interacting with the product or service. The key difference is that accessibility accomplishes its goal through making the product usable to a larger population, including people with disabilities.

External Beta Testing

External beta testing offers developers their first glimpse at how users may actually interact with a program. Copies of the program or a test URL, sometimes accompanied by a letter of instruction, are sent out to a group of volunteers who try out the program and respond to questions in the letter. Beta testing is black-box, real-world testing. However, beta testing can be difficult to manage, and the feedback that it generates normally comes too late in the development process to contribute to improved usability and functionality. External beta-tester feedback may be reflected in a README file or deferred to future releases.

Dates Testing

A program's ability to handle the year change from 1999 to 2000 is tested to ensure that internal systems were not scrambled on dates that are later than December 31, 1999, such as in Y2K testing. However, Y2K-related considerations will remain an issue well beyond the year 2000 due to future leap-year and business-calendar changeovers. Also, programs compiled in C and C++ as well as 32-bit UNIX systems will rollover on January 19, 2038. Rollover meaning the day after 2038 will be 1901. Many computer scientists predict this problem to be much more serious than the Y2K problem.

Security Tests

Security measures protect Web systems from both internal and external threats. Security testing is done to determine if the application features have been implemented as designed. Within the context of software testing, the focus of the work is on functional tests, forced-error tests, and to a certain extent, penetration tests at the application level. It means that you should seek out vulnerabilities and information leaks due primarily to programming practices and, to a certain extent, to misconfiguration of Web servers and other application-specific servers. Test for the security-side effects or vulnerabilities caused by the functionality implementation. At the same time, test for functional side effects caused by security implementation. See Chapter 18, "Web Security Testing," for more information on planning and testing for security.

PRIMARY COMPONENTS REQUIRING SECURITY TESTING

- Client and server software, Databases and software components
- Server boxes
- Client workstations
- Networks

Unit Tests

Unit tests are tests that evaluate the integrity of software code units before they are integrated with other software units. Developers normally perform unit testing. Unit testing represents the first round of software testing, when developers test their own software and fix errors in private.

Phases of Development

The software development process is normally divided into phases. Each phase of development entails different test types, coverage depth, and demands on the testing effort. Refer to Chapter 7, Table 7.1, "Test Types and Their Place in the Software Development Process," for a visual representation of test phases and corresponding test types.

Development phases should be defined by agreed-upon, clearly communicated and measurable criteria. Often, people on the same development team will have different understandings of how particular phases are defined. For example, one phase might be defined such that an application cannot officially begin its beta phase of development until all crash or data-loss bugs have been fixed. Alternatively, *beta* is also commonly defined as being a product that is functionally complete (though bugs may still be present, all features have been coded).

Disagreement over how a phase is defined can lead to problems in perception of completeness and product stability. It is often the role of the test team to define the milestone or completion criteria that must be met for a project to pass from one phase to another. Defining and agreeing upon milestone and completion criteria allows the testing, development, and marketing groups to work more effectively as a team. The specifics of the milestones are not as important as the fact that they are clearly communicated. It is also a concern that developers usually consider that they have reached a milestone when the build is done. In practice, testing still must confirm that this is true, and the confirmation process may take from a few days to a few weeks.

COMMON EXAMPLES OF PHASES OF SOFTWARE DEVELOPMENT

Alpha. A significant and agreed-upon portion (if not all) of the product has been completed (the product includes code, documentation, additional art, or other content, etc.). The product is ready for in-house use.

Pre-beta (or beta candidate). A build that is submitted for beta acceptance. If the build meets the beta criteria (as verified by the testing group), then the software is accepted into the beta phase of development.

Beta. Most, or all, of the product is complete and stable. Some companies send out review copies (beta copies) of software to customers once software reaches this phase.

UI freeze. Every aspect of the application's UI is complete. Some companies accept limited changes to error messaging and repairs to errors in help screens during this phase.

Prefinal (or golden master candidate (GMC)). A final candidate build has been submitted for review to the testing team. If the software is complete and all GMC tests are passed, then the product is considered ready for final testing.

Final test. This is the last round of testing before the product is migrated to the live Web site, sent to manufacturing, or posted on the Web site.

Release (or golden master). The build that will eventually be shipped to the customer, posted on the Web, or migrated to the live Web site.

OTHER SOFTWARE TESTING TERMS

Test case. A test that (ideally) executes a single well-defined test objective (e.g., a specific behavior of a feature under a specific condition). Early in testing, a test case might be extremely simple; later, however, the program is more stable, so you will need more complex test cases to provide useful information.

Test script. Step-by-step instructions that describe how a test case is to be executed. A test script may contain one or more test cases.

Test suite. A collection of test scripts or test cases used for validating bug fixes (or finding new bugs) within a logical or physical area of a product. For example, an acceptance test suite contains all the test cases that are used to verify that software has met certain predefined acceptance criteria. A regression suite, on the other hand, contains all the test cases that are used to verify that all previously fixed bugs are still fixed.

Test specification. A set of test cases, input, and conditions that are used in the testing of a particular feature or set of features. A test specification often includes descriptions of expected results.

Test requirement. A document that describes items and features that are tested under a required condition.

Test plan. A management document outlining risks, priorities, and schedules for testing. (See Part Three for more information.)

Test-Case Development

There are many methods available for analyzing software in an effort to develop appropriate test cases. The following subsections focus on several methods of establishing coverage and developing effective test cases. By no means is this a complete and comprehensive list of test case design methods. It's merely a means for us to share the methods that we actually apply and find useful in our day-to-day testing activities. A combination of most, if not all, of the following test design methods should be used to develop test cases for the application under test.

Equivalence Class Partitioning and Boundary Condition Analysis

Equivalence class partitioning is a timesaving practice that identifies tests that are equivalent to one another; when two inputs are equivalent, you expect them to cause the identical sequence of operations to take place or to cause the same path to be executed through the code. When two or more test cases are seen as equivalent, the resource savings associated with not running the redundant tests normally outweigh the risk.

An example of an equivalence class includes the testing of a data-entry field in an HTML form. If the field accepts a five-digit zip code (e.g., 22222), then it can reasonably be assumed that the field will accept all other five-digit ZIP codes (e.g., 33333, 44444, etc.). Because all five-digit zip codes are of the same equivalence class, there is little benefit in testing more than one of them.

In equivalence partitioning, both valid and invalid values are treated in this manner. For example, if entering six letters into the zip code field just described results in an error message, then it can reasonably be assumed that all six-letter combinations will result in the same error message. Similarly, if entering a four-digit number into the zip code field results in an error message, then it should be assumed that all four-digit combinations will result in the same error message.

EXAMPLES OF EQUIVALENCE CLASSES

- Ranges of numbers (such as all numbers between 10 and 99, which are of the same two-digit equivalence class)
- Membership in groups (dates, times, country names, etc.)
- Invalid inputs (placing symbols into text-only fields, etc.)
- Equivalent output events (variation of inputs that produce the same output)
- Equivalent operating environments
- Repetition of activities
- Number of records in a database (or other equivalent objects)
- Equivalent sums or other arithmetic results
- Equivalent numbers of items entered (such as the number of characters entered into a field)
- Equivalent space (on a page or on a screen)
- Equivalent amounts of memory, disk space, or other resources available to a program

Boundary values mark the transition points between equivalence classes. They can be limit values that define the line between supported inputs and nonsupported inputs, or they can define the line between supported system requirements and nonsupported system requirements. Applications are more susceptible to errors at the boundaries of equivalence classes, so boundary condition tests can be quite effective at uncovering errors.

Generally, each equivalence class is partitioned by its boundary values. Nevertheless, not all equivalence classes have boundaries. For example, given the following four browser equivalent classes (Netscape Navigator 4.6 and 4.6.1, and Microsoft Internet Explorer 4.0 and 5.0), there is no boundary defined among the classes.

Each equivalence class represents potential risk. Under the equivalent class approach to developing test cases, at most nine test cases should be executed against each partition. Figure 3.4 illustrates how test cases can be built around equivalence class partitions. In Figure 3.4, *LB* stands for *lower boundary* and *UB* stands for *upper boundary*. The test cases include three tests clustered around each of the boundaries: one test that falls within the partition's boundaries, and two tests that fall well beyond the boundaries.

Figure 3.5 illustrates another boundary condition test-case design example taken from the sample application described in Chapter 8.

To develop test cases via equivalence class partitioning and boundary class analysis, you must do the following:

- Identify the equivalence classes.
- Identify the boundaries.
- Identify the expected output(s) for valid input(s).
- Identify the expected error handling (ER) for invalid inputs.
- Generate a table of test cases (maximum of nine for each partition).

Note that this example is oversimplified; it indicates only two equivalent classes. In reality, there are many other equivalent classes, such as invalid character class (nonalphanumeric characters), special cases such as numbers with decimal points, leading zeros, or leading spaces, and so on. Chapter 11 contains additional information regarding boundary analysis.

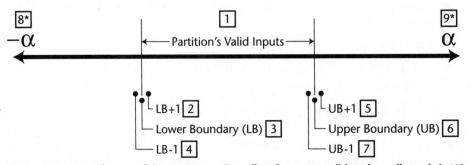

Figure 3.4   Boundary condition test cases (*smallest/largest possible values allowed via UI).
Source: © 1998-2003 LogiGear Corporation. All rights reserved.

Valid Values: 1 to 9999
or 1 to 4-digit value

Test Case	Input	Output
Value Class Partition		
1	Any Valid Input	Functional Result
2	2	Functional Result
3	1	Functional Result
4	0	Error Handling
5	10000	Error Handling
6	9999	Functional Result
7	9998	Functional Result
8	-99999...	Error Handling
9	99999...	Error Handling
Number of Character Class Partition		
1	Any Valid Input	Functional Result
2	2	Functional Result
3	1	Functional Result
4	NULL	Error Handling
5	5	Error Handling
6	4	Functional Result
7	3	Functional Result
8	N/A	N/A
9	99999...	Error Handling

Figure 3.5   Sample application test cases.

State Transition

State transition involves analysis of the transitions between an application's states, the events that trigger the transitions, and the results of the transitions. This is done by using a model of the application's expected behaviors.

A useful resource available on the Internet that contains both articles and links is Harry Robinson's Model-Based Testing Page, www.model-based-testing.org. This Web site contains several articles and useful links on the topic of model-based testing.

GENERAL STEPS FOR STATE TRANSITION TEST-DESIGN ANALYSIS

1. Model, or identify all of an application's supported states. See Figures 3.6 and 3.7.

2. For each test case, define the following:

   ■ The starting state

   ■ The input events that cause the transitions

   ■ The output results or events of each transition

   ■ The end state

3. Build a diagram connecting the states of the application based on the expected behavior. This model is called a *state diagram*. This diagram illustrates the relationships between the states, events, and actions of the application. See Figure 3.8.

4. Generate a table of test cases that addresses each state transition. See Figure 3.9.

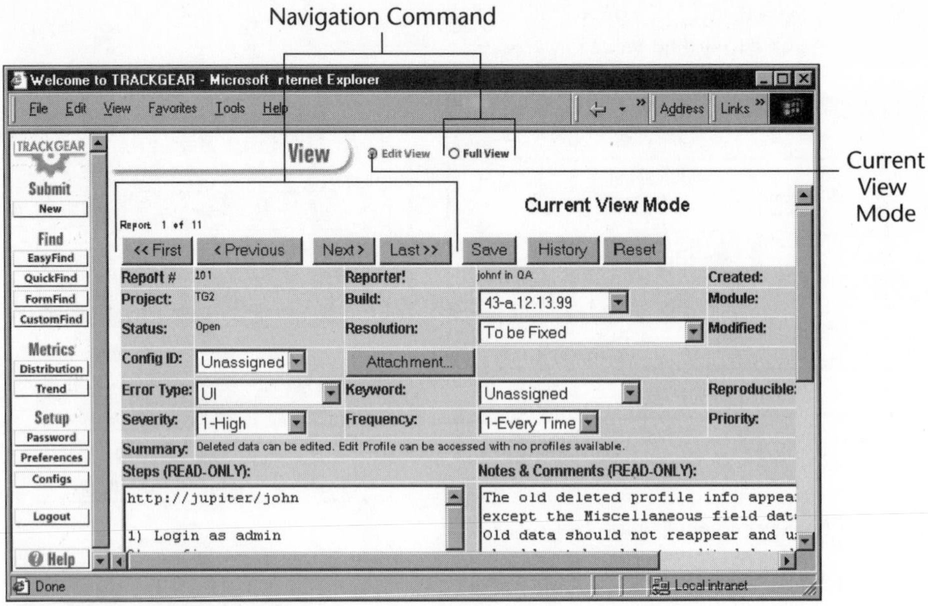

Navigation Command

Figure 3.6   Edit View state.

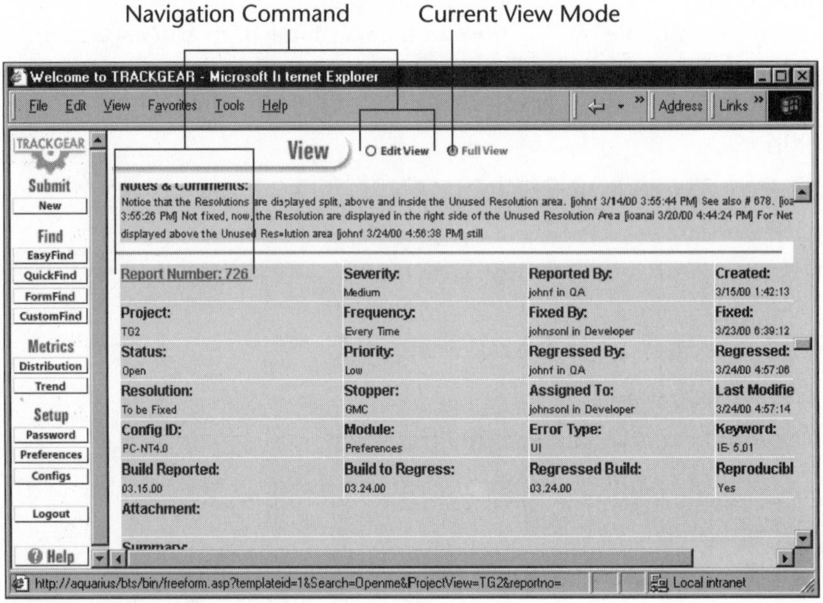

Navigation Command   Current View Mode

Figure 3.7   Full View state.

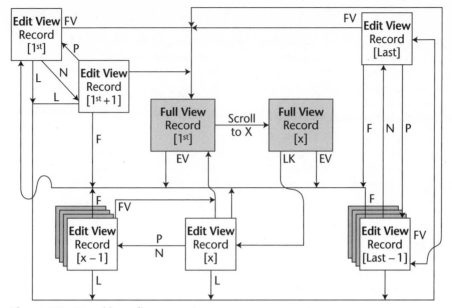

Figure 3.8 Transitions diagram.

Code	VIEW MODE (State)		NAVIGATION COMMAND (Event)	
a	Edit View-Record [1st]	Edit View displaying the 1st record	F	First
b	Edit View-Record [1st +1]	Edit View displaying the 2nd record	P	Previous
c	Edit View-Record [x]	Edit View displaying the record [x]	N	Next
d	Edit View-Record [x -1]	Edit View displaying the record [x -1]	L	Last
e	Edit View-Record [Last]	Edit View displaying the last record	FV	Full View
f	Edit View-Record [Last -1]	Edit View displaying the next to last record		
g	Full View Record [1st]	Full View displaying the 1st record	EV	Edit View
h	Full View Record [x]	Full View displaying the record [x]	LK	Record to ID Link

TEST CASE NO.	1	2	3	4	5	6	7	8	9	10	11	12	13	14	15
Start View Mode	a	a	a	b	b	b	b	c	c	c	c	d	d	d	d
Navigation Command (input)	N	L	FV	F	P	L	FV	F	P	L	FV	F	N	L	FV
End View Mode	b	e	g	a	a	e	g	a	d	e	g	a	c	e	g

TEST CASE NO.	16	17	18	19	20	21	22	23	24	25
Start View Mode	e	e	e	f	f	f	f	g	h	h
Navigation Command (input)	F	P	FV	F	N	L	FV	EV	EV	LK
End View Mode	a	f	g	a	e	e	g	a	a	c

Figure 3.9 Test matrix.

TESTING THE SAMPLE APPLICATION

Figures 3.6 and 3.7 show two different states that are available within the sample application. (See Chapter 8 for details regarding the sample application.) Figure 3.6 shows the application in Edit View mode. Available navigation options from this state include Full View, First, Previous, Next, and Last. Figure 3.7 shows the application in Full View. Available navigation options from this state include Edit View and the Report Number hyperlink. Figure 3.8 diagrams the transitions, events, and actions that interconnect these two states.

Figure 3.9 is a table of test cases that targets each of the transition states. Each test case has a beginning state (Start View Mode), an event or input (Navigation Command), and an event (End View Mode).

Use Cases

A use case is a model of how a system is being used. It is a text description often accompanied by a graphic representation of system users, called *actors*, and the use of the system, called *actions*. Use cases usually include descriptions of system behavior when the system encounters errors.

A typical use case might read:

- An Internet surfer reads reviews for movies in a movie-listing database.
- The surfer searches for a movie by name.
- The surfer searches for theaters showing that movie.

Today, use cases, rightly or wrongly, are most commonly used as requirements from which testers are told to build test cases. Opinions differ greatly as to what a use case is and is not, but this is not the forum for this discussion. Our job is to prepare you for the inevitable task of developing a test strategy or test cases when someone on the team says, "We are now using use cases to aid our development and for you to build your test cases."

A large part of the high growth of the use case method has been the adoption of OMG's UML (Unified Modeling Language) that employs use cases. On Rational Corporation's Web site (www.rational.com/products/whitepapers/featucreqom.pdf) is an excellent white paper, written by Dean Leffingwell, called "Features, Requirements, Use Cases, Oh My!" Though it does not deal with testing issues, it does define use cases and requirements for UML, and puts these items in the context of the software development life cycle.

Use cases describe the functional behavior of the system; they do not capture the nonfunctional requirements or the system design, so there must be other documentation to build thorough test cases.

Use cases generally contain a use case name, scope, or purpose of the use case; the actor executing the action; preconditions for the scenario; postconditions; extensions, sometimes called secondary scenarios; and uses or extends, meaning alternative paths and exceptions giving a description of some error conditions. More detailed use cases might detail the normal course of events as the step-by-step actions on the system. There are two excellent templates to study for this purpose:

- Karl Wiegers from ProcessImpact.com at: www.processimpact.com /process_assets/use_case_template.doc

- Alistar Cockburn's use case template, at: http://members.aol.com /acockburn/papers/uctempla.htm

The degree to which use cases are helpful in designing test cases differs, as usual, according to the author of the use case and how formally or informally the author chose to write them. As with any development documentation, thoroughly detailed use cases can become difficult to maintain and quickly become outdated. Informal use cases may have a longer life, but they often lack adequate information from which to develop detailed test cases.

Since use cases describe how a system is being used, rather than how it is built, they can be a great asset in developing real-world test cases. From them, we can derive process flow, path, functional, and exception-handling information.

Well-written use cases contain, at least, precondition, postcondition, and exception information needed for test case development. Use cases generally contain neither UI-specific nor nonfunctional system information; this information needed for test cases must come from other sources.

You can gain insight from use cases, such as an understanding of which features different users will be using and the order in which they will be used. Often, we expect users to enter at a given point. With Web applications, users may be able to access an application through many points. In event-driven systems, learning about "real-world" activities allows us to model system usage.

Real-world use cases refers not just to the human users but involves modeling other systems with which the application under test will interact. From a security perspective, add cases for unauthorized use.

GENERAL STEPS FOR USE-CASE TEST-DESIGN ANALYSIS

1. Gather all use cases for the area under test.

2. Analyze these use cases to discover the flow of the intended functionality.

3. Analyze each use case based on its normal course of events.

4. Analyze each use case based on secondary scenarios, exceptions, and extends.

5. Identify additional test cases that might be missing.

Example Test Cases from Use Cases

The following example illustrates taking two use cases from a large set of possible use cases to describe a system before developing functional and forced error handling (FET) test cases. The subject of this example is a Web application containing lists of movies, their directors, lead actor/actress, and information on the movie for review. The movie database can be written to and updated by "content editors." The database can be searched or read by users of the Web site. The focus in this example is twofold: an editor writing to the database and an Internet surfer searching the database (see Figure 3.10 for the use case diagram and Figures 3.11 and 3.12 for the use case narrative).

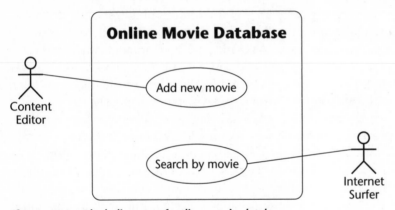

Figure 3.10   Block diagram of online movie database.

Use Case ID:	1.1
Use Case Name:	Search by Movie
Created By:	JW Gibb	Last Updated By:	JW Gibb
Date Created:	5/28/2002	Date Last Updated:	5/28/2002

Actor:	Internet Surfer
Description — Purpose of Case	Describes the process of searching by movie name.
Preconditions	The user is somewhere in the Online Movie Database site.
Postconditions	The Search Results page has been displayed.
Normal Course of Events	1. The user clicks on the Search button. The system displays the Search page. 2. The user enters the Movie name in the Search Text field, then selects Search By Movie from the list of options, then clicks the Search button. The system displays the Search Results page with a list of all the movies that match the search text. 3. Search engine checks for misspellings and variations on title. In order to find "The Lord of the Rings" from "lord of rings."
Secondary Scenarios	1.1.SS.1: In step 2, the user enters the name of a movie that is not in the movie database. The system displays the Search Results page with a message indicating that the movie specified does not exist in the movie database.
Exceptions	1.1.EX.1: In step 2, the user does not enter any text in the Search Text field. The system displays an alert message telling the user that the Search Text field cannot be blank.
Uses/Extends	

Figure 3.11   Use case for Internet surfer.

Use Case ID:	2.1		
Use Case Name:	Add a new movie		
Created By:	JW Gibb	Last Updated By:	JW Gibb
Date Created:	5/28/2002	Date Last Updated:	5/28/2002

Actor:	Content Editor
Description — Purpose of Case	This use case describes the process of adding a new movie to the movie database.
Preconditions	The user is logged in to the content editing interface of the site.
Postconditions	A new movie has been added to the movie database. The system takes the Editor to the Add Movie Actor page.
Normal Course of Events	1. The user clicks the Add a New Movie button. The system displays the Add New Movie page. 2. The user enters the name of the movie in the Movie Name field, then enters the name of the director in the Director field, then enters the year the movie was made in the Year field, then clicks the Save button. The system saves the movie information, then displays the Add Movie Actors page.
Secondary Scenarios	2.1.SS.1: Enter a movie that is already in the database.
Exceptions	2.1.EX.1: In step 2, the user leaves either the Movie Name or Director field blank. The system displays an alert message telling the user to enter text in the appropriate fields. 2.1.EX.2: In step 2, the user enters a movie name and year combination that already exists in the database. The system prompts the user that there is already an entry for the movie in that particular year.
Uses/Extends	

Figure 3.12   Use case for content editor.

Test Cases Built from Use Cases

From the preceding use cases, the tester could produce the following test cases for the Internet surfer (see Figure 3.13).

Use Case ID:	1.1			
Use Case Name:	Search by Movie			
Path or Scenario:	Search			

Test Case Number	1	2	3	4
Initial Condition (Preconditions)	Any Movie site page with Search function available	Any Movie site page with Search function available	Any Movie site page with Search function available	Any Movie site page with Search function available
Actor	Internet Surfer	Internet Surfer	Internet Surfer	Internet Surfer
Action	Enter a Movie name that exists in the Movie Database.	Enter a nonexistent movie name.	Enter extended characters in movie name Text field.	Leave Search text field blank.
Expected Results (Postconditions)	Correct Search results displayed	No Movie found Search result text	Some Error Message – ask Developer for exact message.	Error Message # 47
Pass/Fail/Blocked				
Defect Number				
Notes			Test Data: Â, ß, á iLlegó la Novena	

(continued)

Test Case Number	5	6	7
Initial condition (Preconditions)	Any Movie site page with Search function available	Any Movie site page with Search function available	Any Movie site page with Search function available
Actor	Internet Surfer	Internet Surfer	Internet Surfer
Action	Enter too many characters	Enter illegal characters in Movie Name text field.	Enter maximum 1 character in search.
Expected Results (Postconditions)	Unknown result	Some Error Message ask developer for exact message.	Unknown result
Pass/Fail/Blocked			
Defect Number			
Notes	Not detailed in Use Case 1.1	Test Data: ず, °, ¶	Don't know Maximum. Not in Use Case 1.1

Figure 3.13   Internet surfer search test cases from Search by Movie use case.

A test case for adding a movie to the database can also be created, as shown in Figure 3.14.

Use Case ID:	2.1
Use Case Name:	Add a Movie
Path or Scenario:	Edit Content

Test Case Number	1	2	3
Initial Condition (Preconditions)	User is on Content Edit main page.	User is on Content Edit main page.	User is on Content Edit main page.
Actor	Content Editor	Content Editor	Content Editor
Action	Click to add a movie page.	Click to add a movie page.	Click to add a movie page.
	Enter movie name, director, year.	Enter movie name, director, no year.	Enter movie name, no director, year.
	Click Save.	Click Save.	Click Save.
Expected Results (Postconditions)	Movie added to database. Test by SQL query or search through UI. Page is Add Actor page.	Movie added to Database. Test by SQL query or search through UI. Page is Add Actor page.	Error Message #52- "Please add director name."
Pass/Fail/Blocked			
Defect Number			
Notes		Design Issue: Should a movie be accepted without a year?	

Test Case Number	4	5	6
Initial Condition (Preconditions)	User is on Content Edit main page.	User is on Content Edit Main Page.	User is on Content Edit main page.
Actor	Content Editor	Content Editor	Content Editor
Action	Click to add a movie page.	Click to add a movie page.	Click to add a movie page.
	Enter no Movie Name (leave blank), Director, Year	Enter Movie Name, Director, already in the Database	Enter no Movie Name, no Director, no Year (all blanks)
	Click Save	Click Save	Click Save

(continued)

Expected Results (Postconditions)	Error Message # 53- "Please add Movie Name"	Error Message #54- "That Movie with that Director is already in the database. Do you want to edit that record or enter a different movie?"	Error Message # 53- "Please add Movie Name."
Pass/Fail/Blocked			
Defect Number			
Notes			

Test Case Number	7	8	9
Initial Condition (Preconditions)	User is on Content Edit Main Page	User is on Content Edit Main Page	User is on Content Edit Main Page
Actor	Content Editor	Content Editor	Content Editor
Action	Click to Add a movie Page.	Click to Add a movie Page.	Click to Add a movie Page.
	Enter Movie Name and Year already in the database with different Director	Enter Movie Name and Director already in database with different Year.	Enter Special Characters in any text field.
	Click Save	Click Save	Click Save
Expected Results (Postconditions)	Movie added to Database. Test by SQL query or Search through UI. Page is Add Actor page	Error Message #54- "That Movie with that Director is already in the database. Do you want to edit that record or enter a different movie?"	Unknown Result
Pass/Fail/Blocked			
Defect Number			
Notes	Test Data: Not detailed in Use Case 2.1	Not likely but a test case. What should the expected result be?	Not detailed in Use Case 2.1

Figure 3.14   Add a Movie test cases from content management use cases.

Templates for Use-Case Diagram, Text, and Test Case

Figure 3.15 contains a basic template from Smartdraw.com. Figures 3.16 and 3.17 contain use case templates from Processimpact.com.

Condition Combination

A long-standing challenge in software testing is to find enough time to execute all possible test cases. There are numerous approaches that can be taken to strategically reduce the number of test cases to a manageable amount. The riskiest approach is to randomly reduce test cases without a clear methodology. A better approach is to divide the total test cases over a series of software builds.

The *condition combination* approach involves the analysis of combinations of variables, such as browser settings. Each combination represents a condition to be tested with the same test script and procedures. The condition combination approach involves the following:

- Identifying the variables.

- Identifying the possible unique values for each variable.

- Creating a table that illustrates all the unique combinations of conditions that are formed by the variables and their values.

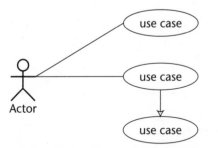

Figure 3.15 Sample use case diagram from www.smartdraw.com.

Use Case ID:	
Use Case Name:	
Created By:	Last Updated By:
Date Created:	Date Last Updated:

Actor:	*Who is using this case?*
Description – Purpose of Case:	*The purpose of the Use Case...*
Preconditions:	*The Use does X, Y, and Z*
Postconditions:	*The user experiences A, B & C*
Normal Course of Events:	*The Use Case begins...*
Secondary Scenarios:	*If the User is not online....*
Exceptions:	*List Here...*
Uses/Extends:	*List Here...*

User Interface Components and Objects for Use Case:

UI Control/Object	Action	Response/Description

Miscellaneous

Special Requirements:	*List Here...*
Notes and Issues:	*List Here...*

Template for Use Case Driven Test Cases

Product Name:	Test Environment:
Test Case Title:	Time:
Test Suite:	Build :
Tester Name:	Version:
Date:	Time to Complete Tests:

Figure 3.16   Use case template from processimpact.com.

Use Case ID: #.#

Use Case Name: Functional Example Area

Path or Scenario: XXX

Test Case Number	1	2
Initial Condition		
(Preconditions)		
Actor		
Action		
Expected Results		
(Postconditions)		
Pass/Fail/Blocked		
Defect Number		
Notes		

Figure 3.17 Test case template from processimpact.com.

Figures 3.18 and 3.19 illustrate an application that includes three variables each with three possible unique values. The number of complete combinations formed by the variables is $3 \times 3 \times 3 = 27$. The 27 unique combinations (test cases) formed by the three variables A, B, and C are listed in Table 3.1. To execute the test cases calculated by these unique combinations, set the values for each A, B, and C variable using the variables listed in the corresponding rows of the tables. Execute the procedures and verify expected results.

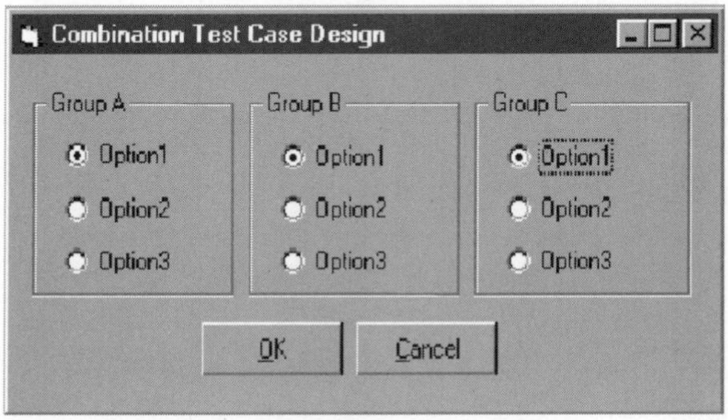

Figure 3.18 Simplified application example.

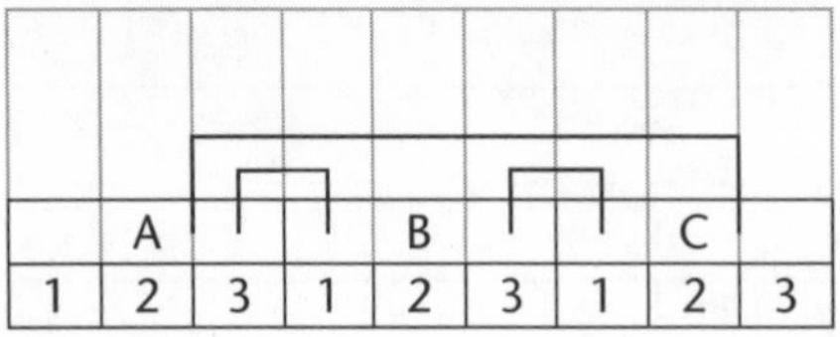

Figure 3.19 Unique combinations.

The Combinatorial Method

The *combinatorial method* is a thoughtful means of reducing test cases via a pairwise shortcut. It involves analyzing combinations of variables, such as browser settings, one pair at a time. Each unique combination pair represents a condition to be tested. By examining and testing pair combinations, the number of total conditions to be tested can be dramatically reduced. This technique is useful when complete condition combination testing is not feasible. The combinatorial method involves the following:

- Identifying the variables.
- Identifying the possible unique values for each variable.
- Identifying the unique combinations formed by the variables, one pair at a time.
- Creating a table that illustrates all of the unique combinations of conditions that are formed by the variables and their values.

Table 3.2 Total Unique Combinations

Case	A	B	C	Case	A	B	C	Case	A	B	C
1	1	1	1	10	2	1	1	19	3	1	1
2	1	1	2	11	2	1	2	20	3	1	2
3	1	1	3	12	2	1	3	21	3	1	3
4	1	2	1	13	2	2	1	22	3	2	1
5	1	2	2	14	2	2	2	23	3	2	2
6	1	2	3	15	2	2	3	24	3	2	3
7	1	3	1	16	2	3	1	25	3	3	1
8	1	3	2	17	2	3	2	26	3	3	2
9	1	3	3	18	2	3	3	27	3	3	3

- Generating the unique combinations formed by the first pair, A-B. As illustrated in Table 3.3, arrange the values in the C column to cover the combinations of the B-C and A-C pairs without increasing the number of cases. Set the value of the variables A, B, and C using the information listed in each row of the table, one at a time. Execute the test procedure and verify the expected output.

For more information on this technique, go to AR GREENHOUSE at www.argreenhouse.com. For a paper on this topic, "The AETG System: An Approach to Testing Based on Combinatorial Design" (Cohen et al., 1997), go to www.argreenhouse.com/papers/gcp/AETGieee97.shtml.

Table 3.3 The Combinatorial Method

Case	A	B	C
1	1	1	
2	1	2	
3	1	3	
4	2	1	
5	2	2	
6	2	3	
7	3	1	
8	3	2	
9	3	3	

Case	A	B	C
10		1	1
11		2	2
12		3	3
13		1	2
14		2	3
15		3	1
16		1	3
17		2	1
18		3	2

Case	A	B	C
19	1		1
20	1		2
21	1		3
22	2		2
23	2		3
24	2		1
25	3		3
26	3		1
27	3		2

Case	A	B	C
1	1	1	1
2	1	2	2
3	1	3	3
4	2	1	2
5	2	2	3
6	2	3	1
7	3	1	3
8	3	2	1
9	3	3	2

Bibliography

Cockburn, Alistair. *Writing Effective Use Cases.* New York: Addison-Wesley, 2001.

Cohen, D.M. Dalal, S.R., Fredman, M.L., Patton, C.G. "The AETG System: An Approach to Testing Based on Combinatorial Design," in *IEEE Transactions On Software Engineering,* Vol. 23, No. 7, July 1997, pp. 437 – 444.

Jacobson, Ivar, and Magnus Christerson, Patrik Jonsson, and Gunnar Övergaard. *Object-Oriented Software Engineering: A Use-Case-Driven Approach,* Wokingham, England: Addison-Wesley, 1992.

Kaner, Cem, Jack Falk, Hung Q. Nguyen. *Testing Computer Software,* 2nd ed. New York: John Wiley & Sons, Inc., 1999.

LogiGear Corporation. *QA Training Handbook: Testing Web Applications.* Foster City, CA: LogiGear Corporation, 2000.

────── *QA Training Handbook: Testing Windows Desktop and Server-Based Applications.* Foster City, CA: LogiGear Corporation, 2000.

────── *QA Training Handbook: Testing Computer Software.* Foster City, CA: LogiGear Corporation, 2000.

QACity.com: www.qacity.com.

CHAPTER

4

Networking Basics

Why Read This Chapter?

Networks hold Web systems together; they provide connectivity between clients and servers. The reliability, bandwidth, and latency of network components such as T1 lines and routers directly influence the performance of Web systems.

Having knowledge of the networking environment enables you to identify configuration and compatibility requirements for your test planning, and enhances your bug-analysis abilities.

TOPICS COVERED IN THIS CHAPTER

- ◆ Introduction
- ◆ The Basics
- ◆ Other Useful Information
- ◆ Testing Considerations
- ◆ Bibliography

Introduction

This chapter delivers a brief introduction to networking technologies; the information supports the effective planning, testing, analysis of errors, and communication that is required for the testing of Web applications. Network topologies, connection types, and hardware components are also discussed. The chapter also offers test examples and testing considerations that pertain to networking.

POSSIBLE ENVIRONMENTAL PROBLEMS THAT MAY CAUSE AN APPLICATION TO OPERATE INCORRECTLY

- Either the client or server may be inaccessible because it is not connected to the network.
- There may be a failure in converting a Domain Name Service (DNS) name to an Internet Protocol (IP) address.
- A slow connection may result in a time-out.
- There may be an authentication process failure due to an invalid ID or password.
- The server or client may be incorrectly configured.
- Firewall may block all or part of the transmitted packets.
- Childproofing software may be blocking access to certain servers or files.

The Basics

The material in this section introduces, in turn, network types, connectivity services, and hardware devices, and provides other useful information on such topics as TCP/IP, IP addresses, DNS, and subnetting/supernetting.

The Networks

Networks comprise the delivery system that offers connectivity that glues clients, servers, and other communication devices together.

The Internet

The Internet's infrastructure is built of regional networks, Internet service providers (ISPs), high-speed backbones, network information centers, and supporting organizations (e.g., the Internet Registry and, recently, the Internet Corporation for Assigned Names and Numbers (ICANN)). Web systems don't exist without the Internet and the networked structures of which the Internet is composed. Understanding how information moves across the Internet, how client-side users gain access to the Internet, and how IPs relate to one another can be useful in determining testing requirements.

As illustrated in Figure 4.1, government-operated backbones or very high-speed Backbone Network Services (vBNSs) connect supercomputer centers together, linking education and research communities. These backbones serve as the principal highways that support Internet traffic. Some large organizations, such as NASA, provide Internet backbones for public use.

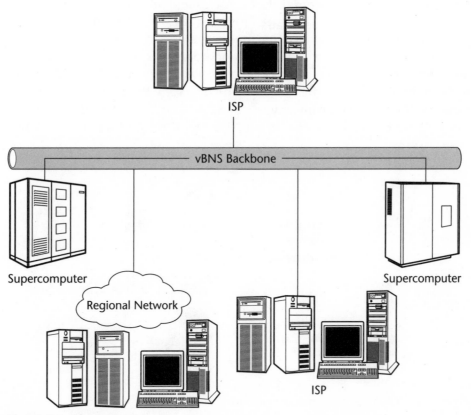

Figure 4.1 The Internet.

Internet service providers and regional networks connect to the backbones. Internet service providers are private organizations that sell Internet connections to end users; both individuals and companies can gain Internet access through ISPs. Online services such as America Online sell access to private sectors of the Internet, in addition to the general Internet. Regional networks are groups of small networks that band together to offer Internet access in a certain geographical area. These networks include companies and online services that can provide better service as groups than they can independently.

Local Area Networks (LANs)

Web-based applications operating over the Internet normally run on *local area networks* (LANs). The LANs are relatively small groups of computers that have been networked to one another. Local area networks are often set up at online services; government, business, and home offices; and other organizations that require numerous computers to regularly communicate with one another. Two common types of LANs are *Ethernet networks* and *token-ring networks*. Transmission Control Protocol/Internet Protocol (TCP/IP), the suite of network protocols enabling communication among clients and servers on a Web system, runs on both of these popular network topologies. On an Ethernet LAN, any computer can send packets of data to any other computer on the same LAN simultaneously. With token-ring networks, data is passed in *tokens* (packets of data) from one host to the next, around the network, in a ring or star pattern. Figure 4.2 illustrates simple token-ring and Ethernet networks, respectively.

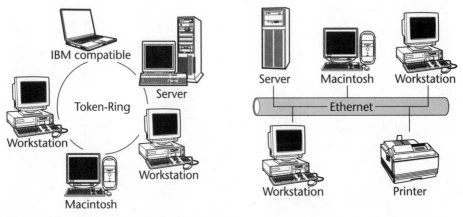

Figure 4.2   Token-ring and Ethernet networks.

Typically, a LAN is set up as a private network. Only authorized LAN users can access data and resources on that network. When a Web-based system is hosted on a private LAN (its services are only available within the LAN) and application access is only available to hosts (computers) within the LAN or to trusted hosts connected to the LAN (e.g., through remote-access service (RAS)), the Web-based system is considered an *intranet* system.

Wide Area Networks (WANs)

Multiple LANs can be linked together through a *wide area network* (WAN). Typically, a WAN connects two or more private LANs that are run by the same organization in two or more regions. Figure 4.3 is an illustration of an X.25 (one of several available *packet-routing service standards*) WAN connecting computers on a token-ring LAN in one geographic region (San Jose, California, for example) to computers on another Ethernet LAN in a different geographic region (Washington, DC, for example).

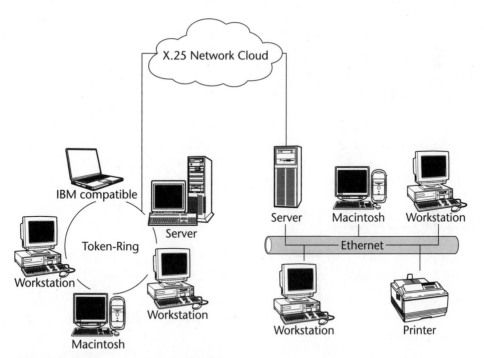

Figure 4.3 Wide area networks (WANs).

Connecting Networks

There are numerous connectivity services and hardware options available for connecting networks to the Internet, as well as to each other; countless testing-related issues may be affected by these components.

Connectivity Services

The two common connection types are *dial-up connection* and *direct connection*, which are discussed in turn next.

Dial-Up Connection

One very familiar connection service type is the dial-up connection, made through a telephone line.

  Plain Old Telephone Service (POTS). POTS is the standard analog telephone line used by most homes and businesses. A POTS network is often also called the *public switched telephone network* (PSTN). Through an analog modem, a POTS connection offers a transmission rate of up to 56 kilobits per second (Kbps).

  Integrated Services Digital Network (ISDN). The ISDN lines are high-speed dial-up connections over telephone lines. The ISDN lines with which we are familiar can support a data transmission rate of 64 Kbps (if only one of the two available wires is used) or 128 Kbps (if both wires are used). Although not widely available, there is a broadband version (as opposed to the normal baseband version) of ISDN, called *B-ISDN*. The B-ISDN supports a data transmission rate of 1.5 megabits per second (Mbps), but it requires fiber-optic cable.

Direct Connection

In contrast to dial-up, another series of connection service type is direct connection such as leased-line, including T1, T3, cable modem, and DSL.

  T1 connection. T1s (connection services) are dedicated, leased telephone lines that provide point-to-point connections. They transmit data using a set of 24 channels across two-wire pairs. One-half of each pair is for sending, the other half is for receiving; combined, the pairs supply a data rate of 1.54 Mbps.

  T3 connection. T3 lines are similar to T1 lines except that, instead of using 24 channels, T3 lines use 672 channels (an equivalent of 28 T1 lines), enabling them to support a much higher data transmission rate: 45 Mbps. Internet service providers and Fortune 500 corporations that connect directly to the Internet's high-speed backbones often use T3 lines. Many start-up Internet companies require bandwidth comparable with a T3 to support their e-business infrastructures, yet they cannot afford the associated costs; the alternative for these smaller companies is to share expensive high-speed connections with larger corporations.

DS connection services. DS connection services are fractional or multiple T1 and T3 lines. T1 and T3 lines can be subdivided or combined for fractional or multiple levels of service. For example, DS-0 provides a single channel (out of 24 channels) of bandwidth that can transmit 56 Kbps (kilobits per second). DS-1 service is a full T1 line; DS-1C is two T1 lines; DS-2 is four T1 lines; DS-3 is a full T3 line.

Digital subscriber line (DSL). The DSL offers high-bandwidth connections to small businesses and homes via regular telephone lines. There are several types of DSL, including Asymmetric Digital Subscriber Line (ADSL), which is more popular in North America, and Symmetric Digital Subscriber Line (SDSL). The ADSL supports a downstream transmission rate (receiving) of 1.5 to 9 Mbps, and an upstream transmission rate (sending) of 16 to 640 Kbps. The DSL lines carry both data and traditional voice transmissions; the data portion of the bandwidth, however, is always connected.

Cable connection services. Through a cable modem, a computer can be connected to a local cable TV service line, enabling a data transmission rate, or *throughput*, of about 1.5 Mbps upstream (sending) and an even much higher rate for downstream (receiving). However, cable modem technology utilizes a shared medium in which all of the users served by a node (between a couple hundred to a couple thousand homes, depending on the provider) share bandwidth. Therefore, the throughput can be affected by the number of cable modem users in a given neighborhood and the types of activities in which those users are engaged on the network. In most cases, cable service providers supply the cable modems and Ethernet interface cards as part of the access service.

Internet Connection Hardware

To connect a terminal or a network to the Internet, a hardware device such as a modem must be used to enable the communication between each side of the connection. With POTS dial-up connections, analog modems are used. With ISDN, ISDN (digital) modems are used. With DSL and cable connections, DSL modems and cable modems are used.

With leased lines such as T1, T3, and other DS connection services, a channel service unit/data service unit (CSU/DSU) device is used. Though actually two different units, they are often packaged as one. You may think of CSU/DSU as an expensive and powerful version of a modem that is required at both ends of the leased-line connection.

Other Network Connectivity Devices

Local area networks employ several types of connectivity devices to link them together. Some of the common hardware devices include:

Repeaters. Used to amplify data signals at certain intervals to ensure that signals are not distorted or lost over great distances.

Hubs. Used to connect groups or segments of computers and devices to one another so that they can communicate on a network, such as a LAN. A hub has multiple ports. When a data packet arrives at one port, it is replicated to the other ports so that computers or devices connected to other ports will see the data packet. Generally, there are three types of hubs.

- *Bridges.* Used to connect physical LANs that use the same protocol into a single, logical network. Bridges examine incoming messages and pass the messages on to the appropriate computers, on either a local LAN or a remote LAN.

- *Routers.* Used to ensure that data are delivered to the correct destinations. Routers are like bridges, except that they support more features. Routers determine how to forward packets, based on IP address and network traffic. When they receive packets with a destination address of a host that is outside of the network or subnetwork, they route the packets to other routers outside of the network or subnetwork so that the packets will eventually reach their destination. Routers are often not necessary when transmitting data within the same network, such as over a LAN.

- *Gateways.* Used like routers, except that they support even more features than routers. For example, a gateway can connect two different types of networks, enabling users from one network (Novell IPX/SPX, for example) to exchange data with users on a different network type (for example, TCP/IP).

Figure 4.4 illustrates a sample configuration in which a bridge, router, or gateway is used to connect the two networks or subnetworks.

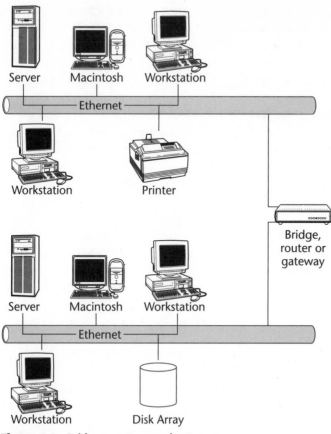

Figure 4.4 Bridges, routers, and gateways.

TCP/IP Protocols

The Internet is a *packet-switched* network, meaning that all transmitted data objects are broken up into small packets (each less than 1,500 characters). The packets are sent to the receiving computer where they are reassembled into the original object.

The TCP is responsible for breaking up information into packets and reassembling packets once they reach their destination. Each packet is given a header that contains information regarding the order in which packets should be reassembled; the header also contains a *checksum*, which records the precise amount of information in each packet. Checksums are used to determine, on the receiving end, if packets were received in their entirety.

The IP is responsible for routing packets to their correct destinations. The IP puts packets into separate IP *envelopes* that have unique headers. The envelope headers provide such information as the receiver's and the sender's addresses. The IP envelopes are sent separately through routers to their destination. The IP envelopes of the same transmission may travel different routes to reach the same destination—often arriving out of order. Before reassembling the packets on the receiving end, TCP calculates the checksum of each packet and compares it with the checksum of the original TCP headers. If the checksums do not match, TCP discards the unmatched packets and requests the original packets to be resent.

The TCP/IP Architecture

For computers to communicate over the Internet, each computer, client or server, must utilize a standard set of protocols called TCP/IP. This suite of protocols is referred to as a TCP/IP *stack* or *socket*. There are numerous versions of TCP/IP stack available, for every target platform and operating system (UNIX, PC, Macintosh, handheld devices, etc.). The TCP/IP stack, as illustrated in Figure 4.5, is composed of five layers: application, transport, Internet, data link, and physical.

The Application Layer

The top layer of the TCP/IP protocol is the *application layer.* End-user applications interact with this layer. The protocols in this layer perform activities such as enabling end-user applications to send, receive, and convert data into their native formats, and establishing a connection (session) between two computers.

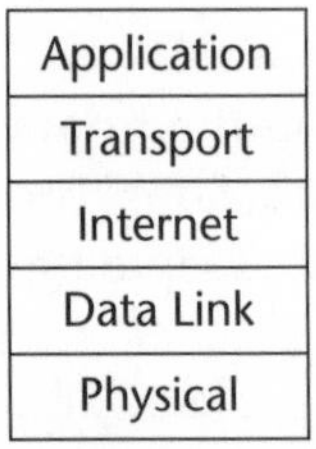

| Application |
| Transport |
| Internet |
| Data Link |
| Physical |

Figure 4.5   TCP/IP stack architecture.

Examples of several common protocols associated with the application layer include:

HyperText Transfer Protocol (HTTP). Commonly used in browsers to transfer Web pages and other related data between clients and servers across the Internet.

File Transfer Protocol (FTP). Commonly used in browsers or other applications to copy files between computers by downloading files from one remote computer and uploading them to another computer.

Network News Transfer Protocol (NNTP). Used in news reading applications to transfer USENET news articles between servers and clients, as well as between servers.

Simple Mail Transfer Protocol (SMTP). Used by e-mail applications to send e-mail messages between computers.

Dynamic Host Configuration Protocol (DHCP). Used in server-based applications to allocate shared IP addresses to individual computers. When a client computer requires an IP address, a DHCP server assigns the client an IP address from a pool of shared addresses.

For example, a network may have 80 workstations, but only 54 IP addresses available. The DHCP allows the 80 workstations to share the 54 IP addresses in a way that is analogous to an office with 80 employees who share a phone system with only 54 trunk lines. In this scenario, it is expected that in normal operation no more than 54 employees will be on the phone at the same time. That is, the 55th employee and beyond will not be able to get onto the system.

The Transport Layer

The *transport layer* breaks data into packets before sending them. Upon receipt, the transport layer ensures that all packets arrive intact. It also arranges packets into the correct order.

Examples of two common protocols associated with the transport layer are the Transmission Control Protocol (TCP) and User Datagram Protocol (UDP). Both TCP and UDP are used to transport IP packets to applications and to flow data between computers. TCP ensures that no transported data is dropped during transmissions. Error checking and sequence numbering are two of TCP's important functions. TCP uses IP to deliver packets to applications, and it provides a reliable stream of data between computers on networks. Once a packet arrives at its destination, TCP delivers confirmation to the sending and receiving computers regarding the transmitted data. It also requests that packets be resent if they are lost.

- TCP is referred to as a *connection-oriented* protocol. Connection-oriented protocols require that a channel be established (a communications line between the sending and receiving hosts, such as in a telephone connection) before messages are transmitted.

- UDP is considered a *connectionless protocol.* This means that data can be sent without creating a connection to the receiving host. The sending computer simply places messages on the network with the destination address and "hopes" that the messages arrive intact.

UDP does not check for dropped data. The benefit of being connectionless is that data can be transferred more quickly; the drawback is that data can more easily be lost during transmission.

The Internet Layer

The *Internet layer* receives data packets from the transport layer and sends them to the correct network address using the IP. The Internet layer also determines the best route for data to travel.

Examples of several common protocols associated with the Internet layer include the following:

Internet Protocol (IP). Responsible for basic network connectivity. Every computer on a TCP/IP network has a numeric IP address. This unique network ID enables data to be sent to and received from other networks, similar to the way that a traditional street address allows a person to send and receive snail mail.

Address Resolution Protocol (ARP). Responsible for identifying the address of a remote computer's network interface card (such as an Ethernet interface) when only the computer's TCP/IP address is known.

Reverse Address Resolution Protocol (RARP). The opposite of ARP. When all that is known is a remote computer's network interface card hardware address, RARP determines the computer's IP address.

The Data Link Layer

The *data link layer* moves data across the physical link of a network. It splits outgoing data into frames and establishes communication with the receiving end to validate the successful delivery of data. It also validates that incoming data are received successfully.

The Physical Layer

The *physical layer* is the bottom layer of the TCP/IP stack. It supports the electrical or mechanical interface of the connection medium. It is the hardware layer and is composed of a network interface card and wiring such as coaxial cable, 10/100-Based-T wiring, satellite, or leased-line.

Testing Scenarios

Normally, with Web-based systems, we may not have to be concerned with issues related to connection services, connectivity devices, or how the TCP/IP stack may affect the applications. When an HTTP-based (i.e., Web browser-based) application runs within the context of a third-party browser (e.g., Netscape Navigator or Microsoft Explorer), one can argue that how a TCP/IP connection is established, which hardware components are used on the network, or the connection throughput does not seem to matter. But when we understand the basics of the technologies, we can more accurately determine which parts need testing and which parts can be left alone.

HOW TCP/IP PROTOCOLS WORK TOGETHER

Figure 4.6 illustrates a simplified version of the data-flow processes that occur when a user sends an e-mail message. The process on the sender's end begins at the top layer, the application layer, and concludes at the physical layer, where the e-mail message leaves the sender's network.

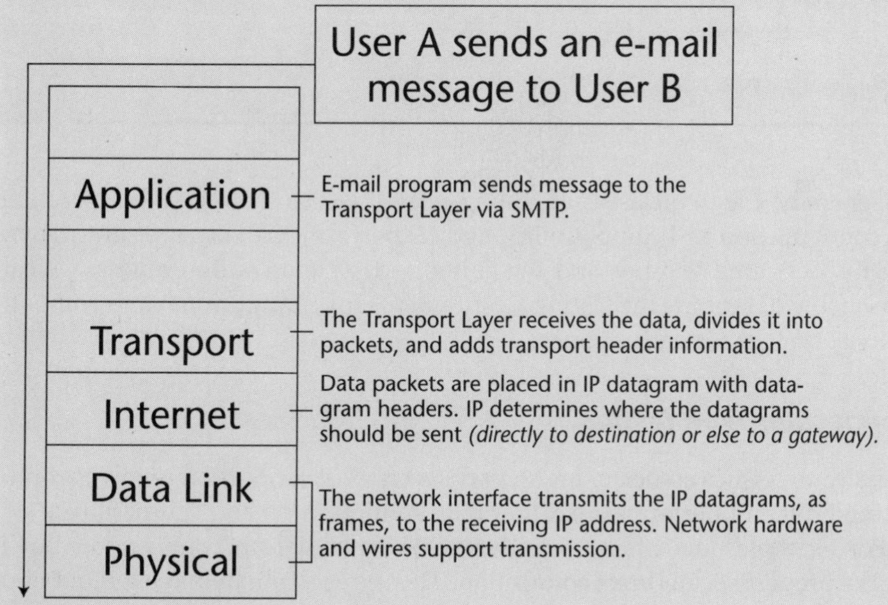

User A sends an e-mail message to User B

| Application | E-mail program sends message to the Transport Layer via SMTP. |

| Transport | The Transport Layer receives the data, divides it into packets, and adds transport header information. |

| Internet | Data packets are placed in IP datagram with datagram headers. IP determines where the datagrams should be sent *(directly to destination or else to a gateway)*. |

| Data Link | The network interface transmits the IP datagrams, as frames, to the receiving IP address. Network hardware and wires support transmission. |

| Physical | |

Figure 4.6   E-mail sent.

(continued)

HOW TCP/IP PROTOCOLS WORK TOGETHER (continued)

The process continues on the receiver's end, working in reverse order. The physical layer receives the sender's message and passes it upward until it reaches the receiver's application layer (see Figure 4.7).

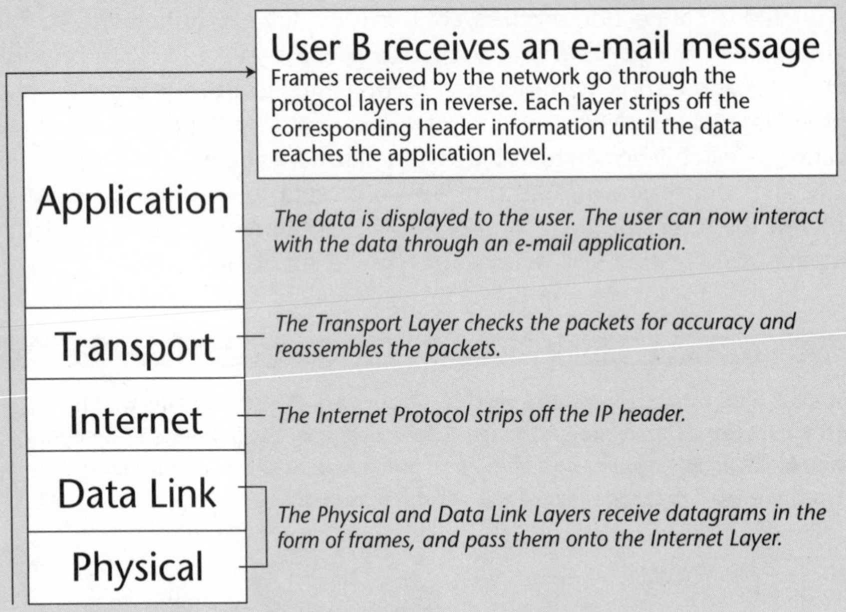

User B receives an e-mail message
Frames received by the network go through the protocol layers in reverse. Each layer strips off the corresponding header information until the data reaches the application level.

Application
The data is displayed to the user. The user can now interact with the data through an e-mail application.

Transport
The Transport Layer checks the packets for accuracy and reassembles the packets.

Internet
The Internet Protocol strips off the IP header.

Data Link

Physical
The Physical and Data Link Layers receive datagrams in the form of frames, and pass them onto the Internet Layer.

Figure 4.7   E-mail received.

Generally, the two classes of testing-related issues that need coverage are: (1) configuration and compatibility, and (2) performance. By carefully analyzing the delivered features and the supported system configurations, we can reasonably determine the testing requirements for configuration and compatibility as well as for performance.

Connection Type Testing

Usually, the issues associated with various types of connection revolve around throughput and performance rather than configuration and compatibility.

For example, login fails to authenticate with dial-up connections, but it works properly with direct connection. This symptom may have a number of causes, but one common issue is that the slow connection causes a time-out in the login or authentication process. With slow connections such as dial-up, it may take too long (longer than the script time-out value) for the client-server to send/receive packets of data; thus, the script will eventually time-out, causing the login or authentication process to fail. The problem cannot, however, be reproduced when the same procedure is retried on an intranet or a LAN connection.

As described earlier, we often work with two types of connections that offer us various throughput rates: direct connection and dial-up connection. Common direct connection configurations to consider include:

- Standard LAN and/or WAN connections (intranet)
- Standard LAN and/or WAN connections with a gateway to the Internet using T1, T3, and DS services; DSL; or cable services
- Stand-alone connections to the Internet using DSL or cable services

Common dial-up connection configurations to consider include:

- Stand-alone connections to the Internet through an ISP directly, using POTS lines or ISDN lines (see Figure 4.8 for an example)

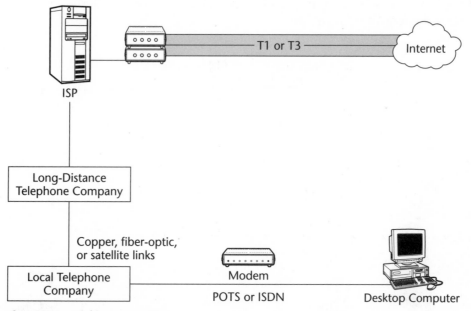

Figure 4.8 Dial-up connection.

In the standard dial-up model (Figure 4.8), the client is a PC that is connected to a modem. Through a local telephone line or ISDN, a connection is made to an ISP. Depending on whether the ISP is local or not, the local phone company may have to connect (via satellite, copper, or fiber-optic cable) to the ISP through a long-distance carrier. The ISP also has a modem to receive the phone call and to establish a connection to the PC.

- Stand-alone connections to the intranet (LAN) through RAS, using POTS lines or ISDN lines

- Stand-alone connections to the intranet (LAN) through virtual private network (VPN) services, using POTS lines or ISDN lines

- Stand-alone connections to the intranet (LAN) through RAS, using POTS lines or ISDN lines, and then to the Internet using a leased line (see Figure 4.9 for an example)

Differing from the model in which the client dials up through an ISP is the model of the client dialing up through an RAS. If a LAN is connected directly to the local phone company, there is no need for a long-distance telephone connection. In Figure 4.9, the modem on the server-side receives the connection from the local phone company and translates it for the RAS; after proper authentication, LAN resources are made available to the user. If the LAN has a leased line, the user can link to an ISP and, ultimately, to the Internet through the local phone company.

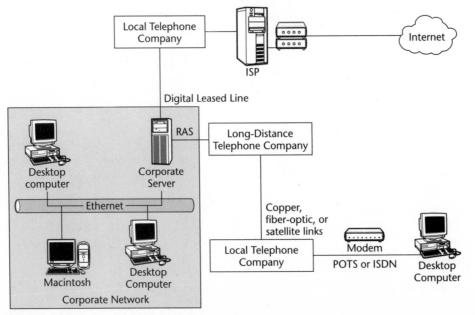

Figure 4.9 Dial-up and leased-line connections.

Potential Modem Compatibility Issues

Users of the Web system under test may be dialing in with a modem that translates digital computer signals into analog signals; the analog signals are carried over POTS lines. The brand names and baud rates (generally ranging from 14.4 to 56 Kbps) of these modems may affect the perceived performance of the Web system under test.

Generally, a modem is a "doesn't matter" issue to a Web application. However, if your application is an embedded browser that also provides drivers for users to connect to certain modems, then the connection type and modem brands may be an issue for testing. If modem compatibility issues are a concern for the system under test, then both client- and server-side modems should be tested.

Potential Dialer Compatibility Issues

Dialer compatibility testing is often required when a Web system interacts with a dialer. Some ISPs, such as EarthLink and AOL, supply users with proprietary dialers. Dialup Networking has more than one version of its dialer. Some ISPs supply their new users with CD-ROMs that replace existing browsers and dialers so that users can connect to their services. Such CDs often install new components, which can cause incompatibility or conflict problems that may lead to errors such as a system crash.

Some dialers also offer users a couple of protocol options from which to choose. Two common dial-up protocols are *Serial Line Internet Protocol* (SLIP) and *Point-to-Point Protocol* (PPP). The SLIP is the older of the two, but Point-to-Point is the most popular, as well as the most stable; it enables point-to-point connections and, when necessary, can retransmit garbled data packets. If the Web application under test is an embedded application that also delivers a dialer that supports more than one dial-up protocol, compatibility testing should be considered. Otherwise, this is usually a "doesn't matter" issue to standard browser-based application testing.

Connectivity Device Testing

Do we need to test our HTTP-based application with various brands and models of hubs, repeaters, bridges, routers, and gateways under various configurations? Hopefully, the answer is no, because a standard Web browser-based application does not interact directly with such devices. However, if a Web application under test is a custom-embedded application that supports several protocols at different layers of the TCP/IP stacks, incompatibility issues may be introduced in interactions with the connectivity devices. For example, assume that an embedded HTTP-based application uses Reverse Address Resolution Protocol (RARP) at the Internet layer of the TCP/IP stacks to determine the computer's IP address; in this case, compatibility tests should be conducted with connectivity devices that support RARP, such as routers and gateways.

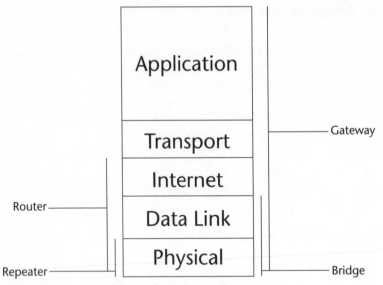

Figure 4.10   Network layer/device interaction.

Many hardware devices do interact with different layers of the TCP/IP stack. Figures 4.10 and 4.11 illustrate the differences in intelligence and network layer interaction that these devices exhibit. Understanding the implementation and support of Web-based applications in the context of TCP/IP layering allows you to determine if configuration and compatibility testing of hardware devices (such as gateways and routers) will be necessary.

	Hubs	Repeaters	Bridges	Routers	Gateways
Network Layer Protocols					
Application	No	No	No	No	Yes
Transport	No	No	No	No	Yes
Internet	No	No	No	Yes	Yes
Data Link	No	No	Yes	Yes	Yes
Physical	Yes	Yes	Yes	Yes	Yes
Address Recognized					
IP	No	No	No	Yes	Yes
Hardware Interface	No	No	Yes	Yes	Yes

Figure 4.11   Network layer protocols and recognized addresses.

Other Useful Information

This section offers an overview of how IP addresses, DNS, and network subnets work; the intent here is to help testers become better at analyzing errors, as well as troubleshooting network-/Web-related issues.

IP Addresses and DNS

Every network device that uses TCP/IP must have a unique domain name and IP address. Internet Protocol addresses are 32-bit numbers—four fields of 8 bits each, each field separated by a dot (Figure 4.13). To better understand IP addresses, it is helpful to review the binary model of computer data storage (Figure 4.12).

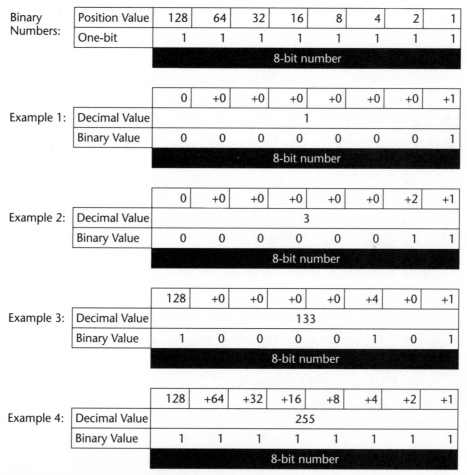

Figure 4.12 Binary model of computer data storage.

Binary is *base two*; it differs from the standard numerical system, which is *base ten*. Base two (binary) dictates that each digit, or *bit*, may have one of two values: 1 (meaning *on*) and 0 (meaning *off*). The value of a bit depends on its position. Figure 4.12 includes four examples of standard numerals expressed in the binary model: 1, 3, 133, and 255.

Starting from right to left, each of the 8-bit positions represents a different number. Depending on the numeral being expressed, each bit is set either to on or off. To calculate the expressed numeral, the on-bit positions must be added up. In the fourth example, note that all positions are set to on, and the resulting value—the maximum value for an 8-bit number—is 255.

IP Address

Internet Protocol addresses are segmented into two numbers: a *network number* and a *host number*. The network number identifies a specific organization's network that is connected to the Internet. Within that network there are specific host computers on individual desktops. These host computers are identified by host numbers. The number of hosts that a network can support depends on the *class* of the network. Figure 4.13 is an example of a Class C IP address.

Network Classes

The Internet is running low on available IP addresses. This is not due to a limitation of the Internet itself or even of software; rather, it is a limitation of the naming convention, or *dotted-decimal notation*, the industry has established to express IP addresses. Simply put, there are mathematical limitations to the amount of numbers that can be expressed in the 32-bit model.

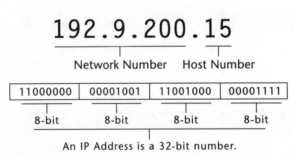

Figure 4.13   Class C IP address.

THREE CLASSES OF TCP/IP NETWORKS

- *Class A networks.* There are only 126 class A network addresses available. Class A networks can support an enormous number of host devices—16,777,216. Not many organizations require access to such a large number of hosts. America Online, Pacific Bell, and AT&T are some of the organizations that have class A networks. Class A networks use only the first 8 bits of their IP addresses as the network number. The remaining 24 bits are dedicated to host numbers.

- *Class B networks.* Class B networks can support approximately 65,000 hosts. The Internet can support a maximum of 16,384 class B networks. Class B networks are quite large, but nowhere near as large as class A. Universities and many large organizations require class B networks. Class B networks use the first 16 bits of their IP addresses as the network number. The remaining 16 bits are dedicated to host numbers.

- *Class C networks.* Class C networks are both the most common and the smallest network class available. There are more than 2 million class C networks on the Internet. Each class C network can support up to 254 hosts. Class C networks use the first 24 bits of their IP addresses as the network number. The remaining 8 bits are dedicated to host numbers.

Domain Name System (DNS)

Although identifying specific computers with unique 32-bit numbers (IP addresses) makes sense for computers, humans find it very challenging to remember network and host names labeled in this way. That is why Sun Microsystems developed the Domain Name Service (DNS) in the early 1980s. DNS associates alphabetic aliases with numeric IP addresses. The *DNS servers* match simple alphabetic *domain names,* such as logigear.com and netscape. com, with the 32-bit IP addresses that the names represent. With this method, Internet users only have to remember the domain names of the Internet sites they wish to visit. If a domain server does not have a certain IP address/ domain name match listed in its database, that server will route a request to another DNS that will, hopefully, be able to figure out the IP address associated with the particular domain name.

E-mail addresses are made up of two main components that are separated by an @ symbol. The far right of every e-mail address includes the most general information, the far left includes the most specific. The far left of every e-mail address is the user's name. The second part, to the right of the @ symbol, is the domain name. For example, in webtester@qacity.com, *webtester* is the user name and *qacity.com* is the domain name.

The domain name itself can be broken down into at least two components, each separated by a period. The far right component of the domain name is the *extension*. The extension defines the domain as being commercial (.com), network-based (.net), educational (.edu), governmental (.gov), small business (.biz), resource Web sites (.info), content rich Web sites (.tv), or military (.mil). Countries outside the United States have their own extensions: Canada (.ca), Great Britain (.uk), and Japan (.jp) are a few of these.

To the left of the domain extension is the name of the host organization, or ISP (.logigear, .compuserve, etc.). Often, domain names are further subdivided, as in webtester@montreal.qacity.com. In this example, *montreal* is the *host name;* this is the specific host computer that acts as the "post office" for webtester's e-mail. Figure 4.14 shows examples of domain names.

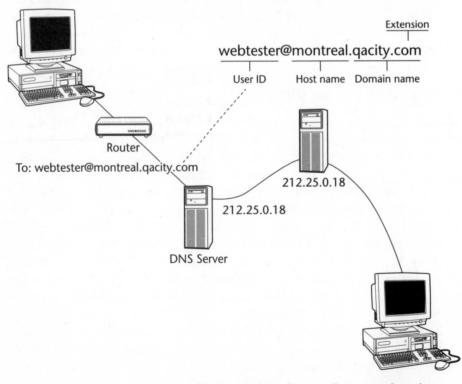

Figure 4.14   Domain names.

When an e-mail is sent to, for example, webtester@montreal.qacity.com, a DNS server translates the letters of the domain name (qacity.com) into the associated numerical IP address. Once in numeric form, the data is sent to the host computer that resides at the domain. The host computer (montreal) ultimately sends the e-mail message to the specific user (webtester).

Subnet

Subnets divide a single network into smaller networks, or network segments. Routers are used to send information from one subnet to another. Subnets are useful in managing IP address allotment. For example, assume an organization, with two physical locations, has a class C network and, therefore, has only 254 IP addresses available to distribute to its employees. This organization could request a second class C network to service the second location. But what if the organization is not currently using all of its IP addresses? Getting a second network address would be wasteful. Instead, a subnet would enable this organization to partition its existing class C network into two subnetworks. Figure 4.17 shows a network divided into two subnets with two IP addresses (192.9.200.100 and 192.9.200.200).

MISSING A DNS ENTRY

When you are outside of the intranet and click on the QA Training or TRACKGEAR button in the page illustrated, the browser appears to hang, or you don't get any response from the server. However, when you report the problem, the developer who accesses the same links cannot reproduce it. One of the possible problems is that the DNS entry for the server referenced in the link is only available in the DNS table on the intranet; that is, it is not known to the outside world. (See Figure 4.15.)

Figure 4.15 LogiGear screen capture.

(continued)

MISSING A DNS ENTRY *(continued)*

TIPS

1. Use the View Source menu command to inspect the HTML source.

2. Look for the information that's relevant to the links. In this example, you will find that clicking on the QA Training and the TRACKGEAR button will result in requests to the server authorized in the *qacity.com* domain. (See Figure 4.16.)

```
...
<td>
<map name=01b238de91a99ed9>
<area shape=rect coords="0,0,88,20" href=https://authorize.qacity
        .com/training-login.asp?>
<area shape=rect coords="0,20,88,40" href=https://authorize.qacity
        .com/trackgear-login.asp?>
...
...
</td>
```

Figure 4.16   Checking the HTML Source.

3. Try to ping authorize.qacity.com to see if it can be pinged (see the section "Discovering Information about the System" in Chapter 13).

4. If the server cannot be pinged, tell your developer or IS staff so the problem can be resolved.

The benefits of subnetting an existing network over getting an additional network include:

- The same network number is retained for multiple locations.
- The outside world will not be aware that the network has been subdivided.
- A department's network activities can be isolated from the rest of the network, thereby contributing to the stability and security of the network as a whole.
- Network testing can be isolated within a subnet, thereby protecting the network from testing-based crashes.
- Smaller networks are easier to maintain.
- Network performance may improve due to the fact that most traffic remains local to its own subnet (for example, the network activities of business administration and engineering could be divided between two subnets).

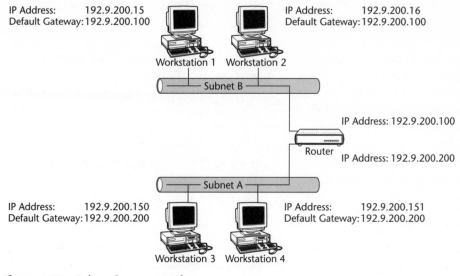

Figure 4.17   Subnetting a network.

Subnet Masks

Subnet addresses are derived from the main network's *network number* plus some information from the host section in the network's IP address. *Subnet masks* tell the network which portion of the host section of the subnet address is being used as the network address.

Subnet masks, like IP addresses, are 32-bit values. The bits for the network section of the subnet address are set to 1, and the bits for the host section of the address are set to 0. Each network class has its own default subnet mask (see Figure 4.18). Every computer on a network must share the same subnet mask, otherwise, the computers will not know that they are part of the same network.

Default Subnet Masks

     Class A Default
     255.0.0.0 or
11111111.00000000.00000000.00000000

     Class B Default
     255.255.0.0 or
11111111.11111111.00000000.00000000

     Class C Default
     255.255.255.0 or
11111111.11111111.11111111.00000000

Figure 4.18   Subnet masks.

As stated earlier, class C IP addresses have 24 bits to the left devoted to network address; class B IP addresses have 16 bits, and class A IP addresses have 8 bits.

Internet Protocol addresses that are included in incoming messages are filtered through the appropriate subnet mask so that the network number and host number can be identified. As an example, applying the class C subnet mask (255.255.255.0) to the class C address (126.24.3.11) would result in a network number of 126.4.3 and a host number of 11.

The value of 255 is arrived at when all bits of an IP address field are set to 1, or *on*. If all values in an IP address are set to 255, as in the default subnet masks, then there are no subnets at all.

Custom Subnets

Subnet masks may be customized to divide networks into several subnets. To do this, some of the bits in the host portion of the subnet mask will be set to 1s. For example, consider an IP address of 202.133.175.18, or 11001010.10000101. 10101111.00010010: Using the default mask of 255.255.255.0, or 11111111. 11111111.11111111.00000000, the network address will be 202.133.175.0, and the host address IP address will be 18. If a custom mask, such as 255.255.255.240, or 11111111.11111111.11111111.11110000, is used, the network address will then be 202.133.175.16 (because 28 bits are used for the subnet address instead of 24 as in the default mask), and the host address will still be 18.

A Testing Example

Following is an example of an embedded HTTP-based application handheld device that involves testing the host name and IP address resolution logics.

Host Name and IP Resolution Tests

CONSIDERATIONS FOR THE SYSTEM UNDER TEST

- Adapter address
- IP address
- Subnet mask
- Host name resolved by DNS, WINS, or other technologies
- Dynamic Host Configuration Protocol (DHCP)
- Default gateway IP address

By the way, you often need to configure your network stack with the correct information for each of the items listed here to enable your computer or any devices connected to the network to operate properly.

TESTING EXAMPLE SPECIFICATIONS

- There are two applications: one running on the remote host and the other running on the target host.

- The product supports Windows 9x, NT, 2000, or Chameleon TCP/IP stack.

- The remote host connects to the private network via a dial-in server.

- The product supports RAS and several popular PPP- or TCP/IP-based dial-in servers.

- From the remote host, a user enters the phone number, user name, and password that are required to connect to the desired dial-in server.

- The remote host establishes a connection with the target host. Therefore, information about the target host name, IP, and subnet mask must be registered on the remote host.

- The product supports static-based, as well as dynamic-based, IP addresses.

- The product also supports WINS- and DNS-based name/IP resolution.

When the target host IP changes, the product has code that relies on the host name alone, or on the host name and the subnet mask information, to dynamically determine the new IP address.

In developing test cases to validate the functionality under various possible scenarios to which the system under test can be exposed, the following attributes are examined:

The host name. May or may not be available on the device.

IP address. May or may not be available on the device.

Subnet mask. May be a standard or a custom mask.

Name server—IP/name-resolving. Configured to use either WINS or DNS.

Type of IP address. May be static or dynamic.

A table is then developed to represent various unique combinations formulated by these five attributes and the possible values for each attribute. There are 32 combinations generated (see Table 4.1). Each combination is then configured and tested accordingly. Figure 4.19 shows a testing example.

In considering testing for compatibility issues, six operating environments are identified, three of which are Windows 9x, NT, and 2000, with Microsoft default TCP/IP stack; the other three comprise the same set of operating systems with the latest version of Chameleon TCP/IP stack.

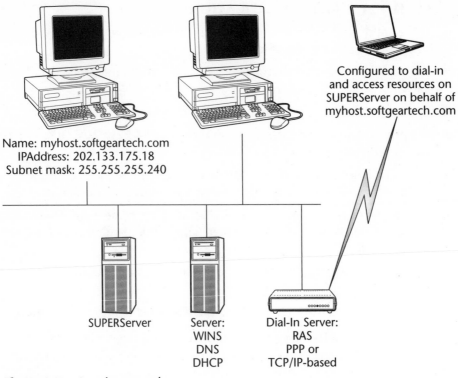

Figure 4.19   A testing example.

Testing Considerations

- If the application under test runs in its own embedded browser, analyze the application to determine if it utilizes any protocols beyond those at the application level. If it does, how would it affect your configuration and compatibility testing requirements with respect to connectivity devices?

- Determine the hardware and software configuration dependencies of the application under test. Develop a test plan that covers a wide mix of hardware and software configurations.

- Examine the Web application as a whole and consider the connection dial-up and direct connection methods. How would each type of connection affect the performance and functionality of the product?

- Will users be accessing the system via dial-up connections through an ISP? If so, connectivity may be based upon proprietary ISP strings, such as the parsing of a login script. Will remote users be accessing through an RAS?

- Will the application be installing any special modules, such as a dialer and associated components, that may introduce conflicts? Consider dialer platforms, versions, and brand names.

Table 4.1   The 32 Unique Combinations

No=0 | Yes=1
No=0 | Yes=1
No=0 | Yes=1
WINS=0 | DNS=1
Static=0 | Dynamic=1

	1	2	3	4	5	6	7	8	9	10	11	12	13	14	15	16	17	18	19	20	21	22	23	24	25	26	27	28	29	30	31	32
Host Name	0	0	1	1	0	0	1	1	0	0	1	1	0	0	1	1	0	0	1	1	0	0	1	1	0	0	1	1	0	0	1	1
IP	0	1	0	1	0	1	0	1	0	1	0	1	0	1	0	1	0	1	0	1	0	1	0	1	0	1	0	1	0	1	0	1
Subnet Mask	0	0	0	0	1	1	1	1	0	0	0	0	1	1	1	1	0	0	0	0	1	1	1	1	0	0	0	0	1	1	1	1
Name Server	0	0	0	0	0	0	0	0	1	1	1	1	1	1	1	1	0	0	0	0	0	0	0	0	1	1	1	1	1	1	1	1
Static/Dynamic IP	0	0	0	0	0	0	0	0	0	0	0	0	0	0	0	0	1	1	1	1	1	1	1	1	1	1	1	1	1	1	1	1

VALIDATING YOUR COMPUTER CONNECTION

Ensure that your test machines are properly configured and connected to the network before you begin testing. To check host connection and configuration in a Windows environment, read the following instructions. Windows NT offers a utility named ipconfig. Windows 9x has winipcfg, which has more of a user interface.

1a. For Windows NT, run IPCONFIG/ALL.

1b. For Windows 9x, run WINIPCFG.

2. Ping the exact value that is received from IPCONFIG and WINIPCFG. To make sure the DNS is working properly, also ping by the domain name. If positive responses are received, then there is a good TCP/IP connection.

3. To ensure that there is a proper TCP/IP connection, ping the loopback IP address: PING 127.0.0.1 or PING YourMachineIPAddress.

Bibliography

Comer, Douglas. *Internetworking with TCP/IP Vol. I: Principles, Protocols, and Architecture,* 4th Ed. Upper Saddle River, NJ: Prentice-Hall PTR, 2000.

Gralla, Preston. *How the Internet Works.* Emeryville, CA: Ziff-Davis Press, 1997.

LogiGear Corporation. *QA Training Handbook: Testing Web Applications.* Foster City, CA: LogiGear Corporation, 2003.

———— *QA Training Handbook: Testing Windows Desktop and Server-Based Applications.* Foster City, CA: LogiGear Corporation, 2003.

———— Foster City, CA: LogiGear Corporation, 2003.

Orfali, Robert, Dan Harkey, Jeri Edwards. *Client/Server Survival Guide,* 3rd Ed. New York: John Wiley & Sons, Inc., 1999.

CHAPTER

5

Web Application Components

Why Read This Chapter?

Having an understanding of a Web application's internal components and how those components interface with one another, even if only at a high level, leads to better testing. Such knowledge allows for the analysis of a program from its developer's perspective—which is invaluable in determining test strategy and identifying the cause of errors. Furthermore, analyzing the relationship among the components leads to an understanding of the interaction of the work product from the perspective of several independent developers, as opposed to from only the individual developer's perspective. Thus, you analyze the work product from a perspective that is not evident from the analysis of any individual component. You are asking how all these components interact with each other to make up the system. The gray-box tester provides this capability. You look at the system at a level that is different from that of the developer. Just like the black-box tester, you add a different perspective and, therefore, value.

Generally, we learn about an application's architecture from its developers during walk-throughs. An alternate approach is to do our own analysis by tracing communication traffic between components. For example, tests can be developed that hit a database server directly, or on behalf of actual user activities, via browser-submitted transactions. Regardless, we need to have a firm grasp of typical Web-based application architecture at the component level if we are to know what types of errors to look for and what questions to ask.

Introduction

This chapter explores the software components of a typical Web-based system—from client-based components on the *front end* (such as Web browsers, plug-ins, and embedded objects) to server-side components on the *back end* (such as application server components, database applications, third-party modules, and cross-component communication). It offers insight to what typically happens when users click buttons on browser-based interfaces. It also explores pertinent testing questions such as:

- Which types of plug-ins are used by the application under test? What are the testing implications associated with these plug-ins? What issues should be considered during functionality and compatibility testing once these plug-ins have been integrated to the system?

- How should the distribution of server-side components affect test design and strategy?

- Which Web and database servers are supported by the application? How is Web-to-database connectivity implemented and what are the associated testing implications?

- How can testing be partitioned to focus on problematic components?

Overview

A Web-based system consists of hardware components, software components, and users. This chapter focuses on the software components of Web-based systems.

Distributed Application Architecture

In a distributed architecture, components are grouped into clusters of related services. Distributed architectures are used for both traditional client-server systems and Internet-based client-server systems.

Traditional Client-Server Systems

A database access application typically consists of four elements:

1. *User interface (UI) code.* The end-user or input/output (I/O) devices interact with this for I/O operations.
2. *Business logic code.* Applies rules, computes data, and manipulates data.
3. *Data-access service code.* Handles data retrieval and updates to the database, in addition to sending results back to the client.
4. *Data storage.* Holds the information.

Thin- versus Thick-Client Systems

When the majority of processing is executed on the server-side, a system is considered to be a *thin-client* system. When the majority of processing is executed on the client-side, a system is considered to be a *thick-client* system.

In a thin-client system (Figure 5.1), the user interface runs on the client host while all other components run on the server host(s). By contrast, in a thick-client system (Figure 5.2), most processing is done on the client-side; the client application handles data processing and applies logic rules to data. The server is responsible only for providing data access features and data storage.

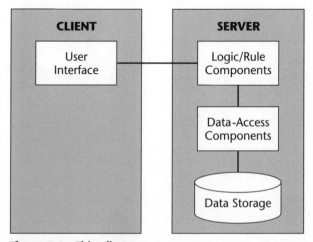

Figure 5.1 Thin-client system.

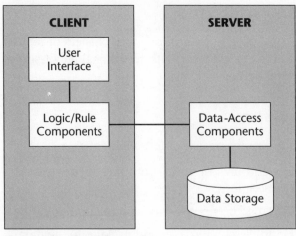

Figure 5.2   Thick-client system.

Web-Based Client-Server Systems

Web-based client-server system components typically can be grouped into three related tiers: (1) *User service components* (client), (2) *business service components* (server), and (3) *data service components* (server). Processing, performance, scalability, and system maintenance are all taken into account in the design of such systems.

An example of a three-tiered Web application is shown in Figure 5.3. The components shown in this example are discussed in later sections of this chapter.

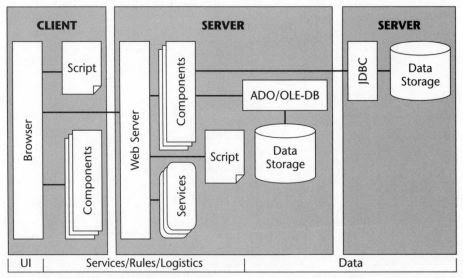

Figure 5.3   Three-tiered Web-based system.

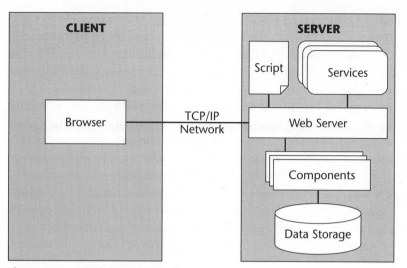

Figure 5.4 A Web-based thin client.

Figures 5.4 and 5.5 illustrate thin-client and thick-client Web applications, respectively. In the thin-client example, the server is responsible for all services. After retrieving and processing data, only a plain HTML page is sent back to the client. In contrast, in the thick-client example, components such as ActiveX controls and Java applets, which are required for the client to process data, are hosted and executed on the client machine. Each of these models calls for a different testing strategy.

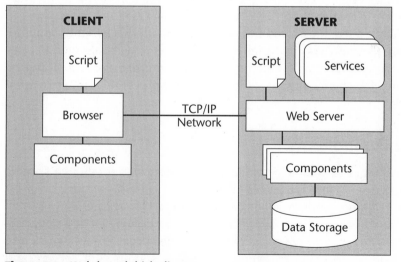

Figure 5.5 Web-based thick client.

In thick-client system testing, tests should focus on performance and compatibility. If Java applets are used, the applets will be sent to the browser with each request (unless the same applet is used within the same instance of the browser). If the applet is a few hundred kilobytes in size, it will take a fair amount of bandwidth to download it with reasonable response time.

Although Java applets are, in theory, designed to be platform-independent, they should be tested with various supported browsers because they may have been created with different versions of the *software development kit* (SDK). Each SDK supports a different set of features. In addition, applets need to be interpreted by a *Java Virtual Machine* (JVM). Different browsers, on different platforms, with their respective versions, have different built-in JVMs, which may contain bug incompatibilities. With ActiveX controls, the network-specific performance hit should occur only once. There may, however, be incompatibility issues with browsers other than Microsoft Internet Explorer and platforms other than Microsoft Windows.

In thin-client systems, incompatibility issues are less of a concern. Performance issues do, however, need to be considered on the server-side, where requests are processed, and on the network where data transfer takes place (sending bitmaps to the browser).

The thin-client model is designed to solve incompatibility problems as well as processing power limitations on the client-side (the thin-client model concentrates work on the server). Additionally, it ensures that updates happen immediately, because the updates are applied at that server only. Personal Digital Assistants (PDAs), for example, due to their small size, are not capable of handling much processing (See Chapter 6, "Mobile Web Application Platform," and Chapter 20, "Testing Mobile Web Applications," for more information). The thin-client model serves PDAs well because it pushes the work to servers, which perform the processing and return results back to the client (the PDA). Desktop computers (in which the operating systems deliver a lot of power and processing) enable much more processing to be executed locally; therefore, the thick-client approach is commonly employed to improve overall performance.

Software Components

A *component* is any identifiable part of a larger system that provides a specific function or group of related functions. Web-based systems, such as e-business systems, are composed of a number of hardware and software components. *Software components* are integrated application and third-party modules, service-based modules, the operating system (and its service-based components), and application services (packaged servers such as Web servers, SQL servers, and their associated service-based components). *Component testing* is the testing of individual software components, or logical groups of components, in an effort

TESTING THE SAMPLE APPLICATION

To illustrate how functionality implementation can affect testing efforts, consider the metric generation feature of the sample application (see Chapter 8, "Sample Application," for more information). The sample application enables users to generate bug-report queries that specify search criteria such as bug severity and the names of engineers. Query results are tabulated and ultimately plugged into graphic charts, which are displayed to users. This functionality is implemented by having the user send a query to the Web server (via a Web browser). The Web server in turn submits the query to a database. The database executes the query and returns results. The Web server then sends the resulting data, along with a Java applet or ActiveX control that is to be installed on the client machine. The client-side, after downloading the component, converts the data into a graphically intuitive format for the user. If the downloaded component executes on the client machine, then the system is a thick-client system.

If the processing is done on the server (i.e., the Structured Query Language (SQL) server gets results from the database, a GIF graphic is created on the server-side, and the GIF is sent back to the browser), then the system is a thin-client system. These alternate functionality implementations will have different consequences on the testing effort.

to uncover functionality and interoperability problems. Some key software components include operating systems, server-side application service components, client-side application service components, and third-party components.

Operating Systems

Operating systems extend their services and functionality to applications. The functionality is often packaged in binary form, such as standard dynamic link libraries (DLLs). When an application needs to access a service, the application does it by calling a predefined *application program interface* (API) set. In addition, with object-based technology, these components extend their functionality by also exposing events (e.g., when a certain applied event is double-clicked, perform the following action), properties (e.g., when the background color is white and the foreground color is black), and methods (e.g., remove or add a certain entry to the scroll list) for other applications to access.

Application Service Components

Server-side packaged servers. A *server* is a software program that provides services to other software programs from either a local host or a remote host. The hardware box in which a server software program runs is also often referred to as a *server.* Physical hardware boxes, however, can support multiple client programs, so it is more accurate to refer to the software as the *server,* as opposed to the hardware that supports it. Packaged servers offer their services and extend their functionality to other applications in a manner that is similar to the extended model of operating systems. Two common packaged servers that are used in Web-based systems are *Web servers* and *database servers.* Web servers typically store HTML pages that can be sent, or served, to Web clients via browsers. It is common for packaged Web servers to offer functionality that enables applications to facilitate database activities. Such features can be packaged in a binary module such as a DLL. Access to these features is achieved via predefined APIs. See Table 5.1 for examples of server-side service components.

Table 5.1 Possible Scenario of Software Component Segmentation

APPLICATION SERVICE COMPONENTS	THIRD-PARTY COMPONENTS
Server-side	Java components
Web server	ActiveX controls
Scripting	Standard EXEs
Java VM	Standard DLLs
Database server	CGIs
Data-access service	etc.
Transaction service	
Client-side	
Web browser	
Scripting	
Java VM	
Other	
INTEGRATED APPLICATION COMPONENTS	
HTML, DHTML, JavaScript, VBScript, JScript, Perl Script, and others	
Standard EXEs	
CGIs	
API-based components	
Java components	
ActiveX controls	
Standard DLLs	

Client-side services. On the client-side, a typical browser supports a variety of services, including Java VM, which runs Java applets, script interpreters that execute scripts. See Table 5.1 for examples of client-side services.

Third-Party Components

Software applications are subdivided into multiple components, otherwise referred to as *units* or *modules*. In object-oriented programming and distributed software engineering, components take on another meaning: *reusability*. Each component offers a template, or self-contained piece to a puzzle that can be assembled with other components, to create other applications. Components can be delivered in two formats: (1) *source-based,* as in an object-oriented programming class, and (2) *binary-based,* as in a DLL or Java Archive file format (JAR). Binary-based components are more relevant to the testing concerns discussed in this book.

Integrated Application Components

An *integrated application* consists of a number of components, possibly including a database application running on the server-side, or a Java-based chart-generation application running on the server-side in an HTML page that is running on the client-side, as shown in Figure 5.6. In the Java applet example shown in this figure, the software component executes within the context of the Web browser, or a *container.* A container can also be a Web-server-based application, a database application, or any other application that can communicate with the component via a standard interface or protocol. Typically, software components are distributed across different servers on a network. They, in turn, communicate with each other via known interfaces or protocols to access needed services. See Table 5.1 for a sample list of integrated software components.

Dynamic Link Library (DLL)

Understanding DLLs and the potential errors that may be associated with them is essential in designing useful test cases. In the early years of software development, the only way that a developer could expose created functionality to another developer was to package the functionality in an object file (.OBJ) or library files (.LIB). This method required the recipient developer to link with the .OBJ or .LIB file. The functionality was therefore locked in with the executable. One of the implications of this approach was that if several executables used the same set of functionality, each executable had to link individually to the object. This was repetitive, and the linked code added to the size of the executable file, which resulted in higher memory requirements at runtime. More important, if new versions of the object or library files became available, the new code had to be relinked, which led to the need for much retesting.

The dynamic link library was introduced to improve the method of sharing functionality. A DLL is a file that contains functions and resources that are stored separately from, and linked to on demand, by the applications that use them. The operating system maps the DLL into the application's address space when the application, or another DLL, makes an explicit call to a DLL function. The application then executes the functions in the DLL.

Files with .DLL extensions contain functions that are either exported or available to other programs. Multiple applications or components may share the same set of functionality and, therefore, may also share the same DLLs at runtime. If a program or component is linked to a DLL that must be updated, in theory all that needs to be done is to replace the old DLL with the new DLL. Unfortunately, it is not this simple. In certain situations, errors may be introduced with this solution. For example, if a DLL that is referenced in the import library links to a component that is not available, then the application will fail to load. (See the error message example in Figure 5.10.)

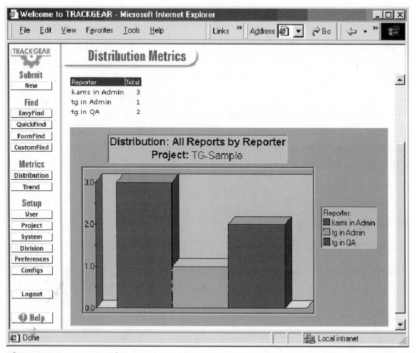

Figure 5.6   Java applet.

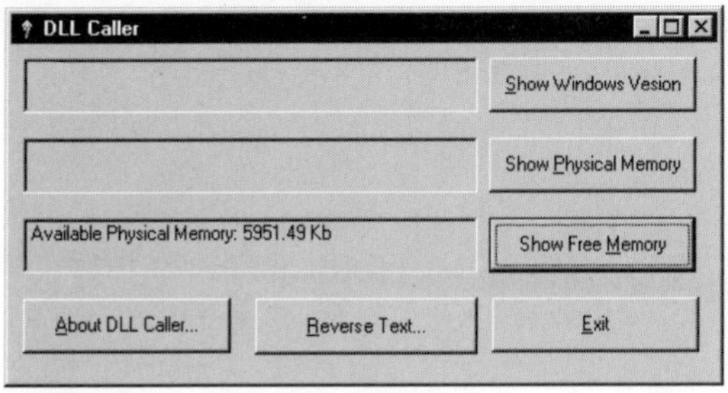

Figure 5.7   DLL caller program.

Here is another example. The DLL caller application illustrated in Figure 5.7 is a Visual Basic application. It uses a few functions that are exported by the system DLL named KERNEL32.DLL. After loading the application, clicking the Show Free Memory button displays the current available physical memory.

To implement this feature, the code that handles the click event on the Show Free Memory button has to be written. Because there is an exported function named *GlobalMemoryStatus,* which is available in the Windows system DLL named KERNEL32.DLL, a developer can simply call this function to retrieve the information. The process of using a function in a DLL is illustrated in Figures 5.8 and 5.9. You call the DLL function when there is a click event on the Show Free Memory button.

```
            Data Structure
                   |
Type MEMORYSTATUS
        dwLength As Long
        dwMemoryLoad As Long
        dwTotalPhys As Long
        dwAvailPhys As Long
        dwTotalPageFile As Long
        dwAvailPageFile As Long
        dwTotalVirtual As Long
        dwAvailVirtual As Long
End Type
```

Figure 5.8   DLL function declaration.

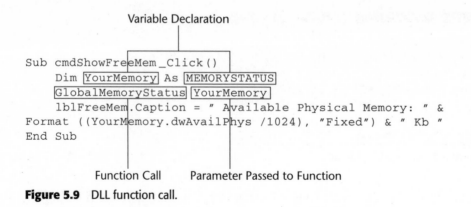

Variable Declaration

```
Sub cmdShowFreeMem _Click()
    Dim YourMemory As MEMORYSTATUS
    GlobalMemoryStatus YourMemory
    lblFreeMem.Caption = " Available Physical Memory: " &
Format ((YourMemory.dwAvailPhys /1024), "Fixed") & " Kb "
End Sub
```

Function Call   Parameter Passed to Function

Figure 5.9   DLL function call.

Potential DLL-Related Errors

Missing required DLL. For example, when the application DLLCALLER .EXE is executed on the developer's machine, everything works fine. When it is first executed on a system other than the developer's, however, the error message shown in Figure 5.10 displays. As it turns out, the application was created with Visual Basic 4.0 and depends on the DLL named VB40032.DLL. If that DLL is not installed, the application will not load properly. The application did not complain about KERNEL32.DLL, because it is a system DLL, which is expected to be there. If it were not, even the operating system would not work.

API-incompatible DLL. There may be two versions of the same DLL, and if the data type, structure, or number of parameters has been changed from one version to another, an error will result.

Other incompatibility issues. One of the benefits of using DLL is that when the author of a DLL needs to change the implementation of a function (to improve performance, for example) but not the API, the change should be transparent to the DLL callers—that is, no problems should result. This is not, however, always the case. You need to test to confirm the compatibility with your application.

Figure 5.10   Error caused by missing DLL.

NOTE The preceding section is not intended to suggest that you should start testing at the API level, unless you are specifically asked to do so. It is intended to give you enough background information to design powerful test cases that focus on interoperability issues. See the "Testing Considerations" section later in this chapter for more DLL-related issues.

Scripts

On the server-side, scripts are often used to convert data from one form to another form, thus using the output from one program to be used by a different program. This is called "glue code." A simple script to take data from a database and send it to a report writer is a common example. Today this is used extensively in Active Server Page (ASP), a Microsoft technology, and Java Server Page (JSP), a Sun Microsystems technology: data is taken from the Web server and formatted for the user's browser. More on ASP and JSP later in the chapter.

Related to glue code are *filters*. Filters are scripts (or programs) that remove unwanted data. An example is an e-mail filter that removes or routes messages based on the user's selection rules. E-mail client applications often contain a scripting language built into the application. Scripts can also be used for many different tasks such as data validation and UI manipulation on the client-side. In Web applications, scripts are used on both the server- and the client-side.

Web Application Component Architecture

Generally, Web applications consist of server-side and client-side components, including operating systems, browsers, packaged servers, and other associated software. A sampling of these components, along with their associated testing issues, follows.

Server-Side Components

Any computer that provides services to other computers is a server. A single physical computer can house multiple servers (software programs). Servers can also be distributed across multiple physical computers. Testing considerations vary, depending on the number and distribution of servers and other software components associated with a system.

Web systems often have several servers included at their back end, allowing users to gain access from a client computer (via a browser) and get the services they need (Web page content or database records). On the hardware side, the characteristics that distinguish server host quality are similar to those qualities considered favorable in all computers: high performance, high data through-put, scalability, and reliability.

Server operating systems need to be more robust than desktop workstation operating systems. Windows 95 and Windows 98, for example, do not offer the reliability or performance required by most servers. Operating systems such as UNIX, Windows NT, and Windows 2000 Advanced Server offer strong security features and administrator tools, in addition to the scalability and reliability required by servers.

Core Application Service Components

Web Servers

Web servers, or HTTP servers, store Web pages or HTML files and their associated contents. Web servers make their contents available to client computers, and are the most essential type of server for Web-based systems. Many software companies develop Web servers: Novel, Netscape, Microsoft, Sun Microsystems, and others. Web servers also serve advanced technology components such as Java servlets, ActiveX controls, and back-end database connectors. Web servers may work with protocols such as FTP and Gopher to pass data back to users.

Database Servers

Database servers act as data repositories for Web applications. Most Web systems use *relational database servers* (RDBSs). Database servers introduce a variety of testing complexities, which are discussed in Chapter 14, "Database Tests."

Prominent database server manufacturers include Microsoft, Oracle, and Sybase. The Structured Query Language (SQL) is the coding language used in *relational database management servers* (RDBMS). Refer to Chapter 14 for more information regarding SQL and databases.

Application Servers

Application server is a term used to refer to a set of components that extend their services to other components (e.g., ASP) or integrated application components, as discussed earlier. Web applications support users by giving them access to data that is stored on database servers. Web applications coordinate the functionality of Web servers and database servers so that users can access database content via a Web browser interface.

The sample application provided in Chapter 8 "Sample Application" is a Web-based bug-tracking system. It is an example of an application server that utilizes component-based technologies. See Chapter 8 for more information.

Markup Language Pages

HTML (Hypertext Markup Language) is the standard markup language used in creating Web pages. Similar to HTML is XML (eXtensible Markup Language), which provides a standard way of flexibly describing the data format that enables systems supporting XML to "talk" to each other by sharing the described format and its data. In short, XML defines the guidelines for structuring and formating data. It is used to facilitate the generation and interpretation of data, and to ensure that other XML-compliant Web systems will not unambiguously interpret and use that data.

Both XML and HTML contain markup symbols to describe the display and the interaction of contents on a Web page or data file. Where they differ is in HTML; the meaning of the content is dependent of the predefined HTML tags. For example, the predefined <b> symbol signifies that the data following will be displayed with a boldface font. XML, in contrast , is extensible, meaning that, for example, if the word "cardnumber" is placed within the markup tags, and an application programmer has defined the data following "cardnumber" as a 16-digit credit card number, any XML-complied Web system interacting with that application will understand how to interpret that data, display it, store it, or encrypt it.

(For information, support tools, mailing lists, and support in languages other than English, go to www.w3.org/XML. For a more in-depth description and additional information, go to www.w3.org/XML/1999/XML-In-10-points.)

XML with SOAP

The Simple Object Access Protocol (SOAP) makes it possible for different software applications running on different computers with different operation systems to call and transfer information to each other. SOAP was originally meant for use with decentralized and distributed environments. The protocol uses a combination of HTTP/HTTPS protocols (widely available for use by many operating systems) and XML (the mechanism to describe the data format and data) to facilitate this information exchange. Since SOAP uses HTTP to transfer data, the requests are more likely to get through firewalls that screen out other requests except HTTP. (For more information, go to www .w3.org/TR/SOAP.)

Web-to-Database Connectivity

The value of data-access applications is that they allow interaction between users and data. Communication between users, Web servers, and database servers is facilitated by certain extensions and scripting models.

On the back end, data resides in a database. On the front end, the user is represented by requests sent from the Web server. Therefore, providing connectivity between Web server requests and a database is the key function of Web-based applications. There are several methods that can be employed to establish such connectivity. The most common are Common Gateway Interface- (CGI) based programs with embedded SQL commands, Web server extension-based programs, and Web server extension-based scripts.

Common Gateway Interface (CGI)

The CGI is a standard communication protocol that Web servers can use to pass a user's request to another application and then send the application's response back to the user. CGI applications allow Web servers to interact with databases, among other things. CGI applications are usually implemented in *Practical Extraction and Reporting Language* (PERL), although they can be written in other programming languages such as C, C++, and Visual Basic.

Once a CGI program has been written, it is placed in a Web server directory called a *CGI bin*. Web server administrators determine which directories serve as CGI bins.

Common Gateway Interface programs must be placed in their correct directories if they are to run properly. This security feature makes it easier to keep track of CGI programs and to prevent outsiders from posting damaging CGI programs.

After a CGI program has been placed in a CGI bin, a link to the bin is embedded in a URL on a Web page. When a user clicks the link, the CGI program is launched. The CGI program contacts a database and requests the information that the user has requested. The database sends the information to the CGI program. The CGI program receives the information and translates it into a format that is understandable to the user. This usually involves converting the data into HTML, so that the user can view the information via a Web browser.

The main drawback of CGI scripts is that they run as separate executables on Web servers. Each time a user makes a request of a database server by invoking a CGI script, small amounts of system resources are tied up. Though the net effect of running a single CGI script is negligible, consider the effect of 1,000 concurrent users launching even one CGI script simultaneously; the effect of 1,000 simultaneous processes running on a Web server would likely have disastrous consequences to system memory and processing resources.

Web Server Extension-Based Programs

An alternate, and sometimes more efficient, means of supplying Web-to-database connectivity is to integrate with *Web server-exported library functions*. The Netscape server API, NSAPI, and the Microsoft Internet API for IIS, ISAPI, commonly referred to as NSAPI/ISAPI, can be *in-process* applications that take advantage of a Web server's native API. Library functions work off of features and internal structures that are exposed by Web servers to provide different types of functionality, including Web-to-database connectivity.

The NSAPI/ISAPI-based applications can be DLLs that run in the same memory space as Web server software. Netscape Server uses NSAPI; Microsoft Internet Information Server uses ISAPI. Both NSAPI and ISAPI effectively offer a similar solution; they are APIs that offer functions in DLL format. These APIs expose the functionality of the Web server software of which they are a part so that required processes can be performed by the server software itself, rather than by a separate executable (such as a CGI script).

Web server extension-based applications, although more efficient from a resource perspective, are not always the best choice for invoking Web server functionality. For example, a Web application might be distributed to multiple server platforms, and it often makes sense to write different code for each platform. A CGI script might be written to interface with a UNIX server, whereas NSAPI code might be used to invoke functions on a Netscape server running in the same system. A third server (e.g., Microsoft Internet Information Server (IIS)) might require either a CGI script or ISAPI code. The development of every Web system, as far as Web-to-database connectivity goes, requires a careful balance between tolerable performance levels, compatibility, and perceived effort of execution.

A drawback of Web server extension-based applications is that, because they are written in compiled languages such as C, C++, or Visual Basic, they are binary. Whenever changes are made to code—for example, during bug fixing—the code has to be recompiled. This makes remote changes to the code more cumbersome. Furthermore, a scripting language is easier to use and, therefore, many new developers can be trained quickly.

Web Server Extension-Based Scripts

Active Server Page (ASP) is a Microsoft technology that allows for the dynamic creation of Web pages using a scripting language. The ASP is a programming environment that provides the capability to combine HTML, scripting, and components into powerful Internet applications. Also, ASP can be used to create Web sites that combine HTML, scripting, and other reusable components. Active Server Page script commands can also be added to HTML pages to create HTML interfaces. In addition, with ASP, business logic can be encapsulated into reusable components that can be called from scripts or other components.

ASP scripts typically run on servers, and unlike the binary code model, they do not have to be compiled; therefore, they can be easily copied from distributed software unless encryption measures are undertaken. However, keep in mind that encryption measures add more components and processing requirements to Web servers—not to mention the need for additional testing.

The ASP scripts interact with the DLL layer through an interpreter (asp.dll). The DLL layer in turn interacts with the ISAPI layer to provide functionality, such as gateway connectivity. An HTML page that contains a link to an ASP file often has the file name suffix of .ASP.

Java Server Page (JSP) is a Sun Microsystems technology similar to ASP for the dynamic creation and control of the Web page content or appearance through the use of servlets, small programs that run on the Web server to generate the Web page before it is sent to the requested user. JSP technology is also referred to as the *servlet API*. Unlike ASP, which is interpreted, JSP calls a Java program (servlet) that is run on the Java Web Server. An HTML page that contains a link to a Java servlet often has the file name suffix of .JSP.

ASP/JSP versus CGI

- The CGI programs require Web server operating systems to launch additional processes with each user request.

- As an in-process component, ASP/JSP can run in the same memory space as Web server applications, eliminating additional resource drain and improving performance.

ASP/JSP versus Web Server Extension-Based Programs

- Because NSAPI/ISAPI applications are in-process applications that use a Web server's native API, they run at a speed comparable to that of ASP.

- NSAPI/ISAPI applications must be compiled.

- ASP/JSP uses scripting languages.

- ASP/JSP is faster to develop and deploy than NSAPI/ISAPI.

Other Application Service Components

Search Servers

Often referred to as *search engines, search servers* catalog and index data that is published by Web servers. Not all Web systems have search servers. Search servers allow users to search for information on Web systems by specifying *queries*. A query, simply put, is a request to find certain data that has been submitted to a search server by a user. Users submit queries so that they can define the goal and scope of their searches—often specifying multiple search criteria to better refine search results.

As new information is introduced into a Web system, search servers update their indices. Robust search servers have the capability to handle large amounts of data and return results quickly, without errors.

Proxy Servers and Firewalls

Proxy servers are sometimes employed by companies to regulate and track Internet usage. They act as intermediaries between networks and the Internet by controlling packet transmissions. Proxy servers can prevent files from entering or leaving networks; they log all traffic between networks and the Internet and speed up the performance of Internet services; and they log IP addresses, URLs, durations of access, and numbers of bytes downloaded.

Most corporate Web traffic travels through proxy servers. For instance, when a client computer requests a Web page from the Internet, the client computer contacts the network's proxy server with the request. The proxy server then contacts the network's Web server. The Web server sends the Web page to the proxy server, which in turn forwards the page to the client computer.

Proxy servers can speed up performance of Internet services by *caching* data. Caching involves keeping copies of requested data on local servers. Through caching, proxy servers can store commonly viewed Web pages so that subsequent users can access the pages directly from the local server, rather than accessing them at slower speeds over the Internet.

Firewalls are shields that protect private networks from Internet intruders; that is, they prevent unauthorized users from accessing confidential information, using network resources, and damaging system hardware, while allowing authorized insiders access to the resources they require. Firewalls are combinations of hardware and software; they make use of routers, servers, and software to shield networks from exposure to the Internet at large. Two common types of firewalls are *packet-filtering* firewalls (such as routers) and *proxy-based* firewalls (such as gateways). Chapter 18, "Web Security Testing," has more information regarding proxy servers and firewalls.

Communication-Related Servers

Numerous communication server types are available to facilitate information exchange between users, networks, and the Internet. If a Web system under test includes a remote-access server, e-mail, a bulletin board, or chat feature, then communication server components are present and should be tested.

E-Commerce-Related Servers

E-commerce servers provide functionality for retail operations (they are not truly a separate type of server, but rather a specialized use of Web server technologies). Via Web applications, they allow both merchants and customers to access pertinent information through client-side Web browsers.

TASKS PERFORMED BY E-COMMERCE SERVERS

- Order taking and order processing
- Inventory tracking

- Credit card validation
- Account reconciliation
- Payment/transaction posting
- Customer orders/account information

COMMON E-COMMERCE SERVER BRANDS

- Ariba
- BroadVision
- Calico
- Vignette

Multimedia-Related Servers

Multimedia servers provide support for high-speed multimedia streaming, enabling users to access live or prerecorded multimedia content. Multimedia servers make it possible for Web servers to provide users with computer-based training (CBT) materials.

Client-Side Components

The client-side of a Web system often comprises a wide variety of hardware and software elements. Multiple brand names and product versions may be present in a single system. The heterogeneous nature of hardware, networking elements, operating systems, and software on the client-side can make for challenging testing.

Web Browsers

Web browsers are applications that retrieve, assemble, and display Web pages. In the client-server model of the Web, browsers are clients. Browsers request Web pages from Web servers. Web servers then locate requested Web pages and forward them to the browsers, where the pages are assembled and displayed to the user. There are multiple browsers and browser versions available for PCs, Macintosh computers, and UNIX computers.

Browsers issue HTML requests (although they can also issue requests for ASP, DHTML, and others). The HTML code instructs browsers how to display Web pages to users. In addition to HTML, browsers can display material created with Java, ActiveX, and scripting languages such as JavaScript and VB Script.

When Web pages present graphics and sound files, the HTML code of the Web pages themselves does not contain the actual multimedia files. Multimedia files reside independently of HTML code, on multimedia servers. The HTML pages indicate to Web browsers where requested sounds, graphics, and multimedia are located.

In the past, browsers required separate applications, known as *helper applications,* to be launched to handle any file type other than HTML, GIF, and JPEG. *Plug-ins,* such as RealPlayer and QuickTime, are more popular today. They allow streaming media and other processes to occur directly within browser windows. RealPlayer, by RealNetworks, is a popular streaming sound and video plug-in. Windows Media Player is a sound and video plug-in that is built into Windows operating systems. QuickTime, made by Apple, can play synchronized content on both Macintosh computers and PCs.

Newer browsers are bundled with complete suites of Internet applications, including plug-ins, e-mail, utilities, and "what you see is what you get" (WYSIWYG) Web page-authoring tools. Netscape Communicator, of which Netscape Navigator is a component, is such a suite. Internet Explorer 5.x and 6.x allow users to view their entire desktops using HTML; Web links are used to interact with the operating system, and live Web content can be delivered directly to the user desktop.

Add-on/Plug-in Components

Additional software may reside on the client-side to support various forms of interactivity and animation within Web pages. Macromedia Shockwave, Java applets and ActiveX controls are examples of such add-on applications. Java, a full-featured object-oriented programming language, can be used to create small applications, known as applets, within Web pages. ActiveX is a Microsoft technology that behaves similarly to both Java applets and plug-ins. ActiveX controls offer functionality to Web pages. Unlike applets, however, they are downloaded and stored on the user's hard disk and run independently of Web browsers. Microsoft Internet Explorer is the only browser that supports ActiveX controls. Java applets and ActiveX controls can also reside on and be executed from servers.

Communication-Related Components

The client-sides of Web systems often contain applications that facilitate various methods of communication. Such applications take advantage of server-based communication components such as remote-access dial-up, chat (IRC), discussion groups, bulletin boards, and videoconferencing.

NOTE For a discussion on mobile Web application components, see Chapter 6, "Mobile Web Application Platform."

USING THE JAVA CONSOLE TO SUPPORT TESTING

The Java Console provides a facility by which we can monitor running Web systems. With limited views and functions, the console is designed as a logging and analysis tool to aid the debugging process. System.out and System.err can be logged and displayed in the console window. The logged information is helpful in further analyzing any odd or erroneous behavior. Figure 5.11 shows a browser display of a Web page with a missing Java applet. The message line at the bottom of the window states that the tgchart applet could not be found. Figure 5.12 shows the Java Console window where information is given about what happened; in this case, it reads: # Unable to load archive http://209.24.0.39/lib/chart360.jar.java.io.IOException<null>.

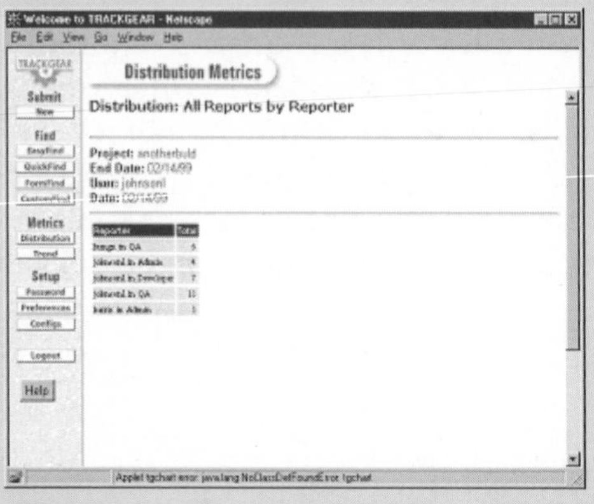

Figure 5.11   The server fails to locate the tg.chart Java applet.

Figure 5.12   Java console shows the location where the server was looking for chart360.jar.

To launch the Java Console with Netscape Navigator:

1. From the browser's menu bar, select Communicator> Tools> Java Console.

To launch the Java Console with Internet Explorer on Windows Systems:

1. From the browser's menu bar, select Tools> Internet Options> Advanced.

2. Scroll to Microsoft VM and check Java console to enable it.

3. Close and restart the browser.

To launch the Java Console with Internet Explorer on Macintosh Systems:

1. From the browser menu bar, select Edit> Preferences.

2. Under Web Browser, select Java.

3. Select to enable the following check-boxes: Alert on exception, Log Java output and Log Java exceptions.

4. From the browser menu bar, select View> Java Messages.

Testing Discussion

The following component architecture example is useful in illustrating effective testing strategies. Figure 5.13 details the chart generation example that was mentioned earlier in this chapter in the section, "Distributed Application Architecture." The pseudodesign for the transaction process runs as follows:

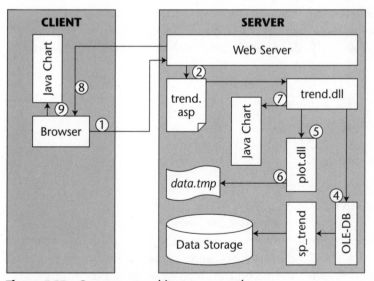

Figure 5.13 Component architecture example.

1. User submits a request for a trend chart that compares daily totals of open bugs with closed bugs over the past five days.

2. Web server requests the file named trend.asp.

3. Trend.dll is called to do some processing work.

4. Trend.dll connects to the database server and calls a stored procedure named sp_trend to pull the requested data.

5. Upon receiving the requested data, trend.dll calls plot.dll and passes the data for calculation and formatting in preparation for drawing the trend chart.

6. The formatted data is then written to a file named data.tmp in comma-delimited format.

7. A third-party Java charting component with the file name data.tmp is requested so that a line chart can be drawn.

8. The Java applet is sent to the client; data.tmp is then deleted.

9. The Java applet is loaded into the user's browser, and a trend chart with the appropriate data is drawn.

Based on the program logic and its component architecture, we will analyze this design to determine potential problems. Then, in an effort to expose possible faults and errors, we will design test cases around the potential problems.

NOTE The potential issues and test cases discussed in this section are by no means definitive. They were designed to encourage you to think more about the possibility of errors in component-based systems. They will help you to think beyond black-box testing from the end user's point of view. Some of the testing issues mentioned in this example are discussed in greater detail in later chapters.

Test-Case Design Analysis

Submitting the request.

- *What happens if the input data is invalid?*

  You want to determine if there is any error-handling code. Hopefully, there is. You will then need to devise test cases that test the error-handling logic, which consist of three parts: (1) error detection, (2) error handling, and (3) error communication. You also want to know if errors are handled on the client-side, the server-side, or both. Each approach has unique implications. You may want to know if error handling is done through scripts or through an embedded component (e.g., if a Java applet or an ActiveX control is used for the input UI).

- *What happens if there is too much data for the last five days?*

    Look for potential boundary condition errors in the output.

- *What happens if there is no data for the last five days?*

    Look for potential boundary condition errors in the output.

- *What happens if there is a firewall in front of the Web server?*

    Look for potential side-effects caused by the firewall, such as dropping or filtering out certain data packets, which would invalidate the request.

trend.asp is requested.

- *Is the Web server environment properly set up to allow ASP to be executed?*

    The environment can be set up manually by the system administrator or programmatically via an installation program or setup utility. Regardless, if a script is not allowed to execute, trend.asp will fail.

- *Will the ASP be encrypted? If so, has it been tested in encrypted mode?*

    The application under test may be using third-party technology to encrypt the ASP files. Incompatibility, performance, time-related, and other environment-related issues may affect functionality.

trend.dll is called.

- *Is trend.dll a standard DLL or a COM-based DLL? If it is a COM-based object, how is it installed and registered?*

    You cannot access a standard DLL directly from within ASP code, so trend.dll must be a COM-based DLL. Trend.dll is registered using the regsvr32 system utility.

- *What are the exported functions in the DLLs upon which trend.dll depends? Are they all available on the local and remote host(s)?*

    There are numerous errors related to DLLs that should be considered. (See the "Dynamic Link Library" section earlier in this chapter for more information.)

Calling sp_trend.

- *The application needs to make a connection to the SQL server before it can execute the stored procedure sp_trend on the database. What issues might cause the connection to fail?*

    There are numerous reasons why this process might fail. For example, there may be an error in authentication due to a bad ID, password, or data source name.

TESTING THE SAMPLE APPLICATION

Please see Chapter 8 for details on the sample application. Following is an example of a real bug that was discovered in the testing of the sample application: trend.dll crashed an ISAPI-based DLL that, in turn, generated error messages on the application server console. However, the end user at the client-side received no communication regarding the error. The user was not notified of the error condition.

- *When an attempt to connect to the database fails, how is the error condition communicated back to the user?*

  The user may receive anything from a cryptic error message to no message at all. What are acceptable standards for the application under test?

- *Is the stored procedure properly precompiled and stored in the database?*

  This is typically done through the installation procedure. If for some reason the stored procedure is dropped or fails to compile, then it will not be available.

- *How do you know that the data set returned by the stored procedure is accurate?*

  The chart might be drawn correctly but the data returned by the stored procedure might be incorrect. You need to be able to validate the data. (See Chapter 14 for more information.)

Calling plot.dll. The functions in this DLL are responsible for calculating and formatting the raw data returned by sp_trend in preparation for the Java chart application.

- *Is data being plotted correctly to the appropriate time intervals (daily, weekly, and monthly)?*

  Based on the user's request, the data will be grouped into daily, weekly, and monthly periods. This component needs to be thoroughly tested.

- *Does the intelligence that populates the reports with the appropriate time periods reside in plot.dll or in sp_trend?*

  Based on what was described earlier, some of the logic can be implemented in the stored procedure and should be tested accordingly.

Write data to file data.tmp.

- *What happens if the directory to which the text file will be written is write-protected?*

  Regardless whether the write-protected directory is a user error or a program error, if data.tmp is not there, the charting feature will not work.

■ *What happens if plot.dll erroneously generates a corrupt format of the comma-delimited file?*

The data formatting logic must be thoroughly tested.

■ *What happens if multiple users request the trend chart simultaneously or in quick succession?*

Multiuser access is what makes the Web application and client-server architectures so powerful, yet this is one of the main sources of errors. Test cases that target multiuser access need to be designed.

Calling the Java charting program.

■ *What happens if a chart program is not found?*

The Java applet must be physically placed somewhere, and the path name in the code that requests the applet must point to the correct location. If the applet is not found, the charting feature will not work.

■ *What happens if there is a missing cls (class) in a JAR?*

A JAR file often contains the Java classes that are required for a particular Java application. There is a dependency concept involved with Java classes that are similar to what was described in the "Dynamic Link Library" section earlier in this chapter. If one or more of the required classes are missing, the application will not function.

Sending results back to the client. The Java applet is sent to the browser, along with the data in data.tmp, so that the applet can draw the chart in the browser; data.tmp is then deleted from the server.

■ *What is the minimum bandwidth requirement supported by the application under test? How big is the applet? Is performance acceptable with the minimum bandwidth configuration?*

Check the overall performance in terms of response time under the minimum requirement configuration. This test should also be executed with multiple users (for example, a million concurrent users, if that is what the application under test claims to support). (See Chapter 19, "Performance Testing," for more information.)

TESTING THE SAMPLE APPLICATION

A hard-to-reproduce bug that resulted in a blank trend chart was discovered during the development of the sample application. It was eventually discovered that the data.tmp file was hard-coded. Whenever more than one user requested the chart simultaneously or in quick succession, the earlier request resulted in incomplete data or data intended for the subsequent request. The application's developer later designed the file name to be uniquely generated with each request.

■ *Has the temp file been properly removed from the server?*

Each charting request leaves a new file on the server. These files unnecessarily take up space.

Formatting and executing the client-side component. The browser formats the page, loads the Java applet, and displays the trend chart.

■ *Is the applet compatible with all supported browsers and their relative versions?*

Each browser has its own version of the "sandbox," or JVM, and does not necessarily have to be compatible with all other browsers. This incompatibility may have an effect on the applet.

■ *What happens when security settings, either on the browser-side or on the network firewall side, prohibit the applet from downloading? Will there be any communication with the user?*

Look for error conditions and see how they are handled.

Test Partitioning

Given the distributed nature of the Web system architecture, it is essential that test partitioning be implemented. For example, at the configuration and compatibility level, if the application under test requires Microsoft IIS 4.0, 5.0, and 6.0, and Microsoft SQL versions 7.0 and 8.0 (MS SQL 2000), then the test matrix for the configuration should look something like this:

TESTING THE SAMPLE APPLICATION

The sample application utilizes a third-party Java charting component that enables the generation of charts. The component offers numerous user interaction features, so it is a rather large object to be sent to a browser. Because the sample application required only basic charts, the developer decided to remove some of the classes in the jar that were not required by the application. The size of the jar was thereby slimmed down to about half its original size, greatly improving performance.

After about a week of testing, in which the testing team had no idea that the number of Java classes had been reduced, the test team discovered a unique condition that required some handling by the applet. The applet, in turn, was looking for the handling code in one of the classes that had been removed. The test team wrote a bug report and subsequently talked to the developer about the issue. The developer explained what he had done and told the test team that they should make sure to test for this type of error in the future. Several test cases that focused on this type of error were subsequently designed. The test team ultimately found five more errors related to this optimization issue.

TEST CONFIGURATION ID	MS-IIS	MS-SQL
1	4.x	7.0
2	4.x	8.0
3	5.0	7.0
4	5.0	8.0
5	6.0	7.0
6	6.0	8.0

Regarding performance, you might wish to compare SQL 7.0 with SQL 8.0. Such a test matrix would look something like this:

TEST CONFIGURATION ID	MS-IIS	MS-SQL
1	Doesn't Matter	7.0
2	Doesn't Matter	8.0

Using the sample application's charting feature as an example (refer back to Figure 5.6), assume that plot.dll has been recompiled with a later version of the compiler; but other than that, not a single line of code has been changed. How can test requirements be determined? Here are a few suggestions:

- Reexamine the specific functionality that plot.dll offers and look for error scenarios.
- For each potential error scenario, consider the consequences.
- Use a utility such as Dependency Walker to determine any new dependencies that plot.dll has and the potential implications of those dependencies.
- Examine other components to make sure that trend.dll is the only component using plot.dll.
- Focus testing on the creation of data.tmp and the data integrity.
- Confine testing to the context of the trend chart features only.
- Retest all other functionality.
- Retest browser compatibility (the Java applet remains the same, so there is no need to be concerned with its compatibility).
- Focus testing on the stored procedure sp_trend (because nothing has changed there).

DIFFERENT CONCEPTUAL LEVELS OF PARTITIONING

- *High-level partitioning.* If the goal of testing is to measure server-side response time, then there is no need to run data through the Internet, firewall, proxy servers, and so on. With a load-testing tool (see Chapter 19 for more information), a load generator can be set up to hit the Web server directly and collect the performance data. Figure 5.14 shows an example of high-level partitioning.

- *Physical-server partitioning.* If the goal of testing is to measure per-box performance, then each physical server can be hit independently with a load generator to collect performance data.

- *Service-based partitioning.* If the goal of testing is to test the functionality of the data application and the overall performance of the database server that is providing services to the application, then testing should focus on the database server.

- *Application/component-based partitioning.* The focus of such testing is on the component level (refer to the preceding Java chart-generation tests for examples). The testing here is focused at the component level, as previously described in the charting example.

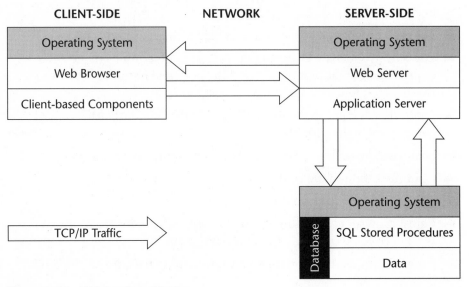

Figure 5.14   High-level partitioning.

Testing Considerations

- Determine the server hardware requirements of the system under test. Then generate a matrix of the supported configurations and make sure that these configurations are tested.

- Determine the server software component requirements (Web servers, database servers, search servers, proxy servers, communications servers, application servers, e-commerce servers, multimedia servers, etc.) and design interoperability tests to look for errors.

- Determine how the server software components are distributed and design interoperability tests to look for errors.

- Determine how the server software components interact with one another and design interoperability tests to look for errors.

- Determine how the Web-to-database connectivity is implemented (CGI, NSAPI/ISAPI, ASP, or other technologies) and design interoperability tests to look for errors.

- Determine the hardware/software compatibility issues and test for those classes of errors.

- Determine how the processing is distributed between client and server (thin client versus thick client).

- Test partitioning involves testing pieces of a system both individually and in combination. Test partitioning is particularly relevant in the testing of Web systems due to the communication issues involved. Because Web systems involve multiple components, testing them in their entirety is neither an easy nor effective means of uncovering bugs at an early stage.

- Design test cases around the identified components that make up the client-side of a Web application, including browser components, static HTML elements, dynamic HTML elements, scripting technologies, component technologies, plug-ins, and so on.

- One way of evaluating integration testing and test partitioning is to determine where the components of an application reside and execute. Components may be located on a client machine or on one or more server machines.

DLL Testing Issues

- Use a utility such as Microsoft Dependency Walker to generate a list of DLLs on which the application under test (and its components) depends. For each DLL, determine its version number and where it is located. Determine if the version number is the latest shipping version.

Here is an example of a component-recursive dependency tool, Microsoft Dependency Walker. If the utility is run and DLL.CALLER.EXE is loaded (the example DLL mentioned in the "Dynamic Link Library" section in this chapter), its dependencies will be analyzed (as shown in Figure 5.15). To download Dependency Walker and other related utilities, go to the Microsoft site and search for Dependency Walker, or visit www.dependencywalker.com.

A comparable utility called QuickView is available for Windows 9.x and NT systems. To access this utility, right-click on a component that you would like to view and choose QuickView from the context menu list.

There are at least four categories of DLLs and components:

1. *Operating system-based DLLs.* In Windows environments, this includes USER32.DLL, GDI32.DLL, and KERNEL32.DLL.

2. *Application service-based DLLs.* In Windows environments, this includes ASP.DLL, CTRL3D32.DLL, VB40032.DLL, and so forth.

3. *Third-party DLLs.* For example, CHART.DLL offers charting functionality to other applications.

4. *Company-specific DLLs.* For example, Netscape Navigator includes the NSJAVA32.DLL.

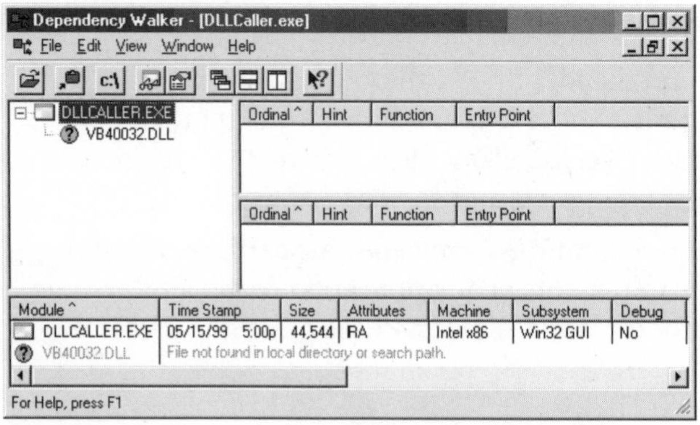

Figure 5.15 Component-recursive dependency tool.

In testing for DLL-related errors, do the following:

- Ensure that nonsystem DLLs are properly installed and that their paths are properly set so that they can be found when the components call them.

- Look for potential incompatibility errors, such as API incompatibility or functional incompatibility among various versions of the same DLL.

- If there are other applications installed on the system that share the same DLL with components, determine how the installation and uninstallation processes will be handled.

- Determine what will happen if the DLL is accidentally erased or overwritten by a newer or older version of the same DLL.

- Determine what will happen if more than one version of the same DLL coexists on the same machine.

- Recognize that explicitly loaded DLLs must be unloaded when applications and processes no longer need them. Typically, this should occur upon the termination of the calling application.

- Test with a *clean* environment (a system with only the operating system installed on it), as well as a *dirty* environment (a system loaded with common applications).

- Decide what to do if a third-party DLL needs certain files that are not available (printer initialization, for example).

- With Windows-based applications, consider looking for errors related to the creation and removal of DLL keys during installation and uninstallation.

Script Testing Issues

Characteristics of a Script

An interpreted language is parsed and executed directly from the source code each time it is executed. The parsing is done on a statement-by-statement basis; syntax error detection occurs only when the statement is about to be executed. Different interpreters for the same language will find different errors. Each interpeter will also execute the script in a slightly different manner. Thus, running Perl script may produce different results when executed on different UNIX hardware. This same script may also produce different results on a Windows NT or Macintosh system. This means that a script needs to be tested on every system on which it will be deployed.

There are several advantages to using scripted languages, which make them an ideal tool to solve many common problems. Scripts are fast to write. This makes them a valuable tool. Scripting languages usually provide features, such as automatic string-to-number conversion, which makes coding many functions quicker and easier.

Use of Scripts in Web Applications

Today's applications contain increasing amounts of scripted code, both on the server- and on the client-side computer. Sometimes this code is only a couple of lines placed in an HTML Web page, as shown here:

```
<SCRIPT LANGUAGE="JavaScript">
bla...
</SCRIPT>
```

Other times the code is very complex. Web severs allow scripts to process HTML forms, provide cookie support, sort and format data, and produce reports.

Or the code can appear to be simple but hide complexity and potential problems; For example, here is a common use of scripts in a web page:

```
<SCRIPT LANGUAGE="JavaScript">
var supported = navigator.userAgent.indexOf("Mozilla")==0 &&
navigator.userAgent.substring(8,9) >= 4;

function openWindow() {
      if(supported) {...}
}
</SCRIPT>
```

The first line of HTML tells the browser that JavaScript follows. The next two lines test if the browser is Mozilla- (Netscape) compliant and if it is version 4.0 or higher. It does so by using the navigator object, and creates a variable named *supported*. These lines set the Boolean variable (*supported*); they contain a logical operation (&&) and the string compare (.substring(8,9) > = 4), which tests the ninth character of the string to see if the version of Mozilla is greater than or equal to 4.0. This defines a function call (openWindow()), and starts a branch (if). The *if* branch could follow as if the *supported* variable were true, meaning Mozilla-compliant and greater than version 4.0 display or as an HTML page in a certain way, or display the page in another way. This code occurred in a company's homepage. It was considered simple, straightforward, and didn't require testing.

Interpreted programs can be several hundred lines of code, as when the page will set, update, and check Web page cookies. For examples look at the source code of http://my.yahoo.com.

To view the source of an HTML page, choose the View pull-down menu and choose Source (IE) or Page Source (NS).

JavaScript is not the only interpreted language; nor is the use of interpreted languages limited to the client-side of Web applications. Many scripts, written for the server-side to process HTML forms or communicate with legacy or back-office systems, are written in Perl, sed, or Tcl. SQL statements are used to request information from relational databases (see Chapter 14). These statements are generated on-the-fly and incorporate data generated by end users. For example a script can grab a piece of data from an HTML page and dynamically insert it to an SQL query.

Testing Scripts in Web Applications

Scripts can appear in many different places. Scripting languages are commonly used on the client-side in browsers. Server-side scripts are used to start, stop, and monitor Web servers, application servers, databases, mail servers, and many other applications. Scripts are used to move data, transform data, and clean up file system directories. Scripts are a part of installation procedures, daily application maintenance, and the uninstall process.

Coding-Related Problems

A script can have all the coding problems of any computer language, hence needs to be tested just like all other code. Testing interpreted code raises additional concerns over testing compiled code, as there is no compiler to check the syntax of the program. Therefore, to find syntax problems, the code must be executed. You should test 100 percent of the code, that is, every line of the code. Testing every line of a script is laborious, and very few commercial tools provide line or branch coverage for scripting languages.

The most common coding problem will be syntax errors. Syntax errors are caused when the programmer forgets to include a line terminator or some other minor formatting requirement of the language. Many of these syntax errors will cause the program to stop execution and display a message of the form shown in Figure 5.16. In this case, the proper use of an apostrophe in the text of the message inadvertently caused a fatal syntax error. Many scripts contain hard-coded data as part of the program, rather than keeping data external to the executable code. Often this means that as the conditions change the code will stop working or start behaving in unexpected ways.

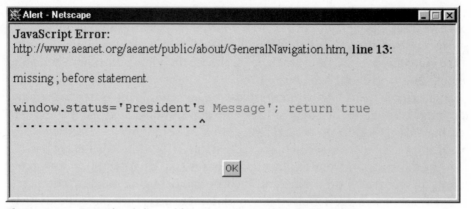

Figure 5.16   Example of client-side script error.Hard-Coded Problems.

The following sample of code exhibits hard-coding of data into the program. If the name "Mozilla" ever changes or the location of the release value (8,9) changes, tracking down all possible occurrences will be difficult.

```
<SCRIPT LANGUAGE="JavaScript">
var supported = navigator.userAgent.indexOf("Mozilla")==0 &&
navigator.userAgent.substring(8,9) >= 4;

function openWindow() {
    if(supported) {...}
}
</SCRIPT>
```

Moreover, users will probably get new versions of the browser before the developers and testers become aware that the new browser is available. With new browsers constantly being released, testing this code has to become an ongoing activity. This is a good opportunity for test automation.

Hard-coding and dependence on data formats may cause problems to occur at unexpected times. One example is awk, a UNIX utility used to process records. *Piping*, or sending, the output of the ls command into awk is a common way to sort and select file system data. The ls command lists the files, subdirectories, and their contents of the current directory. However, the ls command returns a slightly different organization of information depending on the operating system. This means that migrating the application to a new UNIX machine may cause failures. The symptom might be a crash or getting a text field instead of a numeric field. The symptom might be subtle, such as returning the wrong value. Testing scripts also requires checking each supported platform for data integrity.

Script Configuration Testing

Each server type will have a different script interpreter based on the manufacturer. Different interpreters will handle scripts differently. Script testing requires configuration testing as much as browser configuration testing. For a discussion of configuration and compatibility testing see Chapter 17 "Configuration and Compatibility Tests."

Bibliography

Binder, Robert V. *Testing Object-Oriented Systems: Models, Patterns, and Tools.* Reading, WA: Addison Wesley Longman, 2000.

LogiGear Corporation. *QA Training Handbook: Testing Web Applications.* Foster City, CA: LogiGear Corporation, 2003.

———— *QA Training Handbook: Testing Windows Desktop and Server-Based Applications.* Foster City, CA: LogiGear Corporation, 2003.

Orfali, Robert, Dan Harkey, Jeri Edwards. *Client/Server Survival Guide, 3rd Ed.* New York: John Wiley & Sons, Inc., 1999. Reilly, Douglas J. *Inside Server-Based Applications.* Redmond, WA: Microsoft Press, 2000.

Mobile Web Application Platform

Why Read This Chapter?

In the previous chapter we discussed the differences between traditional software systems and Web systems. Those differences, in turn, call for new testing techniques and processes. Mobile Web applications present a new set of challenges in which new types of clients beyond the desktop PCs are introduced. It's also essential to examine the various pieces that make up the Web application systems deployed on mobile devices, such as Personal Digital Assistant

(PDA) devices and Web-enabled wireless phones. With this knowledge, we can begin to understand how mobile Web applications are different from desktop Web applications, the limits of testing, and how to focus our testing resources on well-identified areas of risks.

Introduction

This chapter presents the mobile device platform and shows how it applies to mobile Web systems, which can be wired or wireless. It explores the technological similarities as well as differences between a desktop Web system and mobile Web system. Testing considerations that are suited to mobile Web platforms are also discussed. More testing methods will be covered in Chapter 20, "Testing Mobile Web Applications." Although many of the traditional software testing practices can be applied to the testing of wired and wireless mobile Web application, there are numerous technical issues that are specific to mobile platforms that need to be considered.

In the same way that other chapters are not about testing a PC and its operating system, this chapter is not about testing the handheld or mobile device (meaning its hardware and embedded operating system). It is about testing the Web applications running in a microbrowser and about the accompanying issues in their connection to the Web.

What Is a Mobile Web Application?

A mobile Web application is a Web-based application with one key difference: Standard Web-based applications typically run on a desktop PC as the client; mobile Web-based applications run on a mobile device as the client. Currently, the common mobile devices include wireless phones, PDAs, and smart phones (that is, wireless phone/PDA combos).

The main difference between a mobile and a desktop Web application is the size of a typical mobile device; the browser running on it, which interprets the Web-based content, has many restrictions that do not exist in a typical desktop PC. One of the implications is the Web content; the UI must be compressed to accommodate the size restrictions imposed by the mobile device. Often, a lightweight version of the Web content and UI must be created for the mobile client.

Various Types of Mobile Web Client

Generally, we can group mobile devices into five categories: PDAs, handheld computers, mobile phones, messaging products, and specialized devices. In addition, we will also touch on i-Mode device. At the time of this writing, i-Mode is a very popular device in Japan, but its market share is expanding to other countries. We expect that it will be available in the United States some time in the near future.

> **NOTE** The messaging products are based on technologies such as SMS (Short Messaging Service), which is an inexpensive method for communicating through text messages of up to 160 characters each. Many of the mobile devices today also have the messaging capability built in. Because we are primarily interested in the browser-based applications, we will exclude messaging products from this chapter.

Palm-Sized PDA Devices

PDAs are palm-sized electronic organizers that can run software to connect to the Web using, for example, a landline modem; this is similar to the way a desktop computer has software to connect to the Web using a modem, or increasingly, a wireless modem. These devices are known by many different names, including Palm, PalmPilot, Palm PC, Pocket PC, and handheld organizers, to mention a few. Figure 6.1 shows examples of three PDA devices available on the market today. By default, a PDA will offer a full suite of Personal Information Management (PIM) applications, which should include a date book, an address book, a to-do list, and a notebook.

These PDAs may have Web-enabling capability via a wired or wireless connection to the Web. There are two ways to get connected to the Web: Download during data synchronization or connect through a modem.

Figure 6.1 Examples of Palm-sized PDA devices.

Data Synchronizing

An essential feature contributing to the great success of the PalmPilot is the capability to easily synchronize data between the handheld device and the desktop, and vice versa. The Palm HotSync Manager is designed to do two-way data synchronization between the device and the desktop (commonly referred to as *conduit software*), in this case using functions exported from a number of dynamic link libraries (DLL). HotSync Manager is the conduit manager. Each data type, whether an address book, calendar, or Web content, needs its own conduit to handle synchronization of that specific data type.

To sync your data to or from your PDA to your desktop, you need HotSync Manager on your desktop PC. Then you connect the PDA to your PC via a serial or USB cable, a modem, infrared radiation (IR) or wireless connection. When a HotSync operation is initiated, the sync software compares the record on the PDA to the one stored on your PC and accepts the most recent one (in most cases; these rules can be determined via the HotSync Manager.) Although they might have different names, most PDA devices have a synchronization feature similar to that of HotSync Manager for data transfer between the device and the PC. This feature becomes an essential element for offline Web browsing capability, which we will discuss later in this chapter. Depending on the type of application that you are testing, it will dictate how much testing you will need to focus on data synchronization. For example, if you are testing a mobile Web application that will be used in both the online and offline scenarios, then you will need to consider how the offline scenario will affect data updating between the client and the PC and/or server-side. If you are testing a conduit or a mobile application that includes a data conduit, then your testing should focus more on data integrity, based on various data conditions between the device and the PC and/or the server-side.

Web Connectivity

It's also worth mentioning that in the early days of PDA development and manufacturing, a PDA was considered a wired device, meaning that, in order to make a connection to the Internet, you needed to connect to a data line via a modem. Nowadays, PDA devices can connect to the network or Internet via a wireless card or modem connection, an IR connection, or mobile phone connection, in addition to a landline phone connection. Figure 6.2 shows examples of a PDA connecting to the Internet through a wireless and wired connection. (For more information on wired connectivity, refer back to Chapter 4, "Networking Basics"; wireless networking is discussed more fully later in this chapter.)

Support for wireless connectivity means you will need to take several wireless-specific issues into your testing considerations; these include security issues, a higher probability of losing connectivity when moving about while staying connected, and lower bandwidth availability for data transferring.

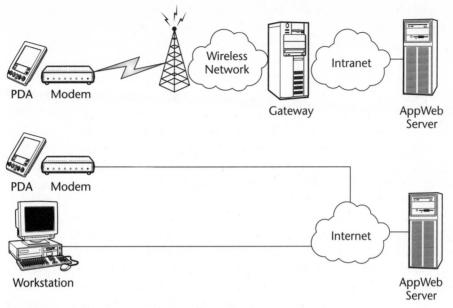

Figure 6.2   Wired and wireless Internet connection.

Various Types of Palm-Sized PDA Devices

One way to differentiate the different flavors of PDA devices is to identify the operating system embedded in the device. At the time of this writing, there are four major operating system players:

- Palm OS, produced by Palm, Inc.
- Windows CE, produced by Microsoft
- BlackBerry, produced by Research in Motion
- EPOC, produced by Symbian

Palm (which at the time of this writing had split into two companies, Palm Computing and Palm Source) not only produces the operating system but also manufactures the PalmPilot devices that have the OS and basic applications already embedded. Several major manufacturers also license the operating systems from Palm then build their PDA devices around the licensed software. Two examples in the commercial space are Handspring's Visor and Sony's CLIE devices. Symbol Technologies is another example of a manufacturer that licenses the Palm OS to build PDA devices that target vertical markets (e.g., health care, transportation, and fulfillment). Palm OS is a strong leader in the commercial or consumer space. One of the reasons for its success is its simplicity. At least in its early days, Palm wanted to design a device that was small (pocket size), inexpensive, and power-efficient, and that performed its few tasks very well. For those reasons a powerful processor, multitasking, color display, and standard applications normally used on the desktop were all considered unnecessary.

Many other devices are built with Microsoft Windows CE operating systems. Examples of these include Casio's Cassiopeia, Compaq's iPAQ, and HP's Jornada. In contrast to Palm's designs, Window CE is designed to leverage users' familiarity with the Windows operating system and applications. It is more like migrating the desktop environment to the palm-size computer, extending its normal use. Therefore, navigating in a Windows CE environment is less natural than in the Palm environment. At the time of this writing, Windows CE devices support multithreaded applications, enabling more powerful applications to multitask on the device. On the flip side, it means that the devices consume more power and therefore demand more processing power.

Symbian's EPOC-based devices comprise another set of PDA devices built around an operating system other than Palm's or Microsoft's. Symbian is owned by a joint venture that includes Ericsson, Matsushita (Panasonic), Motorola, Nokia, Psion, Siemens and Sony Ericsson. The operating system was originally developed by Psion, therefore all PDA devices manufactured by Psion used this operating system. A few examples include the Psion Revo, Psion Series 5, and Psion Series 5mx. Today, there are many other PDAs produced by the joint venture owners. Examples include the Ericsson R380 and Nokia 7650 smart phones.

Finally, Research in Motion's (RIM) BlackBerry OS-based devices are keyboard-based PDAs that also have support for wireless connectivity and for Web browsing. Examples of devices produced by RIM include RIM 957 and BlackBerry 5810.

Handheld PCs

As illustrated in Figure 6.3, handheld PCs are trimmed-down and lightweight versions of a laptop. They often look like miniature laptops and are tiny enough to carry around in your hand; their keyboards are big enough to make typing functional, although not necessarily natural. The two major operating system players in the handheld PC market are: Microsoft with Windows CE, Windows for Handheld PC, and Symbian with EPOC. Windows CE or Windows for Handheld PC are the trimmed-down versions of the standard operating systems. Some people prefer using a laptop instead of the handheld PC since laptops are getting smaller and lighter; and they use the standard version of the OS, which offers full capabilities with lots of applications available.

Figure 6.3   Handheld PC example.

WAP-Based Phones

WAP, an acronym for Wireless Application Protocol, is the technology used to connect mobile devices such as mobile phones to the Web by transforming the information on the Web so that it can be displayed more effectively on the much smaller screen of a mobile phone or other mobile device. Figure 6.4 shows an example of a WAP-based phone.

Recall that in Chapter 2, "Web Testing versus Traditional Testing," we discussed various flavors of the client-server configurations for which the client is assumed to be a desktop PC. WAP-based systems work much like a client-server system with one major difference: The client is a mobile device such as a mobile phone. To make this WAP-based client system work, there are two other elements involved.

First, there must be an intermediary server, called a *WAP gateway*, sitting between the Web server and the client. The WAP gateway is responsible for converting client requests from a mobile device to regular Web requests, and in turn, converting the Web response information from the Web server back to the format that can be transmitted to and displayed on the mobile device or a client. In addition, the mobile device such as the mobile phone must be WAP-enabled; that is, the embedded software used to turn the device into a WAP client must exist on the device. Figure 6.5 illustrates a WAP-enabled phone connected to a Web server via a WAP gateway. (There are several phone manufacturers that produce WAP-enabled phones, including Ericsson, Hitachi, Motorola, Nokia, and Sanyo, to name a few.) An obvious physical difference between a WAP-enabled phone and a regular mobile phone is the size of its screen, which is normally larger, enabling more display real estate for Web content.

Figure 6.4   Example of WAP-based phone.

Second, to make your Web pages viewable by WAP-enabled devices, the HTML pages must be converted into either HDML (Handheld Device Markup Language) or WML (Wireless Markup Language) format. HDML is a simplified version of HTML designed to reduce the complexity of a regular HTML page, which can be large, hence time-consuming to transfer over the wireless network with a bandwidth that is rather limited. WML is similar to HDML except it is based on XML (eXtensible Markup Language), enabling the use of many commercially available XML tools to generate, parse, and manipulate WML. WML can also use XSL (eXtensible Stylesheet Language) and XSLT (XSL Transformations) to construct *WML decks* from XML metalanguages. A WML deck is a collection of WML cards, each of which is a single block of WML code containing text or navigation items, which is part of the interface for a WML-based application. Another difference is that HDML does not allow scripting, while WML supports its own version of JavaScript, called WMLScript, enabling client-side scripting. Unlike JavaScript in HTML, however, WMLScript is treated much like graphics in HTML; that is, the script files must be saved separately from the WML files.

Converting HTML pages to WML pages can be done using conversion tools (which saves time), or manually (which is more elegant because this process takes usability into consideration). WML pages also take into consideration that the screen size is smaller, therefore pages with large graphics and a lot of scrolling text are not easy to view on the mobile devices.

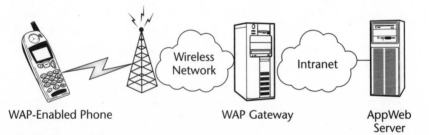

WAP-Enabled Phone   WAP Gateway   AppWeb Server

Figure 6.5   WAP-based client-server architecture.

NOTE More information on WAP and WML can be found on the Mobile Links page of www.qacity.com, which contains links including www.wapforum.com, www.nokia.com, and www.motorola.com, and offers additional reference information.

i-Mode Devices

In 1999, NTT DoKoMo the leading telecommunications operator in Japan, launched a new service called i-Mode (short for information-mode). It has become very popular with more than 20 million subscribers today, and still growing. The i-Mode technology is similar to WAP technology, but instead of using WML contents on the server-side, i-Mode pages are produced with cHTML (Compact HTML), a well-defined subset of standard HTML, which is designed for small information appliances. Similar to WAP, i-Mode client-server architecture requires a gateway to translate wireless requests from a mobile phone to the Web server, and vice versa.

A typical i-Mode client is an i-Mode-enabled phone, which is a regular wireless phone with a larger screen (on average, between 96×90 pixels to 96×255 pixels), often supporting up to 16-bit color. Like a WAP-based phone, it has an embedded microbrowser for browsing i-Mode sites that are tagged in cHTML. There are thousands of i-Mode-compatible Web sites on the Internet today. Another characteristic of i-Mode phone and service is that it's always on. However, since data transmission is packet-based (similar to TCP/IP), users are charged by the size of data transmitted, not by the connection duration. That means i-Mode users can enjoy a variety of typical Internet activities, such as Web browsing, making travel arrangements, buying movie tickets, getting driving directions, e-mailing, video-phoning, and so on.

At the time of this writing, i-Mode services and devices are not yet available outside Japan, though they are slowly being introduced in Europe and, hopefully, in the United States in the near future. This is important, because i-Mode phones use a microbrowser to interpret cHTML tags; and as it turns out, cHTML-based browsers are also used in many other types of small information appliances such as wireless PDAs and wearable communicating devices. Since the i-Mode technology has applications that cross many types of devices, it may become more common, hence, it is important to study. It is in our interest to understand the different types of browser markup languages to plan for our test coverage more adequately.

Smart Phones or Mobile Phone/PDA Combos

A *smart phone* is a wireless phone with extended capabilities that enable access to digital data. Think of a smart phone as a mobile device that combines wireless phone features together with PDA features. This means that it can handle wireless phone calls; support access to the Internet; send and receive voicemails, e-mails, and faxes, usually through unified messaging or UMS (Unified Messaging

System), similar to a Web-enabled phone; and manage personal information, just like a PDA. Other features that a smart phone might offer include LAN connectivity, pen-style data-entry method, wired or wireless data transfer between phone sets and computers through synchronization, remote access to desktop computers, and remote control of electronic systems at home or in the office. In sum, a smart phone is designed to offer similar functionality as a data-enabled phone or i-Mode phone, with these differences: a smart phone has a larger screen display, touch-screen support, more CPU power (relative to the WAP-based phone), more RAM, and more secondary storage (static RAM or flash memory).

This raises the question: Is a smart phone a cellular phone with PDA capabilities, or a PDA with cellular phone capabilities? As the industry evolves, it is really hard to say, and, ultimately, it may be irrelevant. Consider that Handspring, Inc. introduced the VisorPhone Springboard module to add wireless mobile phones and Internet/network connectivity to its PDA device. Shortly after that, the Treo series was introduced as the company's new line of products called Communicators that have both PDA and wireless phone and data connectivity built in. Kyocera licensed the Palm OS from Palm to build its series of smart phones by adding the PDA capabilities to its wireless phones. (Figure 6.6 shows examples of smart phones produced by Handspring and Kyocera, respectively.) These represent efforts to bring PDA functionality to wireless phones by adding larger displays. But regardless of which direction these producers take, their goal is the same: to combine the mobile phone and PDA functionality. It's also essential to point out that there are devices built with operating systems other than Palm OS. As mentioned earlier, two other major players are Symbian EPOC and Microsoft Windows CE. Note that the wireless phone can act as a wireless modem to a PDA, enabling wireless network connectivity. A PDA with a phone is like a PDA with connectivity.

Figure 6.6   Examples of smart phones.

It is fascinating to watch the race among developing technologies, and to monitor market acceptance for the most functional cellular smart phone. However, it is not our job to be concerned with which company ultimately wins this race. Our job is to continue learning the evolving technologies. By equipping ourselves with adequate knowledge, we will be in a better position to offer the best testing strategies to product teams.

Mobile Web Application Platform Test Planning Issues

In addition to learning about the various mobile device platforms available, it's also useful to examine another set of variables that influence testing strategies:

- Various types of microbrowsers embedded in the devices
- Hardware and software attributes
- Wireless networks that deliver the mobile Web application functionality and data
- Service platforms and support infrastructure needed by mobile Web applications

Microbrowsers

Like standard desktop browsers, a microbrowser is designed to submit user requests, receive and interpret results, and display the data received on the screen, enabling users to browse the Web on palm-sized or handheld devices. The key difference is that a microbrowser is optimized to run in the low-memory, lower-power CPU and small-screen environment, such as those presented in PDAs, WAP-based phones, and other smart phones and handheld devices.

In comparison to a desktop PC browser, a microbrowser might have either much less-sophisticated graphics or no graphics support at all. We can classify microbrowsers using the following categories:

- Text-only browsers
- WAP-based browsers that support HDML, WML, or both
- Palm OS-based Web Clipping Application that supports PQA-based (Palm Query Application) Web pages and standard HTML pages
- AvantGO browser that supports its Web Channel formatted pages
- i-Mode-based Web browser that supports cHTML pages
- Browsers that support standard HTML

Let's examine how the relationship between Web site content and Web browsers might affect the output. Figure 6.7 displays a Web page from www .imodecentral.com. Note that the page has support for both HTML and cHTML, but not WML. Four Web browsers used in this example are:

- Window Internet Explorer browser (HTML).
- Palm OS-based browser Blazer by Handspring (HTML/WML/cHTML) runs in an emulator.
- PIXO Internet Microbrowser (cHTML/HTML) runs in an emulator.
- Windows WinWAP browser (WML).

In this case, the WinWAP browser has problems displaying the content formatted for HTML because it supports WML only. The PIXO Internet Microbrowser displays the cHTML version of the Web page correctly. Blazer and Internet Explorer display the HTML version of the Web page correctly.

Figure 6.8 shows the OpenWave.com home page, which has support for both HTML and WML (using the same set of browsers as in Figure 6.7). Note that WinWAP displays the WML version of the content. Blazer displays the WML version of the content instead of HTML. Internet Explore and PIXO display the HTML version of the content.

Finally, Figure 6.9 shows the PIXO i-Mode browser displaying the same HTML content with the Images option turned off.

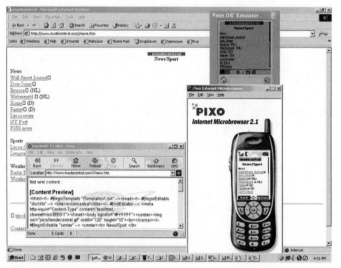

Figure 6.7 Example of a Web site with support for HTML and cHTML.

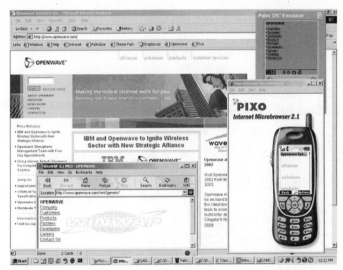

Figure 6.8   Example of a Web site with support for HTML and WML.

Web Clipping Application: How Does It Work?

Because wireless bandwidth is limited (see Table 6.2 for a sample of various wireless network transfer rates), waiting for a normal Web page to download can be a disappointing experience. Furthermore, the typical screen of a PDA device is so small that it is not efficient for displaying regular Web pages.

Figure 6.9   i-Mode browser displaying HTML content with the Images option turned off.

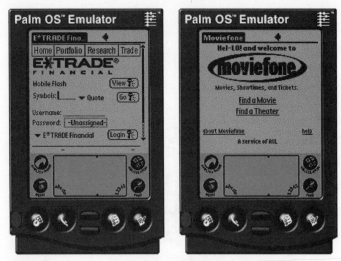

Figure 6.10   Examples of PQAs, Palm query applications.

Palm's solution to this problem was to specifically design Web pages for display on the smaller screens and then to enable them to be preloaded on the device via the HotSync process. These tiny Web pages are templates with complete layouts, form input and output, UI elements, and so on, but no actual data. So, when you need up-to-date information, you request the Web page, and the device sends the query to the Web Clipping Proxy server. In turn, only the actual requested information of that page is sent back to the device. The rest of the static elements of the page, such as images, animation, templates, and so on, already reside on the device.

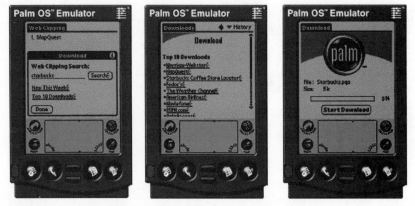

Figure 6.11   Searching, selecting, and downloading a PQA.

Installed PQA

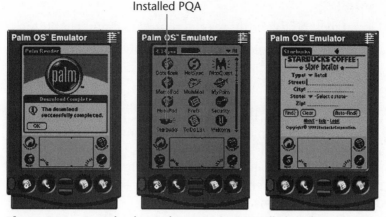

Figure 6.12   Download complete, PQA icon installed, and PQA launched.

This scheme enables a huge reduction of data transferred across the network. The process is referred to as *Web clipping*, and the tiny Web pages are called Palm query applications, PQAs, or Web Clipping Applications. The PQAs are HTML pages that have been processed through a program called PQABuilder, which converts the HTML and graphics into PQAs. Examples of two different PQAs are shown in Figure 6.10. (More information on Web Clipping can be found at these Palm Web sites: www.palmos.com/dev/tech/web-clipping and www.palmos.com/dev/support/docs/webclipping/.)

Predesigned Web Clipping Applications are available for download and installation on your PalmPilot. Following is an example of how a predesigned PQA can be located, downloaded, and used. Figure 6.11 shows the searching and downloading steps.

Continuing from Figure 6.11, Figure 6.12 shows the Starbucks PQA displayed as an Application icon, and how the PQA can be used to locate the nearest store by entering the address information.

Handheld Device Hardware Restrictions

Some of the hardware restrictions that make development and testing of mobile Web applications different from desktop PC Web applications include:

- Small screen display
    - Limited screen resolutions
    - Grayscale display (although color display is becoming more widely available)
- Low-power CPU

- Limited RAM
- Restricted input method (typically, several control and number buttons)
- Restricted character fonts (typically, support for only a single font)
- No secondary storage

Table 6.1 itemizes the differences among samples of various types of devices. The characteristics of these devices demand specific considerations in designing Web applications for display in the restricted environments, beyond markup language incompatibility issues. For example, a large image will not be useful when it displays on a small screen; add-in modules such as plug-ins might not be supported. (In Chapter 20, we will discuss several other testing issues surrounding these limitations.)

Software-Related Issues

Operating system differences. As discussed earlier, each mobile device will adopt a certain operating system to be part of its platform, whether it's Palm OS, Windows-based OS, EPOC, or any other flavor. Each operating system has its own feature-rich offerings, as well as certain limitations. These factors will affect the overall capabilities of the device.

Device-specific microbrowser. Mobile devices that support Web browsing capabilities often supply a device-specific default browser. The default browser is in general designed to interpret the target Web content whether it's Web Clipping, WAP-based DHML or WML, cHTML, or just standard HTML.

Installed microbrowsers. If the device supports installed microbrowsers, there are several commercial microbrowsers available on the market for a particular device.

Supported Web server content. In addition to interpreting markup language content, certain browsers may support additional functionality such as JavaScript, cookies, SSL, WTLS (Wireless Transport Layer Security), and so on.

Online and offline. Due to bandwidth limitations of the current wireless network, it is useful to be able to cache Web content by storing it on a secondary storage device so that users can read news or browse site content offline. This content downloading can be done via the data synchronization process. During the sync operation, the desktop PC can be connected to a wired network, which often has much higher bandwidth that speeds download Web content to the device, by just a simple push of a button.

Table 6.1   Examples of Hardware Device Differences

	PALM-BASED EXAMPLE	POCKET PC EXAMPLE	WAP PHONE EXAMPLE	I-MODE EXAMPLE	DESKTOP PC EXAMPLE	LAPTOP EXAMPLE
Model	Palm m100	Audiovox Maestro PDA1032	Nokia 7110	DoCoMo 502i	Dell Optiplex Optiplex GX240	Apple iMac
Screen Display	LCD integrated	TFT	LCD	LCD	CRT	LCD
Resolution	160×160	320×240	95×65	120×130	1024×768	1024×768
Color	2-bit (four gray levels)	16-bit	2-bit (four gray levels)	Grayscale	32-bit	32-bit
Input method	Touchscreen	Touchscreen	Phone keypad	Phone keypad	Keyboard and mouse	Keyboard and mouse

Wireless Network Issues

As in any client-server system there are three players: the client, the server, and the network. In the case of mobile Web application, the client happens to be a palm-size or handheld device. In order to support this mobility, a wireless network is needed, in addition to the wired network already in place. In this discussion, we will touch on the wireless network installed and managed by leading operators in the telecommunication industry, as well provide an overview of LAN-based wireless technologies.

If you are testing the mobile device itself, which consists of the software and hardware, and their interactions with the network supported in certain localities, there is little you can do to test the interactions unless you are in the locality where the application will be deployed. However, if you are testing locality-independent Web applications, you do not have to worry about network incompatibility issues. The main testing issue you should take into consideration is the bandwidth (or lack thereof) and how it affects the performance and behavior of your mobile Web applications.

Generally, testing with various networks, such as for WAP-based phones, is only concerned with the WAP-gateway compatibility and, in some cases, compatibility with the local networks such as GSM and CDMA. Nevertheless, a brief discussion is in order on the wireless network technologies used today in various parts of the globe (see Table 6.2).

Wireless Network Standards

One way to help understand the evolution of wireless technology is to briefly examine the different network standards and learn what the generation designations (1G, 2G, 3G, and 4G) mean.

1G

As illustrated in Table 6.2, AMPS stands for Advanced Mobile Phone Service. AMPS, introduced in the early 1980s, became, and currently still is, the most widely deployed cellular or wireless system in the United States. AMPS is considered the first generation of wireless technology designed for voice transfer or 1G.

2G

The second-generation, or 2G, protocols added digital encoding capability, which is support for limited data communications, including fax, Short Messaging Services (SMS), and various levels of encryption and security. Examples of 2G protocols include GSM (Global System for Mobile Communications), TDMA (Time Division Multiple Access), and CDMA (Code Division Multiple Access). GSM is the most widely used system; in fact, it is the primary wireless telephone standard in Europe. GSM now has been deployed in close to 150 countries in the world.

It's important to point out that GSM operates on the 900-MHz and 1800-MHz bands throughout the world, except in the United States, where it operates on the 1900-MHz band. Unless you have a triband phone, this difference introduces incompatibility among mobile devices used in the United States versus other locals. TDMA and CDMA are more popular in North America, South America, and other parts of the world, including Central America, South Africa, and Asia Pacific. Although adding limited digital data transfer is a major improvement, one inherent limitation to 2G is its data transfer rate, which is, at top, 9600 bps. Given this limitation, it explains why technology such as WAP is needed for mobile Web applications. WAP was designed to pay attention to bandwidth limitations. Of course, other mobile devices such as palm-size PDAs and handheld computers suffer the same limitations of the wireless data transfer. However, these types of devices have more CPU power, RAM, and secondary storage in comparison to traditional mobile phone solutions.

NOTE A related issue to 2G and 3G/2.5G is that, currently, there are limitations that frequently prevent simultaneous use of voice and TCP/IP on mobile phones. These limitations are imposed by the NOM (Network Operation Mode) of the carrier's network and the phone's own hardware. On many systems, you cannot receive incoming phone calls or make outgoing phone calls while you're on a data call, and vice versa.

3G/2.5G

No one can deny that we live in a world of information overload. To advance mobile computing, one major bottleneck must be resolved: wireless bandwidth limitations. The third generation, or 3G, standards are designed to do just that. Whether the eventual standard used will be UMTS (Universal Mobile Telecommunication System), WCDMA (Wideband Code-Division Multiple Access), or Cdma2000 (Multicarrier Radio Transmission Technology), 3G promises to boost data transmission rate up to 2 Mbps, good enough to keep mobile users in contact at all times and to run most widely used multimedia applications.

3G isn't expected to reach maturity and be fully deployed until around 2005, so many operators are also looking into a possible middle-of-the-road solution. That's where 2.5G comes in. The two major contenders for 2.5G are GPRS (General Packet Radio Service) and EDGE (Enhanced Data GSM Environment).

A number of GSM operators in the United States and Europe are migrating to GPRS. In addition to promising to boost the transfer rate from 9600 bps to 114 Kbps (or, to be more realistic, up to as high as 28 Kbps to 64 Kbps), another benefit of GPRS is that data is sent in packets similar to TCP/IP, rather than via a circuit switch connection. This means that users can connect in the "always-on" mode without being charged. Telecom operators can then charge users based on the data transfer size, rather than connection time.

Table 6.2   Various Wireless Network Standards

STANDARD NAME	GENERATION	DATA TRANSFER RATE	OPERATES ON BAND(S)	STANDS FOR	OPERATES IN
AMPS	1G	Analog only	800 MHz to 900 MHz	Advanced Mobile Phone Service	United States and other countries
D-AMPS (TDMA)	2G	9.6 Kbps	800 MHz and 1,900 MHz	Digital-Advanced Mobile Phone System	North, South, and Central America
GSM (uses a variation of TDMA)	2G	9.6 Kbps	900 MHz, 1.8 GHz, and 1.0 GHz	Global System for Mobile Communications	Europe and more than 140 other countries. United States supports 1.9-GHz band only
CDMA	2G	9.6 Kbps	800 MHz and 1.9 GHz	Code Division Multiple Access	North America, Africa, South America, Pacific Asia, and others
GPRS*	2.5G	56 to 114 Kbps (approx.)	900 MHz, 1.8 GHz, and 1.9 GHz	General Packet Radio Service	Upgrade path for GSM or TDMA
EDGE	2.5G	Up to 384 Kbps	900 MHz, 1.8 GHz, and 1.9 GHz	Enhanced Data GSM Environment	Upgrade path for GSM or TDMA
1XRTT (first phase of Cdma2000)		Up to 144 Kbps (approx.)	800 MHz and 1.9 GHz	(Single-Carrier) Radio Transmission Technology	North America primarily and other countries
WCDMA	3G	384 Kbps to 2 Mbps (approx.)	1.885 GHz to 2.2 GHz	Wideband Code-Division Multiple Access	Upgrade path for GSM or TDMA (possibly for CDMA in some cases)
UMTS	3G	Up to 2 Mbps	1.885 GHz to 2.2 GHz	Universal Mobile Telecommunication System	Japan (2001), moving into Europe, Asia Pacific, and then United States

Table 6.2 *(continued)*

STANDARD NAME	GENER- ATION	DATA TRANSFER RATE	OPERATES ON BAND(S)	STANDS FOR	OPERATES IN
Cdma2000 (3XRTT)	3G	144 Kbps to 2 Mbps	1.885 GHz to 2.2 GHz	N/A	Upgrade path for CDMA
–TBD	4G	20 to 40 Mbps	Expected to be deployed between 2006-2010		

*For more information on GPRS worldwide coverage, go to: www.gsmworld.com/roaming/gsminfo.

EDGE is another significant player in the 2.5G movement. EDGE enables operators to upgrade their systems through software that promises to boost the data transfer rate up to 384 Kbps. This is a very significant improvement. In fact, some operators planning to upgrade to 3G will still be competing against the bandwidth capability delivered by EDGE.

Ready for 4G?

What is the future beyond 3G? It's 4G, of course. Fourth-generation wireless is expected to follow 3G within a few short years. The major improvement of 4G over 3G communications is, again, increased data transmission rate, reaching between 20 to 40 Mbps. 4G is expected to deliver more advanced versions of the same improvements promised by 3G, including worldwide roaming capability, enhanced multimedia and streaming video, universal access, and portability across all sorts of mobile devices.

Wireless Modem

Another important wireless technology is Cellular Digital Packet Data (CDPD), a standard designed to work over AMPS for supporting wireless access to the Internet and other packet-switched networks. Phone carriers and modem producers together offer CDPD-based network connectivity, enabling mobile users to get access to the Internet at the data transfer rate of up to 19.2 Kbps. The Minstrel series of wireless modems is an example of popular and commercially available modems for various PDA devices, including for PalmPilot and Pocket PC.

Wireless LAN and Bluetooth

Two technologies that we predict will have success in their own niche in the mobile movement are 802.11 and Bluetooth. Although these technologies are more applicable to WLAN (Wireless Local Area Network), they deserve mention here.

802.11 is a family of specifications for WLAN that includes 802.11, 802.11a, 802.11b, and 802.11g. Rather than explaining the differences among these standards, for the purpose of this discussion, we can generalize that these standards offer a data transfer rate of somewhere between 11 Mbps to 54 Mbps, or more realistically, up to 60 percent of that expected transfer rate. 802.11 can operate within a distance of a few hundred feet.

Bluetooth, in contrast, is designed to operate at a much shorter distance (about 50 feet). It is a specification that describes how, using a short-range wireless connection, mobile phones, computers, and PDAs can easily interconnect with each other and with home and business phones and computers. Bluetooth requires that a transceiver chip be installed in each device. Data can be exchanged at a rate of 1 Mbps. Users take advantage of Bluetooth technology by using it to interconnect various mobile devices including cellular phones and mobile communicators such as SMS devices, PDAs, portable audio players, and desktop computers. For example, a PDA device can do data synchronization with the desktop wirelessly; and Bluetooth earphones can be used with Bluetooth mobile phones.

Given the possibilities of various available wireless connectivity, the main impact on testing will be to take into consideration the different bandwidths that the majority of the target customers will have. In particular, we need to focus on the lowest common denominator to ensure that performance of the mobile Web application under test will meet the customer's expectations. In addition, we should also take into account the higher probability of losing connection in a wireless network and make sure to develop scenarios to test the handling of those undesirable conditions.

Other Software Development Platforms and Support Infrastructures

If your company develops and deploys a wireless solution, similar to building an e-business application with wireless solutions, the application will have additional dependencies on the software development platforms. These platform solutions include Sun's J2ME (Java 2 Micro Edition) and QUALCOMM's BREW (Binary Run-time Environment for Wireless).

There will also be content management issues to deal with: Specifically, how will you effectively deliver the content to a mobile device? If you have a standard Web application, for example, you will have to massage the content to work on a mobile device. Your company may need a solution specifically designed to deliver in the trimmed-down environments. With respect to back-office applications such as ERP and front-office applications such as CRM, your application will also need a data-access solution for mobile devices. Finally, the wireless infrastructure will also be needed to complete the mobile application deployment.

To accelerate the development and find a cost-effective solution, your company might opt to invest in third-party development platform software, content management client-server software, or data-access client-server solutions; or your company might opt to outsource an ASP (Application Service Provider) solution. While utilizing third-party technologies enables development teams to shorten time-to-delivery, these technologies also cause problems of their own, such as bugs, configuration and incompatibility issues, performance issues, and vendor-centric issues. In either, case, you have to consider that all of these technologies will have an effect on the application under test, as we have experienced in the past in standard Web applications.

The Device Technology Converging Game: Who Is the Winner?

As wireless data transfer rates improve, the mobile device industry players are in hot competition to bring better products and services to the target audience. This includes delivering more power and features to a promised much smaller device. In this race, the lines are blurring among mobile devices such as wireless PDAs, handheld computers, handheld communicators, smart phones, and WAP-based phones.

PDA devices are adding built-in wireless connectivity, mobile phone, Web access features, audio and video playing, and recording capabilities. An example is the aforementioned Handspring Treo product line, which is positioning itself as a communicator rather than a PDA. Alternative solutions for adding features include extending the device capabilities through expansion module technologies, such as the Handspring Secure Digital Card, Multimedia Card, or Type II PC Card technology, to offer wireless connectivity, wireless voice phone, wireless video phone, digital camera, and video recording capabilities.

From the opposite direction, there are the so-called smart phones—Cellular phone vendors are licensing (or using their own) PDA operating systems, such as Palm OS, Microsoft Windows CE, and EPOC to include in the phone. This is done in an effort to add PDA features and local computing and data storage capabilities. Data synchronization capabilities must be added to support data transferring via a desktop host solution.

Certainly, the two-device solution (a phone and a data-centric device connecting to each other and ultimately to the Web) through Bluetooth or IR technology will continue to be a growing path in its own right.

Finally, we expect to see more of the Web on mobile appliances, as well as wearable devices, introduced into the market, which might complement or replace some of the existing or emerging product categories.

Whatever direction the industry at large, and your company in particular, takes, rest assured that, in the future, you will learn more about these new technologies as they are introduced.

Bibliography and Additional Resources

Bibliography

Arehart, Charles, Nirmal Chidambaram, Shashikiran Guruprasad, Alex Homer, Ric Howell, Stephan Kasippillai, Rob Machin, Tom Myers, Alexander Nakhimovsky, Luca Passani, Chris Pedley, Richard Taylor, Marco Toschi. *Professional WAP*. Birmingham, United Kingdom: Wrox Press Inc., 2000.

Collins, Daniel, and Clint Smith. *3G Wireless Networks.* New York: McGraw-Hill Professional, 2001.

Garg, Vijay Kumar. *Wireless Network Evolution: 2G to 3G.* Upper Saddle River, NJ: Prentice Hall PTR, 2001.

Lin, Yi-Bing, and Imrich Chlamtac. *Wireless and Mobile Network Architectures.* New York: John Wiley & Sons, Inc., 2000.

Pogue, David, and Jeff Hawkins. *PalmPilot: The Ultimate Guide*, 2nd ed. Sebastopol, CA: O'Reilly & Associates, 1999.

Rhodes, Neil, and Julie McKeehan. *Palm OS Programming: The Developer's Guide*, 2nd ed. Sebastopol, CA: O'Reilly & Associates, 2001.

Additional Resources

Compact HTML for Small Information Appliances

www.w3.org/TR/1998/NOTE-compactHTML-19980209

CTIA—The Cellular Telecommunications & Internet Association

www.wow-com.com

Developer Resources Page on pencomputing.com

www.pencomputing.com/developer

GSM, TDMA, CDMA, & GPRS. What is it?

www.wirelessdevnet.com/newswire-less/feb012002.html

HDML or WML

www.allnetdevices.com/developer/tutorials/2000/06/09/hdml_or.html

i-Mode FAQ

www.eurotechnology.com/imode/faq.htm

i-Mode FAQ for Developers

www.mobilemediajapan.com/imodefaq

i-Mode Compatible HTML

www.nttdocomo.co.jp/english/i/tag/imodetag.html

Internet.Com Wireless Page

www.internet.com/sections/wireless.html

mBusiness Magazine (wireless technology magazine and books)
www.mbusinessdaily.com

Mobile Computing Magazine (news magazine for mobile computing)
www.mobilecomputing.com

Mobile Information Device Profile (MIDP)
http://java.sun.com/products/midp/

Mobile Software Resources (For i-Mode/HTML Development)
www.mobilemediajapan.com/resources/software

Mobile Technology Resources
www.jmobilemediajapan.com/resources/technology

mpulse-nooper.com—An article: "Application Testing in the Mobile Space"
http://cooltown.hp.com/mpulse/0701-developer.asp

Nokia Forum
www.forum.nokia.com

Online WAP Testing Tool
www.wapuseek.com/checkwap.cfm

Pen Computing Magazine
www.pencomputing.com

QACity.Com | Mobile
www.qacity.com/Technology/Mobile

WAP Devices Metrics
www.wapuseek.com/wapdevs.cfm

WAP FAQs
www.wapuseek.com/wapfaz.cfm

WAP Testing Papers
www.nccglobal
www.nccglobal.com/testing/mi/whitepapers/index.htm

WAP Testing Tools

  http://palowireless.com/wap/testtools.asp

WAP Tutorials

  www.palowireless.com/wap/tutorials.asp

Web-based WAP Emulator: TTemulator

  www.winwap.org

WinWAP: Mobile Internet Browser for Windows

  www.winwap.org

YoSpaces's Emulator

  www.yospace.com

CHAPTER

7

Test Planning Fundamentals

Why Read This Chapter?

A crucial skill required for the testing of Web applications is the ability to write effective test plans that consider the unique requirements of those Web applications. This skill is also required to write the sample test plan for the sample application. (See Chapter 8, "Sample Application," and Chapter 9, "Sample Test Plan," for details.)

TOPICS COVERED IN THIS CHAPTER

- ◆ Introduction
- ◆ Test Plans
- ◆ LogiGear One-Page Test Plan
- ◆ Testing Considerations
- ◆ Bibliography

Introduction

This chapter discusses test documentation, including test plan templates and section definitions. It also explains the efficiencies of the *LogiGear One-Page Test Plan*, details the components of issue and weekly status reports, and lists some helpful testing considerations.

Test planning for Web applications is similar to test planning for traditional software applications; that is, careful planning is always critically important to effective structuring and management. Test planning is an evolutionary process that is influenced by numerous factors: development schedules, resource availability, company finances, market pressures, quality risks, and managerial whim.

Test planning begins with the gathering and analysis of information. First, the product under test is examined thoroughly. Schedules and goals are considered. Resources are evaluated. Once all associated information has been pulled together, test planning begins.

Despite the complex and laborious nature of the test planning process, test teams are not generally given much direction by management. If a company-approved test-plan template does not exist, test teams are often simply instructed to "come up with a test plan." The particulars of planning, at least for the first draft of the test plan, are normally left up to the test team.

Test Plans

A test plan is a document, or set of documents, that details testing efforts for a project. Well-written test plans are comprehensive and often voluminous in size. They detail such particulars as testing schedules, available test resources, test types, and personnel who will be involved in the testing project. They also clearly describe all intended testing requirements and processes. Test plans often include quite granular detail—sometimes including test cases, expected results, and pass/fail criteria.

One of the challenges of test planning is the need for efficiency. It takes time to write these documents. Although some or all of this time might be essential, it is also time that is no longer available for finding and reporting bugs. There is always a trade-off between depth/detail and cost, and in many of the best and most thoughtful test groups, this trade-off is a difficult and uncomfortable one to make.

Another challenge of test planning is that it comes so early in the development process that, more than likely, no product has yet been built on which to base planning. Planning, instead, is based on product specifications and requirements documents (if such documents exist, and to whatever extent that they are accurate, comprehensive, and up-to-date). As a consequence, planning must be revised as the product develops, often moving in directions that are different from those suggested by original specifications.

Assuming that they are read (which often is not the case), test plans support testing by providing structure to test projects and improving communication between team members. They are invaluable in supporting the testing team's primary responsibility: to find as many bugs as possible.

A central element of test planning is the consideration of test types. Although every test project brings with it its own unique circumstances, most test plans include the same basic categories of tests: acceptance tests, functionality tests, unit tests, system tests, configuration tests, and regression tests. Other test types (installation tests, help tests, database tests, usability, security, load, performance, etc.) may be included in test plans, depending on the type of Web application under test. Sometimes, testing groups also need to determine how much automation and which automated testing tools to use. How will test coverage be measured, and which tools will be used? Other tasks that testing groups are often asked to do include designing and implementing defect tracking, configuration management, and build-process ownership.

Table 7.1 details when standard test types are normally performed during the software development process. (Refer back to Chapter 3, "Software Testing Basics," for definitions of these test types.) Note that Release Acceptance Tests (RATs), Functional Acceptance Simple Tests (FASTs), and Task-Oriented Functional Tests (TOFTs) are generally run in each phase of testing. Web systems may require additional test types, such as security, database, and load/stress.

The next phase of test planning is laying out the tasks. After all available resources and test types have been considered, it's possible to begin to piece together a *bottom-up schedule* that details which tests will be performed and how much time each test will require (later, delegation of tasks to specific personnel should be incorporated into the test plan). A bottom-up schedule is developed by associating tasks with the time needed to complete them—with no regard to product ship date. A *top-down schedule*, in contrast, begins with the ship date and then details all tasks that must be completed if the ship date is to be met. Negotiations regarding test coverage and risk often involve elements of both top-down and bottom-up scheduling.

Test plans must undergo peer management and project management review. Like engineering specs, test plans need to be approved and signed before they are implemented. During a test-plan review, the testing group may need to negotiate with management over required resources, including schedule, equipment, and personnel. Issues of test coverage and risk-based quality or life-critical and 24/7 uptime quality may also come into play. (Refer back to Chapter 1, "Welcome to Web Testing," for more information on test coverage and risk-based quality.) Ultimately, a test plan will be agreed upon, and testing can begin.

Table 7.1   Test Types and Their Place in the Software Development Process

TIME →		
Begin Alpha Testing	**Begin Beta Testing**	**Begin Final Testing**
Alpha Phase	Beta Phase	Final Phase

TYPES OF TESTS RECOMMENDED		
TOFT	TOFT	TOFT
FAST	FAST	FAST
RAT	RAT	RAT
Configuration	Real-World User Test	Install/Uninstall Test
Compatibility*	Exploratory Test	Real-World User-Level Test
Boundary Test	Forced-Error Test	Exploratory Test
Stress	Full Configuration	
Installation Test	Compatibility Test	
Exploratory Test	Volume Test	
	Stress Test	
	Install/Uninstall Test	
	Performance Test	
	User Interface	
	Regression	
	Documentation	

* Test one representative from each equivalence class.

Test-Plan Documentation

Test-plan documentation should detail all required testing tasks, offer estimates of required resources, and consider process efficiencies. Unless you are creating a test plan with the intention of distributing it to a third party—either to prove that proper testing was performed or to sell it along with software—it is best to keep test plans focused on only those issues that support the effort of finding bugs. Enormous, heavily detailed test plans—unless required by a customer or third-party regulating body—are only valuable insofar as they help you find bugs.

The unfortunate reality is that the majority of test plans sit unread on shelves during most of the testing process. This is because they are unwieldy and dense with information that does not support the day-to-day effort of finding bugs. Even if they are read, they are seldom updated as regularly as they should be, to reflect current changes to schedule, delegation of tasks, test coverage, and so on.

The LogiGear One-Page Test Plan (included later in this chapter) is designed specifically to avoid the troubles that more traditional test plans suffer; one-page test plans are more easily read and updated.

When read, test-plan documentation improves communication regarding testing requirements by explaining the testing strategy to all members of the product development team. Documentation is, of course, also valuable in conveying the breadth of a testing job to testing staff and in providing a basis for delegating tasks and supervising work.

Documentation generates feedback from testing team members and members of other departments. Debates are often sparked over the contents of test documentation. For example, project managers may insist on different levels of testing from those proposed by the testing group. Therefore, it is always a good idea to make test plans available for review as early in the development process as possible so that managers, programmers, and members of the marketing team can assess risk and priorities before testing begins. Debates are also more fruitful when team members can focus discussions on a clearly laid-out test plan that includes specific goals.

Issues of test coverage often arise midway through the testing process. Requiring managers to approve and sign test plans (before testing begins) brings managers into the test coverage decision process; moreover, it places responsibility on management to approve any compromises of test coverage that may arise from test-plan negotiations.

Accountability is also increased by good test documentation. Clearly defined responsibilities make it easier for both managers and staff to stay focused. Detailed lists of tests that must be performed, along with clearly defined expectations, go a long way toward ensuring that all foreseeable areas of risk are addressed.

Proper test documentation requires a systematic analysis of the Web system under test. Your understanding of the interdependencies of a system's components must be detailed and thorough if test planning is to be effective. As a test project is analyzed, a comprehensive list of program features should be compiled. It is common for a feature list to detail the complete set of product features, all possible menu selections, and all branching options. It is a good idea to begin writing a feature list as early in the test-planning phase as possible.

Test plans take into consideration many of the risks and contingencies that are involved in the scheduling of software development projects. For example, product documentation testing (e.g., online help, printed manuals) cannot be completed until the documentation itself nears completion. Documentation, however, cannot be in its final phase until after the user interface (UI) has been frozen. The UI, in turn, cannot be frozen until at some point in beta testing, when functional errors affecting the UI have been fixed. Another example of testing interdependency includes not being able to execute performance testing until all debugging code has been removed.

Compiling a list of features that are *not* to be tested will also be of value. Such a list sometimes smokes out resistance within the product team that might not otherwise have been voiced until midway through the testing process. It also clearly marks what you believe to be out of scope.

NOTE For more in-depth information regarding test planning, refer to *Testing Computer Software* by Cem Kaner, Jack Falk, Hung Q. Nguyen (John Wiley & Sons, Inc., 1999).

Test-Plan Templates

One effective means of saving time and ensuring thoroughness in test-plan documentation is to work from a *test-plan template*. A test-plan template is, essentially, a fill-in-the-blank test plan into which information that is specific to the system under test is entered. Because they are generic and comprehensive, test-plan templates force test team members to consider questions that might not otherwise be considered at the beginning of a test project. They prompt testers to consider numerous test types—many of which may not be appropriate for the test project—in addition to pertinent logistical issues, such as which test tools will be required and where testing will take place. Test templates can also impose a structure on planning, encouraging detailed specifications on exactly which components will be tested, who will test them, and how testing will proceed.

Appendix A contains the complete LogiGear Test Plan Template. After looking it over, review some of the many other test templates available. A good place to begin looking for a test-plan template is the planning section of the LogiGear Test Resource Web site (www.qacity.com). A standard test-plan template used by the software testing industry is the *ANSI/IEEE Standard 829-1983 for Software Test Documentation*. It defines document types that may be included in test documentation, including test cases, feature lists, and platform matrices. It also defines the components that the IEEE believes should be included in a standard test plan; so among other uses, it serves as a test-plan template. (For information regarding the *ANSI/IEEE Standard 829-1983*, visit www.computer.org, or phone (202) 371-0101.)

Test-Plan Section Definitions

The following lists define a number of standard test-plan sections that are appropriate for most test projects.

OVERVIEW SECTION

Test-plan identifier. Unique alphanumeric name for the test plan. (See Appendix A, "LogiGear Test Plan Template," for details.)

Introduction. Discussion of the overall purpose of the project. References all related product specifications and requirements documents.

Objective. Goals of the project, taking quality, scheduling constraints, and cost factors into consideration.

Approach. The overall testing strategy. Answer: Who will conduct testing? Which tools will be utilized? Which scheduling issues must be considered? Which feature groups will be tested?

TESTING SYNOPSIS SECTION

Test items. Lists every feature and function of the product. References specifications and product manuals for further detail on features. Includes descriptions of all software application, software collateral, and publishing items.

Features to be tested. Cross-references features and functions that are to be tested with specific test design specifications and required testing environments.

Features not to be tested. Features of the product that will not undergo testing. May include third-party items and collateral.

System requirements. Specifications on hardware and software requirements of the application under test: computer type, memory, hard-disk size, display type, operating system, peripheral, and drive type.

Entrance/exit. *Application-specific*: description of the application's working environment; how to launch and quit the application. *Process-specific:* description of criteria required for entering and exiting testing phases, such as alpha and beta testing.

Standard/reference. List of any standards or references used in the creation of the test plan.

Types of tests. Tests to be executed. May include acceptance tests, feature-level tests, system-level tests, regression tests, configuration and compatibility tests, documentation tests, online help tests, utilities and collateral tests, and install/uninstall tests.

Test deliverables. List of test materials developed by the test group during the test cycles that are to be delivered before the completion of the project. Includes the test plan itself, the bug-tracking system, and an end-of-cycle or final release report.

TEST PROJECT MANAGEMENT SECTION

The product team. List of product team members and their roles.

Testing responsibilities. Responsibilities of all personnel associated with the testing project.

Testing tasks. Testing tasks to be executed: The order in which tasks will be performed, who will perform the tasks, and dependencies.

Development plan and schedule. Development milestone definitions and criteria—detailing what the development group will deliver to testing, and when.

Test schedule and resource. Dates by which testing resources will be required. Estimates on amount of tester hours and personnel required to complete project.

Training needs. Personnel and training requirements. Special skills that will be required and number of personnel that may need to be trained.

Environmental needs. Hardware, software, facility, and tool requirements of testing staff.

Integration plan. How the integration plan fits into overall testing strategy.

Test suspension and resumption. Possible problems or test failures that justify the suspension of testing. Basis for allowing testing to resume.

Test completion criteria. Criteria that will be used to determine the completion of testing.

Issue-tracking process. Description of the process, the issue-tracking database, bug severity definitions, issue report formats (see the "Issue Reports" section in this chapter for an example).

Status tracking and reporting. How status reports will be communicated to the development team, and what the content of status reports will be (see the "Weekly Status Reports" section in this chapter for an example).

Risks and contingencies. All risks and contingencies, including deliverables, tools, and assistance from other groups—even those risks and contingencies that are detailed in other parts of the test plan.

Approval process. Test-plan approval and final release approval.

LogiGear One-Page Test Plan

It is often a challenge for testing groups to communicate their needs to other members of the software development team. The myriad test types, the testing sequence, and scheduling considerations can be overwhelming when not organized into a comprehensible plan that others can read at a glance. The LogiGear One-Page Test Plan is a distillation of test types, test coverage, and resource requirements that meets this need.

The LogiGear One-Page Test Plan is task-oriented. It lists only testing tasks, because some members of the product team may not be interested in "testing approach," "features not to be tested," and so on. They just want to know what is going to be tested and when. Because one-page test plans are so easy to reference, if they are adequate for your process, they are less likely to be disregarded by impatient team members.

The LogiGear One-Page Test Plan does not require additional work. It is simply a distillation of the standard test-plan effort into an easily digestible format. The LogiGear One-Page Test Plan is effective because it details the testing tasks that a testing team should complete, how many times the tasks should be performed, the amount of time each test task may require, and even a general idea of when the tasks should be performed during the software development process.

The LogiGear One-Page Test Plan is easy to reference and read. Twenty-page test plans are regularly ignored throughout projects, and 100-page test plans are rarely read at all. One-page test plans, on the other hand, are straightforward and can easily be used as negotiating tools when it comes time to discuss testing time and coverage—the usual question being, "How much testing time can be cut?" The test team can point to test tasks listed on a one-page test plan and ask, "Are we prepared to accept the risk of not performing some of these tests to their described coverage?"

Developing a One-Page Test Plan

The process of completing a one-page test plan is described in the following steps:

Step 1: Test Task Definition

Review the standard test types that are listed in Chapter 3 and in Table 7.1. Select the test types that are required for the project. Base decisions on the unique functionality of the system under test. Discussions with developers, analysis of system components, and an understanding of test types are required to accurately determine which test types are needed.

Step 2: Task Completion Time

Calculate the time required to perform the tests. The most difficult aspect of putting together a test plan is estimating the time required to complete a test suite. With new testers, or with tests that are new to experienced testers, the time estimation process involves a lot of guesswork. The most common strategy is divide and conquer; that is, break down the tasks into smaller subtasks. Smaller subtasks are easier to estimate. You can then sum up from those. As you gain experience, you miss fewer tasks and you gain a sense of the percentage of tasks that you typically miss so you can add an *n* percent for contingency or missing-tasks correction.

Informed estimates may also be arrived at if testing tasks are similar to those of a past project. If time records of similar past testing are not available, estimates may be unrealistic. One solution is to update the test plan after an initial series of tests has been completed.

A 20 percent contingency or missing-tasks correction is included in this example. As testing progresses, if this contingency does not cover the inevitable changes in your project's schedule, the task completion time will need to be renegotiated.

Step 3: Placing the Test Tasks into Context

Once the task list has been developed and test times have been estimated, place the tasks into the context of the project. The development team will need to supply a build schedule.

Determine how many times tests will be run during development. For example, documentation testing may be performed only once, or it may be reviewed once in a preliminary phase and then again after all edits are complete. A complete cycle of functionality tests may be executed once, or possibly twice, per development phase. Acceptance tests are run on every build. Often, a full bug regression occurs only once per phase, though partial regression tests may happen with each build.

Step 4: Table Completion

Finally, multiply the numbers across the spreadsheet. Total the hours by development phase for an estimate of required test time for the project. Add time for management, including test-plan writing/updating, test-case creation, bug database management, staff training, and other tasks that are needed for the test team and for completion of the project.

Step 5: Resource Estimation

Take the total number of hours required for the alpha phase, divide that by the total number of weeks in the alpha phase, and then divide that by 30 hours per week. That gives you the number of testers needed for that week. For example, if you need total testing hours for an alpha of 120, a four-week alpha phase, and testers have a third-hour testing week, your project requires only one tester [(120 ÷ 4) ÷ 30 = 1]. Apply this same process to arrive at estimates for the beta phase and project management. Note that, here, only a 30-hour testing week was used for a full-time tester because experience has shown that the other 10 (overhead) hours are essentially used for meeting, training, defect tracking, researching, special projects, and so on.

Using the LogiGear One-Page Test Plan

The LogiGear One-Page Test Plan can be invaluable in negotiating testing resource and testing time requirements with members of the product team. Figure 7.1 provides an example of the LogiGear One-Page Test Plan. Descriptions of each of the tests are included in Chapter 3.

Milestone	Type of Test	Number of Cycles	Hours per Cycle	Estimated Hours
Alpha			Total:	
Beta			Total:	#
Final			Total:	#
	Testing Project Management Test Planning & Test Case Design Training Test Automation		Total:	#

PROJECT TOTAL DAYS	XX
PERSON WEEKS	XX
20% Contingency (wks)	XX
Total person weeks	**XX**
Testers for Alpha	**XX**
Testers for Beta	**XX**
Testers for Final	**XX**
Project Management	**XX**

Figure 7.1 LogiGear One-Page Test Plan.

Testing Considerations

As part of the test planning process, you should consider how the bug reporting/resolution cycle will be managed and the procedure for status reporting. In addition, you should give some thought to how to manage milestone criteria, as well as whether to implement an automated testing program. This section touches on those issues.

Issue Reports

An *issue report*, or *test incident report*, is submitted whenever a problem is uncovered during testing. Figure 7.2 shows an example of an online issue report that is generated by the sample application. The following list details the entries that may be included in a complete issue report:

ISSUE REPORT FIELDS

Project. A project may be anything from a complex client-server system with multiple components and builds to a simple 10-page user's guide.

Build. Builds are versions or redesigns of a project that is in development. A given project may undergo numerous revisions, or builds, before it is released to the public.

Module. Modules are parts, components, units, or areas that comprise a given project. Modules are often thought of as units of software code.

Configuration. Configuration testing involves checking an application's compatibility with many possible configurations of hardware. Altering any aspect of hardware during testing creates a new testing configuration.

Uploading attachments. Attachments are uploaded along with issue reports to assist QA and developer groups in identifying and re-creating reported issues. Attachments may include keystroke captures or macros that generate an issue, a file from a program, a memory dump, a corrupted file on which an issue report is predicated, or a memo describing the significance of an issue.

Error types. The category of error into which an issue report falls (e.g., software incompatibility, UI, etc.).

Keyword. Keywords are an attribute type that can be associated with issue reports to clarify and categorize an issue's exact nature. Keywords are useful for sorting reports by specific criteria to isolate trends or patterns within a report set.

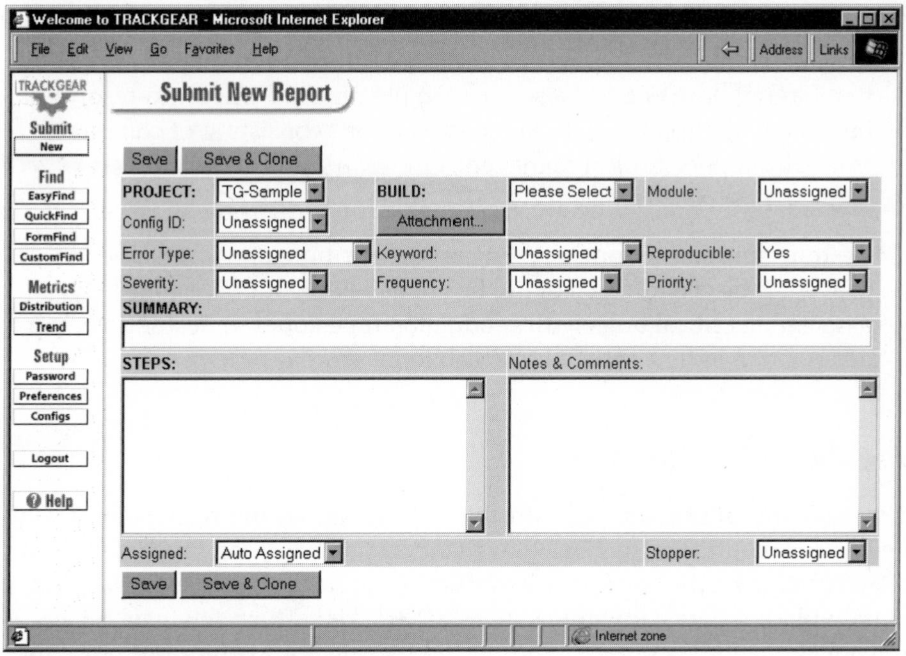

Figure 7.2 Online issue report form.

Reproducible. Specifies whether a reported issue can be recreated: *Yes, No,* with *Intermittent* success, or *Unconfirmed.*

Severity. Specifies the degree of seriousness that an issue represents to users. For example, a typo found deep within an online help system might be labeled with a severity of low, and a crash issue might qualify for a severity of high.

Frequency. Frequency, or how often an issue exhibits itself, is influenced by three factors:

1. How easily the issue can be reached.
2. How frequently the feature that the issue resides in is used.
3. How often the problem is exhibited.

Priority. An evaluation of an issue's severity and frequency ratings. An issue that exhibits itself frequently and is of a high severity will naturally receive a higher-priority rating than an issue that seldom exhibits itself and is only of mild annoyance when it does appear.

Summary. A brief summary statement that concisely sums up the nature of an issue. A summary statement should convey three elements: (1) symptoms, (2) actions required to generate the issue, and (3) operating conditions involved in generating the issue.

Steps. Describes the actions that must be performed to re-create the issue.

Notes and comments. Additional pertinent information related to the bug that has not been entered elsewhere in the report. Difficult-to-resolve bugs may develop long, threaded discussions consisting of comments from developers, project managers, QA testers, and writers.

Assigned. Individuals who are accountable for addressing an issue.

Milestone stopper. An optional bug report attribute that is designed to prevent projects from achieving future development milestones. By associating critical bugs with production milestones, milestone stoppers act as independent criteria by which to measure progress.

Weekly Status Reports

At the conclusion of each week during testing, the testing team should compile a status report. The sections that a status report normally includes follow.

Weekly status reports can take on critical importance because they are often the only place where software changes are tracked. They detail such facts as prerequisite materials not arriving on time, icons not loading onto desktops properly, and required documentation changes. Once archived, they, in effect, document the software development process.

Consideration must be given to what information will be included in weekly status reports and who will receive the reports. Just as test plans need to be negotiated at the beginning of a project, so do weekly status reports. The manner in which risks will be communicated to the development team needs to be carefully considered because information detailed in these reports can be used against people to negative effect. Possibly, milestone status reports only should be disseminated to the entire product team, leaving weekly status reports to be viewed only by a select group of managers, testers, and developers. (See Appendix B, "Weekly Status Report Template.")

Following are descriptions of sections that are typically included in weekly status reports:

TESTING PROJECT MANAGEMENT

Project schedule. Details testing and development milestones and deliverables.

Progress and changes since last week. Tests that have been run and new bugs that have been discovered in the past week.

Urgent items. Issues that require immediate attention.

Issue bin. Issues that must be addressed in the coming weeks.

To-do tasks by next report. Tasks that must be completed in the upcoming week.

PROBLEM REPORT STATUS

Bug report tabulation. Totals of open and closed bugs; explanation of how totals have changed in past week.

Summary list of open bugs. Summary lines from issue reports associated with open bugs.

TREND ANALYSIS REPORT

Stability trend chart. Graph that illustrates the stability of a product over time.

Quality trend chart. Graph that illustrates the quality of a product over time.

NOTE Numerous other document types may be included in test-plan documentation. For definitions of other test documentation types (including test-design, test-procedure, and test-case specifications; test transmittal reports; and test logs), refer to *Testing Computer Software* by Kaner, et al. (1999).

Automated Testing

The sample One-Page Test Plan given in Chapter 9 can be analyzed to uncover areas that may be well suited to automated testing. Considerations regarding staffing, management expectations, costs, code stability, UI/functionality changes, and test hardware resources should be factored into all automated testing discussions.

Table 7.2 categorizes the testing tasks called for in the sample one-page test plan by their potential adaptability to automated testing; further evaluation would be required to definitively determine whether these testing tasks are well suited to automation.

Table 7.2 Test Types Suited for Automation Testing

IDEALLY SUITED	NOT SUITABLE
RAT	Documentation
FAST	Boundary
Performance, load, and stress	Installation
Metrics/charting	Most functionality
Regression	Exploratory
Database population	Import utility
Sample file generation	Browser compatibility
	Forced-error

When evaluating test automation, do the following:

- Look for the tests that take the most time.
- Look for tests that could otherwise not be run (e.g., server tests).
- Look for application components that are stable early in development.
- Consider acceptance tests. Consider compatibility/configuration quick-look tests.

NOTE For more information on automated test planning, see *Integrated Test Design and Automation: Using the Testframe Method*, 1st ed., by Hans Buwalda, Dennis Janssen, Iris Pinkster, and Paul A. Watters (Boston: Addison-Wesley, 2001).

Milestone Criteria and Milestone Tests

Milestone criteria and milestone tests should be agreed upon and measurable (for example, you might decide that alpha testing will not begin until all code is testable and installable and all UI screens are complete—even if they contain errors). Such criteria can be used to verify whether code should be accepted or rejected when it is submitted for milestone testing.

Milestone criteria and accompanying tests should be developed for all milestones, including *completion of testing, entrance,* and *exit*. Ideally, these tests will be developed by the test team and approved by the development team; this approach may reduce friction later in the development project.

Bibliography

Kaner, Cem, Jack Falk, Hung Q. Nguyen. *Testing Computer Software*, 2nd ed. New York: Wiley, 1999.

Kaner, Cem, James Bach, and Bret Pettichord. *Lessons Learned in Software Training*, 1st ed., New York: John Wiley & Sons, Inc., 2001.

LogiGear Corporation. *QA Training Handbook: Lead Software Test Project with Confidence*. Foster City, CA: LogiGear Corporation, 2003.

——— *QA Training Handbook: Testing Web Applications*. Foster City, CA: LogiGear Corporation, 2003.

——— *QA Training Handbook: Creating Excellent Test Project Documentation*. Foster City, CA: LogiGear Corporation, 2003.

——— *QA Training Handbook: Testing Windows Desktop and Server-Based Applications*. Foster City, CA: LogiGear Corporation, 2003.

——— *QA Training Handbook: Testing Computer Software*. Foster City, CA: LogiGear Corporation, 2003.

——— *QA Training Handbook: Test Automation Planning and Management*. Foster City, CA: LogiGear Corporation, 2003.

CHAPTER

8

Sample Application

Why Read This Chapter?

Some of the testing concepts covered in this book may seem abstract until they are applied in practice to an actual Web application. By seeing how the features of the sample application are accounted for in the sample test plan (see Chapter 9, "Sample Test Plan," for details) readers can gain insights into effective Web application test planning.

TOPICS COVERED IN THIS CHAPTER

- ◆ Introduction
- ◆ Application Description
- ◆ Technical Overview
- ◆ System Requirements
- ◆ Functionality of the Sample Application
- ◆ Bibliography

Introduction

This chapter details the features and technologies that are associated with the sample application, including system overview and application functionality.

The sample application, called TRACKGEAR, is helpful in illustrating test planning issues that relate to browser-based Web systems; it places into context many of the issues that are raised in upcoming chapters. TRACKGEAR is a Web-based defect-tracking system produced by LogiGear Corporation. Throughout the book you will see TRACKGEAR used to exemplify various topics. These examples are both in the chapter discussions as well as in boxed text. In Chapter 9, it serves as a baseline from which a high-level test plan is developed.

NOTE At the time of this writing, TRACKGEAR 2.0 had been released. This version offers many new features and improvements over version 1.0. For the latest information on this product, please visit www.logigear.com.

Application Description

The sample application, TRACKGEAR, is a problem-tracking system designed for software development teams. It is used to manage the processing and reporting of change requests and defects during software development. The sample application allows authorized Web users, regardless of their hardware platform, to log in to a central database over the Internet to remotely create and work with defect reports, exchange ideas, and delegate responsibilities. All software development team members (project management, marketing, support, QA, and developers) can use the sample application as their primary communications tool.

The sample application offers a relatively complex system from which to explore test planning. TRACKGEAR supports both administrator and user functionality. To use it requires a database server, a Web server, and an application server. The sample application's features include:

- Defect tracking via the Internet, an intranet, or extranet
- Customizable workflow that enforces accountability among team members
- Meaningful color metrics (charts, graphs, and tables)
- E-mail notification that alerts team members when defects have changed or require their attention

Technical Overview

Following are some key technical issues that relate directly to the testing of the sample application:

- The application server should be installed on the same physical hardware box as the Web server. Such a configuration eliminates potential performance issues that may result from the application accessing the Web server on a separate box. Figure 8.1 shows the recommended configuration of a system.

- The sample application uses Active Server Page (ASP) technology (refer back to Chapter 5, "Web Application Components," for details about ASP). Web servers process ASP scripts, based on user requests, before sending customized pages back to the user. The ASP scripts are similar to server-side and includes Common Gateway Interface (CGI) scripts, in that they run on the Web server rather than on the client-side. The ASP scripts do not involve a client-side install. This thin-client model involves the browser sending requests to the Web server, where ASP computes and parses requests for the application, database server, and Web server.

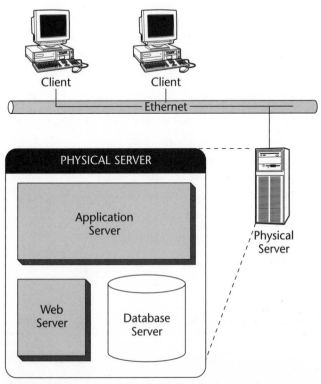

Figure 8.1   Recommended system configuration.

- The CGI scripts are not used in the sample application.

- The database activities (queries and stored procedures) are supported via Microsoft SQL 7 or higher.

- A single Java applet runs on the client browser to display defect metrics (charts and graphics). Only fourth-generation browsers (4.0 or higher) are supported by the sample application.

- Both the Web server and the application server must utilize Microsoft technology (IIS, NT, etc.).

System Requirements

The hardware and software requirements of the sample application are as follows:

SERVER REQUIREMENTS

- *Computer.* PC with a Pentium processor (Pentium II or higher recommended)

- *Memory.* 128Mb (256 recommended)

- *Disk space.* 100Mb for the server application and 200Mb for the database

- *Operating system.* Microsoft Windows NT Server 4.0 with most recent service pack, or Windows 200 Server Service Pack 2

- *Web server software.* Microsoft Internet Information Server (IIS) 4.0 or higher

- *SQL server software.* Microsoft SQL Server 7.0 with Service Pack 2

- *Microsoft Internet Explorer.* 5.5 Service Pack 2 or higher (installed on the server)

- *Microsoft Visual SourceSafe.* 6.0 or higher

CLIENT REQUIREMENTS

- Active LAN or Internet connection

- Netscape Navigator 4.7 or higher on Windows-based PCs *only*

- Windows PC-based Microsoft Internet Explorer 5.5 SP2 or higher

Functionality of the Sample Application

The material in this section helps detail the functionality of the sample application.

Installing the Sample Application

The sample application utilizes a standard InstallShield-based installation program that administrators (or IS personnel) must run to set up the databases that are required by the application. This installation wizard automates the software installation and database configuration process, allowing administrators to: identify preexisting system components (Web server, IIS server, physical hardware boxes, etc.), determine where new components should be installed, and define how much disk space to allocate for databases.

Getting Started

The sample application allows users to define workflow processes that are customized for their organization's defect-tracking needs. Workflow dictates, among other things, who has the privilege to assign resolutions (i.e., defect states) and who is responsible for addressing defect-related concerns. The sample application allows administrators to hardwire such resolution management processes and to enforce accountability. User, group, division, and project assignments dictate the screen layouts and functionality that administrators and different user types can access.

The administrator of the application has access to administrator-level functions, such as user setup, project setup, and database setup, in addition to all standard user functionality, including report querying, defect report submission, and metrics generation.

Division Databases

The sample application acts as an information hub, controlling data flow and partitioning defect-tracking data. A company may use as many division-specific databases as it wishes. Some information will be shared globally—for example, the application itself. Other information, including reports and functional groups, will be relevant only to specific projects or divisions, and therefore will not be shared globally across division databases.

Importing Report Data

The sample application works with an import utility (part of MS SQL Server) that allows administrators to import existing databases. Specifically, the program allows the import of comma-separated values (CSV) files. These CSV files can be exported from other database programs, such as Microsoft Access, Excel, and Oracle. In order for the sample application to properly process imported data, it is important that MS SQL's guidelines be adhered to when creating the CSV files.

System Setup

Many of the sample application's attributes can be customized. Customizable system attributes include the following:

- Keywords
- Error types
- Resolutions
- Severity
- Phases
- Milestone stoppers
- Frequency
- Priority
- Workflow (the method by which reports are routed)

Project Setup

The key components of every project are project name, project members, project modules, project builds, and optional e-mail notification.

E-Mail Notification

The sample application utilizes e-mail to notify and inform individuals of their responsibilities regarding defects that are tracked. E-mail notification settings are flexible and can be customized for each project. For example, one project team might require notification for all defects that could prevent their product from going beta. This team's e-mail notification settings could then be set up to alert them only when a received defect has a milestone-stopper value of *beta*. Likewise, a team whose product is nearing release date could choose to have hourly summaries of every defect report in the system sent to them.

The sample application uses the Simple Mail Transfer Protocol (SMTP) to deliver notifications (most popular e-mail clients are compatible: Eudora, Microsoft Exchange, Microsoft Outlook Express, and others).

Submitting Defect Reports

Users of the sample application must go to the report screen to submit new defect reports (Figure 8.2). The report screen includes fields for recording relevant defect-tracking information. To get to the report screen, users click the New button on the navigation bar.

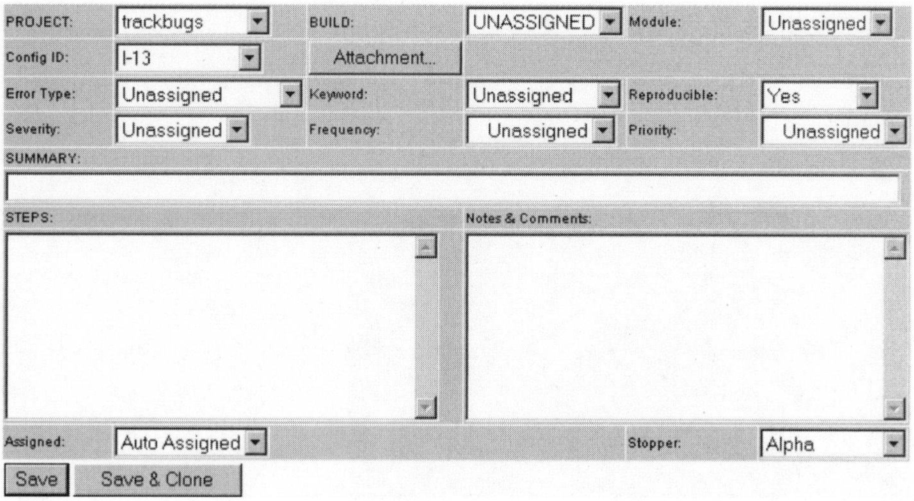

Figure 8.2   Sample application report screen.

Generating Metrics

The sample application includes a third-party Java applet that allows users to generate metrics (charts, graphs, and tables of information) to gain global perspective over defect reports. Project managers, developers, and software-quality engineers in particular can gain insight into defect-fixing trends, personnel workload, and process efficiency by viewing trend and distribution metrics.

The sample application generates two types of metrics: (1) distribution metrics and (2) trend metrics. Figure 8.3 shows the distribution metrics setup screen. Figure 8.4 shows a typical distribution metric. Figure 8.5 shows the trend metrics setup screen. Figure 8.6 shows a typical trend metric.

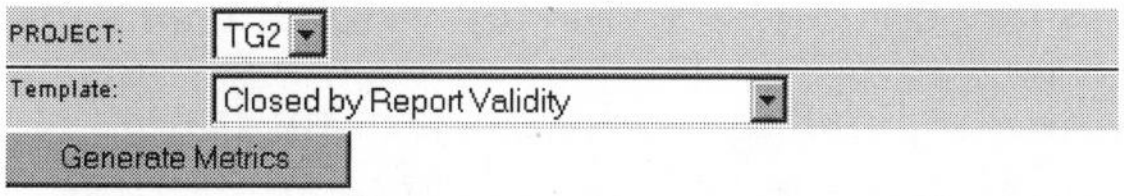

Figure 8.3   Distribution metrics setup screen.

Distribution: Closed by Report Validity

Project: TG2
User: karris
Date: 04/06/00

Report Validity	Total
Invalid	90
Valid	704

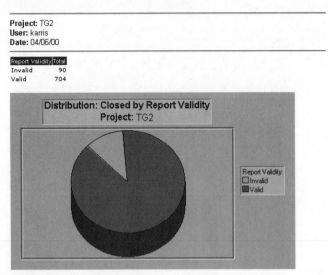

Figure 8.4 Distribution metrics example.

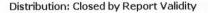

Figure 8.5 Trend metrics setup screen.

Documentation

Documentation for the sample application comes in the following three forms:

1. *Administrator's guide.* A printed manual that provides administrators with the information they need to set up and manage the sample application.

2. *User's guide.* A printable Adobe Acrobat Reader .pdf manual that provides software testers and product team members with the information they need to submit reports, find reports, and advance workflow.

3. *Online help.* A context-sensitive help system that resides within the sample application. The help system is accessible via the Help button on the navigation bar.

Trend: Total vs. Open vs. Closed - Over Time

Project: TG2
Weekly: From 09/29/99 To 11/8/99
User: karris
Date: 04/06/00

Date	Closed	Open	Total
10/03/99	14	7	21
10/10/99	48	11	59
10/17/99	54	18	72
10/24/99	54	18	72
10/31/99	54	18	72
11/07/99	54	18	72

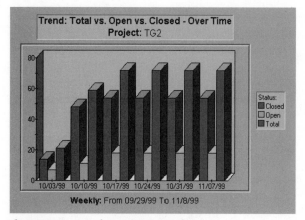

Figure 8.6   Trend metrics example.

Bibliography

LogiGear Corporation. *QA Training Handbook: Testing Web Applications.* Foster City, CA: LogiGear Corporation, 2003.

——— *TRACKGEAR Administrator Guide.* Foster City, CA: LogiGear Corporation, 2001.

CHAPTER

9

Sample Test Plan

Why Read This Chapter?

In this chapter we take the knowledge gained so far in "Software Testing Basics" (Chapter 3) and "Test Planning Fundamentals" (Chapter 7) and apply it to the "Sample Application" (Chapter 8). In this chapter we will use TRACK-GEAR, to gain test planning experience as it applies to Web applications. Therefore, it is recommended that you read both Chapters 7 and 8 before proceeding with this chapter.

The test types listed in this chapter are explored in more detail in Part Three. The sample application is also referenced throughout upcoming chapters.

TOPICS COVERED IN THIS CHAPTER

- ◆ Introduction
- ◆ Gathering Information
- ◆ Sample One-Page Test Plan
- ◆ Bibliography

Introduction

This chapter discusses the test types that are appropriate for the sample application. It includes both a test schedule and a one-page test plan that are designed for the sample application.

> **NOTE** The sample test plan is *high level* by design. A complete test plan for the sample application is not feasible within the constraints of this book.

The information conveyed in Chapter 8 serves as a technical baseline for the test planning purposes of this chapter. As far as planning for other projects, getting involved early in the development process and discovering reliable sources of information is the best way to gather required technical data. Product prototypes, page mock-ups, preliminary documentation, specifications, and any marketing requests should be evaluated; such information, combined with experience and input from application developers, comprises the best means of determining required testing. Input from the project team should focus the test-plan effort on potential problem areas within the system under test.

Preliminary project schedules and an estimated number of builds should be considered in the development of any testing schedule.

With basic QA knowledge, the information about Web testing conveyed in this book, input from the development team, and an understanding of product functionality, a test planner can confidently develop a list of test types for the system under test (refer back to Table 7.1 for details on test scheduling). Once a list of test types has been developed, staffing needs can be evaluated by considering the number of hours and types of skills that will be required of the testing team. Keep in mind, however, that required tester hours and skills will undoubtedly fluctuate as development progresses. Estimates of testing hours required for testing the sample project are detailed later in this chapter.

Gathering Information

The information-gathering process consists of four steps: (1) Establishing testing-task definitions, (2) estimating time required to complete the testing tasks, (3) entering the information into the project plan, and (4) calculating the overall resource requirements.

Step 1: Testing-Task Definitions for the Sample Application

Step 1 in the one-page test planning process involves assembling a list of tasks for the project at hand. First, define the test types. The basic tests for Web applications are acceptance (both release acceptance test (RAT) and functional acceptance simple test (FAST)), functionality (task-oriented functional test (TOFT)), installation, user interface (UI), regression, forced-error, configuration and compatibility, server, security, documentation, and exploratory.

By reviewing the product description detailed in Chapter 8, you can see a need for specific test types that are not included in the preceding list of basic test types. For example, tests should be developed that test the functionality of the databases, data import utility, e-mail notification, and third-party Java applet (metrics charting). The screenshots indicate functionality that should be tested. Some security features that should be tested are also mentioned (login/logout, views, and user permissions). By reviewing the product's system requirements, you can also glean information about test platforms, possible configuration tests, and other technologies that will require testing: Java applets, Microsoft NT (required), and Active Server Page (ASP), rather than Common Gateway Interface (CGI).

The general descriptions given in Chapter 8 do not provide enough information to help you develop an informed testing schedule and list of testing tasks. Much more detail than can be conveyed in this book is required to make such projections. For example, information regarding the number of error messages (and their completion dates) would be required, as would details of the installation process. Complete product descriptions, specifications, and marketing requirements are often used as a starting point from which you can begin to seek out the specific technical information that is required to generate test cases.

Step 2: Task Completion Time

The test times listed in Table 9.1 reflect the actual testing of the sample application. These test times were derived based on input from the test team.

Table 9.1 Task Completion Time

TEST TYPE	FUNCTIONAL AREA	TIME ESTIMATE	NOTES
RAT		30 minutes for each build	
FAST		2 hours for each build	

(continued)

Table 9.1   (continued)

TEST TYPE	FUNCTIONAL AREA	TIME ESTIMATE	NOTES
TOFT	**Admin Functionality** User setup Project setup System setup Division setup **User Functionality** Submit new report Easy find Quick find Form find Custom find Configuration profiles Preferences Metrics **Miscellaneous** Upload attachments Password Editing reports Views Tabular layouts	80 hours for a complete run	These tests represent the majority of testing that must be performed. The entire suite of TOFT tests should be run once during alpha testing, twice during beta testing, and once during final testing. Testing should be segmented as coding is completed and as bugs are fixed.
Installation	Full installation Uninstaller Database initialization Division creation	40 hours	Test functionality, not compatibility. These tests should be performed once at the end of alpha testing, once during beta testing, once during beta testing when the known installer bugs have been closed, and once again during final testing. Often, installers are not ready to be tested until well into alpha testing, or even at the beginning of the beta phase.
Data import utility		16 hours	CSV test data is required.
Third-party functionality testing	Metrics/chart-generation feature	20 hours	Sample input data is required for the metrics function to generate charts.

Table 9.1   *(continued)*

TEST TYPE	FUNCTIONAL AREA	TIME ESTIMATE	NOTES
Exploratory		16 hours per build	These are unstructured tests.
User interface	Every screen		Tested while testing functionality.
Regression		4 hours	Test suites are built as errors are uncovered.
Forced-error	Confirm all documented error messages	20 hours	Run suite twice. Can only be performed after all messages have been coded. There are 50 error messages in the sample application.
Configuration and compatibility	**Browser Settings** Cookies Security settings Java Preferences **Browser Types for Macintosh, Windows, and UNIX** Netscape Navigator Internet Explorer **Browser Functions** Back Reload Print Cache settings Server installation Compatibility E-mail notification	80 hours	Quick-look tests must be developed. A matrix of browsers, operating systems, and hardware-equivalent classes must be developed.
Server	Performance, load, and stress tests	100 hours	
Documentation	Printed manual Online help system Downloadable user guide (PDF file)	80 hours	Functionality and content.
Y2K and boundary testing			Test cases included in functionality tests (TOFT).

(continued)

Table 9.1 *(continued)*

TEST TYPE	FUNCTIONAL AREA	TIME ESTIMATE	NOTES
Database	Database integrity	20 hours	
Security	Login Logout Permissions Views Allowable IP addresses (firewall) Trusted servers (intranet) Password Preferences	40 hours	

As part of evaluating tasks for completion time, you should evaluate resources such as hardware/software and personnel availability. Some test types require unique resources, tools, particular skill sets, assistance from outside groups, and special planning. Such test types include:

- *Configuration and compatibility testing.* Configuration and compatibility testing require a significant amount of computer hardware and software. Because the cost of outfitting a complete test lab exceeds the financial means of many companies, outsourcing solutions are often considered. See Chapter 17, "Configuration and Compatibility Tests," for more information.

- *Automated testing.* Automated testing packages (such as Segue SilkTest and Mercury Interactive's WinRunner) are valuable tools that can, when implemented correctly, save testing time and other resources and ensure tester enthusiasm. See Chapter 21, "Web Testing Tools," for information about available automated testing tools.

- *Milestone tests.* Milestone tests are performed prior to each development milestone. They need to be developed, usually from TOFT tests, and scheduled according to the milestone plan.

- *Special functionality tests (TOFT).* In addition to the specified functionality of the application, SMTP tests (e-mail notification) are also included in the TOFT suite. These tests may require assistance from other groups or special skill sets.

- *Web- and client-server-specific tests.* Performance, load, and stress tests, in addition to security and database tests, normally require specialized tools and skills.

All required tests should be identified as early in the development process as possible so that resource needs for tools, staffing, and outsourcing can be evaluated.

Step 3: Placing Test Tasks into the Project Plan

For the purposes of the sample test plan, a development schedule of 20 calendar weeks has been assumed. Testable code is expected early in July. According to the development team, there will be one build per week.

PRELIMINARY BUILD SCHEDULE

Alpha	12 weeks
Beta	6 weeks
Final	2 weeks

Again referring back to Table 7.1, you can see which test phases are appropriate for each test type. Table 9.2 delineates the development phases and test panning. (Test types from this table are examined in detail in the upcoming chapters of Part Three.)

WHERE TO FIND MORE INFORMATION

- For information about RAT, FAST, TOFT, regression, and forced-error tests, please see Chapter 11, "Functional Tests."

- For information about configuration and compatibility tests, please see Chapter 17, "Configuration and Compatibility Tests."

Table 9.2   Development Phases and Test Planning

7/12/2002	TIME LINE	11/26/2002
7/12/2002 TWELVE WEEKS = 60 BUSINESS DAYS ALPHA PHASE	10/04/2002 SIX WEEKS = 30 BUSINESS DAYS BETA PHASE	11/15/2002 TWO WEEKS = 10 BUSINESS DAYS FINAL PHASE SHIP
	Types of Tests to Be Executed	
RAT	RAT	RAT
FAST	FAST	FAST
TOFT (User and Admin.)	TOFT (User and Admin.)	TOFT
Configuration and compatibility	Server Testing: Stress/Load/ Performance	Regression
Install	Complete configuration and compatibility	Exploratory
Exploratory	Regression	
	Install	
	Forced-Error	
	Documentation	
	Database	
	Exploratory	
	Third-party component integration	
	Security	

- For information about install tests, please see Chapter 16, "Installation Tests."

- For information about database tests, please see Chapter 14, "Database Tests."

- For information about exploratory tests and an example of a third-party component, please refer back to Chapter 3, "Software Testing Basics."

- For information about security testing, please see Chapter 18, "Web Security Testing."

- For information about documentation tests, please see Chapter 15, "Help Tests."

- For information about server testing, please see Chapter 12, "Server-Side Testing," and Chapter 19, "Performance Testing."

Step 4: Calculate Hours and Resource Estimates

Multiply and total test times (refer to section "Developing a One-Page Test Plan" in Chapter 7, for details). Then calculate resource estimates. The one-page test plan is now complete!

Sample One-Page Test Plan

Table 9.3 is a one-page test plan that addresses the special needs of the sample application. Note that time has been budgeted for issue reporting, research, meetings, and more.

Table 9.3 Sample Test Plan

MILESTONE	TYPE OF TEST	NUMBER OF CYCLES	HOURS PER CYCLE	ESTIMATED HOURS
Alpha	RAT: Release Acceptance Test	12	0.5	6
	FAST: Functional Acceptance Simple Test	12	2	24
	TOFT: Task-Oriented Functional Test	2	80	160
	Configuration Compatibility	1	80	80

Table 9.3   *(continued)*

MILESTONE	TYPE OF TEST	NUMBER OF CYCLES	HOURS PER CYCLE	ESTIMATED HOURS
	Install	1	40	40
	Exploratory Testing	12	16	192
			Total:	**502**
Beta	RAT: Release Acceptance Test	6	0.5	3
	FAST: Functional Acceptance Simple Test	6	2	12
	TOFT: Task-Oriented Functional Test	1	80	80
	Server Tests (Performance, Stress, and Load)	2	100	200
	Compatibility/ Configuration (Browser, Install)	1	80	80
	Regression Testing	6	4	24
	Install	1	40	40
	Forced-Error Test	2	20	40
	Documentation/Help (function and content)	1	80	80
	Database Integrity Test	1	20	20
	Exploratory Testing	6	16	96
	Data Import	1	16	16
	Third-party Component Integration	3	20	60
	Security	1	40	40
			Total:	**791**
Final	RAT: Release Acceptance Test	2	0.5	1
	FAST: Functional Acceptance Simple Test	2	2	4

(continued)

Table 9.3   (continued)

MILESTONE	TYPE OF TEST	NUMBER OF CYCLES	HOURS PER CYCLE	ESTIMATED HOURS
	TOFT: Task-Oriented Functional Test	1	80	80
	Regression Testing	1	20	20
	Exploratory Testing	1	16	16
			Total:	**121**
Testing Project Management	Test Planning and Test Case Design Training		40 20	40 20
			Total:	**60**
			PROJECT TOTAL HOURS	1,474
			PROJECT TOTAL DAYS	184
			Person Weeks (30 hrs/wk)	49
			20 Percent Contingency Weeks	10
			Total Person Weeks	59
			Testers for Alpha	1.25
			Testers for Beta	4.4
			Testers for Final	2
			Project Management	1

Bibliography

Kaner, Cem, Jack Falk, Hung Q. Nguyen. *Testing Computer Software*, 2nd ed. New York: John Wiley & Sons, Inc., 1999.

Kaner, Cem, James Back, and Bret Pettichord. *Lessons Learned in Software Testing*, New York: John Wiley & Sons, Inc., 2001.

LogiGear Corporation. *QA Training Handbook: Lead Software Test Project with Confidence.* Foster City, CA: LogiGear Corporation, 2003.

———*QA Training Handbook: Testing Computer Software.* Foster City, CA: LogiGear Corporation, 2003.

——— *QA Training Handbook: Creating Excellent Test Project Documentation.* Foster City, CA: LogiGear Corporation, 2003.

Testing Practice

CHAPTER

10

User Interface Tests

Why Read This Chapter?

To effectively test the user interface (UI) design and implementation of a Web application, we need to understand both the UI designer's perspective (the goals of the design) and the developer's perspective (the technology implementation of the UI). With such information, we can develop effective test cases that target the areas within an application's design and implementation that are most likely to contain errors.

TOPICS COVERED IN THIS CHAPTER

- ◆ **Introduction**
- ◆ **User Interface Design Testing**
- ◆ **User Interface Implementation Testing**
- ◆ **Usability and Accessibility Testing**
- ◆ **Testing Considerations**
- ◆ **Bibliography and Additional Resources**

Introduction

This chapter explores the two primary classes of UI testing issues: (1) the *design* of UI components and (2) the *implementation* of UI components. Web technologies that are used to deliver UI components or controls (graphic objects that enable users to interact with applications) are also discussed, as are considerations for the effective testing of both UI design and implementation.

User interface testing normally refers to a type of integration testing in which we test the interaction between units. User interface testing is often done in conjunction with other tests, as opposed to independently. As testers, we sometimes explicitly conduct UI and usability testing (see the "Usability and Accessibility Testing" section for more information on usability testing), but more often, we consider UI issues while running other types of testing, such as functionality testing, exploratory testing, and task-oriented functional testing (TOFT).

> **NOTE** The discussions in this chapter focus on the testing of Web browser-based applications that run on a desktop, workstation, or laptop computer. For information on testing mobile Web applications, refer to Chapter 6, "Mobile Web Application Platform," and Chapter 20, "Testing Mobile Web Applications."

User Interface Design Testing

User interface design testing evaluates how well a design "takes care of" its users, by offering clear direction, delivering feedback, and maintaining consistency of language and approach. Subjective impressions of *ease of use* and *look and feel* are carefully considered in UI design testing. Issues pertaining to navigation, natural flow, usability, commands, and accessibility are also assessed in UI design testing.

During UI design testing, you should pay particular attention to the suitability of all aspects of the design. Look for areas of the design that lead users into error states or that do not clearly indicate what is expected of them.

Consistent aesthetics, feedback, and interactivity directly affect an application's usability, and should therefore be carefully examined. Users must be able to rely on the cues they receive from an application to make effective navigation decisions and understand how best to work with an application. When cues are unclear, communication between users and applications can break down.

It is essential to understand the purpose of the software under test (SUT) before beginning UI testing. The two main questions to answer are:

1. Who is the application's target user?
2. What design approach has been employed?

With answers to these questions, you will be able to identify any program functionality and design elements that do not behave as a reasonable target user would expect them to. Keep in mind that UIs serve users, not designers or programmers. As testers, we represent users, hence we must be conscious of their needs. (To learn more about Web UI design and usability, several useful books are recommended in "References and Additional Resources" at the end of this chapter.)

Profiling the Target User

Gaining an understanding of a Web application's target user is central to evaluating the design of its interface. Without knowing the user's characteristics and needs, you cannot accurately assess how effective the UI design is.

User interface design testing involves the profiling of two target-user types: (1) server-side users and, more important, (2) client-side users. Users on the client-side generally interact with Web applications through a Web browser. More than likely they do not have as much technical and architectural knowledge as users on the server-side of the same system. Additionally, the application features that are available to client-side users often differ from the features that are available to server-side users (who are often system administrators). Therefore, client-side UI testing and server-side UI testing should be evaluated by different standards.

When creating a user profile, consider the following four categories of criteria for both client-side and server-side users: *computer experience, Web experience, domain knowledge*, and *application-specific experience*.

Computer Experience

How long have the intended users been using a computer? Do they use a computer professionally or only casually at home? What activities are they typically involved with? What assumptions does the SUT make about user skill level, and how well do the expected users' knowledge and skills match those assumptions?

For client-side users, technical experience may be quite limited, though the typical user may have extensive experience with a specific type of application, such as instant messaging, spreadsheet, word processor, desktop presentation program, drawing program, or instructional development software. In contrast, system administrators and information services (IS) personnel who install and set up applications on the server-side probably possess significant technical experience, including in-depth knowledge of system configuration and script-level programming. They may also have extensive troubleshooting experience, but limited experience with typical end-user application software.

Web Experience

How long have the users been using the Web system? Web systems occasionally require client-side users to configure browser settings. Therefore, some experience with Web browsers will be helpful. Are users familiar with Internet jargon and concepts, such as *Java, ActiveX, HyperText Markup Language* (HTML), *eXtensible Markup Language* (XML), *proxy servers,* and so on? Will users require knowledge of related helper applications such as Acrobat Reader, File Transfer Protocol (FTP), and streaming audio/video clients? How much Web knowledge is expected of server-side users? Do they need to modify the Practical Extraction and Reporting Language (Perl) or Common Gateway Interface (CGI) scripts?

Domain Knowledge

Are users familiar with the subject matter associated with the application? For example, if the program involves building formulas into spreadsheets, it is certainly targeted at client-side users with math skills and some level of computing expertise. It would be inappropriate to test such a program without the input of a tester who has experience working with spreadsheet formulas. Consider as another example a music notation–editing application. Determining whether the program is designed for experienced music composers who understand the particulars of musical notation, or for novice musicians who may have little to no experience with music notation, is critical to evaluating the effectiveness of the design. Novice users want elementary tutorials, whereas expert users want efficient utilities. Is the user of an e-commerce system a retailer who has considerable experience with credit-card–processing practices? Is the primary intended user of an online real estate system a realtor who understands real estate listing services; or is the user a first-time homebuyer?

Application-Specific Experience

Will users be familiar with the purpose and capabilities of the program because of past experience? Is this the first release of the product, or is there an existing base of users in the marketplace who are familiar with the product? Are there other popular products in the marketplace that have a similar design approach and functionality? (See the "Design Approach" section later in this chapter for information.)

Table 10.1   Evaluating Target-User Experience

EXPERIENCE GRADES
None = 0
Low = 1
Medium = 2
High = 3

ATTRIBUTE	MINIMUM EXPERIENCE
Computer experience	
Web experience	
Domain knowledge	
Application experience	

Keep in mind that Web applications are a relatively different class of application compared to a traditional software application or a mobile Web application. It is possible that you may be testing a Web application that is the first of its kind to reach the marketplace. Consequently, target users may have substantial domain knowledge but no application-specific experience.

With answers to these questions, you should be able to identify the target users for whom an application is designed. There may be several different target users. With a clear understanding of the application's target users, you can effectively evaluate an application's interface design and uncover potential UI errors.

Table 10.1 offers a means of grading the four attributes of target-user experience. User interface design should be judged, in part, on how closely the experience and skills of the target users match the characteristics of the SUT.

TESTING THE SAMPLE APPLICATION

Consider the target user of the sample application, which is designed to support the efforts of software development teams. When we designed the sample application, we assumed that the application's target user would have, at a minimum, intermediate computing skills, at least beginning-level Web experience, and intermediate experience in the application's subject matter (bug tracking). We also assumed that the target user would have at least beginning experience with applications of this type. Beyond these minimum experience levels, we knew that it was also possible that the target user might possess high experience levels in any or all of the categories. Table 10.2 shows how the sample application's target user can be rated.

(continued)

TESTING THE SAMPLE APPLICATION *(continued)*

Table 10.2   Evaluating Sample Application Target User

EXPERIENCE GRADES
None = 0
Low = 1
Medium = 2
High = 3

ATTRIBUTE	MINIMUM EXPERIENCE
Computer experience	2–3
Web experience	2–3
Domain knowledge	1–3
Application experience	0

Once we have a target-user profile for the application under test, we will be able to determine if the design approach is appropriate and intuitive for its intended users. We will also be able to identify characteristics of the application that make it overly difficult or simple. An overly simplistic design can result in as great a loss of productivity as an overly complex design. Consider the bug-report screen in the sample application. It includes numerous data-entry fields. Conceivably, the design could have divided the functionality of the bug-report screen into multiple screens. Although such a design might serve novice users, it would unduly waste the time of more experienced users—the application's target.

Considering the Design

The second step in preparing for UI design testing is to study the design employed by the application. Different application types and target users require different designs.

For example, in a program that includes three branching options, a novice computer user might be better served by delivering the three options over the course of five interface screens, via a *wizard*. An information services (IS) professional, in contrast, might prefer receiving all options on a single screen, so that he or she could access them more quickly.

TOPICS TO CONSIDER WHEN EVALUATING DESIGN

- Design approach (discussed in the following section)
- User interaction (data input)
- Data presentation (data output)

Design Approach

Design metaphors are cognitive bridges that can help users understand the logic of UI flow by relating them to experiences that users may have had in the real world or in other places. An example of an effective design metaphor includes Web directory sites that utilize a design reminiscent of a library card catalog. Another metaphor example is of scheduling applications that mirror the layout of a desktop calendar and address book. Microsoft Word uses a document-based metaphor for its word-processing program—a metaphor that is common to many types of applications.

EXAMPLES OF TWO DIFFERENT DESIGN METAPHORS

- Figure 10.1 depicts an application that utilizes a document-based metaphor. It includes a workspace where data can be entered and manipulated in a way that is similar to writing on a piece of paper.
- Figure 10.2 exemplifies a device-based metaphor. This virtual calculator includes UI controls that are designed to receive user input and perform functions.

Figure 10.1   Document-based metaphor.

Figure 10.2   Device-based metaphor.

TWO DIFFERENT APPROACHES TO CONVEY IDENTICAL INFORMATION AND COMMANDS

- Figure 10.3 conveys navigation options to users via radio buttons at the top of the interface screen.

- Figure 10.4 conveys the same options via an ActiveX or Java applet pull-down menu.

Neither design approach is more correct than the other. They are simply different.

Regardless of the design approach employed, it is usually not the role of testers to judge which design is best. However, that does not mean that we should overlook design errors, especially if we work for an organization that really cares about subjective issues such as usability. Our job is to point out as many design deficiencies early in the testing as possible. Certainly, it is our job to point out *inconsistency* in the implementation of the design; for example, if the approach uses a pull-down menu, as opposed to using radio buttons, a pull-down menu should then be used consistently in all views.

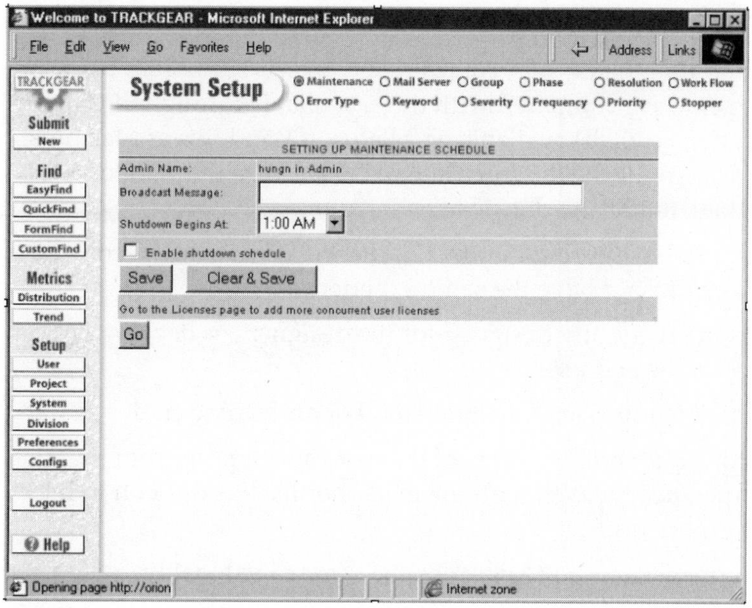

Figure 10.3 Navigation options via radio buttons.

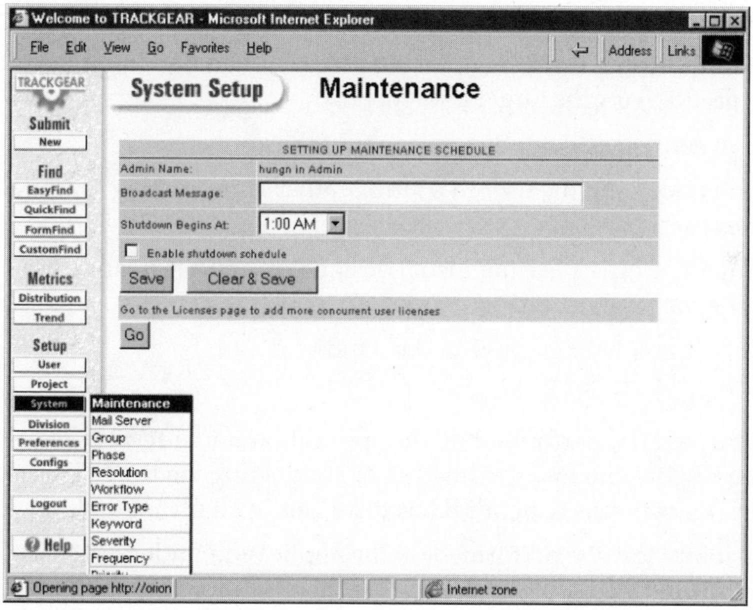

Figure 10.4 Navigation options via pull-down menu.

Think about these common issues:

- Keep in mind that the UI tags, controls, and objects supported by HTML are primitive compared with those available through the Graphical User Interface (GUI) available on Microsoft Windows or Macintosh operating systems. If the designer intends to emulate the Windows UI metaphor, look for design deficiencies.

- If you have trouble figuring out the UI, chances are it's a UI error, and your end users would have the same experience.

- The UI was inadvertently designed for the designers or developers rather than for the end users.

- The important features are misunderstood or are hard to find.

- Users are forced to think in terms of the design metaphor from the designer's perspective, although the metaphor itself is difficult to relate to real-life experience.

- Different terms were used to describe the same functionality.

Ask yourself these questions:

- Is the design of the application under test appropriate for the target audience?

- Is the UI intuitive (you don't have to think too much to figure out how to use the product) for the target audience?

- Is the design consistently applied throughout the application?

- Does the interface keep the user in control, rather than reacting to unexpected UI events?

- Does the interface offer pleasing visual design (look and feel) and cues for operating the application?

- Is the interface simple to use and understand?

- Is help available from every screen?

- Will usability tests be performed on the application under test? If yes, will you be responsible for coordinating or conducting the test? This is a time-consuming process, hence it has to be very well planned.

- Will accessibility tests be performed on the application under test? (See the "Usability and Accessibility Testing" section for more information.)

User Interaction (Data Input)

Users can perform various types of data manipulation through keyboard and mouse events. Data manipulation methods are made available through on-screen UI controls and other technologies, such as cut-and-paste and drag-and-drop.

User Interface Controls

User interface controls are graphic objects that enable users to interact with applications. They allow users to initiate activities, request data display, and specify data values. Controls, commonly coded into HTML pages as form elements, include radio buttons, check boxes, command buttons, scroll bars, pull-down menus, text fields, and more.

Figure 10.5 includes a standard HTML text box that allows limited text input from users, and a scrolling text box that allows users to enter multiple lines of text. Clicking the Submit button beneath these boxes submits the entered data to a Web server. The Reset buttons return the text boxes to their default state.

Figure 10.5 also includes radio buttons. Radio buttons are mutually exclusive; that is, only one radio button in a set can be selected at a time. Check boxes, on the other hand, allow multiple options in a set to be selected simultaneously.

Figure 10.6 includes a pull-down menu that allows users to select one of multiple predefined selections. Clicking the Submit button submits the user's selection to the Web server. The Reset button resets the menu to its default state. The push buttons (Go Home and Search) initiate actions (e.g., CGI scripts, search queries, submit data to a database, hyperlinks, etc.). Figure 10.6 also includes examples of images (commonly referred to as *graphics* or *icons*) that can serve as hyperlinks or simulated push buttons.

Figures 10.7 and 10.8 illustrate the implementation of several standard HTML UI controls on a Web page. Figure 10.7 shows the objects (graphic link, mouse-over link titles, or ALT, and a text link) as they are presented to users. Figure 10.8 shows the HTML code that generates these objects.

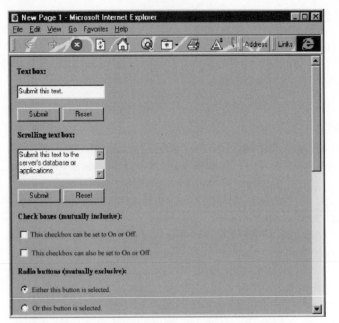

Figure 10.5 Form-based HTML UI controls, including a standard HTML text box and a scrolling text box.

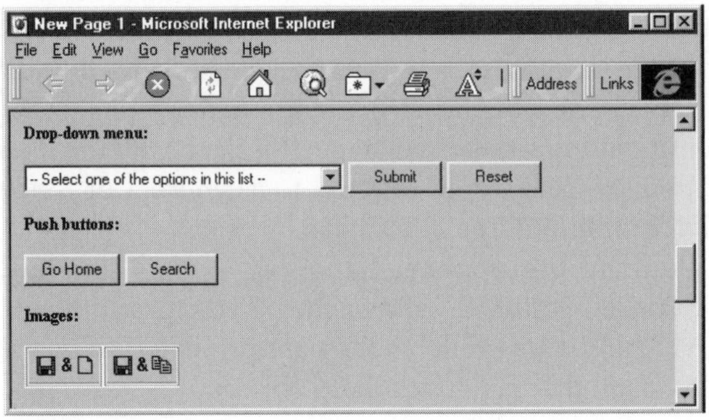

Figure 10.6 Form-based HTML UI controls, including a pull-down menu.

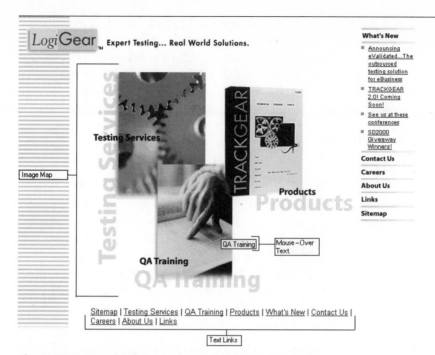

Figure 10.7   Graphic links, mouse-over text, and text links.

Image Map

```
<html>
<head>
<title>LogiGear Corporation, the Software Testing Expert</title>
...
  <tr>
        ...<a href="sitemap.html">Sitemap</a>  |  <a
        href="testing/testing_services.html">Testing Services</a> | <a
        href="training/courses_overview.html">QA Training</a> | <a
        href="products/trackgear.html">Products</a> | <a
        href="whats_new.html"> What's New</a> |  <a
        href="contact_us.html">Contact Us</a>  |  <a
        href="careers.html">Careers</a> | <a
        href="about_us.html">About Us</a> | <a
        href="testing_resources.html">Links</a></font></p>
     </td>
  </tr>
</table>
<a href="products/products_index.html"></a> <a href="testing/testing_index.html"></a>
<a href="training/training_index.html"></a> <map name="divisions">
  <area shape="poly" coords="113,158,229,158..."
        href="training/courses_overview.html" alt="QA Traiping">
  <area shape="poly" coords="230,23,368,23..."
        href="products/trackgear.html" alt="LogiGear QA Products">
  <area shape="poly" coords="1,0,197,0..."
        href="testing/testing_services.html" target="_top" alt="Testing Services">
</map>
</body>
</html>
```

Text Links

Mouse-Over Text

Figure 10.8   HTML code for graphic links, mouse-over text, and text links.

Standard HTML controls, such as tables and hyperlinks, can be combined with images to simulate conventional GUI elements such as those found in Windows and Macintosh applications (navigation bars, command buttons, dialog boxes, etc.). The left side of Figure 10.9 (taken from the sample application) shows an HTML frame that has been combined with images and links to simulate a conventional navigation bar.

Dynamic User Interface Controls

The HTML multimedia tags enable the use of dynamic UI objects, such as Java applets, ActiveX controls, and scripts (including JavaScript and VBScript).

Scripts. Scripts are programming instructions that can be executed by browsers when HTML pages load or when they are called based on certain events. Some scripts are a form of object-oriented programming, meaning that program instructions identify and send instructions to individual elements of Web pages (buttons, graphics, HTML forms, etc.), rather than to pages as a whole. Scripts do not need to be compiled and can be inserted directly into HTML pages. Scripts are embedded into HTML code with <SCRIPT> tags.

Scripts can be executed on either the client-side or the server-side. Client-side scripts are often used to dynamically set values for UI controls, modify Web page content, validate data, and handle errors.

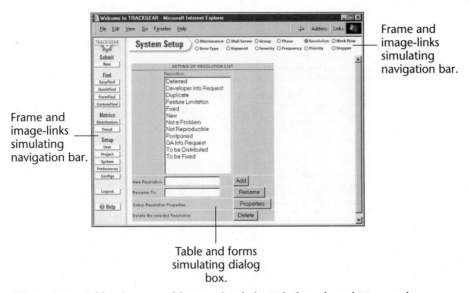

Frame and image-links simulating navigation bar.

Frame and image-links simulating navigation bar.

Table and forms simulating dialog box.

Figure 10.9 Tables, forms, and frames simulating Windows-based UI controls.

There are a number of scripting languages supported by popular browsers. Some browsers support particular scripting languages and exclude others. JavaScript, produced by Netscape, is one of the more popular scripting languages. Other popular scripting languages include Microsoft's version of JavaScript (Jscript) and Visual Basic Script (VBScript).

Java. Java is a computing language developed by Sun Microsystems that allows applications to run over the Internet (though Java objects are not limited to running over the Internet). Java is a compiled language, which means that it must be run through a compiler to be translated into a language that computer processors can use. Unlike other compiled languages, Java produces a single compiled version of itself, called *Java bytecode.* Bytecode is a series of tokens and data that are normally interpreted at runtime. By compiling to this intermediate language, rather than to binaries that are specific to a given type of computer, a single Java program can be run on several different computer platforms for which there is a Java Virtual Machine (JVM). Once a Java program has been compiled into bytecode, it is placed on a Web server. Web servers deliver bytecode to Web browsers, which interpret and run the code.

Java programs designed to run inside browsers are called *applets.* When a user navigates to a Web site that contains a Java applet, the applet automatically downloads to the user's computer. Browsers require Java bytecode interpreters to run applets. Java-enabled browsers, such as Netscape Navigator and Internet Explorer, have Java bytecode interpreters built into them.

Precautions are taken to ensure that Java programs do not introduce malicious code to the users' computers. Java applets must go through a verification process when they are first downloaded to users' machines to ensure that their bytecode can be run safely. After verification, bytecode is run within a restricted area of RAM on users' computers. In addition, unlike a Java application, which uses a JVM on the target operating system, and ActiveX, Java applets cannot make application or system function calls. This restriction was designed to ensure better security protection for client users.

ActiveX. ActiveX is a Windows custom control that runs within ActiveX-enabled browsers (such as Internet Explorer), rather than off servers. Similar to Java applets, ActiveX controls support the execution of event-based objects within a browser. One major benefit of ActiveX controls is that they are components, which can be easily combined with other components to create new, features-rich applications. Another benefit is that once users download an ActiveX control, they do not have to download it again in the future; ActiveX controls remain on users' systems, which can speed up load time for frequently visited Web pages.

Disadvantages of ActiveX include that it is dependent on the Windows platform; and some components are so big that they use too much system memory. Furthermore, ActiveX controls, because they reside on client computers and generally require an installation and registration process, are considered by some to be intrusive.

Figure 10.10 shows a calendar system ActiveX control. Figure 10.11 shows the HTML code that generated the page in Figure 10.10. An HTML <OBJECT> tag gives the browser the ActiveX control class ID so that it can search the registry to determine the location of the control and load it into memory. Sometimes, multiple ActiveX controls are required on the same HTML page. In such instances, controls may be stored on the same Web server or on different Web servers.

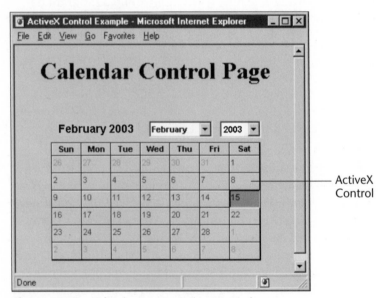

Figure 10.10 Calendar system ActiveX control.

ActiveX
Class ID

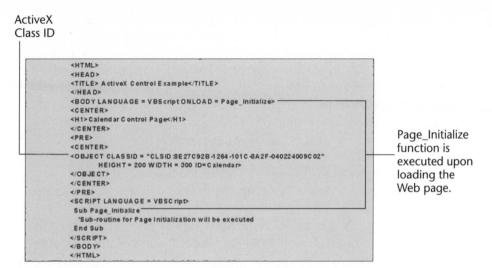

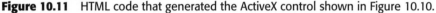

Page_Initialize
function is
executed upon
loading the
Web page.

```
<HTML>
<HEAD>
<TITLE> ActiveX Control Example</TITLE>
</HEAD>
<BODY LANGUAGE = VBScript ONLOAD = Page_Initialize>
<CENTER>
<H1> Calendar Control Page</H1>
</CENTER>
<PRE>
<CENTER>
<OBJECT CLASSID = "CLSID:8E27C92B-1264-101C-8A2F-040224009C02"
        HEIGHT = 200 WIDTH = 300 ID=Calendar>
</OBJECT>
</CENTER>
</PRE>
<SCRIPT LANGUAGE = VBSCript>
 Sub Page_Initialize
   'Sub-routine for Page Initialization will be executed
  End Sub
</SCRIPT>
</BODY>
</HTML>
```

Figure 10.11   HTML code that generated the ActiveX control shown in Figure 10.10.

Server-Side Includes. Server-side includes (SSIs) are directives to Web servers that are embedded in HTML comment tags. Web servers can be configured to examine HTML documents for such comments and to perform appropriate processes when they are detected. The SSIs are typically used to pull additional content from other sources into Web pages—for example, current date and time information. Following is an example of an SSI (enclosed between HTML comment tags) requesting that the Web server call a CGI script named *mytest.cgi.*

<!--#exec cgi="/cgi-bin/mydir/mytest.cgi"-->

Style sheets. Style sheets are documents that define style standards for a given set of Web pages. They are valuable in maintaining style consistency across multiple Web pages. Style sheets allow Web designers to define design issues such as fonts and colors from a central location, thus freeing designers from concerns over inconsistent format of style presentation that might result from browser display differences or developer oversight. Style sheets set style properties for a variety of HTML elements: text style, font size, and face; link colors; and more. They also define attribute units such as length, percentage, and color.

The problem with traditional style sheets is that they do not take the dynamic nature of Web design into account. Web pages themselves offer multiple means of defining styles without the use of style sheets; for example, style properties can be defined in an HTML page header or inline in the body of an HTML document. Such dynamic style definition can lead to conflicting directives.

Cascading style sheets (CSS) is the most common and most mature style sheet language. CSS offers a system for determining priority when multiple stylistic influences are directed onto a single Web page element. Cascading style sheets dictate the style rules that are to be applied when conflicting directives are present, thus enabling Web designers to manage multiple levels of style rules over an unlimited number of Web pages. For example, a certain line of text on a Web page might be defined as being in blue in the page header, as red in the page body text (inline), and as black in an external style sheet. In this scenario, CSS could establish a hierarchy of priority for the three conflicting color directives. The CSS could be set up to dictate that inline style commands take priority over all other style commands. Following that might be "pagewide" style commands (located in page headers). Finally, external style sheet commands might hold the least influence of the three style command types.

There are different means of referencing style sheets. The browser takes all style information (possibly conflicting) and attempts to interpret it. Figure 10.12 shows a mixture of styles applied to a page. Some of the approaches may be incompatible with some browsers. (For more information about CSS, see WebReview's "Overview of the CSS Specification" at www.webreview.com/style/css1/glossary.shtml. The W3C's CSS Validator is available for download at http://jigsaw.w3.org/css-validator.)

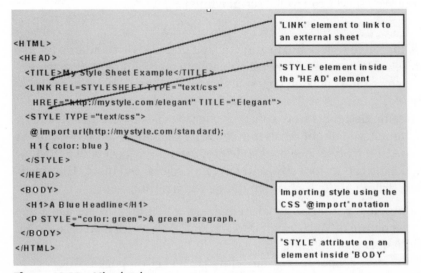

```
<HTML>
 <HEAD>
  <TITLE>My Style Sheet Example</TITLE>
  <LINK REL=STYLESHEET TYPE="text/css"
    HREF="http://mystyle.com/elegant" TITLE="Elegant">
  <STYLE TYPE="text/css">
   @import url(http://mystyle.com/standard);
   H1 { color: blue }
  </STYLE>
 </HEAD>
 <BODY>
  <H1>A Blue Headline</H1>
  <P STYLE="color: green">A green paragraph.
 </BODY>
</HTML>
```

"LINK" element to link to an external sheet

"STYLE" element inside the "HEAD" element

Importing style using the CSS "@import" notation

"STYLE" attribute on an element inside "BODY"

Figure 10.12   Mixed styles.

Some UI control errors that you should look for include:

- The default state of UI control is incorrect.
- A poor choice of default state was made.
- The updated state of UI control is incorrect.
- The default input value is incorrect.
- A poor choice of default value was made.
- The updated input value is incorrect.
- The initial input focus is not assigned to the most commonly used control.
- The most commonly used action button is not the default one.
- The form or dialog box is too wide or long under minimum support display resolution (e.g., 800×600).
- The HTML code is often generated dynamically. It's essential to understand how the HTML code is generated. Don't assume that you have already tested that page and won't have to do it again until something changes.
- Set View Text Size to the Largest and the Smallest to see how each setting might affect the UI.
- Check for ALT attributes. One of the tricks black-box testers use to quickly spot missing ALT tags is to turn off the Show Pictures option in a Web browser. When a Web page displays, you will simply see graphics in a page and can quickly determine whether the ALT tag or text is missing.
- Check for correct descriptions in ALT attributes.
- Avoid reporting multiple broken links or missing images used by the same error (e.g., the same image used in 20 HTML pages is missing).
- Invalid inputs are not detected and handled at client-side.
- Invalid inputs are not detected and handled at server-side.
- Scripts are normally used to manipulate standard UI (form) controls (e.g., set input focus, set default state, etc.). This is a tedious program chore, and the process normally produces errors. Look for them.
- Scripts, CSS, Java applets, and ActiveX controls commonly cause incompatibility errors among different releases of browser produced by different vendors. Make sure to run compatibility tests for all supported browsers. See Chapter 17 "Configureation and Compatibility Test" for more information.

- If your application uses scripts, Java applets, and ActiveX controls, and the users might have disabled one or more of these features, determine whether your application will function at some capacity or will simply stop functioning.

- To quickly determine whether a Web page contains scripts, Java applets, or ActiveX controls, set these options (script, Java applet, or ActiveX control) in the browser to Prompt. When the browser tries to display a Web page that needs the options enabled, it will prompt you.

- To test for script (such as JavaScript) incompatibility problems between different browser brands and versions, first identify which pages use script, and for what purposes. Once these pages are cataloged, run these pages through one of the HTML authoring tools that has built-in support for checking script incompatibility based on a static analysis method. One tool that provides this support is Macromedia's Dreamweaver.

- Determine whether the Web pages will display correctly on handheld devices, which often do not support graphics and have relatively small screen real estate.

Navigation Methods

Navigation methods dictate how users navigate through a Web application or Web pages, from one UI control to another within the same page (screen, window, or dialog box) and from one page to the next. User navigation is achieved through input devices, such as the keyboard and mouse. Navigation methods are often evaluated by how easily they allow users to access commonly used features and data.

Ask yourself these questions:

- Is the application's navigation intuitive?

- Is accessibility to commonly used features and data consistent throughout the program?

- Can users always tell where they are in the program and which navigation options are available to them?

- How well is information presented to the user?

- If the program utilizes a central workspace, does the workspace remain consistent from screen to screen?

- Do navigation conventions remain consistent throughout the application (navigation bars, menus, hyperlinks, etc.)?

- Examine the application for consistent use of mouse-over pop-ups, clicks, and object dragging. Do the results of these actions offer differing results from one screen to the next?

- Do the keyboard alternatives for navigation remain consistent throughout the application?

- Are all features accessible via both mouse and keyboard action?

- Click the Tab button repeatedly and examine the highlight path that is created. Is it logical and consistent?

- Click the Shift-Tab button repeatedly and examine the highlight path that is created. Is it logical and consistent?

- Look at the keyboard shortcuts that are supported. Are they functioning? Is there duplication among them?

- Have the navigation features been tested for accessibility?

- If the user clicks a credit card payment button on an e-commerce site numerous times while he or she is waiting for server response, will the transaction be erroneously submitted numerous times?

Mouse/Keyboard Action Matrices

Appendices D and E contain test matrices that detail mouse and keyboard actions. These matrices can be customized to track navigation test coverage for the Web system under test.

Action Commands

Occasionally, the names of on-screen commands are not used consistently throughout an application. This is partially attributable to the fact that the meaning of command names often varies from one program to the next. If the nomenclature of certain commands varies within a single program, user confusion is likely to result. For example, if a Submit command is used to save data in one area of a program, then the Submit command name should be used for all saving activities throughout the application.

Consideration should be given to the action commands that are selected as the default commands. Default action commands should be the least risky of the available options (the commands least likely to delete user-created data).

Table 10.3 lists a number of common confirming-action and canceling-action commands, along with their meanings and the decisions that they imply.

TESTING THE SAMPLE APPLICATION

User navigation within the sample application is achieved via standard UI controls (keyboard and mouse events). Data updates are *submission-based,* meaning that they are achieved by clicking action buttons, such as Submit. Figure 10.13 diagrams how users navigate through the sample application's trend metrics and distribution metrics features.

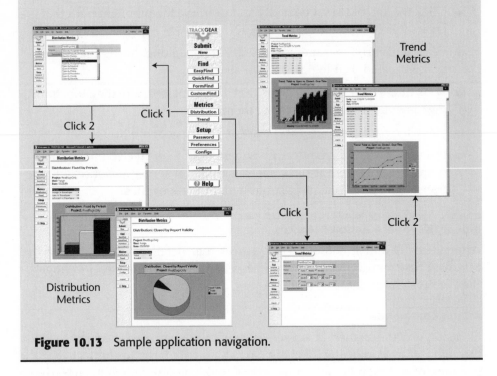

Figure 10.13   Sample application navigation.

Feedback and Error Messages

Consistency in audible and visible feedback is essential for maintaining clear communication between users and applications. Messages (both visible and audible), beeps, and other sound effects must remain consistent and user-friendly to be effective. *Error messaging* in particular should be evaluated for clarity and consistency. (In Chapter 11, "Functional Tests," see the section entitled "Task-Oriented Functional Test (TOFT)" for more information regarding error messages.)

Examine the utilization of interface components within feedback for unusual or haphazard implementations. You can identify commonly accepted guidelines within each computing platform for standard placement of UI elements, such as placing OK and Cancel buttons in the bottom-right corner of dialog boxes. Alternate designs may make user interaction unnecessarily difficult.

Table 10.3   Confirming and Canceling Commands

	DECISION	IMPLIED DECISION
Common confirming-action commands		
Done	Dismiss the current dialog box, window, or page.	
Close	Dismiss the current dialog box, window, or page.	
OK	I accept the settings.	Dismiss the current dialog box, window, or page.
Yes	I accept the stated condition.	Proceed and dismiss the current dialog box, window, or page.
Proceed	I accept the stated condition.	Proceed and dismiss the current dialog box, window, or page.
Submit	Submit the data in the form, page, or dialog box.	
Common canceling-action commands		
Cancel	I do not accept the settings or stated condition.	Return to the previous state and dismiss the current dialog box, window, or page.
No	I do not accept the settings or stated condition.	Proceed and dismiss the current dialog box, or page.
Reset	Return the settings to their previous state.	Clear all unsubmitted changes in the current dialog box, window, or page.

Two types of message-based feedback are available. Figure 10.14 illustrates a typical *client-based error message* (generated by error-checking JavaScript on the client-side) that utilizes a browser-based message box. Figure 10.15 shows typical *server-based feedback*.

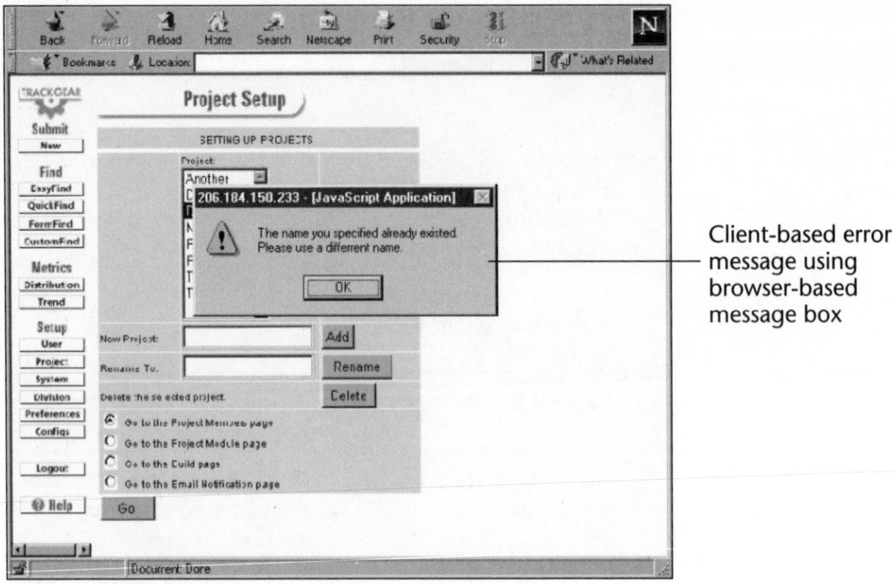

Figure 10.14   Browser-based error message.

Source: ©1999 LogiGear Corporation

Client-based error messages are generally more efficient and cause less strain on servers and the network than do server-based error messages. Server-based error messages require that data first be sent from the client to the server and then returned from the server back to the client, where the error message is displayed to the user.

In contrast, client-based error messages, using script (such as JavaScript) embedded in an HTML page, can prevent such excessive network traffic by identifying errors and displaying error messages locally, without requiring contact with the server. Because scripting languages such as JavaScript behave differently with each browser version, testing of all supported platforms is essential.

As a general rule, simple errors such as invalid inputs should be detected and handled at the client-side. The server, of course, has to detect and handle error conditions that do not become apparent until they interfere with some process being executed on the server-side.

Another consideration is that, sometimes, the client might not understand the error condition being responded to by the server, and might therefore ignore the condition, display the wrong message, or display a message that no human can understand. Additionally, the client might not switch to the appropriate state or change the affected data items in the right way unless it understands the error condition reported by the server.

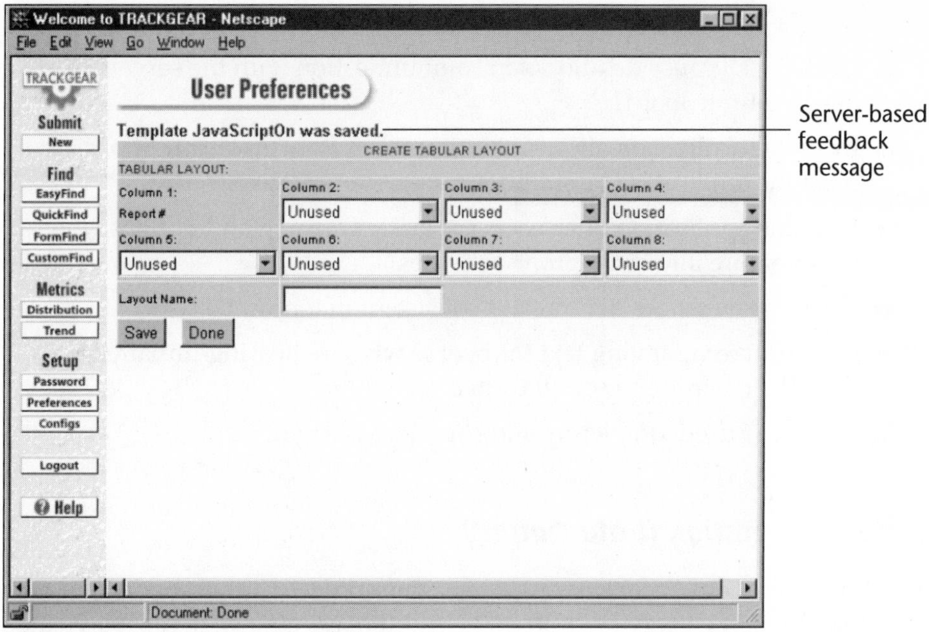

Figure 10.15   Server-based feedback.

Source: © 1999 LogiGear Corporation

Some errors to look for include the following:

- Displaying incorrect error message for the condition.

- Missing error messages.

- Poorly worded, grammatically incorrect, and misspelled errors.

- Messages were not written for the user and, therefore, are not useful to the user. For example, "Driver error 80004005."

- Error message is not specific nor does it offer a plausible solution.

- Similar errors are handled by different error messages.

- Unnecessary messages distract users.

- Inadequate feedback or error communication to users.

- Handling methods used for similar errors are not consistent.

Ask yourself these questions:

- Does the UI cause deadlocks in communication with the server (creating an infinite loop)?

- Does the application allow users to recover from error conditions, or must the application be shut down?

- Does the application offer users adequate warning and options when they venture into error-prone activities?

- Are error messages neutral and consistent in tone and style?

- Is there accompanying text for people who are hearing-impaired or have the computer's sound turned off?

- If video is used, do picture and sound stay in sync?

Data Presentation (Data Output)

In Web applications, information can be communicated to users via a variety of UI controls (e.g., menus, buttons, check boxes, etc.) that can be created within an HTML page (frames, tables, simulated dialog boxes, etc.).

Figures 10.16, 10.17, and 10.18 illustrate three data presentation views that are available in the sample application. Each view conveys the same data through a different template built using HTML frames and tables.

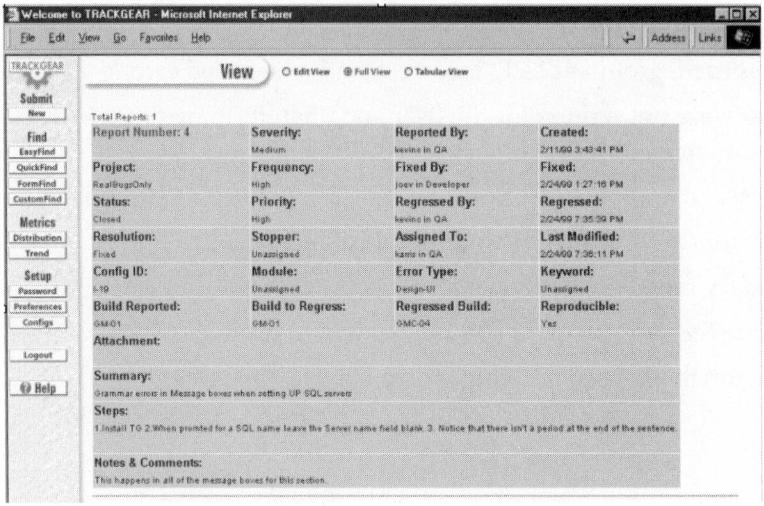

Figure 10.16 Single-issue report presented in Full View.

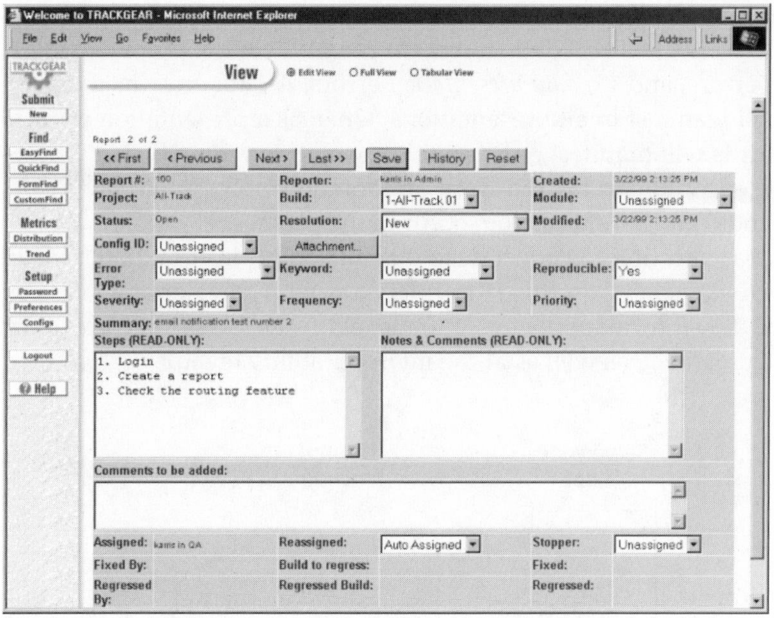

Figure 10.17 Same-issue report presented in Edit View.

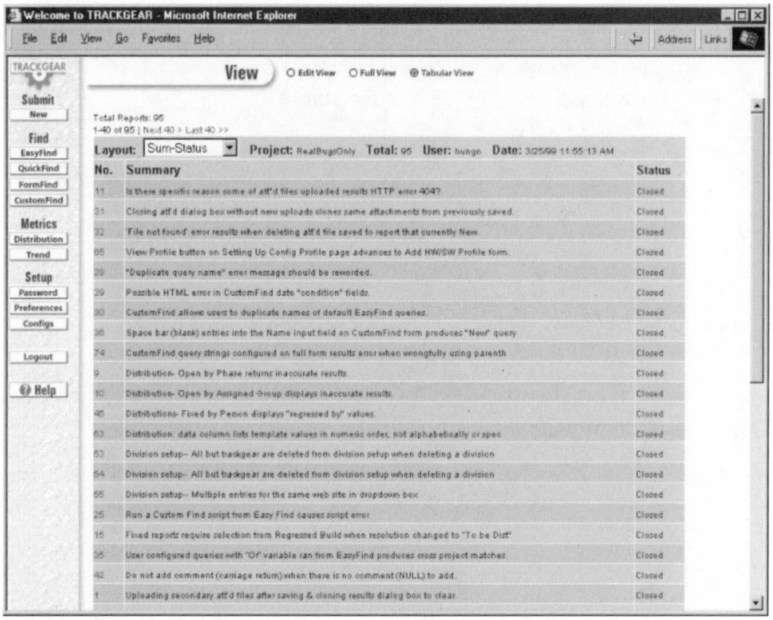

Figure 10.18 Multiple-issue reports presented in Tabular View.

In this sample application example, there are at least three types of potential errors: (1) *data* errors (incorrect data in records caused by write procedures), (2) *database query* errors, and (3) *data presentation* errors. A data error or database query error will manifest in all presentations, whereas a presentation error in server-side scripts will manifest only in the presentation with which it is associated. Figure 10.19 illustrates the data presentation process. Where errors manifest depends on where the errors occur in the process.

Analyze the application to collect design architectural information. One of the most effective ways to do this is to interview your developer. Once you have collected the information, use it to develop test cases that are more focused at the unit level, as well as at the interoperability level.

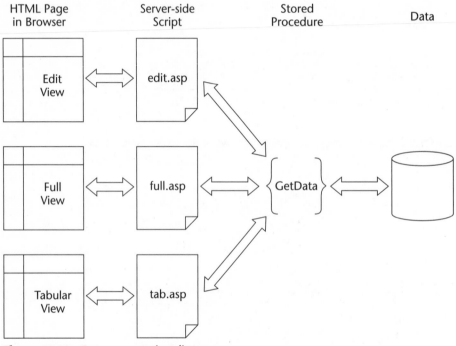

Figure 10.19   Data presentation diagram.

User Interface Implementation Testing

User interface implementation testing examines applications with an eye toward their operation. It evaluates whether UI features work properly. If a UI control does not operate as designed, it will likely fail to deliver accessibility to underlying features, which, independently, may be functioning properly. Functionality testing often takes place simultaneously with UI design testing, but it is helpful to consider the two types of testing separately.

NOTE This section includes some overlap in information with functionality tests that are run specifically on UIs and functionality tests that are run on all other features of an application. The TOFT section in Chapter 11 includes more complete information on the execution of functional tests. The content of this chapter is useful only in supporting functional testing efforts that are specific to UI.

The line between design consistency and design functionality is not always a clear one. An example of a gray area is a text link of a certain color that remains consistent from one screen to the next while the background on which the text is displayed changes. As the background changes, the text becomes illegible on certain screens. Although the text is consistent in this example, the color of the text should be adjusted to improve legibility.

Miscellaneous User Interface Elements

Table 10.4 lists miscellaneous interface elements that require testing.

Table 10.4   Miscellaneous UI Elements

ELEMENT TYPE	ISSUES TO ADDRESS
Instructional and technical information	Accuracy of information and instructions.
Fonts	Consistency of style.
	Legibility of text.
	Difficulty of reading italic and serif fonts.
	Visual clutter resulting from use of multiple fonts in a single document; question of availability of fonts on the targeted platforms.

(continued)

Table 10.4 *(continued)*

ELEMENT TYPE	ISSUES TO ADDRESS
Colors	Suitability of background colors.
	Suitability of foreground colors.
	Suitability of font colors.
	Haphazard use of color can be negative and confusing.
	Subtle, complementary color choices are generally more pleasing than saturated, contrasting colors.
Borders	Three-dimensional effects on command buttons can be effective visual cues for users.
	Use of three-dimensional effects on noninteractive elements can be confusing.
Images	Large images may increase load time.
	Visual cues and design details should blend with background, not compete with it.
	Suitability of background.
	Legibility of labels.
	Legibility of buttons.
	Suitability of size of images.
Frames	Some older browsers cannot display frames.
	Display settings and browser types can affect how frames are displayed.
	Use of back buttons often have unexpected results.
Tables	Nested tables (tables within tables) slow down HTML load time.
	Presentation may vary depending on display settings and browser type (improper scaling or wrapping may result).
	Testing should include all browsers and display settings and browser window sizes.

Complications Specific to Web Applications

- *Web browsers present their own unique set of challenges in functionality testing.* Most significantly, the marketplace is crowded with a number of browser brands and versions. If the goal is to support most browsers, developers often must code for the lowest-common-denominator Web user—meaning those users who have the slowest modems and the least-sophisticated capability, such as text-only browsers or specialized browsers that support accessibility. Even with careful HTML development, variations in graphical presentation are almost inevitable between browsers. For example, when viewing the same table on, alternately, Microsoft's Internet Explorer and Netscape's Navigator, a user may see different results.

- *Browser-server communication is explicit-submission-based.* This means that data entries and updates are not written to the server until the user initiates an action. For example, input data will be lost if a user shuts down a Web application before clicking a submission button, such as Save or Submit.

- *Scripting languages, such as JScript, JavaScript, and VBScript, can be used to simulate limited browser-side, submission-driven event handling.* Without browser-side scripting, error handling must be done on the server-side, which is not always effective. For example, assume someone in Ireland is interacting with a server in California. If the user in Ireland submits data in an incorrect format, the user will be notified immediately only if the scripting is handled on the client-side. If the error is handled on the server-side, the data will have traveled to California and back to Ireland before the user learns of the client-side error.

- *Web applications use a single-page paradigm.* Therefore, they do not have the benefits of hierarchical organization that is found in GUI-based applications (such as Windows applications). Web applications have no provision for the modal dialog box paradigm that is so common in other GUI-based environments; when modal dialog boxes are used to present error messages to users in a Windows environment, they require the user to take an action before control of the application or operating system is returned to the user.

- *The browser's Back button can complicate the dependent relationship between pages in Web applications.* Clicking the Back button, rather than an appropriate explicit-submission button, is a common cause of loss of uncommitted data.

- *Changes to monitor color depth settings (16 colors, 24-bit color, 32-bit color, etc.) often creates unexpected display results, as do changes to screen resolution (640 ¥ 480, 800 ¥ 600, 1280 ¥ 1024, etc.) and font size.* It is recommended that all such combinations of color depth, screen resolution, and font size be addressed in browser-based application testing.

- *Different browser brands and versions on different platforms (Windows, Solaris, Macintosh, etc.) may display HTML elements differently.* Depending on display settings, even a single browser may display elements in multiple ways. Additionally, resetting the size of a browser window can lead to unexpected table and frame presentation. It is recommended that Web applications be tested with all common browser brands and versions.

Figures 10.20 and 10.21 illustrate UI errors that are the result of browser incompatibility. The HTML tags for these examples are specific to one browser. They are not designed to be compatible with other browsers. These errors are a result of the different manner in which the two browsers read standard HTML tables and controls. The browser in Figure 10.21 does not accurately display the scrolling text box and pull-down menu as the browser in Figure 10.20 displays. Both browsers present the same HTML page with different results.

Display Compatibility Matrix

Appendix G, "Display Compatibility Test Matrix," lists variations in display settings that should be considered during browser-based application testing.

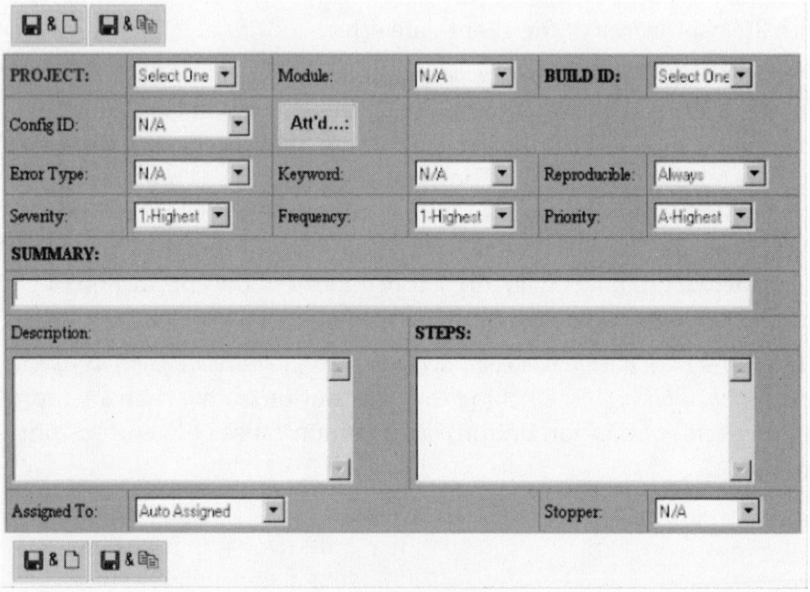

Figure 10.20   Browser incompatibility—Browser A.

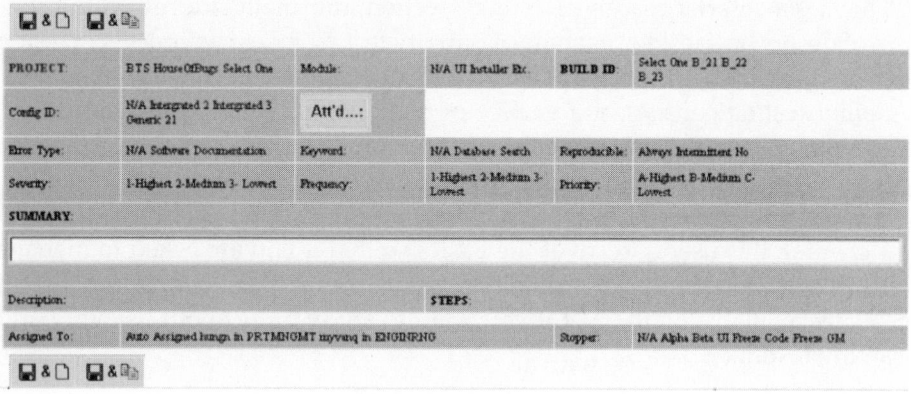

Figure 10.21   Browser incompatibility—Browser B.

Usability and Accessibility Testing

Depending on the charter of a software testing organization, usability testing might be beyond the scope of responsibilities typically assigned to the testing group. That said, sometimes the test group is asked to manage or coordinate the usability testing effort. Regardless, it's important to understand what *usability* means.

Usability is a metric that helps the designer of a product or service (including Web application, software application, and mobile application) determine the users' satisfaction when they interact with a product or service through interfaces, including UI. Simply put, an effective UI design is one that provides the highest usability to the users. In designing for usability, important questions to ask include the following:

- How easy will it be for a user who has never seen the product before to carry out basic tasks?

- How easy will it be for a user who has used the product before to remember how to carry out the same tasks?

- How effective and efficient will it be for a user who has used the product before to quickly carry out frequently used tasks?

- How frequently does a user run into errors while using the product? How serious are those errors? How forgiving is the product—that is, does it enable the user to easily recover from the errors? How informative is the product in communicating the error conditions to the user?

- How good is the user's experience in using the product?

The "User Interface Design Testing" section informally addressed the concept of design and test for usability. Usability testing takes the process one step further, formalizing it to ensure that the design meets the usability objectives. Usability testing consists of a variety of methods for setting up the product, assigning tasks to the users to carry out, having the users carry out the tasks, and observing user interaction and information collection to measure usability.

Although an in-depth discussion of usability testing is beyond the scope of this chapter, it is useful to cover the basics so that if you are asked to manage this task, you can quickly fulfill the responsibility. Following are useful resources available on the Net if you want to study more about usability and usability testing.

Usability.gov. This Web site offers information on how to make health-related information Web sites and other user interfaces more usable, accessible, and useful.

www.usability.gov. This is the web URL for the above description.

QACity.com | Functional UI Testing Link. This page offers articles and links to Web sites that offer information design and test for usability.

www.qacity.com/Test+Types/Functional+UI/. This is the web URL for the above description.

Accessibility Testing

In producing a Web site that is accessible, the designer must take into consideration that the Web content must be available to and accessible by everyone, including people with disabilities. It means that everyone must be able to navigate within a Web page and between Web pages; navigate the content with the use of keyboard only or other specialized input devices other than a mouse; and easily follow the contents and instructions provided. Similar to usability, accessibility is about providing the greatest satisfaction to users. The key difference is that accessibility accomplishes its goal through making the product usable to a larger population, including people with disabilities.

A great deal of information on methods and tools used for designing accessible products are widely available today. The following are good resources to tap:

■ The World Wide Web Consortium (W3C) offers "Web Content Accessibility Guidelines" as an aid to those designing accessible products for people with disabilities. The document also offers a list of checkpoints that can be used to make pages more accessible to everyone, including those who use different browsers, such as microbrowsers on mobile devices. The "Mobile Web Application Platform" standard contains more information on microbrowsers. A copy of this standard can be found at www.w3.org/TR/WAI-WEBCONTENT/.

■ U.S. Federal Regulation 508 requires Web sites to be accessible to all users. For more information on this regulation, go to www.access-board.gov/sec508/508standards.htm.

■ Several tools are available for automating the testing of Web content for accessibility. W3C offers a Web page with links to such tools grouped into three different categories: Evaluation, Repair, and Transformation Tools for Web Content Accessibility. For more information, go to: www .w3.org/WAI/ER/existingtools.html.

Other useful resources available include:

■ Web Accessibility Initiative (WAI) Resources (www.w3.org/WAI/ Resources/#fq). Developed and maintained by W3C, this page offers guidelines, checklists, techniques, tools, and links to information on designing and testing for Web accessibility.

■ Human-Computer Interaction's Accessibility Link Page (www.hcibib .org/accessibility/). This page contains links to information on making computers and software more accessible to persons with disabilities.

■ U.S. Department of Justice—Section 508 Home Page (www.usdoj.gov/ crt/508/). Offers information on requirements for electronic and information technology accessibility for people with disabilities.

■ XML Accessibility Guidelines (www.w3.org/TR/xag.html). W3C's guidelines on accessibility for XML-based content.

Testing Considerations

USER INTERACTION TESTING CONSIDERATIONS

■ How is information presented to the user?

■ Is there a central workspace? If so, does it remain consistent from screen to screen?

■ Is data presented in frames? If so, is there a choice for nonframe browsers?

■ What means of data manipulation are included in the application under test?

- Are data manipulation methods presented intuitively and consistently?

- Are data manipulation methods consistent with Web application standards (possibly platform-specific)?

- Are data manipulation methods consistent with industry standards (possibly product-specific)?

- Is drag-and-drop functionality supported? If so, is the drag-and-drop functionality consistent with industry practices or standards? Is the support compatible across vendors and platform-specific browsers?

UI CONTROL TESTING CONSIDERATIONS

- What are the UI controls used by the application under test: dialog boxes, radio buttons, drop-down menus?

- Are the layout and implementation of UI controls intuitive and consistent throughout the application?

- Are naming conventions for controls and dialog boxes intuitive and consistent?

- Are the default settings for each control the most commonly used and least error-prone settings?

- Do control buttons change position from screen to screen? Are they consistently placed?

- Do data interaction methods vary illogically from screen to screen (drag-and-drop, text entry, queries, etc.)?

- Do the property settings of UI-based HTML tags (color, size, style, alignment, wrapping, etc.) support the design objectives?

- Are properties consistently applied to all HTML elements?

- Are the interface components unusual or confusing in any way?

- What dynamic UI elements (scripts, Java applets, ActiveX controls, SSIs, CSS, DHTML, etc.) are utilized by the application? Consider testing with all supported browsers to uncover vendor- or platform-specific errors.

- Do the dynamic UI elements fit with the overall design approach?

- Are dynamic UI elements implemented intuitively and consistently?

- Are third-party plug-ins, such as QuickTime, ShockWave, RealPlayer, and Adobe Acrobat, included? Which versions of these components does the product claim to support?

UI IMPLEMENTATION TESTING CONSIDERATIONS

- Are all keyboard shortcuts functioning for ActiveX and Java applet components?

- Are combination keyboard/mouse functions operating properly for ActiveX and Java applet components?

- Do all mouse-rollovers (ALT text) operate properly? Is there any missing ALT?

- Does the correct text pop up in mouse-rollovers?

- Are appropriate command buttons default-highlighted?

- Do command buttons perform the actions they purport to?

- Are on-screen or in-place instructions accurate?

- Do graphics and text load as required?

- Do links and static text support the intended design?

Bibliography and Additional Resources

Bibliography

Cluts, Nancy Winnick. *Programming the Windows 95 User Interface.* Redmond, WA: Microsoft Press, 1995.

Goodman, Danny. *Dynamic HTML: The Definitive Reference.* Sebastopol, CA: O'Reilly and Associates, Inc., 1998.

Holzner, Steven. *Web Scripting with VBScript.* New York: M&T Books, 1996.

Meyer, Jon, and Troy Downing. *Java Virtual Machine.* Sebastopol, CA: O'Reilly and Associates, 1997.

McKay, Everett N. *Developing User Interfaces for Microsoft Windows.* Redmond, WA: Microsoft Press, 1999.

Microsoft Corporation. *The Windows Interface Guidelines for Software Design.* Redmond, WA: Microsoft Press, 1995.

Powell, Thomas A. *HTML: The Complete Reference, 2nd ed.* Berkeley, CA: Osborne/McGraw-Hill, 1999.

Simpson, Alan. *Official Microsoft Internet Explorer 4 Site Builder Toolkit.* Redmond, WA: Microsoft Press, 1998.

Recommended Reading

About Face: The Essentials of User Interface Design, by Alan Cooper, IDG Books Worldwide (1995).

Handbook of Usability Testing: How to Plan, Design, and Conduct Effective Tests, by Jeffrey Rubin, John Wiley & Sons, Inc. (1994).

Microsoft Windows User Experience (Microsoft Professional Editions), by Microsoft Corporation, Microsoft Press (1999).

Web Style Guide: Basic Design Principles for Creating Web Sites by Patrick J. Lynch and Sarah Horton, Yale University Press (1999).

Useful Links

Microsoft MSDN UI page

http://msdn.microsoft.com/ui

QA City: More information on Web testing and other software testing–related subjects

www.qacity.com

Web Content Accessibility Guidelines

www.w3.org/TR/WAI-WEBCONTENT/

Yale University: Online style guide

http://info.med.yale.edu/caim/manual/

CHAPTER

11

Functional Tests

Why Read This Chapter?

The purpose of this chapter is to point out several test types and techniques used in functionality testing, whether we have specifications or not. The premise of this testing is to find errors in the process of checking if the product is useful for its intended users and if it would do what a target user reasonably expected it to do. This chapter analyzes a variety of functional tests with an eye on their use during the testing process.

TOPICS COVERED IN THIS CHAPTER

- ◆ Introduction
- ◆ An Example of Cataloging Features in Preparation for Functional Tests
- ◆ Testing Methods
- ◆ Bibliography

Introduction

Functional testing is a broad category of testing. It includes a variety of testing methods such as FAST, TOFT, boundary, FET, exploratory testing, and other attacking techniques. This chapter details some of these functional test types and relates them to Web-testing examples.

To better define the scope of functionality tests, look at various degrees of the functioning of an application:

- *FAST.* Does each input and navigation control work as expected?

- *TOFT.* Can the application do something useful as expected?

- *Boundary.* What happens at the edge of specified use?

- *Forced-error.* What happens when an error condition occurs?

- *Exploratory.* What does experience tell about the potential problematic areas in the application? This involves simultaneous learning, planning, and executing tests.

- *Software attacks.* Why does software fail? How do you turn lessons learned into a series of attacks to expose software failures?

An Example of Cataloging Features in Preparation for Functional Tests

Following is an example of how the features in the sample application described in Chapter 8 "Sample Application " are cataloged.

Testing the Sample Application

We will use the sample project's chart-generation feature to detail some specific test cases for the varieties of functional testing. Chapter 8 describes this feature as a single Java applet running on the client browser to display *bug metrics*.

For the purpose of this example, bug metrics measure bug-report activity or resolution at any one time (*distribution metrics*) or over time (*trend metrics*) to support test project status monitoring. In the sample application, these metrics can be displayed as tables and charts.

This feature under test allows users to generate trend metrics based on a variety of criteria. The function works by choosing (1) a template to specify the type of data or comparisons to graph; (2) the period (daily, weekly, or monthly); and (3) the start and end dates.

Figure 11.1 shows the trend metrics generation page from the sample project. Figure 11.2 illustrates the result table and chart from the criteria chosen in Figure 11.1. Figure 11.3 shows a matrix that lists test cases to target the functionality of the sample project's chart-generation feature.

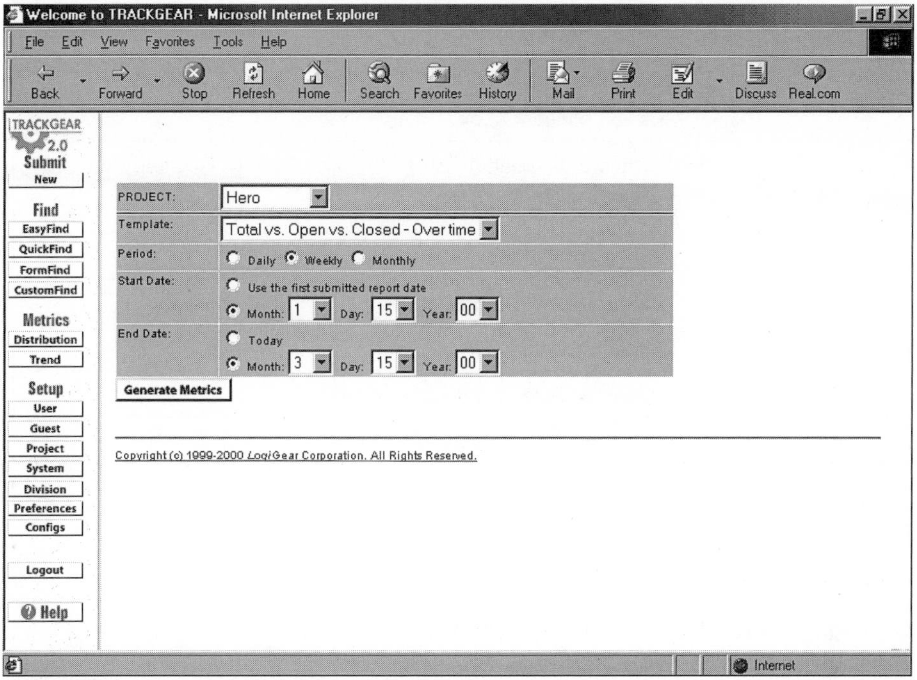

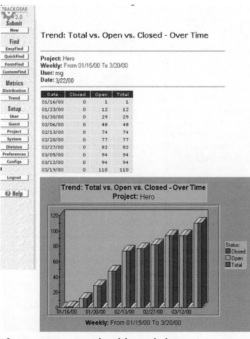

Figure 11.1   Trend metrics generation page.

Figure 11.2   Result table and chart.

		P: Passed	F: Failed	B: Blocked			
		Note:					
		Watch for date boundary conditions such as First/Last Day of Month, Day-of-Week and Minute-of-Day.					
		Watch for sorting order attributes such as Priority, Severity, Frequency, etc.					
		Watch for multiple dimension table.					
		Watch for one or more of the attributes have no records.					
No.	Template	Period	Start Date	End Date		P/F/B	Comments
1	1	Daily	Submitted Date	Today			
2			Submitted Date	Same Date			
3			Spec. Date	Today			
4			Spec. Date	Spec. Date			
5			Spec: Same Date	Spec: Same Date			
6			*No Record-Date*	*No Record-Date*			
7		Weekly	Submitted Date	Today			
8			Submitted Date	Spec. Date			
9			Spec. Date	Today			
10			Spec. Date	Spec. Date			
11			Spec: Same Date	Spec: Same Date			
12			*No Record-Date*	*No Record-Date*			
13		Monthly	Submitted Date	Today			
14			Submitted Date	Spec. Date			
15			Spec. Date	Today			
16			Spec. Date	Spec. Date			
17			Spec: Same Date	Spec: Same Date			
18			*No Record-Date*	*No Record-Date*			
...	...	...	...	...		...	...
87		Monthly	Submitted Date	Today			
88			Submitted Date	Spec. Date			
89			Spec. Date	Today			
90			Spec. Date	Spec. Date			
91			Spec: Same Date	Spec: Same Date			
92			*No Record-Date*	*No Record-Date*			

Figure 11.3   Functionality test cases for the trend-charting feature.

Testing Methods

Several common black-box testing methods that can be applied to functional tests will be discussed in this section. (Please see the "Functional Test" section of www.qacity.com for additional references.)

Functional Acceptance Simple Tests

Functional acceptance simple tests (FASTs) represent the second level of acceptance testing (relative to the release acceptance test (RAT), which was discussed in Chapter 3, "Software Testing Basics"). Rather than including only a small sampling of a program's functionality (as in RAT), FAST coverage is wide in breadth, but shallow in depth. The FAST exercises the lowest level of functionality for each command of a program. The combinations of functions, however, no matter how firmly integrated, are not tested within the scope of FAST. Such issues are considered in task-oriented functional testing (TOFT), which is discussed later in this chapter.

A test team can reject a build after it has been accepted into FAST. However, this is rare. The rejection expresses a determination by the test team that further testing of this build would be a waste of time, either because so many tests are blocked or because the build itself is invalid. More often, the test team continues testing a buggy build but reassigns some testers to other work if their tests are blocked by bugs.

One of the objectives of FAST is to check for the appropriate behaviors of user interface (UI) controls (e.g., text box, pull-down list, radio button, etc.) based on the intended designs. This entails checking for the existence of UI controls on each page, window, or dialog box; checking if the default state (such as enable, disable, highlighted, etc.) is as intended; checking if the default value or selected mode is as intended; checking if the tab order is as intended; and if the behavior of shortcuts (e.g., Ctrl-X, Ctrl-V, etc.) and other access keys (e.g., Alt-O for Open) is as intended. Additionally, in this process, you learn about the developer's thoughts and implementation logic in crafting the functionality delivered to the end user. You use this information later to design test cases that poke into the flaws of the design logic.

In a Web environment, things to check for in a FAST include:

- Links, such as content links, thumbnail links, bitmap links, and image map links
- Basic controls, such as backward and forward navigating, zoom-in and zoom-out, other UI controls, and content-refreshing checks
- Action command checks, such as add, remove, update, and other types of data submission; create user profiles or user accounts including e-mail accounts, personal accounts, and group-based accounts; and data-entry tests

- Other key features such as log in/log out, e-mail notification, search, credit card validation and processing, or handling of forgotten passwords

Some of the simple errors you may find in this process include the following:

- Broken links
- Missing images
- Wrong links
- Wrong images
- Correct links with no or outdated contents
- Errors in ordering/purchasing computation
- Ignoring credit card classifications
- Accepting expired credit
- Accepting invalid credit card numbers
- Incorrect content or context of automated e-mail reply
- No intelligence in address verification
- Server not responding (no server-updating message to user) to Domain Name Service (DNS) errors
- Inability to validate invalid user's e-mail addresses

Task-Oriented Functional Tests

Task-oriented functional tests (TOFTs) check whether the application can do useful tasks correctly. They are "positive" tests that check program functions by comparing the results of performed tasks with product specifications and requirements documents, if they exist, or to reasonable user's expectations. The integrity of each individual task performed by the program is checked for accuracy. If behavior or output varies from what is specified in product requirements, an issue report is submitted.

The TOFTs are structured around lists of features to be tested. To come up with a features-to-be-tested list, the product specification should be carefully dissected. The product itself must also be examined for those features that are not well defined or that are not in the specification at all. In short, every function and feature becomes an entry on the features-to-be-tested list. Consideration should also be given to competitive influences and market demands in developing the details of the list. For example, if competitive pressures dictate that a certain function should execute in less than two seconds, then that requirement should be added to the features-to-be-tested list.

TESTING THE SAMPLE APPLICATION

Functional Acceptance Simple Test Matrix—Trend Metrics checks whether a chart is generated when the tester selects the specified criteria. The FAST does not necessarily check whether the generated chart presents accurate data. The tests are passed even if the content of a metric generated by one of these test cases is incorrect—though an issue report should be written up to track the problem. The FAST, in this scenario, simply ensures that something is drawn, regardless of accuracy. The accuracy or the output would be the focus of TOFT, which is discussed in the next section. For Functional Acceptance Simple Test—Trend Metrics, we choose test cases to exercise a combination of functional choices.

Once your features-to-be-tested list is complete, each entry on it should be used to define a test case that checks whether the feature's requirements have been met.

Forced-Error Tests

Forced-error tests (FETs) intentionally drive software into error conditions. The objective of FETs is to find any error conditions that are undetected and/or mishandled. Error conditions should be handled gracefully; that is, the application recovers successfully, the system recovers successfully, or the application exits without data corruption and with an opportunity to preserve work in progress.

Suppose that you are testing text fields in an online registration form and the program's specification disallows nonalphabetical symbols in the Name field. An error condition will be generated if you enter "123456" (or any other nonalphabetic phrase) and click the Submit button. Remember, for any valid condition, there is always an invalid condition.

A complete list of error conditions is often difficult to assemble. Some ways of compiling a list of error conditions include the following:

- Collect a list of error messages from the developers.
- Interview the developers.
- Inspect the string data in a resource file.
- Gather information from specifications.
- Use a utility to extract test strings from the binary or scripting sources.
- Analyze every possible event with an eye to error cases.
- Use your experience.
- Use a standard valid/invalid input test matrix (such as the one in Appendix F, "Web Test-Case Design Guideline: Input Boundary and Validation Matrix).

TESTING THE SAMPLE APPLICATION

The Task-Oriented Functional Test Matrix—Trend Metrics would include the entire test suite detailed in Figure 11.3 to completely exercise this aspect of the sample project's trend metrics feature. Note that it would take a lot more than this simple matrix to completely exercise this part of the program. Beware of words like "complete."

These test cases check whether output data (the trend metrics and charts) accurately reflect input parameters (in this scenario, a data set that incorporates daily bug-tracking activity). The sample data set includes the number of new reports opened versus the number of reports closed over a given period. The TOFT test cases check whether output metrics mirror the particulars of the input data set.

Once you have a complete list of error conditions, each error condition should be run through the following testing process:

1. *Force the error condition.* Direct the software into the error condition specified in the test case.

2. *Check the error detection logic.* Error handling starts with error detection. If an error goes undetected, there is no handling. From the developer perspective, detection is done through validation. For example, in the code, an input value is validated using some constraints. If the value does not satisfy the constraints, then do something about it (i.e., disallow the input). Test cases should be designed to poke into the flaws of the validation logic.

3. *Check the handling logic.* Now that the detection is in place, we need to check how each detected error condition is handled from the following dimensions:

   ■ Does the application offer adequate forgiveness and allow the user to recover from the mistakes gracefully? For example, if one of the inputs in a 20-field form is invalid, does the application allow the user to reenter valid data to that one field, or does it force the user to start it all over again?

   ■ Does the application itself handle the error condition gracefully? If the program terminates abnormally (e.g., due to a critical error, the application exits without going through the normal exit routines), a variety of cleanup activities might not have been done. For instance, some files might have been left open, some variables might have incorrect data, or the database is in an inconsistent state.

- Does the system recover gracefully? Does the system crash or continue operating with erratic or limited functionality, or compromised security? For example, in a Web-based system, critical errors should be predicted, examined, and handled so that system crashes can be avoided. However, a system crash caused by an error condition might be a better outcome than having the system continue running but produce wrong results or compromised security.

- Keep in mind that if one of the physical servers must reboot for any reason, when the system is restarted, it is possible that not all services (e.g., SMTP service, database services, etc.) will restart successfully. You should check to make sure that the restart routine does what you expect it to do.

4. *Check the error communication.* Do the following:

   - Determine whether an error message appears. If an error message appears, then this part of the test is passed (the accuracy of the message is secondary to the fact that a message has been generated).

   - Analyze the accuracy of the error message. Does the message tell the user what's wrong? Can the user understand it? Do the instructions match the error condition? Will the instructions help users successfully escape the error condition? You also need to ask yourself if the application offers adequate instructions so that the user can avoid an obvious error condition in the first place.

   - Note that the communication does not have to be in an error message. It can be in another medium such as an audio or visual cue. Use your judgment to assess which medium is the most appropriate, and voice your concern accordingly.

5. *Look for further problems.* Are any other related issues uncovered in generating this error condition? For example, there might be a memory leak, a stack corruption, a partially updated data structure or table entry, or a wild pointer. A calculation might have been incorrectly completed. You might use data collected from logging tools to analyze the state of the servers, thereby detecting the implication associated with error messages.

Figure 11.4 walks you through an example of a Web system to demonstrate the error-handling process. First, the user takes certain action and puts the system or application in an error state. This can be done in a variety of ways: simply from invalid keyboard input, disconnecting from an ISP, removing a network connection cable, or attempting to follow an incorrect path through the application.

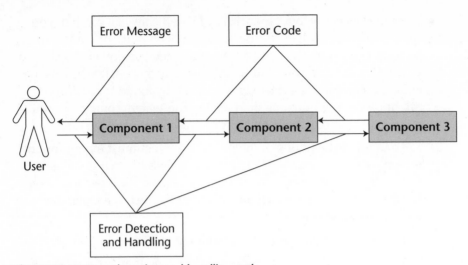

Figure 11.4 Error detection and handling path.

The error must then be detected. There may be code to handle an error, but it's useless if the application does not detect the error. As illustrated in Figure 11.4, the error might be detected at any component in the communication chain involved in executing the request. Does a message go back to the client at all? If not, was there proper silent error handling? Could there be *improper* silent error handling? Which test would have to be created to generate an error behind the client that the client will not be advised of but that will be persistent?

The detected error must then be handled. Will the application fix the error itself? In most cases, some components may return an error code or message. The error condition is usually communicated back to the user in the form of an error message. This can be done either on the client-side (if that is the expected behavior) or on the server-side (after the user sends a request to the server).

For example, the user enters a request and the request is sent to the Web server, which then passes it along to the database server. If the database server experiences an error condition, it will then return an error code. The Web server either generates an error message that is based on the error code or it forwards the error code back to the client. (For more information, see Chapter 10, "User Interface Tests," for an example of client- and server-side error message handling).

In this error-handling scheme, consider the following issues:

- An error condition might occur anywhere in the chain transaction processing.
- Each component within the chain might fail to detect or interpret an error condition correctly.

- Each component within the communication chain might fail to forward an error code to the next component.

- An error condition (code) needs to be translated into an understandable message so that the user will know what happened. For example, "Exception 80065" will not mean anything to the user.

- The user does not know or care where the error happened. He or she only needs to know what the error is (from the human perspective) and how to correct the situation.

- The goal of forced-error tests is to put the application in an error condition. The first level of the test is to make sure an error message is received by the client. The second level is to test that the error message is correct; that is, it should convey the description of the error and tell the user how to resolve the error.

The next step is to check if the error condition was properly handled. This may be instantly apparent, but in most cases, we may not know what has resulted from the error condition. A key for testers is to keep good notes of what actions were taken, and in what order, so that bugs can be better investigated and reproduced.

As discussed earlier, there are numerous ways to collect error condition information. The most systematic way of generating a preliminary error condition test is to compile a list of all error messages from the program's developers. Additional error conditions can be uncovered through guesswork based on past testing experience. You may also discover bugs accidentally while performing other kinds of testing.

A full cycle of FET may require two to three builds to complete, because testers have to perform countless error-generating activities that, in an ideal world, users would never do. Only by creating unexpected situations (e.g., entering special characters into fields that are designed for numerals and by requesting page margin settings that are impossible) can you generate error conditions that are unrelated to the known error conditions.

Boundary Condition Tests and Equivalent Class Analysis

Boundary tests are similar to FETs in that they test the boundaries of each variable. For example, in testing an online registration form, you need to check if a text field with a specified character limit from two to seven characters is, in fact, functioning as expected. Does the field accept two, three, six, and seven characters? What about one character? Or eight? Can the field be left empty? (Boundary and equivalence class test-case design techniques are discussed in Chapter 3.)

Boundary tests are really an extension of TOFTs and FETs, and there is some overlap between the test types. See Table 11.2 at the end of this chapter for a visual representation of the differences and overlap between TOFT, FET, boundary, and FAST.

Exploratory Testing

Exploratory testing* is a process of examining the product and observing its behavior, as well as hypothesizing what its behavior is. It involves executing test cases and creating new ones as information is collected from the outcome of previous tests. Test execution includes setting up an environment, creatively generating input data to attack the program, observing the program's response, evaluating what has been learned, and then starting the next test.

Exploratory testing has many names and can take many forms. It is also referred to as *unstructured* or *ad hoc testing* and is, contrary to some beliefs, a methodical testing strategy. It involves "thinking outside the box," testing behavior that we may not expect but that any user may, mistakenly or intentionally, do.

You do exploratory testing by walking through the program, finding out what it is, and testing it. It is called *exploratory* because you explore. According to James Bach, an author and expert in testing software, exploratory testing means learning while testing. It's the opposite of prescribed testing—like playing 20 questions. If we had to specify all our questions in advance, the game would be nearly impossible, because with each question we learn more about what the next test should be. The elements of exploratory testing include:

- Product exploration
- Test design
- Test execution
- Heuristics
- Reviewable results

NOTE For more on this topic, read James Bach's paper at www.satisface.com. Also go to Brian Marick's site at www.testingcraft.com/exploratory.html; and read Chris Agruss's and Bob Johnson's paper at www.testingcraft.com/ad_hoc_testing.pdf.

---

*According to James Bach, "In operational terms, exploratory testing is an interactive process of concurrent product exploration, test design, and test execution."

TESTING THE SAMPLE APPLICATION

An example of an FET using the sample project includes requesting a metric (or chart) that has a start date that is later than its end date. In effect, this test case requests the impossible, thus, such a chart cannot exist. Nevertheless, the sample project enables users to request such a chart, so the scenario must be tested.

The intent of this test case is not to ensure accuracy of output, but to examine how the program responds to the error condition. Does the system crash? Is the user given a chance to amend his or her request? Is an error message presented to the user (regardless of the accuracy of the error message)?

Compiling a list of all error messages is an effective means of generating test cases for FET. Figure 11.5 shows a straightforward FET with a start date for a chart of September 31. We all know "30 days has September, thus an error message reading, "Start Date Not Found or Invalid," is returned.

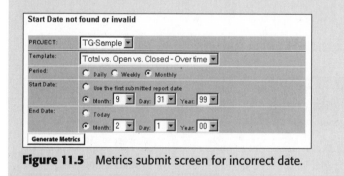

Figure 11.5   Metrics submit screen for incorrect date.

Software Attacks

Particularly useful for designing test cases are the 21 attacks on software described by James A. Whittaker in his book, *How to Break Software: A Practical Guide to Testing* (Addison-Wesley, 2002*).* According to Whittaker, software attacks fall into at least one of three general categories: (1) input/output attacks, (2) data attacks, and (3) computation attacks.

Which Method Is It?

Definition of test types or methods, by itself, is not important. What is important is to make sure that relevant test cases (and their probability of revealing failures) are used to exercise a feature in search for errors.

TESTING THE SAMPLE APPLICATION

Using the sample project's trend metrics feature as an example, boundary tests can be used to check if the program responds appropriately to user requests at the boundaries of the data set. For example, we make a data set in which report data begins on April 1, 1999, and ends on April 30, 1999. The specified limits of this data set are, therefore, 4/1/99 and 4/30/99. Any user requests that specify start and end dates between 4/1/99 and 4/30/99 should not generate errors. Any user requests that specify start dates before 4/1/99 or after 4/30/99 should generate errors.

In this example, the boundary test requires three values for each end of the limits: 3/31/99, 4/1/99, and 4/2/99 for the start date; and 4/29/99, 4/30/99, and 5/1/99 for the end date. Each boundary test must confirm that accurate trend-metric data is returned for requests that specify start and end dates between 4/1/99 and 4/30/99, and that error conditions are handled gracefully for requests that specify start and end dates before 4/1/99 or after 4/30/99. Table 11.1 shows combinations of values that are to be tested in boundary testing for the sample project's trend metrics.

Table 11.1 Value Combinations to Be Boundary Tested for the Sample Project's Trend Metrics

BOUNDARY TEST CASE NUMBER	START DATE	END DATE	EXPECTED RESULT
1	4/1/99	4/30/99	Nonerror (TOFT)
2	3/31/99	4/30/99	Forced-error (FET)
3	4/2/99	4/30/99	Nonerror (TOFT)
. . .	. . .	. . .	Forced-error (FET)

As illustrated in Table 11.2, the lines between boundary tests, TOFTs, and FETs are not always clear. Using the text field example given previously, you can perform any of these three test types, depending on which character you enter into the field with the two- to seven-character limits. It does not matter which method it is. It's important that a test case would have a high probability of finding errors.

Table 11.2 Special Characters and Example Boundary Test Input

CHARACTER TESTING	CORRESPONDING TEST TYPE
0	Boundary, special-case, or forced-error?
2-7	Task-oriented functional testing?

Table 11.2 *(continued)*

CHARACTER TESTING	CORRESPONDING TEST TYPE
1 or <2	Boundary or forced-error?
8 or >7	Boundary or forced-error?
?, + (, #, !, <	Forced-error?
%n, $name, etc.	Forced-error or special cases that are meaningful (used as keyword in that programming environment) to the application under test?

Bibliography

Bach, James. *General Functionality and Stability Test Procedure for the Certified for Microsoft Windows Logo.* Redmond, WA: Microsoft, 2000.

Kaner, Cem, Jack Falk, Hung Q. Nguyen. *Testing Computer Software,* 2nd ed. New York: John Wiley & Sons, Inc., 1999. LogiGear Corporation. *QA Training Handbook: Testing Web Applications.* Foster City, CA: LogiGear Corp., 2003.

———— *QA Training Handbook: Testing Windows Desktop and Server-Based Applications.* Foster City, CA: LogiGear Corp., 2003.

———— QA Training Handbook: Testing Computer Software. Foster City, CA: LogiGear Corp., 2003.

Whittaker, James A., *How to Break Software: A Practical Guide to Testing,* Boston: Addison-Wesley, 2002.

Whittaker, James A., and Alan Jorgensen. "Why Software Fails." *ACM Software Engineering,* Note 24 (1999): 4.

CHAPTER
12

Server-Side Testing

Why Read This Chapter?

Somewhere behind all of the user interfaces that make up a Web application is a server or, more likely, many servers. The server is the brain of the client-server system. Testing the server directly is challenging because you can no longer take advantage of the client interface. Server applications and components talk to each other, as well as to the operating system's services such as file system services, via an application interface or Application Programming Interface (API). Unlike the UI, this interface is not intuitive to use for an end user. Therefore, testing these interfaces often requires a *test harness* or *driver* to be built, or the use of scripts or programs to execute your tests. This chapter shows ways to bypass the normal user interfaces and directly test the server's software.

TOPICS COVERED IN THIS CHAPTER

- ◆ Introduction
- ◆ Common Server-Side Issues
- ◆ Connectivity Issues

(continued)

TOPICS COVERED IN THIS CHAPTER *(continued)*

- ◆ **Resource Issues**
- ◆ **Backup and Restore Issues**
- ◆ **Fail-over Issues**
- ◆ **Multithreading Issues**
- ◆ **Server-Side Testing Tips**
- ◆ **Bibliography and Additional Resources**

Introduction

Many software services and much processing in a Web application happen on the server-side rather than on the client-side. The server software, isolated from the standard user interfaces, often resides on server computers in remote locations. This means that software you test—whether it's a Web server, application server, database server, or back-office system—is difficult to exercise fully via the UI. The UI may also prevent you from doing error condition tests because client-side error checking (if available) will block, accidentally or purposely, bad data from reaching the server. Testing the server-side software will require creative use of the user UI, the creation of some custom client interfaces to reach the server-side software, utilization of tools and utilities, and implementation of new techniques.

What is a server? As defined in Chapter 5, "Web Application Components," "Any computer that provides services to other computers is a server." But also recall from that chapter that,"Physical hardware boxes can support multiple client programs, so it is more accurate to refer to the software as the *server*, as opposed to the hardware that supports it." In Chapter 5 we listed several types of servers and their definitions, illustrating the wide range of servers being used today; we expect many more to come. Most applications are built using several component servers, plus the custom software that makes up the application. You will need to consider testing the interoperability of your application at the many layers of the interface as it interacts with these components.

In Chapter 2, "Web Testing versus Traditional Testing," we touched on some challenges to testing server-based applications. In this chapter, we'll examine more fully some of the common server-side testing issues, including connectivity, resources, fail-over, multithreading, and backup and restore issues. You will learn several server-side testing tips, including:

- How to use monitoring utilities to spot potential bugs.
- How to create test drivers to quickly exercise server-side components.
- How to use log files for analyzing application failures.

- How to automate server restarting procedures to save time.

- Why scripting languages are useful to server testing.

The discussions in this chapter will also prepare you for several follow-up, in-depth server-side testing discussions in the Chapter 14, "Database Tests," Chapter 17, "Configuration and Compatibility Tests," Chapter 18, "Web Security Testing," and Chapter 19, "Performance Testing."

Common Server-Side Testing Issues

Similar to client-server systems, Web systems consist of a client, a server, and the network that connects them. We will discuss a few key issues surrounding these three elements, focusing on the server-side.

Connectivity Issues

In testing Web systems, the two key factors that cause a Web transaction to fail are: (1) the submitted transaction did not reach the destination, or (2) the transaction reached the destination but did not get what it needed. When the transaction did not reach the destination, often there are two explanations: (1) there is a connectivity problem, or (2) something is wrong with the server. Let's talk about some of the common connectivity issues.

Time-Out Issues

In testing the server-side, determine what is the longest possible time delay for the various server-side tasks. Then set up conditions and test the system against those scenarios. During stress or performance testing, these tests will need to be reviewed using various loads on the server. If the application is not architected and implemented well, time-out conditions not only often lead to loss of connection (e.g., the user must log in again), but they can also create data integrity problems. For example, in Web applications, the client never communicates directly with the database; it communicates only through the software application—that is the end-user client can send data to the application server, and the data never makes it all the way to the database server due to a time-out. As a result, the user and the database may then be using different sets of data.

If the database receives an excessive number of requests for data, it may cause long delays when responding to these requests. Some requests may never be returned. It is possible that the database is completely offline and unable to provide any feedback to the Web or application servers. During such conditions, many different failure modes may exist. You want to analyze the system under test to identify test scenarios by trying to understand how each component (e.g., database, Web servers, application servers, browsers, and clients) will behave when there is a time-out.

A request that gets no response from the database may:

- Cause the application server to return to the client a meaningless or misleading error message.
- Cause the application server to drop connection to the client.
- Cause the application to drop all connections to the database.
- Cause the application to fail to free up this connection, thus creating a resource limitation.
- Cause the application to crash, thus not respond to any requests.

Each of these responses is usually a bug. However, each might also be an acceptable response for some applications. The proper handling for an application server when the database doesn't respond will depend on a number of factors, including: how mission-critical the application is; how secure the data must be; how knowledgeable the client is; and how sensitive to error the client will become.

Maintaining State

State is a relationship between the client and server wherein information supplied from previous transactions is available to the server. Many applications use cookies, session IDs, or IP addresses, sometimes coupled with user logins, to establish an application state. State information can be stored in multiple locations. An example of Web-based application state is at the my.yahoo.com Web site: Using your my.yahoo.com account requires many database lookups. Examples include lookups to check for proper logon, to check the weather, maps, stock quotes, and e-mail. When you visit my.yahoo.com from a client machine, your first task is to log in with your user name and password. This establishes state for just this one session. The created state for this session will give you complete access to your account. At a later time, when you use the same machine to contact your yahoo account, cookies residing on your machine identify you to the Web server, allowing the Web server to check its database and present the information you want using the color options and layout you have previously chosen, without asking you to logon again. However, when you need access to your my.yahoo.com account on a new client machine, you will need to go through the logon procedure again because there is no state information on that machine for the server to identify you and your previous activities.

To test state-related problems, you need to understand where and how state information is stored in the application. You also need to understand when and how this state is communicated among various components (e.g., client machines, servers, database, etc.). Testing for state-related problems mostly involves modifying or removing the information that describes different states. Some state-related problems include:

- *Lost information*. This includes data supplied during a previous screen or session and is assumed to be part of the context for the current requests. Testing these conditions may require stopping both the client application and the server. For example, a reservation system would usually allow customers to return to the Web site days or weeks later to confirm or modify reservations. In this case, both the client's machine and the server may have been restarted several times.

- *Stale data*. Collecting and storing credit card data is a common practice, saving repeat customers time, and lowering error rates due to typing and transmission problems. However, expiration dates make formerly good data invalid and can prevent completion of a transaction. Just because the data was once valid does not mean that it is still, or will always be, valid.

- *"Duplicate" data*. How does the system generate the data to determine unique transactions? Many people have the same name, and using credit card numbers fails when members of the same family are traveling. Many corporate firewalls mask their IP address, and most techniques used for generating random IDs are error-prone.

- *Wrong information being sent to a client*. Is the information from the server sent to the correct client? Is the information from the server sent to the client, the correct information? Information stored in a common buffer before being returned to a client can easily be sent to the wrong client. This issue may trigger security or privacy issues (See Chapter 18 for more information").

- *Lost clients*. How long should the server wait for a response from a client? What cleanup work does the server need to do after a session terminates improperly? In the reservation example, what happens if the client just doesn't respond for several minutes?

- *Data integrity*. You also may experience data integrity errors and product inventory problems as a result of lost requests when connectivity is unexpectedly lost (see Chapter 14 for more information).

There are many different protocols for connecting Web clients to the server: HTTP, HTTPS, SMTP, and FTP are among the most common ones. The configuration settings on the server-side will have an effect on the behavior of the application. For example, many systems disable FTP connections to prevent outside users from gaining file-transfer access to the internal network. However, if your Web site allows downloading files via the FTP protocol, FTP needs to be enabled on the server. What is the default configuration that the installation program should use for the Web server during the installation and setup process? Also, keep in mind that most systems evolve over time, so after this application has been operational for a while, the organization may decide to change the system and block FTP, perhaps to use FTP only once a quarter to send material to the board of directors. Changing the protocol configuration may cause the application to fail. Will this mode of failure be acceptable to the users who receive the error messages? Should the server software routinely check the system configuration and report the status?

If your application supports confidential information sent using a secure protocol such as HTTPS, then testing with this protocol should be done. Switching between HTTP and HTTPS mode can be a concern for some users. For example, technically, the Web page that allows you to enter sensitive information such as credit card account information does not need to be sent to the client-side browser using HTTPS. Only the Submit command that sends the sensitive information in that page from the client to the server should transfer the information using HTTPS protocol to take advantage of SSL. However, it is a good idea to send the information-collection Web page using HTTPS mode anyway. Having the Web page display in HTTPS mode gives the user a comfortable feeling of being in a secure environment (although it makes no difference technically). Test cases should also determine if the transitions between protocols occur at the proper conditions, offering users the proper level of comfort.

Resource Issues

A *resource* is anything that an application uses to properly execute given instructions. All software applications need resources such as RAM, disk space, CPU(s), bandwidth, open connections, and so on to carry out their tasks. The following are test issues that you need to be aware of so that proper test planning can be carried out.

- How does the application interact with the operating system to acquire and utilize resources?
- Does it handle lack-of-resource conditions gracefully?
- Does it handle out-of-resource conditions gracefully?

- Does it handle boundary resource conditions gracefully?

- Does it handle the systems with multiple or distributed resources properly? For example, running the application in a computer with multiple CPUs may perform differently than in a single-CPU computer.

As discussed in Chapter 2, distributed server configurations working together provide more resources for the application. However, making it work requires the application to be flexible in handling these additional resources. Systems that have been designed and built to work in the one-box model and have not been able to expand into the two- and three-box models as the workload increases are known as *not scalable*. Examples of failure to build a flexible application include:

- Applications use the host name "localhost" to the specified computer from which the application will get resources. This will work fine as long as the application will run only on a single host. When the workload needs to be distributed over multiple hosts, to leverage additional computing power and other resources, references to "localhost" will be one of the main errors that cause the system to break.

- A more severe error is when the application hard-codes "localhost" in many places in the source code, thereby making debugging and fixing more challenging.

- The application is designed with only one variable to store the host name to avoid hard-coded host names. This will also cause scalability problems because the application is assumed to always go to one computer for resources. Another flavor of this is that a hard-coded name for a log file may become a problem if the server-side is given additional disk resources.

Several types of the tests discussed in Chapter 19 are designed to address resource-related issues with a focus on the server-side. In addition, it is useful to take advantage of a few monitoring utilities so that resource utilization activities can be seen in real time during testing, or logged for failure analysis at a later time. (See the "Using Monitoring Tools" section for more information.)

Backup and Restore Issues

Data on network servers is usually backed up on a regular schedule. Backups take a snapshot of the system at a particular moment. That snapshot can be restored at a later time to bring the application and data back to the state when the snapshot was made. In a dynamic system, such as a Web server or database, restoring to that point in time may not make sense.

Your application's server software may need special handling for the backup process to work. At the minimum, you should check:

- The installation guides and operating guides for instructions related to backup and restore process, such as the user names and directories that need to be backed up.

- On systems using encryption, the private keys will require special handling since normal backups are usually available to a large number of users.

- In a system that is in continual (24/7) use, restoring to the point in time when the backup occurred may not make sense. For example, the program uses disk files to store intermediate values such as running totals for the end-of-month report, and the application needs to recalculate these values. A report that contains restored values from the backup will definitely result in wrong answers. In this case, decisions on how the restore happens, how often the restore happens, and what data is backed up and restored, may or may not be the responsibility of the test team. However, when data is restored from a backup, it has to be understood and tested.

Fail-over Issues

According to Webopedia, the online computer dictionary (www.webopedia .com, June 2002,) fail-over is defined as:

A backup operation that automatically switches to a standby database, server, or network if the primary system fails or is temporarily shut down for servicing. Failover is an important fault tolerance function of mission-critical systems that rely on constant accessibility. Failover automatically and transparently to the user redirects requests from the failed or down system to the backup system that mimics the operations of the primary system.

And, according to www.whatis.com, June 2002:

Failover is a backup operational mode in which the functions of a system component (such as a processor, server, network, or database, for example) are assumed by secondary system components when the primary component becomes unavailable through either failure or scheduled downtime. Used to make systems more fault-tolerant, failover is typically an integral part of mission-critical systems that must be constantly available. The procedure involves automatically offloading tasks to a standby system component so that the procedure is as seamless as possible to the end user. Failover can apply to any aspect of a system: within a personal computer, for example, failover might be a mechanism to protect against a failed processor; within a network, failover can apply to any network component or system of components, such as a connection path, storage device, or Web server.

Originally, stored data was connected to servers in very basic configurations: either point-to-point or cross-coupled. In such an environment, the failure (or even maintenance) of a single server frequently made data access impossible for a large number of users until the server was back online. More recent developments, such as the storage area network (SAN), make any-to-any connectivity possible among servers and data storage systems. In general, storage networks use many paths—each consisting of complete sets of all the components involved —between the server and the system. A failed path can result from the failure of any individual component of a path. Multiple connection paths, each with redundant components, are used to help ensure that the connection is still viable even if one (or more) paths fail. The capacity for automatic failover means that normal functions can be maintained despite the inevitable interruptions caused by problems with equipment.

Fail-over testing is about putting the system in a state to trigger failure so that the design of system error-handling and recovery process can be validated and its implementation can be verified. Some of the questions to consider in testing for fail-over include:

- Do the fail-over configurations work as expected?
- Are both software-only fail-over (failure of the application) scenarios as well as hardware fail-over (failure of all nodes) scenarios tested?
- What are the possible fail-over scenarios that should be tested?
- Upon the occurrence of the fail-over, are users' requests routed to other available servers without losing any sessions?
- Upon failure, does the failed server restart and automatically resume processing without performance degradation?
- When the primary server in the cluster is brought down under heavy load, does the fail-over process work as expected; and, ultimately, does the application recover to its fully functional state?
- After a server in the cluster is down, how long does it take for it to resume processing and to return the site to the service levels of the original throughput? Is that time frame acceptable?

Multithreading Issues

A *thread* is the smallest unit of independently scheduled code that a machine can execute. Often an application will use multiple threads in order to improve an application's efficiency. Threads allow a program to execute multiple tasks concurrently.

For example, a Web server needing to make several requests to a database can be designed to put these requests into separate threads. This allows the database to process each of these requests concurrently, returning each response as soon as possible, allowing the Web server to return answers to its client (the end user) more quickly. Figure 12.1 illustrates such a condition. In this case, the user sends a request for information on a vehicle by filling out a form and submitting the request to the server. The Web server generates four separate threads that execute four separate database searches. Since all four tasks are being executed at the same time, the client's request is completed faster.

If, instead, this example were single-threaded, each task would need to be completed sequentially, and information would have to be fetched from one database at a time. When information from the first database search was returned, the next one would then be started. Do you see the obvious performance differences between the two scenarios?

When threads are created, the normal serial execution of instructions cannot be relied upon. One thread may inadvertently interact with the other threads by changing global variables or by executing in a different order than expected. If one thread fails to complete, then some tasks may only partially fail, causing unexpected results. Thread testing is very dependent on the run-time environment. The system load and types of activities being performed have a strong influence on your ability to detect problems.

Unit testing will often fail to find thread problems. In general, unit tests are concerned with smaller modules of code, hence are less likely to detect problems associated with system-level problems. Design reviews can be very effective, and often an entire review session is devoted to a single threading issue.

Running the various processes (Web server and database in the preceding example) on the same machine will limit the number of thread problems a tester can discover. A single machine is still limited to executing instructions one at a time, but this is far different from a system in which many computers share the load, as in the case of distributed databases. To test for threading problems, you should create complex system environments and try to put server components on as many different machines as possible. You can also modify the test results by using a mixture of fast and slow Ethernet connections. For the preceding example, you could use four machines, as follows:

- Web server
- File system for Web server
- Database engine
- Database file storage

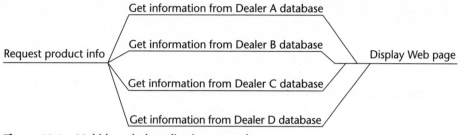

Figure 12.1 Multithreaded application example.

The operating system will schedule threads differently every time the application is executed. System interrupts and processing dependency will cause threads to take varying amounts of time to complete. Many other factors influence each thread's performance as well. Because threads do not execute in the same order or take the same amount of time rerunning, the same test may find a problem on one run but not on other runs of the same test. This means most multithread problems are first reported as "not reproducible." The code may work correctly almost every time; it is the very rare condition that will cause the defect to be shown. The symptoms will also vary, because each time the problem is encountered, a slightly different place in the code will be at fault for the problem. Sometimes data will be wrong; other times the program might halt or throw an exception.

Finding and reporting multithreaded problems will often require running a simple test thousands of times before the problem will appear. If your application uses multiple threads, you should design your tests to be run repeatedly for several days. These tests will have to be able to detect the problem and then save as much information as possible to help trace the problem. Detailed log files are often useful to track down multithread and synchronization problems.

Expect an application's thread usage to be slightly different on every platform you support. Even different versions of an operating system, such as Solaris will vary from one workstation to another. A problem that appears on one system may not be reproducible in another environment.

You can use log files to find problems. In the example log used later in this chapter, the sequence to close down an application contains two log entries concerning threads. If the log should occasionally have another entry between the request to close and confirmation that all threads are closed, then an error may be present. As a general test for proper thread behavior, reading the application's log can show when events occurred in a different order than expected.

Timing and data corruption are not the only multithreading problems that can occur. Another example of a different class of problem is resource contention, which can lead to resource deadlocks. For example, as shown in Figure 12.2, a request to an application requires three threads (here called T1, T2, and T3) to execute code concurrently. Each thread has a need for a pair of resources: T1 needs R1 and R2, T2 needs R2 and R3, and, finally, T3 needs R1 and R3. Imagine that at one moment, the operating system had only one of each resource available, R1, R2, and R3; and that T1 got R1 allocated but was blocked on R2; T2 got R2 allocated but was blocked on R3; and T3 got R3 allocated and was blocked on R1. While each thread possesses only one of the needed resources, none of them can complete its task. Also imagine what would happen if T1, T2, and T3 all decide to hold on to the resource that it has and wait for the missing one: you would have a classic deadlock situation.

Testing multithreaded applications is a challenging task because:

- The behavior of the application can be environment-dependent.

- Unit testing will probably fail to reveal run-time multithreaded problems.

- Running the various processes on the same machine will limit the opportunities to reveal multithreading problems.

- System interrupts and processing dependency will cause threads to take varying amounts of time to complete.

- Failures are hard to reproduce because threads do not execute in the same order. Symptoms will vary because each time the problem is encountered, a different place in the code or different timing of the execution will cause a different failure. Sometimes, data will be wrong. Sometimes, the program might halt, crash, or throw an exception.

- Finding multithreading problems often requires running a simple test thousands of times before the problem will appear.

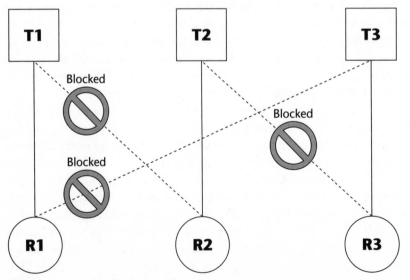

Figure 12.2 A deadlock example.

NOTE You can find examples of problems using threads at these two sites: http://gee.cs.oswego.edu/dl/cpj/jmm.html and www.cs.umd.edu/~pugh/java/memory/Model/DoubleCheckedLocking.html

You can increase your chances of finding threading problems in the following ways:

- Test with multiprocessor server boxes.

- Design your load and stress tests with a variety of timing conditions in mind.

- Logging can be an effective method of tracking down multithreading and synchronization problems, assuming the proper data is logged (see the "Using Log Files" section later in this chapter). In the example log shown in Figure 12.3, the sequence to close down contains two log entries concerning closing down threads: "Asking all threads to close," and "all threads are down." If, somehow, the log shows an entry between the two entries, then something might be wrong. As a general test for proper thread behavior, reviewing the application log enables you to discover when events occurred in a different order than expected.

Server Side Testing Tips

Using Log Files

Operating systems and server-based applications often offer logging mechanisms so that activities among various application and operating system components can be tracked, analyzed, and audited. Programmers create log files to write status and diagnostic information. These log files are often used during program debugging to help isolate problems. After the program is out of development and "in the field," or "live," on your company's production servers, the support organization uses the log files' data to monitor the operation of the program, and to troubleshoot problems.

Understanding the basics of event logging, what information is being written to log files, and how to retrieve the logs will help you a great deal in testing for, and more importantly, analyzing server failures. For example, several different logs are available to the tester, including the operating system log, database logs, audit logs (if turned on), as well as custom logs, which the program can produce. As a tester, you need to understand what information is being written to these files and how to retrieve the logs. You should provide a list of data the test team wants included in these logs. Information you may want to make available includes:

- Time the server is started, stopped, or paused.

- Name of the computer (host name).

- Version and build number of software. If the software contains multiple independent components, list each component and its version number.

- If you go to a code review session, look for case statements. Usually, the last statement is an "otherwise," meaning that no case matched the expected values; the comment in the code reads, "Not possible." Theoretically, a log entry for this case should never be sent to the log. If such a message shows up in the log then that which was thought of as "not possible" is, indeed, possible. For such an entry, it is useful to add the data value used in the case statement such as:

```
Error in function: foo illegal switch value: N
```

- Thread creation and synchronization.

- Transaction *start* and *commit* times.

- Garbage collection *start* and *completion* times.

- Many programs provide varying degrees of data to be logged based on a configuration parameter.

- Debugging information might include recording every time a certain event, such as a mouse movement, occurs or every time a new thread is created.

- Another common log usage is to record every time a particular function is called.

- When testing databases, programmers often write the exact SQL command into the log.

NOTE Chapter 13, "Using Scripts to Test," describes tools you can use to quickly search log files for important information. It is a simple task to automatically search a log file for warning, errors, and other messages.

To avoid writing all information into the log during test execution (which would unduly stress the computer), the two common methods used to select the data to log are compile-time switches and environmental variables. These methods allow some information to be written to the files during construction and testing. However, in production, the logs will not normally be filled with this debugging data.

It is useful to include in the log a timestamp, followed by whatever task was just started or completed.

```
. . .
Mar 18 19:02:48 Initializing application.
Mar 18 20:47:37 Asking all threads to close.
Mar 18 20:47:39 mainWnd::OnEndSession -  all threads are down.
Mar 18 20:47:43 mainWnd::OnEndSession - application terminated.
. . .
```

Figure 12.3   Example log.

In selecting what to write to the log, you should consider capturing all rarely executed or unusual error-handling code. This will help testing in two important ways. First, when you are testing these conditions, you should check the log to determine that you actually did create the condition you were trying to test. (It is often much more difficult to create these conditions than we expect, hence a test we believe is exercising a certain condition never actually executes the intended code.) Second, you can monitor the code during the entire testing process to determine how often these conditions actually occur. (Chapter 13 contains a sample program to automatically search log files.)

Logs data can also be used to infer other problems as well. From the example log shown in Figure 12.3, we can calculate a time of two seconds to close down all threads. But suppose this process, which usually takes two seconds, sometimes takes over 10 seconds to complete: What accounts for all that extra time? Is there an event occurring of which we should be aware? Do the times cluster at two (or more) different times for the same event? The log files can give you insight to the execution of the code.

This can help generate ideas about the actual behavior of the program. Are the times for some events close to system time-outs? Is writing to a log slowing down the process? Have the logs become so big they are filling cache space? Knowing how long different tasks need to execute can help you design new tests to stress these activities.

Performance testing needs to be done both with logging turned on and off. If your application supports different levels of logging, then several tests may be required. In some applications, logging accounts for over 50 percent of the program's execution time. Logging, which requires writing to disk, normally stops execution of the program until the disk status confirms a successful write has occurred.

In addition, you should consider testing the log mechanism itself. Logs can grow very large, so what happens when log files fill the disk? An easy way to test this is to write the log file to a floppy. Do all the events actually get written to the file? When writing data, it is often necessary to flush buffers before the data is actually written to disk. The content of the log is also subject to problems; for example, incorrect grammar or other embarrassing text should be corrected or removed. Or the log file just looks sloppy; for example, the log uses different timestamp formats, and some entries end with punctuation, while others do not. Also keep in mind that computer log files are often viewed by many people or are presented as evidence in court cases.

Using Monitoring Tools

Monitoring utilities are useful tools that give you a view into what's going on inside the system software and hardware. This information is key to gray-box testing because it shows the communication and activities generated by many hidden processes. These processes represent applications and their components talking to each other or to the operating system's service components. This type of information is not understandable to black-box testers unless we educate ourselves as to what is viewable inside the system in real time, and how to interpret the collected data.

The various types of information offered by these monitoring utilities include:

- General system information, such as:
  - The total amount of each type of resource (e.g., various types of memory, threads, handles, etc.).
  - The amount or percentage used/available for each type of resources.
- Specific hardware activities through various metrics against each type of hardware (e.g., percent of time the hard drive is writing or reading, the amount data in bytes transmitted per second, etc.).
- What is where in the current system, such as:
  - Information about the resources and their configuration (e.g., network interface cards, drivers, etc.).
  - What is currently in memory? Which application or module? Produced by whom? What's the release version?
- Who is talking to whom? This refers to the communication between application components or to system components through events or function calls.
- More specific information about which application, module, process, or thread is using which portion of each type of resource.
- Information about the communication between various host and devices over the network.

Additional goodies offered by these utilities include logging capability, graphing, trend charting, alerts, event-based command execution, and so on.

Every operating system comes prepackaged with tools for monitoring system usage. There are also many tools available commercially or as shareware and freeware. These tools allow you to: see what is on your host computer; watch the activity of several servers from your own machine; and monitor traffic over the network.

If, however, you know the type of information you want to monitor but you can't find an appropriate tool readily available, talk to your development team and describe your specific need. They should be able to put one together for you, especially when they understand that it will help them to solve debugging or bug-analyzing problems.

Following are several examples of monitoring utilities available for the Windows operating systems. All have some form of documentation to assist you in understanding the various metrics collected and how to use the tools effectively:

- The System Monitor Utility (shown in Figure 12.4) can track system resource usage.

- The Performance Monitor (see Figure 12.5) can track various types of hardware activities, enabling you to collect and monitor various system metrics, such as process usage, hard disk usage, memory usage, application server transactions, transaction errors, and so on. It also offers additional goodies such as trend charting and alerting capability.

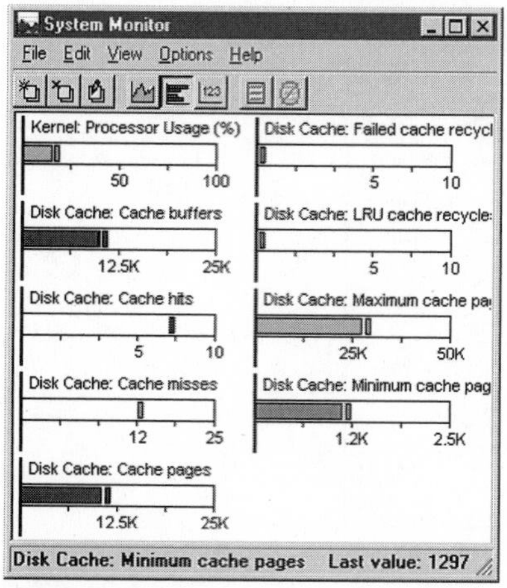

Figure 12.4 Windows System Monitor.

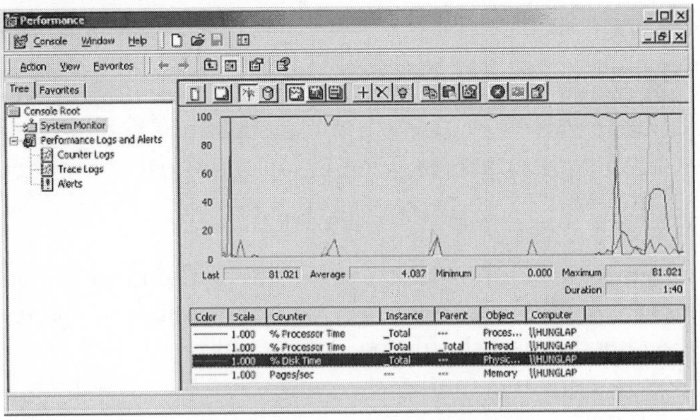

Figure 12.5 Windows Performance Monitor.

- Figure 12.6 shows the Event Viewer, a utility with logging capabilities, including Application Log, Security Log, and System Log. It enables you to configure those events you want to log to a file by setting up filters, views, and events related to an application, security, or system activities.

- Figure 12.7 shows a System Information utility that enables you to determine what is where, including hardware resources and software environment. For example, it shows you all the software modules currently loaded in memory.

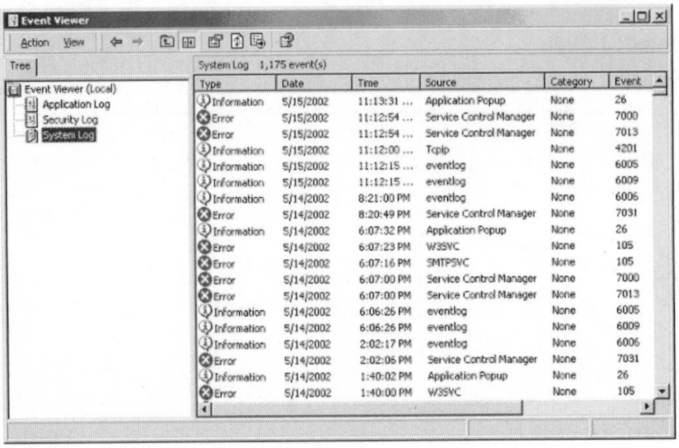

Figure 12.6 Windows Event Viewer.

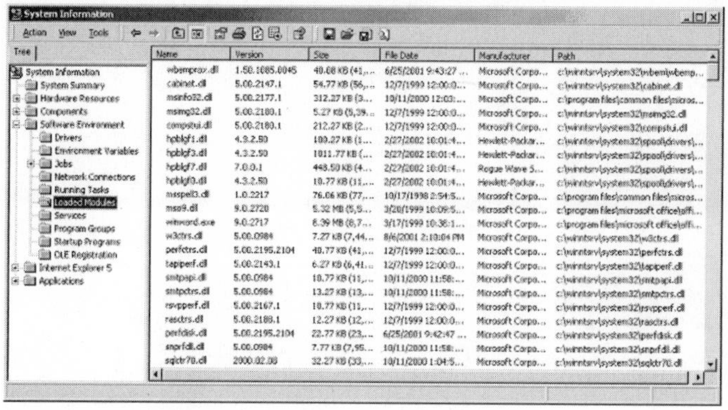

Figure 12.7   Windows System Information.

- Figure 12.8 shows another utility for finding system information.

- Windows Task Manager (shown in Figure 12.9) enables you to examine the current applications and other processes running, as well as CPU and memory usage metrics.

- KS HostMonitor 1.78 (downloadable from www.webattack.com/free-ware/system/fwmonitor.shtml) is a utility that enables you to monitor network and server activities.

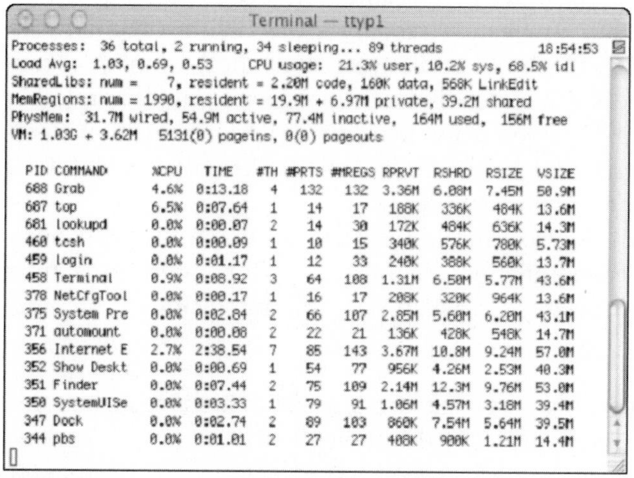

Figure 12.8   Terminal System Information.

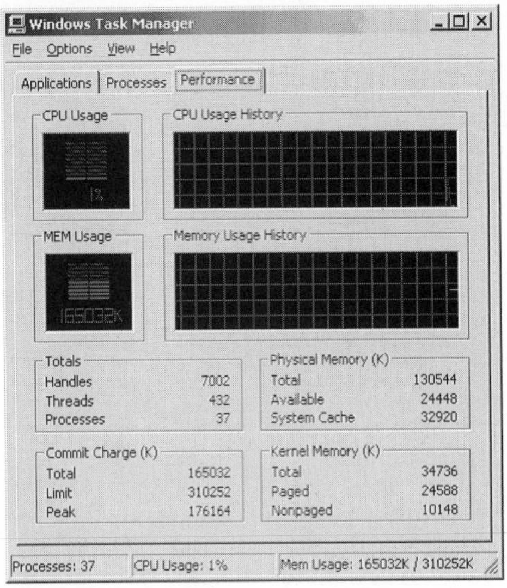

Figure 12.9 Windows Task Manager.

Testing a Web application for resource usage requires designing test cases to stress the usage of the server. During normal server usage, users will not often be accessing the same functions simultaneously; thus, in order to determine whether resources are properly used and released, test cases have to be created that attempt to use the same resource at the same time. Memory usage is usually the key resource. Other interesting resources are disk space, network bandwidth (including internal bandwidth between machines), number of connections to databases, and CPU cycles. External hardware devices are other resources that need to be considered for monitoring. An application hardwired to use only one printer might not be fast enough during peak volume times. (See Chapter 19 for more information.)

Testing for resource limits is also critical for system administration functions. Many system administration functions require stopping other users from accessing the system. The questions to ask in this situation include:

- Will this be acceptable?

- Can you stop or pause the server, allowing these functions to be handled without losing work being done by the other clients?

- Large systems may have several people working as a system administrator at the same time. Can multiple system administrators access the server properly?

Creating Test Interfaces or Test Drivers

Not all testing must be done using the same client interfaces that the final application will use. For our purposes, specific test interfaces can be created. Finished applications contain screens designed to help the user, but these are not the easiest or most complete way for a tester to access the application in order to test the different server-side components.

Typically, the "real" interface will have text and graphics that make rapid data entry difficult. The text and graphics can be removed to make a stream-lined set of screens available for testing. Doing so will enable faster load times and easier data entry. Although this is still black-box testing of the server soft-ware, it enables you to focus solely on the server-side testing without worry-ing about client-side problems.

Likewise, the final production screens may include error checking for data fields. Removing these checks allows a greater range of testing on the server, enabling two types of bad data to be sent to the server:

- *Out-of-range data.* For example, a person's age should not be a negative number. Often the client-side software will check the data for proper format and ranges before sending the data to the server. In addition, forms with missing data can also be sent to the server. For example, leaving a required field blank might cause database problems.

- *Data input tests.* As the application is revised, new screens may not con-tain the same client-side filtering of the data. If the server does not check and filter the data, errors will occur. Also, people will try to hack the system—Hackers will bypass the normal paths to enter data and defeat the client-side checking. So, we should try those techniques first.

Custom interfaces built for testing can also change the default options or add more options. These are useful ways to "tag" test data being put into the system. For example, you can create several new payment types to be used only during testing. Each different test case can have its own payment type. Instead of just Visa and MasterCard, for example, you can create, say, Test Team Card. If several persons are testing different parts of the application, every person can have a different payment type. This allows the testing team to verify test data and to selectively clean up the server's database after running tests.

Custom interfaces for testing also allows additional data to be sent back to the client. Copying log entries, SQL statements, session IDs, or any tracking data can help identify what was happening when a problem occurred. This data is useful for both the tester to spot problems, and for the developer to track down and debug the problem. When the test is successful, this data can be easily ignored.

A custom interface designed for testing can also be text-based, enabling it to be driven from a command-line, script or a Web page. Producing a message that will be sent to the server can be done without a GUI. The message can be sent to the server and the results examined without the need to fill in a screen. For example, assuming that we have a long and complex URL to type in, such as:

www.example.com/cgi-bin/S-zACH8Ztua6/ProdMenu.asp?s-10&c=4

we can make our testing job easier by writing some very simple HTML to make a custom interface to save time (see Figure 12.10). Normally, this URL could be typed in or copied and pasted directly into a browser's URL address field every time we needed to make that request. This saves time and makes the tests easily reproducible. You can produce a file with many different URLs to be tested and quickly edit the text to produce test cases for additional data conditions.

Pasting these URLs also makes client-side testing on multiple browsers much easier. To rapidly test many combinations, you can generate an HTML page wherein each of these test cases is a separate link. By selecting each link, the respective test is executed; the Back button will return you to this page to run the next test.

Figure 12.10 lists five made-up tests that link to complex URLs that, for the purposes of this example, we'll assume we need to run often. Listing 12.1 then shows the custom HTML code written to produce a custom page, or interface, to make testing them easier. Here, www.example.com/cgi-bin/ S-zLACH8ZTua6/ProdMenu.asp?s=10&c=4 forms a request to the server-side to fetch a Web page.

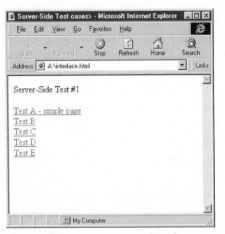

Figure 12.10   Custom test interface example.

```
<head><title>Server-Side Test cases</title></head>
<body>
Server-Side Test #1<p>

<a href="http://www.example.com/cgi-bin/S-
zLACH8ZTua6/ProdMenu.asp?s=10&c=4">
Test A - simple page</a><br>

<a href="http://www.example.com/cgi-bin/S-
zLACH8ZTua6/ProdMenu.asp?s=10&c=5">
Test B</a><br>

<a href="http://www.example.com/cgi-bin/S-
zLACH8ZTua6/ProdMenu.asp?s=10&c=6">
Test C</a><br>

<a href="http://www.example.com/cgi-bin/S-
zLACH8ZTua6/ProdMenu.asp?s=10&c=7">
Test D</a><br>

<a href="http://www.example.com/cgi-bin/S-
zLACH8ZTua6/ProdMenu.asp?s=10&c=8">
Test E</a><br>

</body>
```

Listing 12.1   Custom HTML page to drive server-side tests.

The Testing Environment

A setup for testing server software requires resources, including money. You will need multiple computers, network routers, monitors, cables, and places to put the equipment. You will need software for all these machines, sometimes several different versions of the same product for your compatibility testing. It is usually cheaper in the long run to not have to reinstall operating systems and databases on a regular basis. This may mean purchasing even more hardware.

Getting full-time system administration support will be more expensive. The IT staff of most companies is not prepared to continually reconfigure machines for testing purposes. Nor will restarting a testing database receive their highest priority. Therefore, either you will need dedicated systems administrators in the testing group, or everyone on the test team will need to learn many of these basic skills.

More often, the network you will be testing will belong to a smaller group of developers and testers. However, you still won't have easy control over the system under test. The servers may be in a different building, state, or country. If you crash the server, you may have a hard time getting it restarted. Asking for upgrades and patches will take longer. You will face an impossible obstacle when you request earlier versions to be installed.

Understanding what you will need for your testing environment, building the networks, acquiring all the software products, and getting everything working will take time. Often your equipment will be diverted to higher-priority groups. You will also need time to write your scripts and to build your custom test interfaces.

Fortunately, there are many ways to partition your test. You can start server testing early. Your scripts will drive the server before the client interfaces are ready. The developers will need the database schema early, so you can start testing them as well.

Working with Live Systems

Sometimes you will have to work on live production systems, and because your job is to break the application, when you do your job well, chances are you will bring the live system to its knees. In addition, your developers may be placing new code or patches directly onto the live system, meaning that end users may experience the untested code before you know that your developer has installed it. These issues quickly become high-risk problems for the organization.

Therefore, you may need to become involved in creating a robust release and deployment process to minimize the risks exposed by a poor development process. If it is inevitable that you have to deal with real-time live systems, you will need to build a strong process and devise a well-crafted policy for updating software in a timely but safe manner. The policy must be simple enough to make it easily enforceable. This might mean that you will have to develop staging servers, as well as a means to undo or roll back fixes that don't work.

Resetting the Server

During testing, the server will need to be stopped, reconfigured, and restarted many times. You will have to perform many of the tasks normally done by a system administrator—the difference being, however, that a system administrator typically has to restart a Web server once a month, whereas you, while testing, may need to restart it a dozen times in one afternoon. Thus, you will need to have simple tools to access the server and perform these tasks. These tools can be written before server testing begins. It is often best to have both a GUI tool and a command-line tool available. For example, a Web page can be written with links to applications. These applications will execute scripts to manage the Web server. Knowing the names of the command-line scripts will allow you to directly call the scripts when the browser is unavailable. You may also find that tools created for the system administrator are close to those you need, in which case you can modify them to default to the options you wish. You can also create "wrappers" (one-line scripts) with all the correct values predefined for your test environment.

These tools should include options to change the server's configuration file before restarting the server. A simple script using the command-line interface will enable running an automated test sequence through all the different configurations.

Listing 12.2 shows an example of a UNIX shell script used to start, run a test, and shut down for two different server configurations. Each additional test can be easily cut and paste to repeat the six lines that comprise the basic test structure (not elegant but it does the trick). The only edit required is to change the configuration file name and edit the log entry text.

```
#!/bin/csh
if /test/test_log exists then
      echo "test log exists"
      exit 1
endif

echo "Server Test Log - Testing Server Configurations" > /test/test_log
date > /test_log
server -stop
cp /test/configs/config.1 /server/config.rc
echo "start config 1" > /test/test_log
date  > /test/test_log
server -start
junit tests
server -stop
cp /test/configs/config.2 /server/config.rc
echo "start config 2" > /test/test_log
date  > /test/test_log
server -start
junit tests
echo "end - Testing Server Configurations" > /test/test_log
date  > /test/test_log
      exit
```

Listing 12.2   Example of a script to reset a server.

Using Scripts in Server-Side Testing

Due to the complex nature of server-side testing, it is useful to know how to use scripting languages, become familiar scripting techniques, and know how to apply them to testing software. Read Chapter 13 to learn some of the best practices in testing, as well as to discover scripting resources on the Internet. Be aware that you don't always have to write the script yourself. Knowing what you need and what is possible will enable you to ask developers for the help you need to be more effective.

Bibliography

LogiGear Corporation. *QA Training Handbook: Testing Web Applications.* Foster City, CA: LogiGear Corporation, 2003.
———— *QA Training Handbook: Testing Windows Desktop and Server-Based Applications.* Foster City, CA: LogiGear Corporation, 2003.
Microsoft Corporation. *Microsoft SQL Server 2000 Resource Kit.* Redmond, WA: Microsoft Press, 2001.
Orfali, Robert, Dan Harkey, Jeri Edwards. *Client/Server Survival Guide,* 3rd ed. New York: John Wiley & Sons, Inc., 1999.
Reilly, Douglas J. *Designing Microsoft ASP.NET Applications.* Redmond, WA: Microsoft Press, 2001.
———— *Inside Server-Based Applications.* Redmond, WA: Microsoft Press, 2000.

Additional Resources

"JUnit Best Practices—Techniques for Building Resilient, Relocatable, Multithreaded JUnit," by Andy Schneider,

www.javaworld.com/javaworld/jw-12-2000/jw-1221-junit_p.html.

Written for Java developers, this article discusses good and bad ways to use JUnit, a test framework for building and executing unit tests. The author offers practical recommendations and explains simple mechanisms to support automatic construction of composite tests multithreaded test cases.

"Diagnose Common Runtime Problems with hprof—Track Down the Culprits Behind Your Application Failures," by Bill Pierce,

www.javaworld.com/javaworld/jw-12-2001/jw-1207-hprof_p.html.

This article presents some easy-to-follow examples to demonstrate a useful profiling tool in Java2JDK called hprof's, which can be used to diagnose deadlock and memory leak issues in the code.

"Log It or Lose It—Log Events to the Windows NT Event Log with JNI," by Sunil Kumar and Nitin Nanda,

www.javaworld.com/javaworld/jw-09-2001/ jw-0928-ntmessages_p.html.

This article explains Java event logging in a Windows NT environment and how to enable a Java application to log messages to the NT Event Log.

JavaWorld.Com's Testing Article Listing Page,

www.javaworld.com/ channel_content/ jw-testing-index.shtml.

This page offers a number of articles on the topic of white-box testing, specifically for Java applications.

JavaWorld.Com's Thread Programming Article Listing Page,

www.javaworld.com/channel_content/jw-threads-index.shtml.

This page offers many articles on the topic of thread programming, specifically for Java applications. These articles are written for programmers rather than testers.

JavaWorld.Com's Java Testing Tool Listing Page,

www.javaworld.com/ javaworld/tools/jw-tools-testing.html.

This page lists several Java testing tools for Java developers.

Sitrata JProbe Thread Analyzer,

www.sitraka.com/software/jprobe/jprobethreadalyzer.html.

Java testing tools that can detect several classes of thread problems at the source-code level.

Testing Tools for Run-Time Testing

Microsoft Windows Application Verifier,

http://msdn.microsoft.com/library/default.asp?url=/library/en-us/ dnappcom/html/appverifier.asp.

A Windows application testing tool that offers an option for thread stack size checking.

Microsoft Windows Driver Verifier,

http://msdn.microsoft.com/library/ default.asp?url=library/en-us/ ddtools/hh/ddtools/dv_9pkj.asp.

A Windows driver testing tool that offers an option for deadlock detection.

Compuware JCheck Java Edition,

www.compuware.com/products/ devpartner/ java/jcheck.htm.

JCheck is a thread analyzer in DevPartner Java Edition that helps detect thread deadlocks and identify thread starvation and thrashing conditions.

Using Scripts to Test

Why Read This Chapter?

Using scripts to test Web applications gives us much flexibility in when and how we test. Scripts let us bypass the UI, giving us the ability to begin testing even before a UI is complete, or simply to access the server-side of the application under test directly. Scripts can also be used to automate routine system administration tasks, like copying or deleting files, as well as requesting, or checking on, system services. In addition, repetitive use or execution of the scripts can greatly increase testing productivity; and scripts enable us to accomplish testing tasks that cannot normally be done through the UI.

This chapter starts by discussing scripting in general, and what scripting can do for you. Then it describes a few useful ways you can use scripting as a solution to testing issues. The chapter describes several useful testing practices for scripting, and lists resources for learning a scripting language, places on the Web to download prewritten scripts, and general scripting resource Web sites.

Introduction

Chapter 5, "Web Application Components," discussed the use of scripts to build Web applications. Scripts can handle input forms, text validation, and many requests for Web services. Scripting can offer unique benefits in Web application development, both on the client-side and on the server-side, but as testers, we use scripting under very different circumstances: to test the application or the application server-side. We can use scripts to discover information about the system, such as available memory to make operating system requests through command-line execution; and to examine large amounts of data, such as log files and reports, looking for that proverbial "needle in a haystack."

A script contains an instruction or a sequence of instructions carried out by an interpreter. When we talk about scripts in this chapter, we mean: line commands, batch or shell scripts for Windows, UNIX, Linux, and others that offer an operating-system-specific interpreter; and scripts produced in languages such as Perl, VBScript, JavaScript, and Tcl, among others that require a language-specific interpreter (discussed at the end of the chapter).

System administrators have used scripting facilities for years, and to a lesser degree, so have testers. Many black-box testers are subject-matter experts, not technical experts. For example, you may have been an accountant, and now are testing a Web-enabled ERP (enterprise resource planning) accounting system. Nevertheless, learning and using a scripting language does not have to be a daunting task. After using it for a while, you may wonder how you ever got along without knowing how to script! Even experienced technology-based testers are always looking for new ways to do their work more efficiently.

Batch or Shell Commands

UNIX and DOS (Windows) commands are probably the easiest place to start when adding scripting to your test practice. Individual commands are typed into a command-line interface, which is a text-based interface, a nongraphical interface to the operating system, and an alternative to the graphical user interface (GUI), another common way for end users to "talk to" the computer. In a command-line interface, you type a command along with optional switches and parameters. When you hit the Return key, the command is then executed. For example, this command:

```
rm myfile.txt
```

will remove the file named myfile.txt from the current directory. This can be much quicker than opening a directory window, finding the file, and then dragging it to the trashcan. Every operating system comes with hundreds of commands ready to be used.

The following is a list of some of the basic and useful UNIX commands and their purpose:

cat. Short for concatenate, or show a file's contents to the screen (same as DOS *type*).

cd. Change directories.

chmod. Change file permissions (read- only to read-write, for example).

cksum. Check sum and count the bytes in a file.

cmp. Compares two files. Similar to diff, but works better than diff on binary files.

cp. Copy (in DOS, *copy*).

diff. Find differences between two files (in DOS, *fc*).

echo. Display a line of text.

find. Search for files in a directory hierarchy.

grep, egrep, fgrep. Print lines matching a pattern.

head. Output the first part of files.

tail. Output the last part of files.

ls. List contents of current directory.

ln. Make links between files.

mail. Send and receive mail.

man. Provide a detailed description of a command with examples of usage.

mkdir. Make a directory (same as DOS *md*).

more. Page through text one screen at a time.

mv. Move or delete a file. Rename (or "move") a file (same as DOS *ren*).

ping. Ask another computer if it is running.

ps. Report process status.

pwd. Print name of current/working directory.

rm. Remove a file. Remove (or "delete") a file (same as DOS *del*).

rmdir. Remove a directory (same as DOS *rd*).

sleep. Delay for a specified amount of time.

sort. Sort lines of text files.

touch. Change file timestamps.

tee. Read from standard input and write to standard output and files.

whereis. Locate the binary, source, and manual page files for a command.

who. Show who is logged on.

whoami. Print effective user ID.

which. Show full path of commands.

These are only a sampling among many, many more. For a list containing hundreds of UNIX commands, visit these two sites:

http://publib.boulder.ibm.com/cgi-bin/ds_form?view=Commands

www.rt.com/man

For Windows systems, which use MS-DOS commands, visit these two sites:

www.Microsoft.com/windows2000/en/server/help/ntcmds.htm

www.easydos.com/dosindex.html

These built-in programs are most often run in a *shell*, a program running on a terminal (or a terminal window) that provides access to the operating system. The shell acts as the interpreter between the command and the operating system. In Windows, we think of the familiar DOS prompt, and its command-line prompt: C:> (see Figure 13.1).

Figure 13.1   DOS command-line window.

From this window, you can start any Windows program. For example, enter

```
calc
```

to start the Windows Calculator program (see Figure 13.2).

Each line command executes an action. When you need to execute a series of actions, you can put them together in the form of a text file and save it as a script, or in this case a batch file. The script is a set of instructions and the line commands are the actions.

Batch Files and Shell Scripts

Batch files and shell scripts are text files that contain sequences of commands that allow you to manage files, set and modify system settings, and execute programs. In DOS, a batch file has the file name extension .BAT, as in AUTOEXEC.BAT. It takes several single line commands and bundles them.

Batch files are usually created because testers want to use them repeatedly. If, however, you need the bundle of commands only once, it would save time to execute them as a string of line commands. If you need to run the commands often you can save them in a text file, give it a name, and run it as often as you need. This is where the time-saving factor of using scripts can be tremendous.

Writing scripts also ensures that instructions will be executed the same way each time you run the scripts. With scripts you can also add logic or looping. The scripts you write do not need to be complex. Many useful scripts can be only two or three lines long. For example, the following script written for the C-shell, one of the common UNIX shells available, is used to quickly determine how much the Java source code has changed.

Figure 13.2   Executing Calculator program from the DOS window.

```
#!/bin/csh

set file = `find . -name '*.java' -print`
wc -l $file
```

These two lines of code count the total number of lines in all the Java source code for the project. By comparing the output of this short script with the previous release, you can determine how much new code is in this release and which classes have changed.

Scripting Languages

DOS batch files were designed to string commands together. Although they can become large and complex, they have limits on data manipulation capability and processing logic. We need more powerful scripting languages that provide more features, better control, and greater flexibility to accomplish more complex tasks. For example, assume you have a stored procedure that accesses database tables. You have to connect to the database and call or execute the stored procedure. You can't do that in a batch file, but you can use a scripting language as a facility to call the stored procedure.

There are a variety of scripting languages available today that give testers greater access to applications under test and other Application Programming Interfaces (API) and system services that are robust, powerful, flexible, and in many cases, free!

Writing in a scripting language is, essentially, computer programming in interpreted languages. There are many scripting languages and more are constantly being developed. Some of the most popular scripting languages for testers are: Perl, VBScript, Tcl, JavaScript, awk, sed, and Python, among others. Each language is designed to make it easier to solve certain classes of problems, so many people learn to use several different scripting languages.

Be aware that certain languages are especially good at specific tasks. For example, Perl is known for great text, data processing, and its support for TCP/IP service requests, which makes it very useful for testing Web applications.

Why Not Just Use a Compiled Program Language?

The answer is that compiled languages, like C, C++, Java, and Visual Basic, are more heavy-duty and often can be overkill for the testing tasks that we need to do. Furthermore, these more powerful languages are harder to learn, hence development in them incurs a higher overhead; finally, executables written in these languages may be intrusive to the application under test.

That said, compiled languages can be more appropriate for building test utilities and tools. From a simplistic point of view, programs in scripting languages are faster to write and debug but have much slower execution times and therefore lead to poor performance. Compiled languages execute faster and are more robust, but require much more programming overhead to get the job done.

What Should You Script?

Adding scripts to your testing process can happen gradually. The more you learn about scripting, the more ways you will think of to integrate scripts in your routine testing tasks.

The value of scripting will, undoubtedly, depend on the type of Web application you are testing, the types of tests you plan to execute, the test platform, and how much time you wish to invest in improving your scripting skills.

The next section describes some basic tasks often done in testing Web applications and shows how scripting can make those tasks possible or easier. It is not meant to be a comprehensive list of scripting possibilities, but rather to provide an introduction to the many ways that scripts can be helpful. There are many resources, free tutorials, and books available on using scripts to test, some of which are listed at the end of the chapter.

Application of Scripting to Testing Tasks

This section will take you through these examples of using scripts:

- Using them for system administration tasks.
- Discovering information about the system.
- Testing the server directly.
- Making system requests bypassing the UI.
- Examining logs.
- Comparing two test-result files.
- Executing tests faster and doing tests that could not be done manually.

System Administration: Automating Tasks

It is common practice to maintain the computers or test environments. Learning line commands and writing simple scripts can save you time doing these tasks and can also help you to ensure the tasks are executed the same way each time the script is run. Databases used by an application can also be reset for testing with SQL scripts or stored procedures. Scripts can put the database in a proper state before test execution, by adding, modifying, or deleting records.

A common situation you will face is setting up the test environment before a test. For this example, we'll write a four-line shell script to complete the task. Here is the scenario: Before a test is run, you may need to delete old log files, copy configuration files to the correct place, and download the latest build. All of these tasks can be done with a simple script, as shown here.

```
#!/bin/csh
# clean-up before testing product

cd ~tester/product
rm *.log
rm product.rc
mv /test-cases/product.rc .
```

This script is used before executing a test procedure to ensure the proper starting directory, erase the previous log file, and move the proper configuration file into the current test directory. During testing, it is easy to be distracted and forget one of these steps. Using this script, each step is completed in the correct order. If any of these steps should fail, such as the log file being set to read-only, preventing it from being deleted, a warning will be prompted.

Discovering Information about the System

There is a wealth of information you can learn about your network using line commands. From discovering how much memory is available to who is logged in to the network at any given time, simple line commands open a window into the working of the network.

For example, you may be executing tests and run into error messages reading "server not found" or "unable to locate server." The server under test may be offline, being maintained, or getting a new build installed, or you may have the wrong URL. How do you know if the machines are available or the URL is correct? The ping command can give you the status of a remote computer on the network. Usually, this is a simple command typed at the terminal window. The command requires only a single argument: the name of the remote computer or its IP address, as shown here. The results are shown in Figure 13.3.

```
ping qacity.com
```

In this case, the computer, qacity.com, is running. If your test cases required connecting to several computers, as shown previously in Figure 2.12 (a multi-server system), then you might want to check all the machines before starting your test. In this case, you could write a short script to check each computer, like this:

Figure 13.3   Using ping.

```
ping qacity.com
ping delphi.qacity.com
ping popper.qacity.com
```

CAUTION The same command will behave differently depending on which computer is executed. For example, the ping command will continue to send requests on some UNIX platforms. This requires the user to manually stop the ping program. This version running on DOS will automatically terminate.

Testing the Server Directly: Making Server-Side Requests

Testing Web applications from the client interface is limited, but server-side testing can complement client testing through the use of scripting. By using scripts, server-side functionality can be accessed directly.

In the next application example, the Web application under test has a configuration file that resides on the server to provide data to be used for the particular installation. Values such as administrator user names, e-mail addresses, and log file locations are stored in this configuration file. When the Web server is started, the configuration file is read. However, the file may contain incorrect information, leading to abnormal behavior. In such a case, you can create various configuration files that contain the boundary conditions you wish to test, and then use scripts to automate the process of running the Web server with these various configuration files (see the example script shown here).

Starting the server causes the configuration file to be opened and read. These values are then used to initialize variables in the program (server software). Bad data can cause error messages to the log and erratic behavior, including crashes.

```
#!/bin/csh

server -stop
cp /test/configs/config.1 /server/config.rc
server -start

server -stop
cp /test/configs/config.2 /server/config.rc
server -start

# add additions configurations to be tested here

server -stop
    exit
```

This script starts the Web server using several different configuration files. In order to test a new configuration, all you need to do is modify and save an existing configuration file, then add the necessary lines to the test script to copy the new configuration file to the correct directory and start the Web server.

Be aware that the script may fail silently. The server might not be able to process a certain configuration file and will simply continue to the next test. To determine success of this test, you will need to check something else, possibly the application log files. (See the upcoming section "Examining Data: Log Files and Reports," for more information on log files.)

Working with the Application Independent of the UI

The earlier we can start testing, the better. But one of the problems with starting testing early is that we may have to wait until the UI is functional enough to test. A workaround is to bypass the UI, for example by sending a request to the Web server directly. Using scripting languages like VBScript or Perl, we can broaden our test toolset with powerful capabilities, such as making function calls, thus building our own interfaces to the server's software.

The following sample VBScript is used to create an object to send http requests, in this case to the server www.qacity.com. It checks the http status, that is, whether the file can be found. You probably are familiar with the "Message 404-File not Found." Message 200 means the file is found, and executed correctly, if it is a script such as an ASP or CGI. We normally do not see that message as the requested file will display in the browser. You can write a script to request a set of pages.

This sample script calls an ASP (Active Server Page) function, GET. If the script runs correctly, the response will be that the ASP ran successfully. This script will also write the result—successful or not—to standard output. The result can be read manually or with another script to verify the test output.

```
<job>
<script language="VBScript">

dim objHTTP
set objHTTP = CreateObject("MSXML2.ServerXMLHttp")

objHttp.Open "GET","http://www.qacity.com"
objHttp.Send

if objhttp.Status = 200 then
      WScript.Echo "The page was called successfully"
else
      WScript.Echo "The response status was " & objHttp.Status
end if

'write the response content to a text file
dim objFS,objTS
set objFS = CreateObject("Scripting.FileSystemObject")
set objTS = objFS.CreateTextFile("c:\output.txt")
objTS.WriteLine objHttp.ResponseText

</script>
</job>
```

This VBScript begins by creating an object named MSXML2.ServerXML-Http. Then it calls the page. If the page is found, the status sent as a response to the request will be 200. If the page is not found, the message response will be 404 or some other 4XX or 5XX response. We test to see if the response is 200 or some other response. If the response is other than 200, that response message will be printed to the text file. The end of the script creates the text file on the C: drive.

Examining Data: Log Files and Reports

Logs generated by the system and by the application under test are excellent sources for detecting and analyzing bugs. Operating systems, e-mail servers, database servers, and Web servers all create log files. These data records include many kinds of data that may be important for determining how the system is performing or for who is using the system and what they were trying to do. More specifically, a log file can contain data such as: server requests, warnings, HTML pages visited, counts and IP addresses of unique users of a Web application, events, files created, user activities, which APIs are called, and many other pieces of data, all of which might be timestamped for later analysis. (Refer back to Chapter 12, "Server-Side Testing," for more information on server logs.)

But saving all this information can make the logs very long and hard to read. Instead, you can create scripts to search the log files for specific text strings that might indicate potential problems. The following script is used to routinely check after running the test suite to determine if any unexpected events were written to the log file. The grep command is used to extract all the error, warning, and stack trace log entries from the log and put them into a file to be analyzed. (Later in the chapter, we will use grep again to pull text out of a file and place it in another file to be read or compared.)

```csh
#!/bin/csh
# check product log for errors and warnings

if ( $#argv == 0 ) then
   echo "usage: program-name logfile-name"
   exit 1
endif

set file=$argv[1]
date
grep -ins ' error ' $file
grep -ins ' warning ' $file
grep -ins ' stack trace ' $file
```

During the development phase, this script can be run as part of the nightly build, after unit and regression testing, and any output can be e-mailed to interested developers and testers on the project. Testers can use this script after running test cases to catch some types of abnormal behavior that might or might not have produced a visible defect.

Using Scripts to Understand Test Results

Determining when a test produces the expected result can be difficult. Often, running a test will produce large amounts of output—too much data to be read, compared to the expected result, and understood by the tester. Using scripts, we can extract the relevant data from the output of a test and produce understandable reports.

The most commonly used utility for doing comparisons in UNIX is diff. This utility compares two text files line by line and provides a list of all the differences. Certain Web pages returned to the client's browser should be the same every time. Even when the server must gather information about the user, the returning HTML page should have the same data incorporated into the page. Testing to see that the same information is always returned often means looking at the page, which is both time-consuming and error-prone (not to mention boring). However, the tester can use the diff utility to compare this Web page to a previously known correct version:

```
diff correct-data/thisfile.html current-test/thisfile.html
```

Test comparisons are seldom this simple. The two files may be nearly the same but still have too many differences to make diff useful. You can modify one or both of these files before using diff. This is called *filtering the inputs*. Editing data before inputting, reviewing, or comparing is called *filtering*. You extract the needed data and discard the remainder.

The following script example is used to remove timestamps and other nonrelevant data that may change each time the test is executed. You can also filter the output.

```
diff correct-data/thisfile.html current-test/thisfile.html > current-
test/test-diff.out
diff correct-data/test-diff.out current-test/test-diff.out

rm current-test/test-diff.out
```

In this example, the output of the test is first compared to the output of a correct and verified execution of the test, often called the "Golden Master." You would expect several differences (too many to check by hand); however, these differences are always the same. You can then compare that the current changes are the same as the changes in the previous (good) execution.

The benefit of such a script is that the comparison is quicker and more accurate than trying to view the HTML page. When viewing the page, take notes to remind you what the page should look like. This test will compare everything and let you know if any changes have taken place.

The diff command is not the only way to compare text files. Several commands and tools are available to enable you to compare many different types of files, including binary files. You can also write simple scripts to compare graphics data, text field labels, any files, such as gif or bmp files or database content.

NOTE For an expanded discussion on automated comparison testing, read *Software Test Automation* by Mark Fewster and Dorothy Graham (Addison-Wesley, 1999) Chapter 4, "Automated Comparison."

Using Scripts to Improve Productivity

The most common use of scripts in testing is to improve productivity. This section describes two examples of scripting applications to improve productivity.

A Script to Test Many Files

Sometimes you test to check that the information is correct. Again, a simple script can save you time and help gather all the information. A common but mundane problem for testing Web applications might be to check all the copyright notices on every page. The following script prints out the copyright line from every HTML page in a certain directory. This makes reviewing each copyright a quick task.

```
set file = `find . -name '*.html' -print`
grep -ins 'copyright' $file
```

Grep, a common UNIX command for finding a string in a file, is used in this script to display only those files that contain the word "copyright." The script will not display files that have no copyright information or files where "copyright" is misspelled. Note that this checker can have many grep commands and thus search for many different real or potential problems.

When you hear about a bug in a library or system function, this type of search allows you to quickly check if this feature is being used in your application. Because the feature isn't used today doesn't mean your developer might not need to use this feature or command in the future. Putting these checks into a script that is run on a regular basis will catch the fact that this feature is now being used.

Searching the program files can be used to help the team validate the test planning process. By searching the source code, you can determine which features are being used and how complete your test planning is. For example, in Java, by searching on "throw" and "catch," you can uncover error-handling conditions to test. A search for "synchronization" can help uncover multithread issues that will require additional testing.

A Set of Scripts That Run Many Times

The ability to quickly write a script and then execute that script as a test provides a powerful means to create reusable tests. Once a test is written, a loop can be added to allow the first test to expand, covering many different boundary conditions. For example, in a script to test a mail server, the application must handle many variations for the To: field. A single script can read a data file containing all the names to be tested. This includes checking for special characters, mail lists, multiple names, and separators between names. Because this test is driven from a script, you can easily add more tests when new requirements are added, when requirements change, or when you realize an important test case was forgotten.

Since these tests have been automated, the test case script can be included in the project's acceptance-into-testing suite. These tests can be executed with every new build.

Using Perl, Tcl/Expect, or shell scripts is an effective and low-cost means to produce tests. It also has the advantage that many programmers can quickly review your tests and understand how to reproduce any problems found with these tests. The output of these tests can be written to a file or sent to the standard output. It is a good practice to include timestamps with the output—this allows correlation with system and program logs.

Executing Tests That Cannot Be Run Manually

There are certain tests that cannot be executed manually. The best example of that class of tests is a load test. Placing a load on your application can simply be a matter of repeatedly running your scripts. Scripts can be nested; that is, they can call other scripts. So you can create a simple loop that repeatedly runs your test scripts. The following script executes these scripts: test_001.csh and test_002.csh 1,000 times each.

```csh
#!/bin/csh

@ counter = 0
while (counter <= 1000)
      @ counter++
      test_001.csh
      test_002.csh
end
chk_log.csh
```

In a networked client-server application, running all the scripts from the same machine will limit the testing you can perform. This is because one machine might not be adequate to create race conditions, and is limited in the number of requests it can make. However, a script can be executed simultaneously on several different machines, simulating several clients accessing the server. Care must be taken when performing a load test, as a load test can easily and inadvertently become a denial-of-service attack on your system.

One method of implementing a load test is to use Perl scripts to simulate a Web browser, opening up a port and sending requests to a Web server. One script can open up multiple connections to simulate multiple users accessing a Web server simultaneously. (See Chapter 19, "Performance Testing," for more on performance testing.)

Scripting Project Good Practice

Most scripts are simple, very short pieces of code written to do a simple set of tasks. These scripts do not need a detailed plan or scheduling. As you find scripts becoming more useful, you will start to compile dozens of different scripts, each one tailored to a specific task. Then a naming structure becomes important; you will want to use names that are easy to remember and recognize, as your scripts may become popular, and other testers may want to use them. Good scripts for maintaining the system will soon be shared with developers as well. A few simple suggestions will help you and your team use scripts more effectively and increase the scripts' lifetime.

- *Scripts are code.* When you are writing scripts, you become a developer.
- *Version and source control your code.* Use version-tracking software.
- *Build your scripts for reuse.* You do not have to continually "reinvent the wheel." Short scripts that perform only a limited number of functions can become the reusable building blocks for creating more complex scripts.
- *Download prewritten scripts if possible.* There are a lot of these scripts available (see References for Batch files, Perl scripts, etc., at the end of this chapter).
- *Establish style and convention guidelines (i.e., naming conventions for script variables) before you start scripting.* This will make it easier for different members of the testing team to understand each other's scripts, and may also help you understand your own scripts if you haven't used them for some time.

Scripting Good Practice

- Standardize header format and documentation for all scripts. Some of this information will be standardized by using version-tracking software.
  - Author
  - Date
  - Purpose
  - Parameters
  - Valid input/expected output
  - Other data or files needed
- Set guidelines for applicationwide error handling.
- Keep the size of scripts to a minimum.
- Describe the function. Specifically:
  - List one clear, single purpose.
  - Write common functions for reusability.
- Structure scripts for ease of reading, understanding, and maintenance.
- Avoid hard-coded values by parameterizing data whenever possible. Putting real data—for example, path names, user IDs, passwords, maximum data values, text data, and so on—(into a script will, over time, cause the scripts to fail as those values change, meaning you will need to spend extra time debugging your scripts. Keeping data outside the script will make script maintenance easier.
- Pay attention to results format. Make script output or logs readable and understandable.

Resource Lists

General Resources for Learning More about Scripting

About.com: Batch and scripting tips, help and ideas. Contains many links.
http://windows.about.com/cs/batchscriptingtips/index.htm

Many free tutorials: learn SQL, VBScript, JavaScript, and more
www.w3schools.com

Danny Faught, Tejas Consulting references:
Writing shell scripts:
www.tejasconsulting.com/sqamag/shell.html

Mastering Lessons in Scripting
At STQE Magazine
www.tejasconsulting.com/stqe/a_lesson_in_scripting.pdf

Scripts in My Toolbelt
Pdf downloadable from: www.tejasconsulting.com/#resources

Integrating Perl 5 into Your Software Development Process
www.tejasconsulting.com/papers/iworks98/integrating_perl.html

Windows Script Host (WSH)

http://msdn.microsoft.com/scripting

To get WSH as a download to your computer
www.microsoft.com/msdownload/VBScript/scripting.asp

WSH information, resources and sample scripts from Annoyances.org
www.annoyances.org/exec/show/wsh

Labmice.net: Windows Scripting Host Resources
www.labmice.net/scripting/WSH.htm

Windows Script Host Bazaar: Information, resources, and sample scripts for many languages

www.borncity.com/WSHBazaar/WSHBazaar.htm

win32scripting: Resources and sample scripts in many scripting languages

http://cwashington.netreach.net

Batch and Shell

developerWorks Linux using bash shell scripts for testing for function testing

www-106.ibm.com/developerworks/library/l-bashfv.html

List Site of Batch Links: Batch Bookmarks

www.fpschultze.de/bss.htm

DOS Batch Language: A personal view

http://gearbox.maem.umr.edu/~batch/batchtoc.htm

Horst Schaeffer's Batch Pages: downloadable batch files

http://home.mnet-online.de/horst.muc

Mapping DOS batch files to Unix shell scripts

www.tldp.org/LDP/abs/html/dosbatch.html

Unix Shell Script Tutorial and Reference

www.injunea.demon.co.uk/pages/page203.htm

MS-DOS Help and Commands

www.computerhop.com/msdos.htm

Perl

Perl.com is the publisher: O'Reilly Computer Books Perl reference site

www.perl.com

Perl Mongers: Many links for all Perl users. Perl Mongers is a not-for-profit Perl advocacy group.

www.perl.org

Robert's Perl Tutorial

www.sthomas.net/roberts-perl-tutorial.htm

Learn Perl: a multipart series from Linux Gazette

www.linuxgazette.com/issue61/okopnik.html

Take 10 Minutes to Learn Perl

www.geocities.com/SiliconValley/7331/ten_perl.html

Very detailed reference list from author of *Take 10 Minutes to Learn Perl*

www.geocities.com/SiliconValley/7331/perl.html

Tcl

Tcl and all of these extensions are available on many platforms and are free:

www.scriptics.com

AWK

Working with AWK

www.canberra.edu.au/~sam/whp/awk-guide.html

How to use AWK

http://sparky.rice.edu/~hartigan/awk.html

Learn SQL

A Gentle Introduction to SQL

www.dcs.napier.ac.uk/~andrew/sql

SQL Introduction

www.w3schools.com/sql/sql_intro.asp

Interactive/Online SQL Tutorial with SQL Interpreter and live practice database

www.sqlcourse.com

JDBC Short Course: SQL Primer

http://developer.java.sun.com/developer/onlineTraining/Database/
JDBCShortCourse/jdbc/sql.html

SQL Examples

www.itl.nist.gov/div897/ctg/dm/sql_examples.htm

Where to Find Tools and Download Scripts

Visual Basic Developers Resource Centre

www.mvps.org/vbnet

As listed above for online courses, this site also has tools, sample and
downloadable scripts, and references.

www.w3schools.com

There are several programs available to provide UNIX commands and
shells in the Windows environment:

http://sources.redhat.com/cygwin/download.html

Tools and utilities for debugging and testing to download

www.hotscripts.com/Tools_and_Utilities/Debugging_and_Testing/

Bibliography and Useful Reading

Anderson, Gail, and Paul Anderson. *UNIX C Shell Field Guide.* Englewood
Cliffs, NJ Prentice Hall, 1986.

Fewster, Mark, and Dorothy Graham, *Software Test Automation.* Harlow,
England: Addison-Wesley, 1999.

Barron, David, *The World of Scripting Languages.* New York: John Wiley & Sons,
Inc., 2000.

Libes, D. *Exploring Expert.* Sebastopol, CA: O'Reilly & Associates, 1995.

Ousterhouse, J. *Tcl and the Tk Toolkit.* Upper Saddle River, NJ: Addison-Wesley,
1994.

CHAPTER

14

Database Tests

Why Read This Chapter?

All Web-based data access applications require database servers. To effectively plan for database testing and the analysis of database-related errors, it is useful to understand key database technology concepts, how Web server components interact with the database components, and other testing issues.

Introduction

This chapter offers an introduction to database components, application-database interaction, data warehouses, and data marts. Technical terms and examples that are useful in improving test planning and bug-report communication are also discussed. Databases play an important role in Web application technology. They house the content that Web applications manage—fulfilling user requests for data storage and record queries. Understanding how databases operate within Web applications is essential to effective database testing. Databases are repositories that are organized in such a way that makes it easy to manage and update the data they contain. One of the database technologies commonly used in Web-based applications is the *relational database*. Relational databases are tabular databases that can be easily reorganized and queried. Additionally, in a Web environment, the term *distributed database* is used to refer to databases that are dispersed over multiple servers on a network.

Two common approaches used to address the needs of target users are *online transaction processing* (OLTP) and *online analytical processing* (OLAP). Online transaction processing is transaction-oriented. The design objective is to support users who need access to systems to process sales or other types of transactions. An example of an OLTP-type of application is an e-commerce system where sales transactions are processed between buyers and merchants. In contrast, OLAP is intended for users who need access to systems such as data warehouses and data marts to obtain various types of metrics or analytical reports. Figure 14.1 shows an example of OLTP versus OLAP design. Three databases containing operational information are used for product sales, training registration, and purchasing (OLTP).

A data warehouse collects and transforms the raw data from the operational databases and stores it in a read-only informational database. This information is used to support decision-making processes (OLAP). Data replication executes every hour, 24/7. Data warehouse information is further parsed and distributed to data marts that are designed for sales and fulfillment departments to help in marketing expenditure and inventory control decisions.

Data warehouses are large databases that aggregate and process information from multiple databases. The data is stored in a format that supports various analytical needs. Data marts are customized databases normally derived from a data warehouse that has been formatted to meet the needs of specific workgroups. Data warehouses are structured around data. Data marts are structured around user needs. Data warehouses also allow Web sites to catalog large amounts of user profile data, e-commerce purchases, use and session data information, trends, and statistics. Data warehouses are large databases that aggregate information from multiple databases. Raw data is transformed via a filtering process and stored in a format that accommodates the database designer's informational needs. Generally, the data warehousing process supplies data marts (discussed next) or users with the data they require. Data warehouses are commonly referred to as *informational* databases.

Data marts are informational databases that have been custom-formatted to meet the needs of specific workgroups. They differ from data warehouses, which are structured around data, in that they are built around the needs of users. Generally, both database types are read-only. They may be used to collect database activity statistics, such as numbers of calls, page hits, sources of hits, MIME types, header names, and so on.

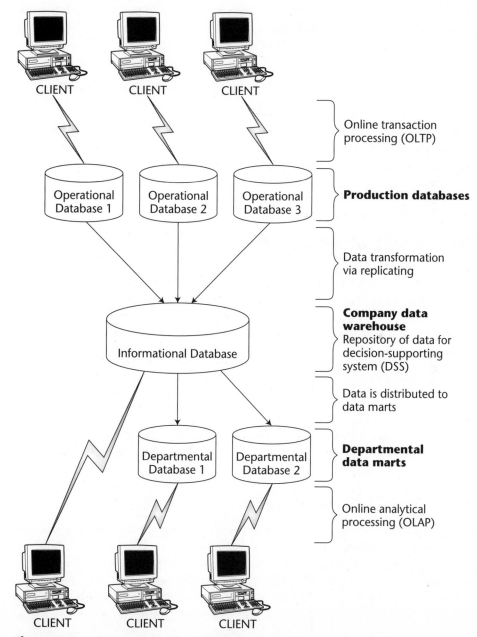

Figure 14.1   OLTP versus OLAP (data warehouse and data mart) example.

There are two ways to copy and update databases. With *synchronous updates,* changes in the operational database immediately affect the informational database. With *asynchronous updates,* changes in the operational database are uploaded to the informational database at regular time intervals.

Data warehouses can be designed to selectively collect data about operational activities in an OLTP system. The data can then be transferred to an OLAP system where it can be used for reporting, analysis, and decision support. Information stored in data warehouses is typically summarized, historical, read-only data. The goal of such a design is to improve query performance for decision-supporting systems (DSSs).

Several different data extraction processes may be implemented:

- Subsets of rows and columns may be configured to copy data from a source database to a target database.

- Aggregations of data, such as summaries or number of hourly transactions, may be copied from a source database to a target database.

- Data that are sent to target databases may be derived via calculations on raw-source data.

Relational Database Servers

Relational databases organize data into tables, records, and fields. They provide data storage and data access to clients upon request. Typical services include table and record creation, deletion, modification, data filtering, and sorting. Relational database servers consist of two components:

- *Structured Query Language (SQL).* Structured Query Language (see the definition in the following subsection) offers front-end query commands used for writing, retrieving, and manipulating data in two-dimensional table formats.

- *Physical data.* Physical data is stored in *relational database management systems* (RDBMSs), which offer powerful storage access schemes.

Structured Query Language

Structured Query Language is a programming language that enables users to access and manipulate data at runtime. Application developers and database administrators use SQL to design data tables, objects, indexes, views, rules, and data access controls. Using English-based commands or statements, SQL can maximize database flexibility and system performance while enforcing certain required security measures. Other programming languages, such as

Java, C, C++, and Visual Basic, can integrate SQL commands to enable data connectivity and data manipulation features.

SQL statements are instructions sent to the database engine. The database engine will parse the statements and execute commands based on these instructions.

The statements are often batched together to perform a task, such as creating a database, creating tables, populating data into tables, and so on. In these cases, the order of the statements may be important. SQL statements also share the problems of other runtime, interpreted languages of not being checked for syntactical correctness before execution.

Database Producers and Standards

The key players of the SQL server application market are Sybase, Microsoft, Oracle, IBM, and Informix. Most SQL server applications support features that are based on one or more of the following standards: ANSI SQL89, SQL92, and SQL99. Although an in-depth analysis of these standards is beyond the scope of this book, brief descriptions of each follow:

SQL89. Published in 1989, this is a revised version of the original SQL standard that was published in 1986 by ANSI and ISO. SQL89 supports the creation of tables, indices, views, and referential integrity (the ability to add constraints using PRIMARY KEY, FOREIGN KEY, and REFERENCE clauses within table and column definitions). Support for Embedded Static SQL was also added with this standard.

SQL92. SQL92 introduced many new features such as support for embedded SQL in additional languages, additional data types, advanced error handling, and so on.

SQL99. This standard added many new features to the existing one.

Database Extensions

Database extensions are proprietary features that increase database functionality. Stored procedures, triggers, and rules are examples of database extensions. Most SQL servers support database extensions of one sort or another. Unfortunately, the extensions supported by one vendor are often incompatible with the extensions supported by other vendors.

Stored procedures are compiled SQL statements. Stored within databases, these procedures can be called upon by name as needed. They also accept input parameters. They are analogous to *subroutines* or *functions* in traditional programming terminology. To improve programming productivity (and, sometimes, to intentionally introduce incompatibility), database vendors often include stored procedures that perform common database services. Stored procedures are used to perform many tasks internal to a database, including selecting, copying, and modifying data in the database; performing audits; or sending notifications by calling triggers when data is changed.

A *trigger* is a type of stored procedure that is executed when an event occurs. For example, a trigger may be executed when a certain table is modified. Databases often use triggers to modify data during SQL updates, inserts, and deletes.

Rules define restrictions on the values of table fields and columns. Rules are used to enforce business-specific constraints. Entered data that do not meet predefined rules (e.g., values that do not fall within an acceptable range) are rejected or handled appropriately.

Defaults are defined values that are automatically entered into fields when no values are explicitly entered.

Example of SQL

Following is a data insertion example that includes data entry for a specific database field. The example includes a subsequent query for the same data, illustrating how SQL databases are created and later utilized.

1. First, create a table to store information about company sales staff. Avoid creating duplicate IDs within the same table.

```
CREATE TABLE staff
(id INT, city CHAR(20), state CHAR(2), salary INT, name CHAR(20))
```

2a. Populate the STAFF table using INSERT statements.

```
INSERT INTO staff (id, city, state, salary, name) VALUES
(13, 'Phoenix', 'AZ', 33000, 'Bill')
INSERT INTO staff (id, city, state, salary, name) VALUES
(44, 'Denver', 'CO', 40000, 'Bob')
INSERT INTO staff (id, city, state, salary, name) VALUES
(66, 'Los Angeles', 'CA', 47000, 'Mary')
```

2b. As an alternate to creating the table directly (as in step 2a), you can populate the STAFF table using a stored procedure.

```
/* Create stored procedure that accepts parameters for inserting
records */
CREATE PROCEDURE add_staff (@P1 INT, @P2 CHAR(20), @P3 CHAR(2), @P4
INT, @P5 CHAR(20))
AS INSERT INTO staff
VALUES (@P1, @P2, @P3, @P4, @P5)
/* Inserting 3 records with created stored procedure */
add_staff 13, 'Phoenix', 'AZ', 33000, 'Bill'
add_staff 44, 'Denver', 'CO', 40000, 'Bob'
add_staff 66, 'Los Angeles', 'CA', 47000, 'Mary'
```

3a. Query for all entries in the STAFF table. SQL statements (see Figure 14.2).

```
SELECT * FROM STAFF
```

ID	CITY	STATE	SALARY	NAME
13	Phoenix	AZ	33000	Bill
44	Denver	CO	40000	Bob
66	Los Angeles	CA	47000	Mary

Figure 14.2 Query results.

3b. Query for all entries in the STAFF table using the stored procedure (see Figure 14.3).

```
/* Create a stored procedure that does not use parameters */
CREATE PROCEDURE all_staff
AS SELECT * FROM staff
/* Query for all entries in the STAFF table */
all_staff
```

ID	CITY	STATE	SALARY	NAME
13	Phoenix	AZ	33000	Bill
44	Denver	CO	40000	Bob
66	Los Angeles	CA	47000	Mary

Figure 14.3 Query results (comparative selection).

4. Query staff with salaries higher than $35,000 (selecting only certain rows that meet the query criteria) (see Figure 14.4).

```
SELECT * FROM staff WHERE salary > 35000
```

ID	CITY	STATE	SALARY	NAME
44	Denver	CO	40000	Bob
66	Los Angeles	CA	47000	Mary

Figure 14.4 Query results (column-based selection).

5. Query only ID, CITY, and STATE columns for all entries (selecting only certain columns) (see Figure 14.5).

```
SELECT id, city, state FROM staff
```

ID	CITY	STATE
13	Phoenix	AZ
44	Denver	CO
66	Los Angeles	CA

Figure 14.5 Query results (column and comparative selection).

6. Query only ID, CITY, and STATE of staff with salary higher than $35,000 (see Figure 14.6).

```
SELECT id, city, state FROM staff
WHERE salary > 35000
```

ID	CITY	STATE
44	Denver	CO
66	Los Angeles	CA

Figure 14.6 Query results.

7. Create a trigger to notify when there is a change to the table.

```
/* Create a trigger to send an email to a Sales Manager
alias when there is a change in the staff table. */
CREATE TRIGGER DataChangeTr
ON staff
FOR INSERT, UPDATE, DELETE
AS
/* Send an email to the address SALESMGR with change status message
*/
EXEC master..xp_sendmail 'SALESMGR', 'Data in the staff table has
been changed.'
GO
```

8. Create and bind (associate) defaults.

```
/* Create a default to be bound (associated) to the name column. It
means that the default value for the name column in the staff table
will be "Unassigned" */
CREATE DEFAULT name_default as 'Unassigned'
```

```
GO
sp_bindefault name_default, 'staff.name'
GO
```

9. Create and bind rules.

```
/* Create a rule to be bound to a new user-defined data type
age_type. By binding the age_rule to the age_type data type, the
entered value will be constrained to > 18 and < 65. */
sp_addtype age_type, int, 'not null'
GO
CREATE RULE age_rule
AS @age_type > 18 and @age_type < 65
GO
sp_bindrule age_rule, age_type
```

This sample code was written for a specific database, Microsoft SQL in this case. While SQL is a standard language, every implementation for every target database often introduces slightly different conventions. For example, PL/SQL is a procedural language extension to SQL for use with Oracle databases. T-SQL (Transact-SQL) is an extension of SQL for use with Microsoft and Sybase databases. An SQL script written for one database product will most likely produce errors when migrated to a new database platform.

Client/SQL Interfacing

Client applications may be built from one of several different programming languages. There are two main approaches to integrating these programming languages with the execution of SQL queries: (1) embedded SQL (ESQL) and (2) SQL call-level interface (CLI).

Embedded SQL statements must be precompiled for the target programming language and target database (using vendor-specific precompilers). Structured Query Language statements must be recompiled for each supported SQL vendor. Every change made to source code requires recompilation of all vendor-specific SQL statements. Therefore, embedded SQL statements complicate application installation and deployment. They make the development of commercial-off-the-shelf (COTS) products more challenging.

With SQL CLI (as opposed to ESQL), applications execute SQL statements and stored procedures to access data.

Microsoft Approach to CLI

Open Database Connectivity (ODBC) is a Microsoft version of SQL CLI. As illustrated in Figure 14.7, it is used for accessing data in heterogeneous environments of relational and nonrelational database management systems (DBMSs). Think of ODBC as a transfer protocol that is used to move data between Web applications and SQL servers. Open Database Connectivity is based on the CLI specifications of the SQL access group. In theory, it provides an open, vendor-neutral means of accessing data that is stored in disparate PC and mainframe databases. With ODBC, application developers may enable an application to simultaneously access, view, and modify the data of multiple database types.

As illustrated in Figure 14.8, Microsoft's object-oriented approach to CLI is through OLE DB's ActiveX Data Objects (ADO). OLE DB is Microsoft's application program interface (API). It offers applications access to multiple data sources. OLE DB offers Microsoft SQL ODBC capabilities and access capabilities to data types other than MS SQL.

ActiveX Data Objects is an object-oriented interface that provides data access features to applications via object and class interfaces instead of procedural APIs. The data request process runs as follows: initialize OLE, connect to a data source object, execute a command, process the returned results, release the data source object, and uninitialize OLE. For example, if the Web application under test supplies data to users with an Oracle database, you would include ADO program statements in an Active Server Page- (ASP-) based HTML file. When a user submits requests for a page with data from the database, the requested page would include appropriate data returned from the database, obtained using ADO code. To make this work, Microsoft and database suppliers provide a program interface layer between the database and Microsoft's OLE DB. OLE DB is the underlying system service of ADO that a developer uses.

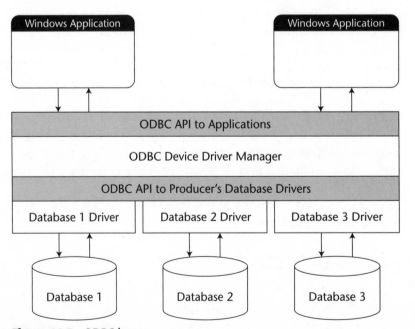

Figure 14.7   ODBC layers.

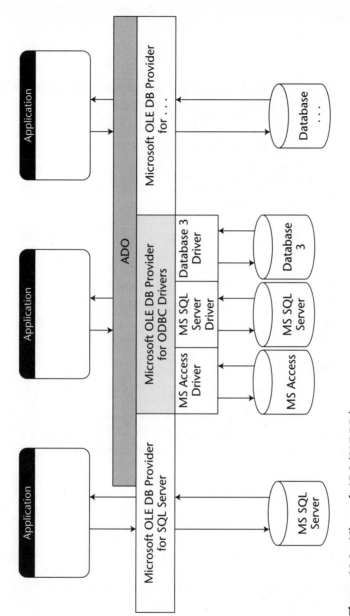

Figure 14.8   Microsoft ADO/OLE DB layers.

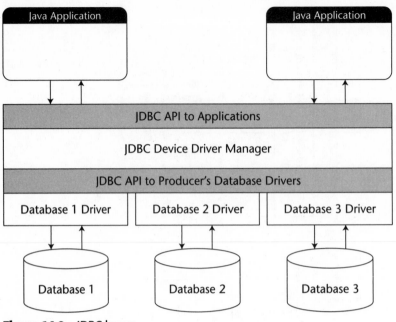

Figure 14.9   JDBC layers.

Java Approach to CLI

As illustrated in Figure 14.9, the Java object-oriented approach to CLI is *Java Database Connectivity* (JDBC). Similar to Microsoft's approach, JDBC provides a CLI that can be accessed via an object interface. The JDBC provides two sets of standard interfaces: one for application developers and the other for database developers.

Testing Methods

Database testing includes the testing of actual data (content) and database integrity, to ensure that data is not corrupted and that schemas are correct, as well as the functionality testing of the database applications (e.g., Transact-SQL components). SQL scripting is generally used to test databases. Although not all databases are SQL-compliant, the vast majority of data hosting is supported via SQL databases, as are most Web applications.

A two-day introduction-to-SQL course is strongly recommended for those who do not have enough basic SQL experience to properly test databases. The SQL testing typically considers the validation of data (i.e., ensuring that entered data shows up in the database). Accessing structured data with SQL is quite different from Web document searches, which are full-text searches. Structured data in the relational DBMS model implies that data is represented in tables of rows and columns. Each row in a table represents a different object, and columns represent attributes of row objects.

Because column values are named and represented in a consistent format, rows can be selected precisely, based on their content. This is helpful when dealing with numeric data. Data from different tables can be joined together based on matching column values. Useful analysis can be performed in this way—for example, listing objects that are present in one table and missing from a related table. Rows can also be extracted from large tables, allowing for regrouping and the generation of simple statistics.

Testing can be applied at several points of interaction. Figure 14.10 shows that failures may occur at several points of interaction: client-side scripts or programs, server-side scripts or programs, database access services, stored procedures and triggers, and data stored in the database table. Therefore, testing can and should be applied at several points of interaction. Although client-side and server-side scripts are independent of the stored procedures and actual data, the scripts or programs that interact with them play a very important role. They are used to validate and handle errors for input and output data.

Common Types of Errors to Look For

Two common classes of problems caused by database bugs are *data integrity errors* and *output errors*.

Data is stored in fields of records in tables. Tables are stored in databases. At the programming level, a data integrity error is any bug that causes erroneous results to be stored, in addition to data corruptions in fields, records, tables, and databases. From the user's perspective, this means that: we might have missing or incorrect data in records (e.g., incorrect Social Security number in an employee record); we might have missing records in tables (e.g., an employee record missing from the employee database); or data might be outdated because it was not properly updated; and so on.

Output errors are caused by bugs in the data retrieving and manipulating instructions, although the source data is correct. From the user's perspective, the symptoms seen in the output can be similar to data integrity errors. In doing black-box testing, it's often a challenge to determine if a symptom of an error is caused by data integrity errors or output errors. (See Chapter 10, "User Interface Tests," Figure 10.19, for a discussion on this topic.)

Instructions for manipulating data in the process of producing the requested output, or storing and updating data, are normally in SQL statements, stored procedures, and triggers. Bugs in these instructions will result in data integrity errors, output errors, or both.

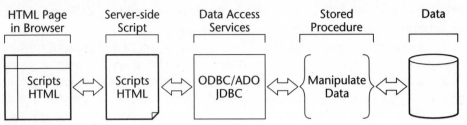

Figure 14.10   Several points of interactions.

Generally, database operations involve the following activities:

■ First-time activities (e.g., the setup process):

　1. Connect to the database server.

　2. Create new databases.

　3. Create tables, defaults, and rules; populate default data.

　4. Compile stored procedures and triggers.

After the setup process has completed successfully, using the database consists of the following activities:

■ Connect to database.

■ Execute SQL statements, stored procedures, and triggers.

■ Disconnect from the database.

The common types of errors uncovered in database activities include:

■ Failures in connecting to the database. Several potential problems that cause this type of failure include the following:

　■ Invalid user name, password, or both.

　■ User has inadequate privileges required for certain data activities, such as creating tables and stored procedures.

　■ Invalid or wrong DSN (Microsoft Windows platform; see examples in Figures 14.22 through 14.25 for more information).

　■ Failure to connect to the server that has the needed file DSN.

Several potential problems that can cause failures in creating databases, tables, defaults, rules, stored procedures, and triggers, as well as failures in populating default data, include:

■ Unable to write to the specified volume.

■ Failure to create files.

■ Inadequate storage required for creating databases and tables.

■ Resource contention keeps one or more stored procedures or tables from being created.

Some of the common errors in the instructions (stored procedures, triggers, etc.) include:

- The database is configured to be case-sensitive, but the code is not.

- Using reserved keywords in the SQL statement. For example:

```
SELECT user FROM mytable.
```

  Since user is the reserved keyword, this can cause a problem.

- NULL is passed to a record field that does not allow NULL.

- Mishandling single quote (') in a string field. See Figure 14.15 for an example.

- Mishandling comma (,) in an integer field. See Figure 14.18 for an example.

- Mishandling wrong data type. For example, if a field such as employee_salary in a record expects an integer, but receives $500 instead, it will complain because 500 is an integer but $500 is not. See Figure 14.19 for more examples.

- A value is too large for the size of the field.

- A string is too long for the size of the field. See Figure 14.17 for an example.

- Time-out: The time it takes the database to complete executing the procedure is longer than the time-out value set in the script (e.g., ASP script).

- Invalid or misspelled field or column, table, or view name.

- Undefined field, table, or view name.

- Invalid or misspelled stored procedure name.

- Calling the wrong store procedure.

- Missing keyword. An example would be the code written as follows:

```
...
create view student_view
select * from student_tbl
...
instead of
...
create view student_view as
select * from student_tbl
...
```

  Notice that *as* was omitted.

- Missing left parenthesis. For example:

  ```
  . . .
  INSERT INTO staff id, city, state, salary, name) VALUES
  (13, 'Phoenix', 'AZ', 33000, 'Bill')
  ```

- Missing right parenthesis. For example:

  ```
  . . .
  INSERT INTO staff (id, city, state, salary, name VALUES
  (13, 'Phoenix', 'AZ', 33000, 'Bill')
  . . .
  ```

- Missing comma. For example:

  ```
  . . .
  INSERT INTO staff (id, city, state, salary, name) VALUES
  (13, 'Phoenix', 'AZ', 33000 'Bill')
  ```

- Missing keyword.

- Misspelled keyword.

- Missing opening or closing parenthesis before the keyword.

- Certain functions are disallowed, to be used with group by. For example, the following statement can cause error:

  ```
  . . .
  group by count (last_name), first_name, age
  . . .
  ```

- Missing arguments for a function.

- Missing values. For example:

  ```
  . . .
  /* Create stored procedure that accepts parameters for inserting
  records */
  CREATE PROCEDURE add_staff (@P1 INT, @P2 CHAR(20), @P3 CHAR(2), @P4
  INT, @P5 CHAR(20))
  AS INSERT INTO staff
  VALUES (@P1, @P2, @P3, @P4, @P5)
  /* Inserting 3 records with created stored procedure */
  add_staff 13, 'Phoenix', 'AZ', 'Bill'
  . . .
  ```

- Insufficient privilege to grant permissions.

- Invisible invalid characters such as ESC.

- Errors in implementing COMMIT TRANSACTION and ROLLBACK TRANSACTION. The COMMIT TRANSACTION statement saves all work started since the beginning of the transaction. The ROLLBACK TRANSACTION statement cancels all the work done within the transaction. COMMIT and ROLLBACK errors cause partial data to be undesirably saved.

There are several approaches to database functionality testing, which we'll discuss in the following sections.

Database Stored Procedures and Triggers

Usually, the code for both triggers and stored procedures is installed at the same time as the database is created. A stored procedure for a database is often loaded into the database when the tables are first created. It is challenging to determine when, or even if, a stored procedure is executed. It is also a challenge to get the database into a constrained condition to execute the stored procedure. Stored procedures are most likely to break when the data is outside the range of expected values. It is difficult to identify boundary condition or corner case data to test a stored procedure. (See Chapter 3, "Software Testing Basics," for more information on boundary test development.)

White-Box Methods

Although an in-depth exploration of white-box testing is beyond the scope of this book, it's worth a brief discussion because several of these methods are quite effective for database testing. More important, the methods offer knowledge that can be useful for black-box testers in designing powerful test cases.

Code Walk-through

Code walk-through is a very effective method of finding errors at the source level. This method is not unique to database testing. It has been used for many programming languages. This is a peer-review process in which the author of the code guides other developers through his or her code, one line at a time. Along the way, reviewers are encouraged to point out any inefficiencies, redundancies, inconsistencies, or poor coding practices they see. The goal of the reviewers should be to carefully examine the code under review and identify as many potential errors as possible (but not necessarily to determine how to fix the identified errors in these sessions). Walk-throughs are effective when black-box testing is impractical for testing stored procedures at the unit level and when debugging programs are unable to track down logic errors in code.

Code walk-throughs tend to work better when they are limited to just a few developers and last no more than a couple of hours. If the reviewed objects require further review, a follow-up walk-through should be scheduled. Although as a black-box tester, one might not have the coding skill to contribute, participating in the walk-through is still extremely useful, for at least three reasons:

1. A black-box tester can gain a great deal of knowledge about how the code works internally. This knowledge becomes of great value in designing black-box test cases.

2. As a tester, one is often very good at asking what-if questions. (What if the data type passed to the parameter is an invalid one?) These questions, in turn, reveal many bugs, as well as information for designing a good error-handling mechanism.

3. The tester can learn to become a good facilitator and record keeper. This helps the group to be better focused on identifying issues rather than on figuring out the fixes for the identified issues. This also helps in tracking the identified issues for later checking to make sure problems are adequately addressed.

As discussed earlier, SQL extensions such as Transact-SQL (supported by Microsoft and Sybase Server database product) and PL/SQL and SQL*Plus (supported by Oracle Server database product) are similar to other programming languages. Therefore, there will be syntactic as well as logic errors to be found in using expressions, conditions, and operators, along with functions such as date and time functions, arithmetic functions, data conversion functions, and so on.

Redundancy Coding Error Example

The following is a simplified example of a redundancy error in the ASP code that can be caught using the code walk-through approach. This error will cause performance degradation. However, it will not expose any visible error at runtime. Therefore, from the black-box testing perspective, we will not see this bug.

```
'Send a query to the SQL database from an ASP
Set RS = Conn.Execute ("Select * from STAFF")
'Now, loop through the records
If NOT RS.EOF Then
'Notice that the If statement is redundant because
'the condition is already covered in the Do while loop.
'From the black-box testing perspective, this error
'will not cause any visible failure.
Do while Not RS.EOF
'The code that manipulates, formats and displays
'records goes here
...
    Loop
End If
```

Inefficiency Coding Error Example

Here is a simplified example of an inefficiency error. This error will cause performance degradation. However, it will not expose any visible error at runtime. Therefore, from the black-box testing perspective, we will not see this bug.

ID	CITY	STATE	SALARY	NAME
13	Phoenix	AZ	33000	Bill
44	Denver	CO	40000	Bob
66	Los Angeles	CA	47000	Mary

Figure 14.11 Query results.

Using data in the staff table similar to the one shown in Figure 14.11, we will be querying the data and displaying results in an HTML page.

Now, suppose that the application under test offers two views, a complete view showing all fields and records and a partial view showing all fields except CITY and all records. For the complete view, the SQL statement to query data should look something like this:

```
SELECT * FROM staff
```

This query statement will be sent to the database. After the database server returns the record set, the application will then format and display the results in an HTML page. The complete view in the Web browser would look like the illustration in Figure 14.12.

For the partial view, instead of sending this SQL statement to query data:

```
SELECT id, state, salary, name FROM staff
```

the application sends the same SQL statement as one in the complete-view case.

After the database server returns the record set, the application will then format and display the results in an HTML page. The partial view in the Web browser would look like the illustration in Figure 14.13. Notice that there is no failure from the user or black-box tester perspective. This type of error only causes the database to do unnecessary extra work. Hence, the overall performance might be affected.

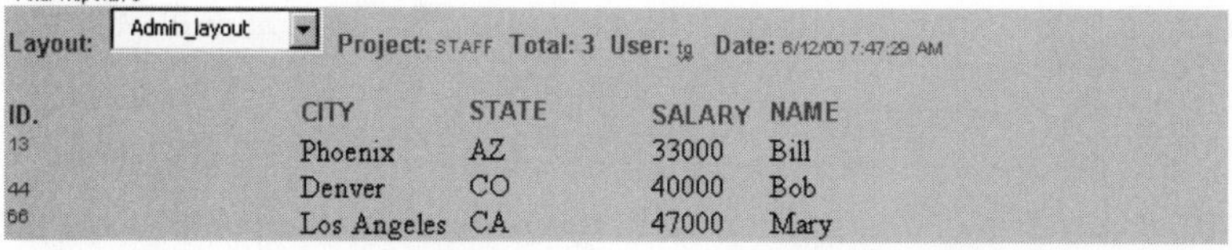

Total Reports: 3

| Layout: | Admin_layout ▼ | Project: STAFF Total: 3 User: tg Date: 6/12/00 7:47:29 AM |

ID.	CITY	STATE	SALARY	NAME
13	Phoenix	AZ	33000	Bill
44	Denver	CO	40000	Bob
66	Los Angeles	CA	47000	Mary

Figure 14.12 The complete view.

Total Reports: 3

| Layout: | NoCity_Layout ▾ | Project: STAFF Total: 3 User: tg   Date: 6/12/00 8:22:58 AM |

ID	STATE	SALARY	NAME
13	AZ	33000	Bill
44	CO	40000	Bob
66	CA	47000	Mary

Figure 14.13   The partial view.

Executing the SQL Statements One at a Time

It is possible to test stored procedures by executing SQL statements one at a time against known results. The results can then be validated with expected results.

This approach is analogous to unit testing. One benefit of this approach is that when errors are detected, little analysis is required to fix the errors. However, this approach is tedious and labor-intensive.

Executing the Stored Procedures One at a Time

Stored procedures often accept input parameters and contain logic. Sometimes, they call other procedures or external functions. Therefore, logic and input dependencies must be taken into account when testing stored procedures. This testing approach is then similar to the testing of functions. For each stored procedure, analyze the data type and constraint of each input parameter: the user-defined return status value and conditional logic code within the stored procedure. To test a stored procedure, try invoking it with no records and with a large number of records. Testing a database with only a few records is not the same as when the database is fully loaded with real data.

Design test cases that cover both valid and invalid data types. In addition, apply equivalent class-partitioned values and boundary conditions in designing input parameters. (See the section entitled "Test-Case Development" in Chapter 3, for more information.) Consider exercising various possible paths based on the conditional logic.

Execute the stored procedure by passing various input parameters into the procedure. Validate the expected results, as well as the user-defined return values, and the handling of error conditions (by rule enforcement, as well as business logic).

For example, we want to test the `add_staff` stored procedure created in example 2b earlier. Using Microsoft SQL 7.0, we launch the SQL Server Query Analyzer. We execute the following statement to call the add_staff stored procedure and pass in the parameters:

```
add_staff 13, 'San Francisco', 'CA', 33000, 'Joe'
```

As shown in Figure 14.14, because the input data is valid, it confirms that the record is added successfully.

Let's try a test case with potential problematic input data. In this case, we will pass 'Mary's' to the `name` parameter (the fifth parameter of this stored procedure). Because it's known that a single quote (') is used by SQL to mark the beginning and end of a string, the extra single quote in 'Mary's' is expected to create a problem if it's not handled properly. We execute the following query to call the `add_staff` stored procedure and pass in the parameters:

```
add_staff 13, 'San Francisco', 'CA', 33000, 'Mary's'
```

As shown in Figure 14.15, a SQL syntax error results.

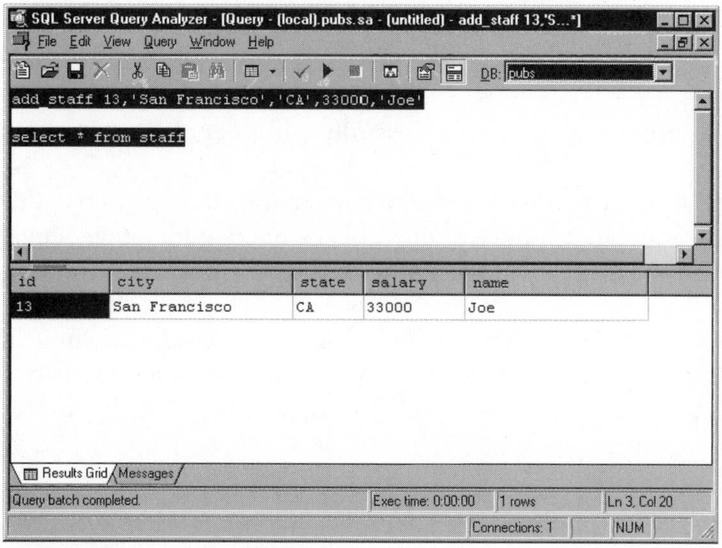

Figure 14.14 Valid input data.

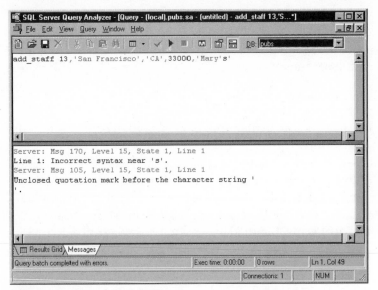

```
add_staff 13,'San Francisco','CA',33000,'Mary's'
```

```
Server: Msg 170, Level 15, State 1, Line 1
Line 1: Incorrect syntax near 's'.
Server: Msg 105, Level 15, State 1, Line 1
Unclosed quotation mark before the character string '
'.
```

Figure 14.15   An SQL syntax error.

Now we'll run the same stored procedure, this time escaping the single quote character by placing an additional single quote character.

```
add_staff 14, 'San Francisco', 'CA', 33000, 'Mary''s'
```

Notice that the record is now added successfully without error, as shown in Figure 14.16.

What this tells us is that we must check all the text parameters passed to this procedure to make sure that single quotes are escaped with other single quotes. This can be done through the scripting or the programming language of your choice.

Let's look at what happens when a string passed in exceeds the limit of the maximum number of characters. In this case, the size of State field is two characters. (See step 1 of the section entitled "Example of SQL," earlier in this chapter.)

```
add_staff 15, 'Albany', 'New York', 33000, 'John'
```

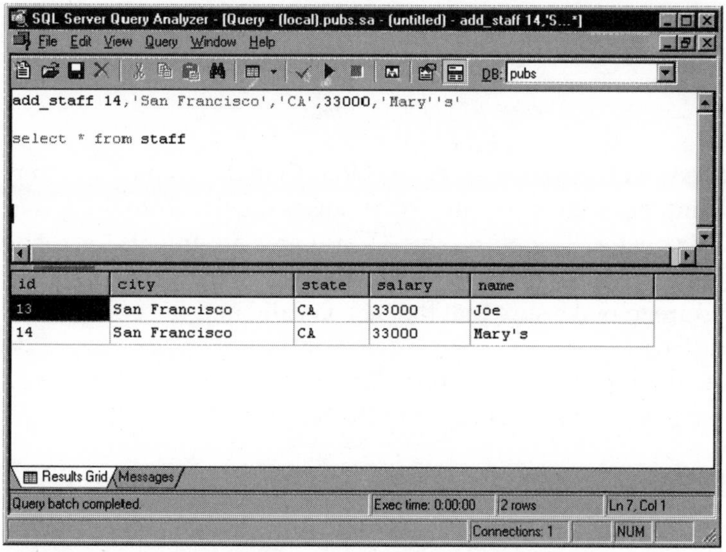

Figure 14.16   Single quote (') is properly handled.

Now, we check the contents of the staff table. Notice that in the State field, as shown in Figure 14.17, "New York" is truncated, becoming "NE" (Nebraska). We can fix this by ensuring that only two characters are allowed in the Web form that the user uses to submit to the database. If more than two characters are typed, the machine can beep. We can do this via client-side scripting with JavaScript or use server-side validation with the scripting or programming language for our application (e.g., Asp, perl, JSP, C++, VB, etc.).

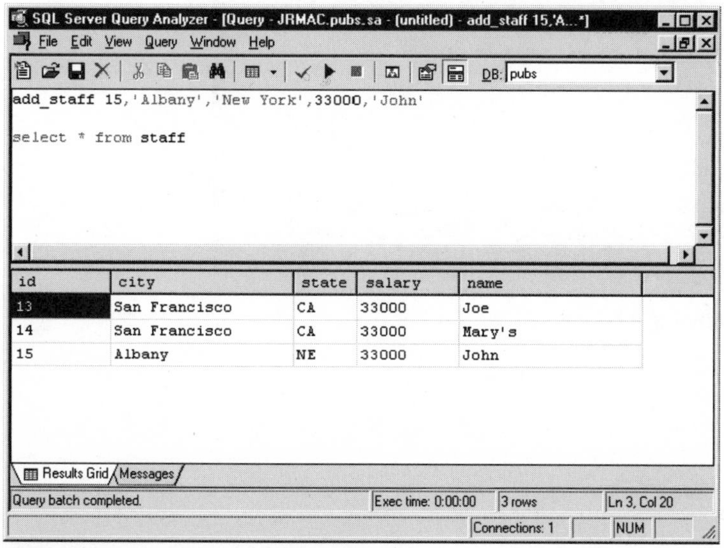

Figure 14.17   The string is too long.

Figure 14.18 shows an example of mishandling a comma. Here, we pass in a supposed integer with a comma (,) used as a thousand separator.

```
add_staff 15, 'Albany', 'New York', 33,000, 'John'
```

Running this query will produce an error. Note that the comma is interpreted as a field delimiter. The comma in 33,000 causes the parser to think that there is an extra parameter. Therefore, the "Too many arguments" error is raised. Similar to other cases, we must check our Web form that passes the data to the stored procedure to make sure that the data is valid and the error condition should be handled.

Finally, let's look at an example of wrong data type passed into the stored procedure. Here, we pass a string data type to the Salary field.

```
add_staff 15, 'Albany', 'New York', '33,000', 'John'
```

Running this query will produce an error. As shown in Figure 14.19, the stored procedure was expecting an integer data type; instead, it received a string.

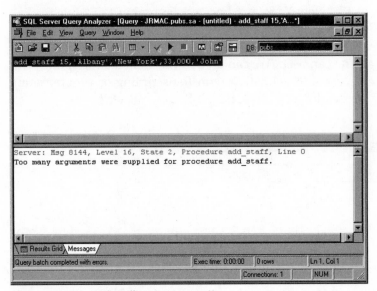

Figure 14.18 Mishandling a comma (,).

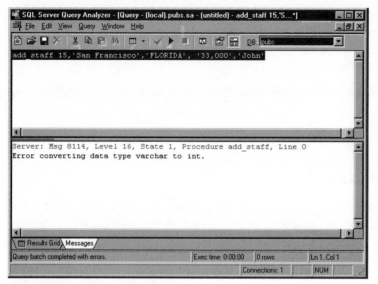

Figure 14.19 Wrong data type.

Testing Triggers

Triggers are executed when certain events such as INSERT, DELETE, and UPDATE are applied to table data. Trigger implementation can be very powerful. For example, a trigger can call itself recursively or call other stored procedures.

We need to identify all the triggers that are part of the application. We then analyze and catalog the conditions under which a trigger will be executed. We try to understand the tasks that each trigger carries out. We then write and execute SQL statements or stored procedures to induce the conditions and validate the expected results.

The testing objectives should include the following:

- Does the stored procedure or trigger meet the design objectives?

- For each conditional statement, does the handling of the condition execute properly?

- For each predefined input, does the procedure produce correctly expected outputs?

- Have all input cases identified in the equivalence class and boundary condition partitioning process been executed (either by walk-through, executing the stored procedure, or calling the stored procedure from other procedures)?

- For each possible error condition, does the procedure detect such condition?

- Is the handling of each detected error reasonable?

External Interfacing

In this method, the analysis of test case design is similar to the white-box and black-box testing approaches. However, instead of executing a stored procedure individually, stored procedures are called from external application functions. Whether an application is implemented with compiled programming languages such as C++ or Visual Basic, or with scripting languages such as Perl, JSP (Java Server Page), or Microsoft ASP (Active Server Page), this method addresses both the testing of the functionality of stored procedures and the interoperability between the application and the stored procedures. Web-based applications offer users a browser-based interface through which they can access and manipulate data records. SQL statements sent to the database are often built by inserting user-supplied data into the various fields of the SQL command. Unless the data coming from the Web browser is checked and verified before sending to the database, an SQL statement or a stored procedure may produce unexpected results due to data errors. This can easily cause data corruption and security problems for the application. (See Chapter 18, "Web Security Testing" for more information.)

The external interfacing method also addresses the testing of proper application-database connectivity and authentication. Several automated testing tools such as Segue SILK and Mercury Interactive WinRunner also provide scripting features that allow for database connection and stored-procedure execution.

Black-Box Methods

In applying black-box testing methods, we will discuss test-case design, preparation for database testing, and setup/installation issues.

Designing Test Cases

Using the traditional black-box testing approach, test cases are executed on the browser-side. Inputs are entered on Web input forms, and data is submitted to the back-end database via the Web browser interface. The results sent back to the browser are then validated against expected values. This is the most common method because it requires little to no programming skill. It also addresses not only the functionality of the database's stored procedures, rules, triggers, and data integrity, but also the functionality of the Web application as a whole. There are, however, two drawbacks to this method. One is that sometimes the results sent to the browser after test-case execution do not necessarily indicate that the data itself is properly written to a record in the table. The second drawback is that when erroneous results are sent back to the browser after the execution of a test case, it does not necessarily mean that the error is a database error. Further analysis will be required to determine the exact cause of the error.

As it turns out, several examples shown in "Executing the Stored Procedures One at a Time" earlier in this chapter, are not realistic. For instance, if we already know that a single quote (') will cause the SQL parser to think that it's the end of the string, when the single quote is not handled properly, SQL will fail. So what's the point of trying something that you already know will fail?

There are at least four important lessons learned in these exercises:

1. There are input/output (I/O) validations and error handlings that must be done outside of the stored procedures. These areas (both client- and server-sides) should be thoroughly analyzed and tested.

2. Based on the acquired knowledge about things that would cause SQL to break, we should do a thorough analysis to design black-box test cases that produce problematic inputs that would break the constraints; feed in wrong data type; pass in problematic characters, such as commas (,), single quotes ('), and so on.

3. Testing the interaction between SQL and other components such as scripts is an equally important task in database testing.

4. Understanding how to use database tools to execute SQL statements and stored procedures can significantly improve our ability to analyze Web-based errors. For instance, it can help us determine whether an error is in the stored procedure code, the data itself, or in the components outside of the database.

Testing for Transaction Logic

Atomic actions are those tasks that must be done as a single action. For example, several tables may need to be updated to complete a purchase. If any of these updates cannot occur, the operation must not perform the other updates. For this purchase, the following tables may need to be updated, as specified here:

- Inventory record for this item needs to be lowered.
- Fulfillment table needs a record added.
- Customer record needs to have a purchase added.
- Billing table needs to be updated.

Several other tables may need to be modified as well. If any of these actions cannot be completed, an error condition exists that should prevent any of the modifications. Transaction logic allows the database designer to bundle SQL statements together to produce the required atomic action. You must carefully check the database tables to determine if the transaction logic is properly covering the atomic actions. For example, if the purchase cannot be completed because a rule in the inventory table does not allow the inventory to become negative; then you must check the other three tables to confirm that those updates did not occur.

Test cases need to be created to test all possible transactions. A matrix showing the atomic action can then list those tables that are affected. This matrix should also list the preconditions for the transaction. For example, to create a purchase, there must be a registered customer that might require additional tables, such as a shipping address and billing address.

Testing for Concurrency Issues

A database can handle many transactions at the same time. Many customers can be buying products totally unaware that other purchases are being conducted or that shipping clerks are updating records as new items arrive and products are shipped. However, these activities need to lock records to prevent concurrent updates and prevent data errors in the database. For example, two customers should not be able to buy the same item. Your application design has to consider when to lock an item so that other customers cannot attempt to purchase. If the first customer does not complete the transaction, the lock needs to be removed.

Many concurrency problems exist. A deadlock exists when two or more users attempt to lock the same records. If user A cannot complete a task that requires updating a record that user B has locked, and user B requires a record that user A has locked, then neither user can complete his or her work. The system will not determine that a conflict exists.

Data inventory errors also occur. For example, a clerk might read the inventory table and then try to update the quantities while a customer is making a purchase. Unless locking and transaction logic are properly designed and implemented, data integrity problems will result. In the past, many of these problems were "solved" by having clerks work at night when customers were gone. Having only a few customers also lowered the chances of many people wanting to access and modify the same record. Web applications running on the Internet may have thousands of concurrent users, both customers and internal staff, using the database at all hours of the day and night.

Preparation for Database Testing

To prepare for database testing, we generate a list of database tables, stored procedures, triggers, defaults, rules, and so on. This will help us to have a good handle on the scope of testing required for database testing. Figure 14.20 illustrates a list of stored procedures in a Microsoft SQL 7.0 database.

1. Generate data schemata for tables. Analyzing the schema will help us determine:

   ■ Can a certain field value be NULL?

   ■ What are the allowed or disallowed values?

   ■ What are the constraints?

   ■ Is the value dependent upon values in another table?

   ■ Will the values of this field be in the lookup table?

   ■ What are the user-defined data types?

   ■ What are the primary and foreign key relationships among tables?

   Figure 14.21 shows a screen shot of a table design that lists all the column names, data types, lengths, and so on, of a Microsoft SQL 7.0 database table.

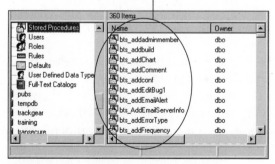

Figure 14.20 A list of stored procedures.

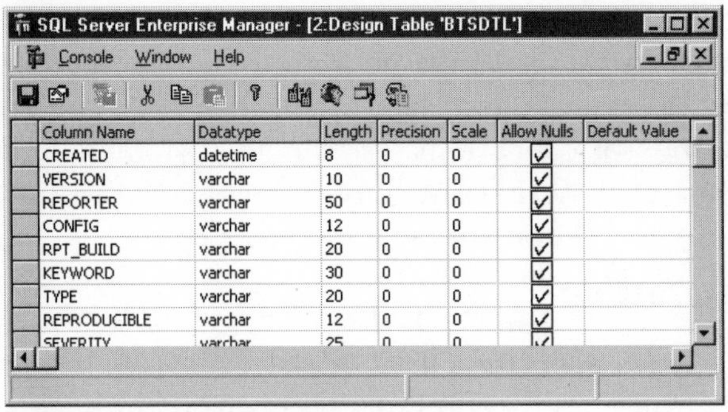

Figure 14.21 Table design view.

2. At a high level, analyze how the stored procedures, triggers, defaults, and rules work. This will help us determine:

   ■ What is the primary function of each stored procedure and trigger? Does it read data and produce outputs, write data, or both? Pay particular attention to procedures that have keywords such as INSERT, DELETE, and UPDATE, because they might have effects on data integrity.

   ■ What are the accepted parameters?

   ■ What are the returned values?

   ■ When is a stored procedure called, and by whom?

   ■ When is a trigger fired?

3. Determine what the configuration management process is. That is how the new tables, stored procedures, triggers, and such are integrated in each build. In other words, how can you determine if stored procedures are added, removed, or updated? This will help us determine the effects on our testing.

Setup/Installation Issues

During the installation process, the installer often needs to establish connectivity with the database server. This process requires authentication, which means that the installer needs to have a proper database-user ID and password to connect to the database. Generally, the user ID and password are entered into the installer screen and passed to the database during the authentication process. The user ID must be one that has adequate rights to create data devices (the physical files that store data), databases, and tables. The ID must also have rights to populate data and defaults, drop and generate stored procedures, and so on. This process is prone to errors. Each step within the process is susceptible to failure. It is quite possible that out of 100 tables created, one or two tables will not be created correctly due to a failure.

Here is an example of data source creation during the installation process. The *data source name* (DSN) used in Microsoft ODBC technology is a reference to the collection of information used by the ODBC manager to connect an application to a particular ODBC database. A DSN can be stored in a file or a file DSN. A DSN can also be stored in a User/System registry or a machine DSN.

Figures 14.22 through 14.25 illustrate the manual process of creating an MS-SQL server DSN. The first step is to launch the ODBC applet. Click the system DSN tab to view a list of currently installed DSNs (see Figure 14.22). Click the Add button to create a new system DSN and follow the on-screen instructions to complete the process. If a DSN is created successfully, a dialog box will display. Once all of the information has been supplied, a summary of the configuration is presented. From the dialog box shown in Figure 14.23, test the data source to see if it has been set up correctly (see Figure 14.24). Suppose that, in this process, the supplied ID or password is incorrect; an error message will display (as shown in Figure 14.25).

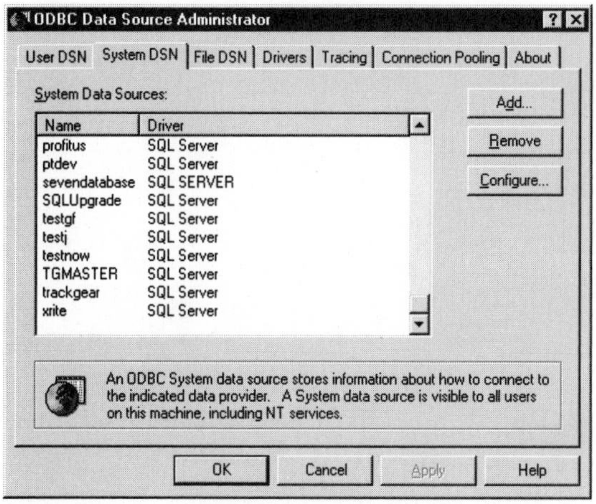

Figure 14.22   ODBC data source administrator.

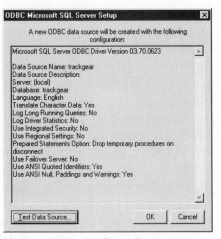

Figure 14.23 Configuration summary.

Figure 14.24 Data source test confirmation.

Figure 14.25 Invalid ID or password error message.

Now consider that the preceding manual process can be implemented (coded) in the installation program—the complete DSN creation procedure can be executed programmatically. Any errors that arise during this process can cause an invalid DSN. An invalid DSN will cause a failure in connecting to the database server. If the installer cannot establish a connection to the database server, and it did not check for such an error, all the code used to create devices, databases, tables, stored procedures, and triggers will fail.

Testing with a Clean Database

The installation script often contains the SQL statements used to create the database, produce the tables, views, install stored procedures, and populate tables with records and initial values. Depending on the complexity of the data schema and the application, the script with SQL can be short or rather long. During the development cycle, it is common for this script to change to reflect specific implementation needs. Repeated testing of the installation process on completely clean databases will be required to ensure that no side-effect is introduced by the changes.

Database Testing Considerations

- Using a call-level interface such as Microsoft ODBC, in theory, applications are not involved with the types of back-end databases because they only interact with the ODBC layer. In practice, however, there are incompatibility issues among different types of back-end databases. Therefore, we should test each supported database individually to ensure that errors specific to incompatibility can be isolated more easily.

- Applications that use Microsoft ASP technology generally rely on DSN to make connections to SQL servers. An invalid DSN will cause a connectivity failure.

- Structured Query Language databases may not be able to accept special characters (', $, @, &, and others) as valid inputs.

- Data sent to a database server may be corrupted due to packet losses caused by slow connections.

- Script time-out issues may cause data corruptions or erroneous outputs. For example, the time it takes the database to complete executing the query is longer than the time-out value set in the script.

- Local browser caching and Web server caching may cause problems in an application's interaction with the database server.

- Do the automatic database backup recovery procedures need to be tested?

- Database rollback logic, if not properly implemented, can cause data corruption. Identify where and how rollback logic is implemented. Design test cases to exercise those areas.

- Running out of hard disk space can cause serious problems to data in an SQL database. What happens when your server runs out of disk space?

- Localized support may require the support of the native version of the operating system, Web server, database server, application server, and browsers. Consider testing the Web application from different countries, using various browsers with language settings.

- The SQL Server Performance Monitor is available as a selection from the MS-SQL Server program group.

- With MS-SQL Server, verify that all DSNs correctly point to the appropriate servers; otherwise, changes may undesirably apply to the wrong database.

- Ensure that new/closed files are assigned correct permissions, owners, and groups. This is a necessity for UNIX and may apply to Windows NT.

- Check for proper permissions on file-based directories. Check for the existence of and proper permissions for the source and target directories.

- Check for accessibility to the machine on which the target directory resides.

- Test for proper error handling when the logs have incorrect permissions. This is a necessity for UNIX and may apply to Windows NT.

- Check for proper loading of all tables in the database.

- Check for proper error handling when database files fail to load.

Bibliography and Additional Resources

Bibliography

Bourne, Kelly C. *Testing Client/Server Systems.* New York: McGraw-Hill, 1997.

Coffman, Gayle. *SQL Server 7: The Complete Reference.* Berkeley, CA: Osborne/McGraw-Hill, 1999.

Kaner, Cem, Jack Falk, Hung Q. Nguyen. *Testing Computer Software,* 2nd ed. New York: John Wiley & Sons, Inc., 1999.

LogiGear Corporation. *QA Training Handbook: Testing Web Applications.* Foster City, CA: LogiGear Corporation, 2003.

——— *QA Training Handbook: Testing Windows Desktop and Server-Based Applications.* Foster City, CA: LogiGear Corporation, 2003.

Microsoft Corporation. *Microsoft SQL Server 2000 Resource Kit.* Redmond, WA: Microsoft Press, 2001.

Orfali, Robert, Dan Harkey, Jeri Edwards. *Client/Server Survival Guide,* 3rd ed. New York: John Wiley & Sons, Inc., 1999.

Reilly, Douglas J. *Designing Microsoft(r) ASP.NET Applications.* Redmond, WA: Microsoft Press, 2001.

——— *Inside Server-Based Applications.* Redmond, WA: Microsoft Press, 2000.

Additional Resources

Articles and information for Microsoft SQL Server

www.databasejournal.com/features/mssql/

The Development Exchange's SQL Zone

www.sql-zone.com/

Microsoft site for information about SQL Server

www.microsoft.com/sql

Microsoft site for information about OLAP services

www.microsoft.com/sql/olap

Microsoft Worldwide SQL Server User's Group

www.sswug.org/

SQL Server Magazine

www.sqlmag.com/

A convienent tool to compare two databases made by Automated Office Systems

www.automatedofficesystems.com/products/dbcompare/

CHAPTER

15

Help Tests

Why Read This Chapter?

Having an understanding of the technologies that are used in the implementation of Web-based help systems (and the potential errors associated with those technologies) is critical to successful test planning.

TOPICS COVERED IN THIS CHAPTER

- ◆ Introduction
- ◆ Help System Analysis
- ◆ Approaching Help Testing
- ◆ Testing Considerations
- ◆ Bibliography

Introduction

Web help testing is a two-phase process. The first phase of testing involves the analysis of the system undergoing testing—determining its type, intended audience, and design approach. Once the particulars of the system have been identified, the second phase of the process begins—the testing phase. The testing phase itself is a two-part process that includes:

1. Testing the system as a stand-alone component.
2. Testing the interaction of the system with the application.

Help System Analysis

Before beginning the testing of a Web-based help system, you should understand the system's intended purpose, the design approach, the technologies used, and the potential errors associated with those technologies. The following sections offer analyses of Web-help design approach, technologies, and potential errors.

Types of Help Systems

There are several types of Web-based help systems. Each type involves unique objectives and benefits. By clearly identifying the type of help system under test, you can apply appropriate testing practices.

NOTE This chapter looks only at the testing of Web-based help systems, not printed documentation or PDF-based help systems.

Application Help Systems

Application help systems reside within, and support, software applications. They commonly support users in operating applications by offering context-sensitive assistance. Context-sensitive help gives users instruction that is relevant to the activities they are actively engaged in. An example of context-sensitive help includes clicking a Help button while a credit card billing information form is displayed. Clicking the Help button in this context generates help content that explains the controls and functionality associated with the billing form. Sometimes, users also get explanations of the intent of the form and the place of the form in a long transaction chain—that is, sometimes they get help that explains the application, not just its buttons.

Reference Help Systems

Reference help systems offer in-depth information about specific subjects, such as building a Web site or digital photography basics. They do not act as how-to guides for specific applications. Web-based reference systems are organized around the subject matter they present in a way that is similar to the way printed reference books are organized into chapters. Unlike printed books, however, online reference systems include cross-referenced hyperlinks between related topics. Although they are generally context-sensitive, they can often be read linearly, like a book, if required. For example, www.CNBC.com has a great deal of reference material on investing and finance that is not part of the feature set of its Web site.

Tutorial Help Systems

Tutorial help systems walk users through specific how-to lessons in an effort to train them in a given subject matter. Occasionally, such systems are used in tandem with books (possibly in a school setting). Tutorial help systems are often interactive, encouraging user input and offering feedback. This type of help system generally lacks context sensitivity. (See www.cnet.com in the section, "Tech Help How-To's and Tips," for examples of tutorials and how-to's.)

Sales and Marketing Help Systems

Sales and marketing tools convey product benefits to potential customers. The goal of *sales and marketing help systems* is to get users to buy certain products or take an action of some kind, such as filling out a Web-based questionnaire or requesting information from a manufacturer via an online form. These systems may include live demonstrations and interactivity. The products being presented may or may not be software applications. This type of help system generally lacks context sensitivity.

Evaluating the Target User

There are four primary skill types that should be tracked when evaluating target users: (1) computer experience, (2) Web experience, (3) subject matter experience, and (4) application experience. (See Chapter 10, "User Interface Tests," for detailed explanations of target-user skill types.) Considering your application, English-reading skill, or grade level may also need to be evaluated. A help system should be evaluated by how closely its characteristics match the experience and skills of its intended users. Discrepancies in experience level between target user and system indicate the potential for error conditions and poor usability. The key question is whether the help system communicates the information that the reader needs, in a way that the reader can understand.

Evaluating the Design Approach

Web-based help system design entails the same testing challenges that are involved in UI testing. Look and feel, consistency, and usability tests all come into play. Means of navigation, UI controls, and visual design (colors, fonts, placement of elements, etc.) should be intuitive and consistent from screen to screen. (Please refer to Chapter 10 for detailed information regarding design approach, consistency testing, and usability testing.) However, the mission is different. Here, the entire point of the application is to present content in a way that is easy to find and easy to understand, but with a slick display.

Evaluating the Technologies

Some of the authoring technologies used for Web-based help systems are described in the following subsections.

Standard HTML (W3 Standard)

Standard HyperText Markup Language (HTML) page technology can be used to build help systems that combine framesets, multiple windows, and hyper-links. As with any HTML-based system, hyperlinks must be tested for accuracy.

Context sensitivity presents complications in HTML-based systems. The correct help page ID must be passed whenever the Help button is clicked. However, HTML does not allow for the same hierarchical architecture that Windows-based applications are built upon. Thus, users may advance to other screens while viewing help content that is no longer applicable; the help browser window might become hidden by the application window; or the wrong page ID might be passed, resulting in incorrect help content.

Some applications, such as eHelp's (formerly Blue Sky Software) WebHelp, support the authoring of Web-based help systems that have Windows-styled help features such as full-text browsing and pop-up windows. WebHelp uses Dynamic HTML and supports both Internet Explorer and Netscape Navigator. To learn more about the functionality of WebHelp and read white papers on many help-authoring subjects, visit:

www.winwriters.com/resource.htm

www.ehelp.com

www.helpauthoring.com/webhelp/webhelp.htm

Refer to Figure 15.1 for an example of RoboHelp's HTML-based WebHelp.

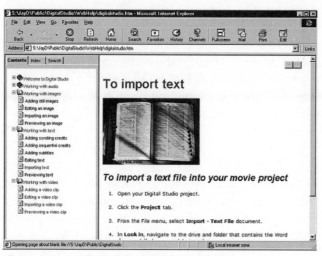

Figure 15.1   RoboHelp's HTML-based WebHelp.

Source: Graphics from "Demystifying Help," a white paper produced by eHelp Corporation. Reproduced with permission from eHelp Corporation.

Java Applets

Java-based help systems can be run from servers while UI is displayed through Web browsers. Sun Microsystem's JavaHelp (supported by eHelp's RoboHelp, Figure 15.1) combines HTML and XML with 100 percent Pure Java. JavaHelp is a platform-independent authoring environment that enables developers to create online help in Web-based applications and Java applets. For more information about JavaHelp, go to:

www.ehelp.com

www.helpauthoring.com/javahelp/javahelp.htm

http://java.sun.com/products/javahelp/

Also, see Figure 15.2 for an example of JavaHelp's Java-based help system.

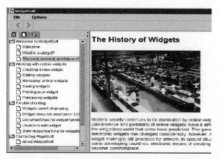

Figure 15.2   JavaHelp's Java-based help system.

Source: Graphics from "Demystifying Help," a white paper produced by eHelp Corporation. Reproduced with permission from eHelp Corporation.

Netscape NetHelp

NetHelp is an HTML-based, cross-platform, online help-authoring environment. It is based on technology that is built into the Netscape Communicator suite. It is compatible only with Navigator. Figure 15.3 shows an example of Netscape's NetHelp help system. For more information about Netscape NetHelp, visit http://home.netscape.com/eng/help.

ActiveX Controls

Microsoft's HTML Help ActiveX control allows for the creation of Web-based help systems that have tables of contents, cross-referencing links, indices, and a splash window that accompanies the HTML Help Viewer. It is compatible only with Internet Explorer. See Figure 15.4 for an example of Microsoft's HTML Help ActiveX control.

Figure 15.3   Netscape NetHelp help system.

Figure 15.4   ActiveX-based Microsoft HTML Help.

Help Elements

Web-based help systems are commonly made up of the following elements. Help systems created with authoring programs such as WebHelp have many design elements that mimic the features of Windows-based help systems. Such elements include the book-and-page metaphor for help topic organization.

Elements to test include:

CONTENTS TAB (OPTIONAL)

- Book links
- Page links

    - Topic page names
    - Topic displayed in main window
    - Topic displayed in secondary window

INDEX TAB

- Single-level

    - With sublist
    - Without sublist

- Multilevel
  - With sublist
  - Without sublist

FIND TAB (OPTIONAL)

- Full-text search
- Associative links

OTHER CUSTOM TABS (OPTIONAL)

- Favorites

GLOSSARY

- Self-defining terms
- Browse sequences

RICH TOPICS

- Video
- Sound
- Links
- Text
- Graphics

DYNAMIC CONTENT

- Scripting
- ActiveX controls
- DHTML
- XML
- Java applets

CONTENT-SENSITIVE HELP

- Pop-up windows (self-sizing)
- Secondary windows (self-sizing)
- Buttons
- Expanding text (DHTML)
- Pull-down text (DHTML)

Approaching Help Testing

Once the technological particulars of the system have been identified, you can begin the testing process.

Two-Tiered Testing

The testing phase is a two-tiered process that includes testing the help system as a stand-alone system and testing the help system's interaction with the application.

Stand-alone Testing

Web-based help systems are subject to the same compatibility and functionality issues as are all applications. They need to be evaluated as stand-alone applications in accordance with the technologies that created them; Java-based systems, for example, should be tested in the same way that any stand-alone Java application would be tested. ActiveX-based systems, like all ActiveX components, should be evaluated for compatibility issues (they should support all the relevant versions of browsers).

Interaction between the Application and the Help System

The help system must be tested in combination with the application to ensure that all context-sensitive IDs are passed and that correct help content is displayed throughout all states of the application. Issues to consider include the *map* file:

- Names of help files
- Topic IDs for Help buttons on dialog boxes
- Accessing help through F1, shortcut keys, buttons, and so on

Types of Help Errors

Following are a number of help-related testing issues and error examples:

UI DESIGN

- Functional testing of a help system checks whether everything is operating as intended. Each link should be operational and lead users to their intended destination. All graphics should load properly.
- Web systems are vulnerable to environmental conditions surrounding platform compatibility, display resolutions, and browser types.

TESTING THE SAMPLE APPLICATION

The help system of the sample application is built with standard HTML. It can be accessed from any screen in the application by clicking the Help button, so it is an application help system. An example is shown in Figure 15.5.

Adding configuration profiles		
Overview To add a hardware/software configuration profile, enter information that describes the profile into any or or all of the following fields:		

Config ID	ROM	DVD
Model	Video Card	Printer
Brand	Video Memory	Modem
O.S.	Hard Disk	Scanner
CPU Brand	Disk Size	CD-ROM
CPU Speed	Sound Card	RAM
Other HW	Other SW	Network Cards

Click the Save button when finished to save the configuration profile. Click the Reset button to reset the profile to its last saved state. Click the Done button to return to the Setting Up Hardware/Software Configure Profile Screen.

Figure 15.5 Sample application's standard HTML help system.

Looking at the design approach of the help system, you see that the system is context-sensitive; clicking the Help button at any time while using the application links users directly to help content that supports the current activities and on-screen options. Each help screen includes a table of contents hyperlink. Users click this link to access the system's table of contents, from which they can access related content and, if they wish, read the entire system's contents from start to finish, like a reference book. Also, hyperlinked keywords within the text link users to related content.

Though client-side users (end users and administrators) have access to differing privileges and UI controls in the sample application, both user types are referred to the same help system. This approach has positive and negative implications. End users may be exposed to administrator-level content that they do not expect or understand.

- As with all Web content, help systems should operate consistently across multiple screen resolutions, color palette modes, and font size settings. This is a particularly important issue for help because these types of legibility errors are common. For information regarding testing of display settings and fonts, see Appendix G, "Display Compatibility Test Matrix." This matrix shows lists of display settings to use during your help testing. It is good practice to change your display settings regularly during the course of your testing, and it is particularly important during help testing as help probably uses different technology to be displayed; formatting and readability issues are key to a useful help system.

CONSISTENCY OF THE HELP SYSTEM

- Help system implementation should be consistent throughout; otherwise, user confusion may result.

- Consistency issues to test for include:

  - *Organization.* Is the system structured in a way that makes sense? Are available options clearly laid out for users? Is the system easy to navigate?

  - *Design approach.* Applications are often designed around familiar structures and patterns to enhance their usability. Many help systems are organized hierarchically; some are context-sensitive. Is the metaphor used by your system consistent from screen to screen? Do methods of searching and navigation remain consistent?

  - *Terminology.* Is there consistency of language throughout the system? A command or term referred to in one context should be referred to in the same way in all other contexts. See the section entitled "Testing for Consistency" in Chapter 10 for a list of synonymous commands that are often mistakenly interchanged.

  - *Fonts and colors.* Are font sizes and styles used consistently throughout the system? Are links, lettering, backgrounds, and buttons presented consistently?

  - *Format.* Text should be formatted consistently.

HELP SYSTEM USABILITY

- Usability concerns how well a help system supports its users. Usability issues are often subjective. Ideally, users should be able to easily navigate through a help system and quickly get to the information they need.

- Does context-sensitive assistance adequately support users from screen to screen?

- Is the system appropriately designed for the skill levels of the target user?

- What about user perception? Will users consider the system to be useful, accurate, and easy to navigate?

- How many clicks does it take users to get to the information they are looking for?

  Please refer to Chapter 10 for more information on consistency and usability testing.

HELP SYSTEM CONTENT

- A help system is only as valuable as the information it conveys. Inaccuracies in procedural instruction lead to confusion. In some instances, technical inaccuracies in help systems can lead to serious data loss.

- Every fact and line of instruction detailed in a help system should be tested for accuracy.

- Content should be tested for correct use of grammar and spelling.

- Has important information been omitted?

FUNCTIONAL ERRORS

- Functional testing of a help system ensures that everything is operating as intended. Each link should be operational and lead the user to the intended destination. All graphics should load properly. The table of contents links should be working.

- Help elements to be tested for proper functionality include:
  - Jumps
  - Pop-ups
  - Macros
  - Keyword consistency
  - Buttons
  - Navigation
  - Context-sensitive links
  - Frames/no frames

TECHNOLOGY-RELATED ERRORS

- Compatibility
- Performance
- Look for and research errors that are common to each technology type, then design test cases that look for those errors.
  - Visit online technical support and issue databases that are specific to each technology type. Such sites list bugs that users have dealt with in the past. They are a great place to begin research for test-case design. For an example, visit eHelp's technical support knowledge base at www.helpcommunity.com.

Testing Considerations

APPLICATION HELP SYSTEMS

- Are there multiple methods available for accessing help from within the application (UI button, navigation bar, menu, etc.)? If so, each method should be tested for proper functionality.
- Does context-sensitive information meet the needs of the intended audience in every situation? Different users have different needs; depending on their skill level and where they are in a program, users will require different information from the help system.
- Does the system include graphics? If so, do the graphics load properly?

REFERENCE HELP SYSTEMS

- Is the system designed to link to other online resources? If so, are the links working properly? Are the other resources active and available?
- Is the subject matter compatible with the knowledge and skill levels of the system's target audience?
- Is the information design of the system intuitive?

TUTORIAL HELP SYSTEMS

- How are users directed through the content? Are the intended navigation paths clearly marked?
- Is appropriate user feedback delivered?
- Does the system respond accurately to user input?

SALES AND MARKETING HELP SYSTEMS

- How will the presentation be delivered? Is the system working properly on all delivery mediums?
- Is the system compatible with the computing skills of the target audience?

ONLINE HELP VERSUS PRINTED HELP

- Though online help systems and printed help serve effectively the same purpose, their testing differs in a few important ways:
  - Online help systems are interactive. Links, navigation, software functionality, and browser settings are complexities not found in traditional printed documentation.
  - Formatting can be dynamic. The diversity of browser types and browser versions leads to variations in content display. Where one browser may display content accurately, another browser may display content with inaccurate font size, unintended background color, and wrapping text.

ENVIRONMENTAL CONDITION TESTING

- Web systems are vulnerable to environmental conditions surrounding platform compatibility, display resolutions, and browser types.
- Environmental variables to pay attention to include:
  - Cross-platform compatibility: Mac, Windows, and UNIX
  - Graphic hotspots
  - Display color (e.g., compiled with 16.8 million color palette, displayed with 16-color palette)
  - Display resolution (e.g., compiled at 1024 × 768, displayed at 640 × 480)

Bibliography

Klein, Jeannine M. E., *Building Enhanced HTML Help with DHTML and CSS*, Upper Saddle River, NJ: Prentice Hall, 2000.

Deaton, Mary, and Cheryl Lockett Zubak. *Designing Windows 95 Help: A Guide to Creating Online Documents*. Indianapolis, IN: Que Corporation, 1997.

Horton, William. *Designing and Writing Online Documentation: Hypermedia for Self-Supporting Products*. New York: John Wiley & Sons, Inc.,1994.

CHAPTER

16

Installation Tests

Why Read This Chapter?

To be effective in testing installation programs, we need to analyze the functional roles of both the installation and uninstallation programs from the designer's perspective. Knowledge of potential issues and common errors that are specific to the operating system and environment in which the installation program will be running contributes to effective test-case design. It is also helpful to learn about available tools and techniques that can be used to track changes to the environment, both before and after installations and uninstalls.

TOPICS COVERED IN THIS CHAPTER

- ◆ Introduction
- ◆ The Roles of Installation/Uninstallation Programs
- ◆ Common Features and Options
- ◆ Common Server-Side-Specific Installation Issues

(continued)

Introduction

This chapter looks at the functional roles of installation and uninstallation programs. Common errors and issues that are associated with these programs in Web environments are discussed. Installation methods for both client-side and server-side installations are explored. Test-case design and test considerations for testing installation and uninstallation programs are also covered. Tips and tools related to tracking changes to the environment (such as the InCtrl utility shown in Figure 16.6) are also discussed.

In an installation process, undetected errors—either server-side or client-side—can prevent robust applications from functioning properly. Web applications involve a server-side software installation of one sort or another. Occasionally, Web applications, even those that utilize Web browsers for their user interface (UI), also involve client-side software installations (installing plug-in components, ActiveX controls, etc.). Some Web applications install platform-specific TCP/IP clients that are used in place of regular browsers.

Effective installation testing requires solid knowledge of the operating system and the environment in which the installer will be running and the application will be installed. Environmental dependencies involving software/hardware configurations and compatibility need to be clearly understood so that failure symptoms can be quickly identified as either software errors or user errors.

Installation program bugs may originate from several sources:

- The detection and interpretation of environment variables. For example: How much disk space is available? Which browser is installed, and where?

- The copying of files. For Web installations, a common source of error is having an intermittent network connection.

- The configuration of the system and the environment.

- Software and hardware incompatibility.

- The user might install the wrong application or the wrong version, or might terminate operation prematurely or do other things that interfere with the installation.

- Background noise. For example, the virus checker that the user runs in the background might interfere with installation in several ways. Sometimes, the installation itself will propagate a virus.

We can improve our effectiveness if we learn as much as possible about what the operating system expects from the installed application and what common application setup errors have already been discovered.

The Roles of Installation/Uninstallation Programs

Following are descriptions of the typical activities that are associated with installation and uninstallation programs. Common errors that installation and uninstallation programs are associated with are also discussed.

Installer

An installer often begins an installation by retrieving user operating environment information. In this process, installers learn about user hardware/software configurations and memory information, such as RAM and disk space availability. Based on its interpretation of collected information, the installer will then create new directories, install files, and configure the system so that the application will run successfully. Typically, the copying of data files includes moving executables (.EXEs), software components such as Java classes (.JAR), dynamic link libraries (DLLs), and so on into appropriate directories on the user's hard disk. Sometimes, compressed files (such as .tar, .zip, or .sit) need to be uncompressed before application files can be copied to the directories. After the copying process is complete, the installer will configure the *application operating environment* by adding or modifying configuration data files and (in Windows-based environments) registry entries.

Here is an example series of activities performed by an installation program:

- Execute the installer from the source host.
- Log in the destination host.
- Interrogate the destination host to learn about its environment.

- Install software components based on the information collected from the user environment and install option selected by the user (such as Full, Compact, or Custom).

- Uncompress the .tar, .zip, or .sit files.

- Search for or create directories.

- Copy application executables, DLLs, and data files, preferably checking for each file whether a more recent copy is already on the destination system.

- Copy shared files (shared with other applications). For example, in a Windows environment, these files are copied to the \Windows\System or \Winnt\System directory.

- Copy shared files (shared within company-only applications). For example, in a Windows environment, these files are copied to the \MyCompany\SharedDLLs\.

- Create registry keys (Windows only).

- Validate registry key values (Windows only).

- Change registry, .INI files, and/or .BAT files (Windows only).

- Reboot the system (Windows only).

- Populate database tables, stored procedures, triggers, and so forth.

- Create or update configuration files.

Following are descriptions of several classes of installer errors, along with examples of those errors.

Functionality errors. Installer functionality errors are miscalculations or failures in an installer's tasks (collecting data, creating folders, installing files, etc.). Examples include an installer not checking for available disk space or failing to complete an installation due to a forced reboot in the middle of the install script.

User interface design errors. User interface design errors are failures in conveying information to the user. Examples include incorrect, incomplete, or confusing instructions; surprising functions for controls; nonstandard menus; and inappropriate error messages.

User interface implementation errors. User interface implementation errors are failures in the installation of UI controls and UI functionality. Examples include incorrect behavior of common function keys (such as ESC, ENTER, F1, etc.) and improper UI updating and refresh during dialog box interaction.

Misinterpreting collected information. Errors in an installer's interpretation of collected information about the user environment include any misidentification of user hardware or software. Examples include an installer not correctly identifying the user's software platform and failing to detect the preexistence of a browser.

Errors by the person installing the program. Typos in file names or directory names can cause files to not be found or to be created in the wrong place. Invalid names, passwords, or e-mail addresses can cause the install or, later, the application to silently fail.

Operating system errors. Operating system errors are failures in user environment settings and file copying. Examples include the installer failing to add a shortcut to the Start menu, inaccurate registry settings, and application fonts being placed in an incorrect folder.

Dynamic-link-library-specific errors. DLL-specific errors include failures in the detection and copying of correct DLLs. Examples include the installation of incorrect versions of DLLs and the failure to check for preexisting required DLLs. Another common problem is trouble installing a DLL that is currently in use (already loaded in memory).

Uninstaller

The role of an uninstaller is to reverse the installation process (reversing the file copying and configurations that were executed by the associated installation program). Uninstallers often remove all data files—including application executables and DLLs—that have been installed by the installer.

Uninstallers generally offer users options for keeping and removing user data. They recover an application environment to the state it was in prior to the software installation. In Windows environments, this process involves modifying files, modifying registry entries, and removing entries that were created by the installer.

Here is an example series of activities performed by an uninstallation program:

- Remove directories.
- Remove application files.
- Remove application EXE and private DLL files.
- Check whether certain files are used by other installed applications.
- Remove shared files (shared with other applications) if no other installed application needs to use it.

- Remove shared files (shared within company-only applications) if no other installed application needs to use it.
- Remove registry keys (Windows only).
- Restore original registry key validations (Windows only).
- Execute the uninstaller via links or command lines.
- Execute the uninstaller via Add/Remove programs (Windows only).

Any of these uninstallation activities may introduce errors. Potential errors include the uninstaller not completely removing files (including program folders, directories, and DLLs) or removing files that shouldn't be removed (such as data files that were created by the application but that the user wants to keep; graphics files that came with the application that the user wants to keep; and files that are not marked as shared system files but are, in fact, used by more than one application and system DLLs).

Common Features and Options

The primary measure of success for an installation program is that the installed application functions as expected under all setup options and supported software/hardware configurations. The secondary measure of success is determined by the quality of the installation program itself—its functionality, accuracy of instruction, UI, and ease of use. Following is an examination of common features and options that are supported by installation programs. An understanding of these functions assists us in identifying and executing adequate test coverage.

User Setup Options

Installation programs often allow users to specify preferred setup options. Here is a sample list of setup options that might be supported by an installer (each option should be fully tested).

Full, typical, or expanded setup. *Typical* is usually the default option. It installs most but not all application files and components. *Full* might install all files and components. *Expanded* might install all files and components, and additionally install files or components that would normally be left with the vendor or on the CD.

Minimum setup. This installs the fewest possible number of files required to operate the application. This option helps conserve disk space.

Custom setup. This offers users the option of specifying only the exact components they wish to have installed (such as additional utilities and certain application features). An example of server-side custom setup options include:

- Application server only.
- Database server setup only.
- Initialize database only.
- Create and initialize database.

Command-line setup. This option uses batch scripts to run the setup without user interaction via the UI.

Testing should start with the typical setup option, because this is the most commonly selected option. Once this setup option is considered to be stable, testing of the other setup options may begin. In theory, the functionality within the code remains unchanged from option to option; based on the setup conditions specified by the user, a subset of the standard functions will be called in a particular sequence to carry out the desired result. However, errors are often introduced in the implementation of this conditional logic. Typical errors in this class range from missing files that should have been copied, skipping a configuration procedure that should have been executed, and missing error detection code that warns users of fatal conditions (such as "not enough disk space to install"). These errors may ultimately prevent an installer from executing successfully, or the installed application from functioning properly.

Installation Sources and Destinations

The following subsections explore the complexities of installing software over distributed-server systems. Source and destination media types (CD-ROM, Web, hard disk) and branching options within installation programs are also covered.

Server Distribution Configurations

In the testing of Web-based applications, all supported server-side installations should be identified and fully tested. Figures 16.1 through 16.3 show examples of possible server distribution configurations. Keep in mind that just because the installation process successfully executes with one server distribution configuration does not mean that the installation process will successfully execute with all other server distribution configurations.

Server-Side Installation Example

In a server-side installation, the user (usually an administrator) must, at a minimum, be able to specify the following:

- The ID of the host (the physical server) where the software is to be installed.
- The ID and password (with adequate login privileges) for the host, so that the installation can successfully complete its tasks.
- The ID and password for the Web server.
- The path to the Web server.
- The ID and password (with adequate login privileges) for the database server residing on the host, so that database setup procedures can be completed.
- The path where the software components are to be installed and the database is to be created.

Installers offer the following functionality through the UI:

- A clickwrap software license agreement. If you choose not to agree with the terms, the installation software will normally stop installation.
- An input field for the host ID.
- Two input fields for the user ID and password that are used to log in to the host.
- Two input fields for the user ID and password that are used to log in to the database server.
- An input field used to specify the application path.

As an example, under a one-host configuration (where both the Web server and the database server reside in the same hardware host), the installation completes successfully (see Figures 16.1 through 16.3). However, under a two-host configuration (where the Web server lives on one host and the database server lives on another host), the installation program no longer works. To understand why this installer error has occurred, we should examine the installer's functionality:

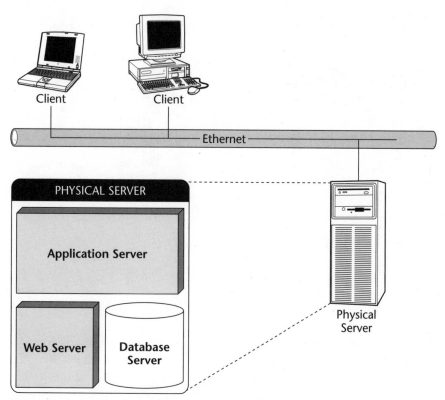

Figure 16.1   One-host configuration.

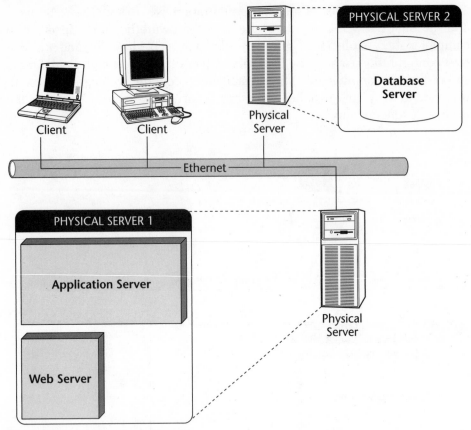

Figure 16.2 Two-host configuration.

- The installer allows only one input field for the host ID and a set of input fields for the user ID and password on that host. Under a two-host configuration, this does not work because another set of input parameters is required to log on to the second host.

- Misinterpretation may result in a two-host configuration when the application path is set to C:\MYAPP. Does C:\MYAPP apply for host 1 or host 2? On UNIX systems, has the configuration used localhost in place of the host name?

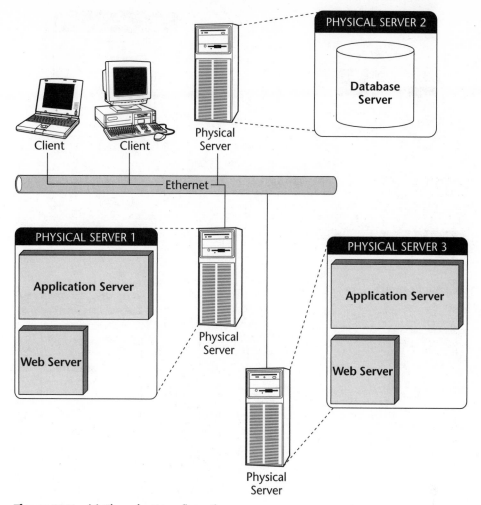

Figure 16.3   (a) Three-host configuration.

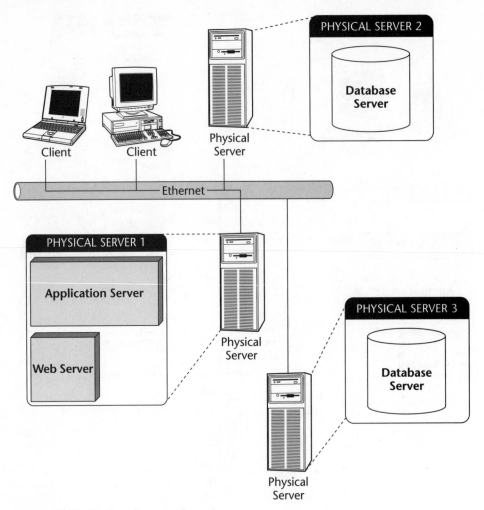

Figure 16.3   (b) Three-host configuration.

Media Types

Installation programs may be run from several different media types, and applications may be installed on several different media types (as well as hosts). Each unique condition should be identified and thoroughly tested:

- Floppy disk installation from a local or remote drive: 1.44 Mb, 120 Mg, 233 Mb

- CD-ROM installation from a local CD-ROM or a remote shared CD-ROM

- DVD-ROM installation (CD from a DVD player)
- Web installation (purchasing a product over the Web, using secure-server technology to get a code that unlocks the software):
  - Downloading and installing over the Web without saving the downloaded file.
  - Downloading and saving the file, then executing the installer from the local or remote host.
- Installing off a hard disk (includes downloadable installers):
  - Local or shared volume, in general
  - Local or shared FAT hard drive
  - Local or shared NTFS hard drive
  - Local or shared compressed NTFS hard drive
  - Local or shared Novell NetWare hard drive
  - Local or shared removable drives (such as Iomega, Zip, and Jazz)

Many installation errors are the result of running installers from, or installing to, different media types. For example, an installer might not autorun off a CD-ROM.

Branching Options

Installation programs typically include numerous branching options, which require users to make decisions about such things as continuing the installation, deciding where software should be installed, and deciding which type of installation should be performed. Figure 16.4 (a) through (d), which spans the next several pages, details a typical software installation process that might be executed on either the server-side or the client-side. It is a good idea to create a flowchart that depicts the branching options and use it to guide the creation of test cases.

This diagram (Figure 16.5) presents the branching options that are illustrated in the preceding installation program example shown in Figure 16.4 (a)–(d). Charting the branching options of an installation program under test is an effective means of guiding testing and determining required test coverage.

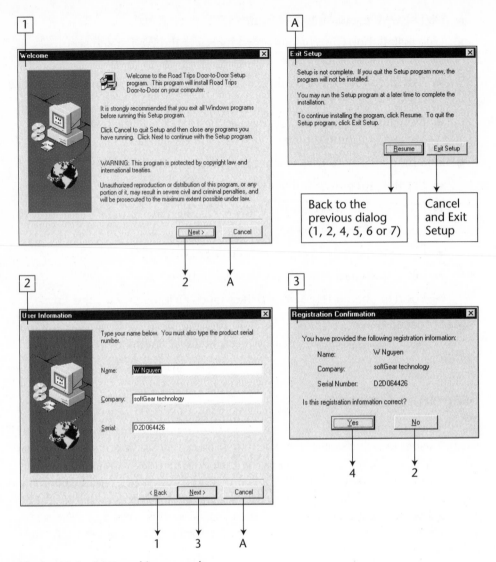

Figure 16.4 (a) Branching example.

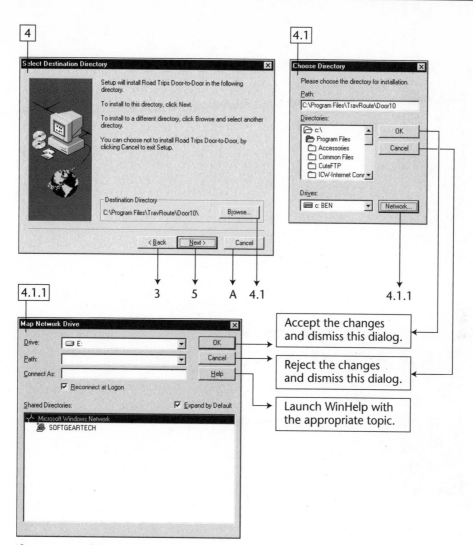

Figure 16.4 (b) Branching example.

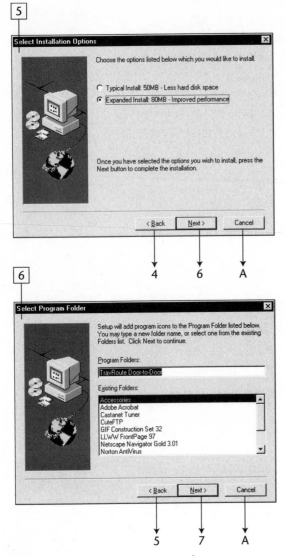

Figure 16.4   (c) Branching example.

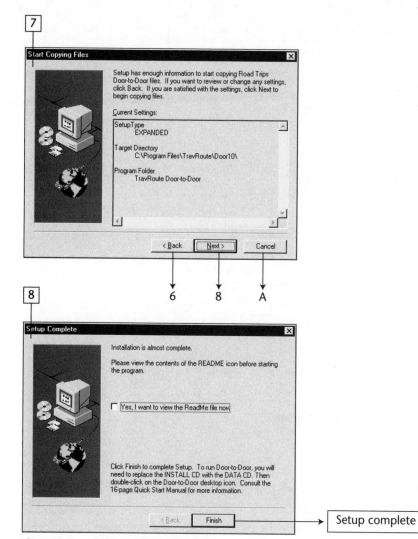

Figure 16.4   (d) Branching example.

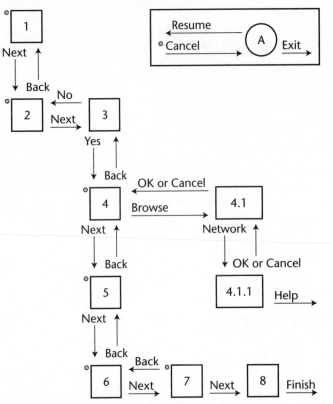

Figure 16.5   Branching options diagram.

Common Server-Side-Specific Installation Issues

All Web applications require some form of server-side software installation. Although there are some Web applications that provide client-side functionality by installing software on the client-side, most do not because their UI functions are supplied via Web browsers (the sample application in Chapter 8 is an example of this sort of application).

Table 16.1 lists a number of common server setup issues that may come up during installation testing.

Table 16.1 Server-Side Installation Issues

SERVER SETUP COMPONENT	DESCRIPTION	ISSUES TO ADDRESS
Server ID	ID used by servers/ processes to access services or components that reside on a server (local or remote host).	Name IP Local | Name | IP (if the target server is local)
Physical Server	Often referred to as a host. This host (physical hardware box) has an OS installed on it and is configured to commu- nicate with other hosts on a network.	Minimum versus maximum configuration issues Service packs Hardware compatibility issues
Server Software Component	Server software or component installed on a physical server.	Web server Database server Application server POP server SMTP server Proxy server Firewall
Accessing Services	The process of logging in to, interacting with, and accessing resources on a server.	Server name Server IP Local | Name | IP (if the target server is local)
Web Server	Server that hosts HTML pages and other Web service components. It receives and processes requests from/to clients and other services.	Distributed servers Vendor/OS/Version Server configuration for operability and security Account ID, password, and privileges Manual versus automated configuration
Database Server	Typically, an SQL DBMS that hosts system and user data. It may host stored procedures and/ or triggers used by the application server or related services.	Distributed servers Vendor/OS/Version Server configuration for operability and security Manual versus automated configuration

(continued)

Table 16.1 *(continued)*

SERVER SETUP COMPONENT	DESCRIPTION	ISSUES TO ADDRESS
ODBC	Object Database Connectivity: A Microsoft application interface that enables applications to access data from a variety of data sources.	Data Source Name (DSN) Server name Login ID and password Account privileges Authentication methods (e.g., NT versus SQL server) Driver version incompatibility issues Target database driver incompatibility issues
Application Server	Typically consists of code packaged in both binary objects (such as .EXEs, .DLLs, .COMs, JavaClass, and scripts) and integrated third-party components. These pieces work in concert with one another (and with other servers) to provide end-product functionality.	Distributed servers Vendor/OS/Version Server configuration for operability and security Manual versus automated configuration

Some common problems in Web application installations include:

- Database rules and permissions.
- Security.
- Server software version issues.
- Time-out/waits.
- Application files being installed on the wrong server (with multiple server systems).
- Drive and path names.
- UNIX paths use forward slash (/), such as Unix/MyDir/.
- Windows paths use backward slash (\), such as Windows\MyDir\.
- UNIX file name is case-sensitive.
- Windows file name is not case-sensitive.
- UNIX file name does not allow space.
- Windows long file name does allow space.
- Problems related to installations occurring while other server software (such as .DLLs) is in use by other applications.

Installer/Uninstaller Testing Utilities

Here are some tools that you should consider for the installation and uninstall phase of your testing project. These comparison-based testing tools compare system attributes and files both before and after installation and uninstalls.

Comparison-Based Testing Tools

Comparison-based testing tools look for the addition, deletion, or change of:

- Directories and files
- Configuration data in specific files (.ini, .cfg)
- Registry information in registry database (Windows-specific)

InControl4 and InControl5

InControl4 and InControl5 track all environment changes that are performed by an installer. They track changes made to the hard disk, registry, and other configuration files (such as WIN.INI and SYSTEM.INI). Figure 16.6 shows InControl4, which can be downloaded for free. Search for InCtrl at www .zdnet.com/products.

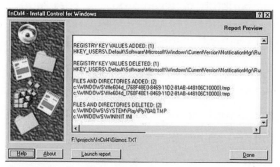

Figure 16.6   InControl4.

Norton Utilities' Registry Tracker and File Compare

These tools provide similar functionality to that of InControl5. However, these products are not shareware.

Testing Considerations

SOME OBJECTIVES OF INSTALLATION TESTING

- Test the functionality and UI of the installer.
- Test the functionality of the application that is installed and set up.
- Test the known error conditions and error handling of the installer and uninstaller.
- Test the impact that the installer and uninstaller have on existing system environments.
- Test software and hardware compatibility.
- Test the installer functionality on multiple server configurations.
- Test the installer functionality using multiple installation options and conditions.
- Test the configurations and modifications that the installer makes to existing files and registry entries.
- Test the uninstall program to see that it removes all data files—including application executables and .DLLs—that are installed by the installer.
- If your company markets multiple products with independent installers, test for installer compatibility between products. For example, can you install both products without conflicts? Can you uninstall individual products without affecting the others?

AREAS OF CONCERN THAT SHOULD BE CONSIDERED DURING INSTALL/UNINSTALL TESTING

- The functionality of the installed application.
- The functionality of the install and uninstall programs.
- The error handling of the install and uninstall programs.
- The UIs of the install and uninstall programs.
- The environment conditions in which the install and uninstall programs (and, ultimately, the installed application) will operate. Test coverage should include application-specific and environment-specific variables (including both dynamic and static conditions).
- Application-specific conditions: all supported user-setup options, all supported upgrade options, and all reinstallation conditions.

- Environment-specific conditions: all supported software and hardware conditions (especially when the installer relies on the existing configuration in determining which setup options to run).

- Does your product require administrative (Admin) privileges to install it? If so, is an explicit error message to this effect given if you try to install it without Admin rights?

TEST SCENARIOS THAT SHOULD BE CONSIDERED

- Installation under minimum configuration.

- Installation and running of application on a clean system. A clean environment consists of only the required components of an operating system.

- Installation and running of an application on a dirty system. A dirty environment consists of the operating system components and other commonly used software, such as various versions for browser, productivity applications, virus checkers, and so on.

- Installation of upgrades that are targeted toward an operating system (e.g., Windows 98 to Windows 2000).

- Installation of upgrades that are targeted toward new application functionality. Did the installer remove the dated files? Did any other applications depend on the dated files?

- Installation of software over multiple operating systems.

- Reducing the amount of free disk space during installation to see if the installer can respond gracefully to an unexpected lack of sufficient space after the installation has begun.

- Canceling the installation midway through to see how well it restores the system to the base state.

- If you change the default target installation path to a different drive, will all the files really be installed in the specified path? For example, changing C:\program files\targetdir to D:\program files\targetdir: some programs will still place some files in the C:\program files\ targetdir path without warning, thus spreading the installation between two or more drives.

FUNCTIONAL INSTALLATION TESTING CONSIDERATIONS

- Execute the test cases in Appendix F, "Web Test-Case Design Guideline: Input Boundary and Validation Matrix I."

- Test a mix of UI navigation and transition paths.

- Look for user-level logic errors. For example, run the installer by following all on-screen instructions and user guide instructions; look for software-to-documentation mismatches.

- Consider test cases for error detection and error handling.

- Make sure that the installer does not prompt inaccurate or misleading error messages.

- Consider whether the installer might obtain incorrect path information, and thereby install shared files in the wrong place or update registry keys with the wrong information.

- Consider incorrect default path errors.

- Check for incorrect file permissions. The install program may provide permissions based on the read/write/execute permissions of the install media.

- Consider the file ownership for the installed files.

- Test with full, compact, and custom installation options.

- Test with various installation branches.

SOME COMMON INSTALLATION FUNCTIONALITY ERRORS

- The main application does not successfully operate in all setup options.

- The installer fails to operate under the minimum configuration.

- The installer fails to operate under the maximum configuration. For example, if the size of the variable used to store the value of free disk space is too small for the actual amount of free disk space, that variable will be overflowed. This error often leads to a negative value reported for free disk space. In turn, it might prevent the installer from executing.

- The installer assumes (via a hard-coded path) that some source files are on floppy drive A. Therefore, installation fails if the user installs from floppy drive B or over the network or from any other drive whose name is not A.

- The installer fails to provide the user with default options.

- The installer does not check for available disk space.

- The installer fails to check whether certain key components (such as Internet Explorer or Acrobat) are already present on the user's system. Instead, it installs a new version (which might be older than the copy on the user's disk) and sets a path to that newly installed version.

- The installer fails to inform the user of how much space the installation requires.

- The installer fails to operate on a clean system.

- The installed application fails to operate after the completion of an install on a clean system.

- The installer fails to complete due to a forced reboot in the middle of the install script.

- The uninstaller fails to remove all program files.

- The uninstaller removes files that the user created without informing the user or offering an alternative.

- The uninstaller moves user files stored in the user directory to a new location without informing the user or offering an alternative.

- The uninstaller fails to remove empty directories left behind by the application.

USER INTERFACE INSTALLATION TESTING CONSIDERATIONS

- Execute the test cases in Appendices D and E (the keyboard and mouse action matrices, respectively).

- Test the default settings of the UI controls.

- Test the default command control for each dialog and message box. Does it lead to a typical installation?

- Check the behavior of common function keys such as ESC, Enter, F1, Shift-F1, WINDOWS, and so on.

- Check for proper UI updating and refresh during dialog box interaction. Also check navigation between dialog boxes (using Back and Next buttons).

- Test the default click path that is generated by clicking the Tab button repeatedly. Is the path intuitive?

- Test the default click path that is generated by clicking the Tab button repeatedly while holding down the Shift button. Is the path intuitive?

- Test the implementation of accelerator keys (underscores beneath letters of menu selection items). Are the keys functional? Have intuitive character selections been made (N for Next, B for Back, etc.)?

- Are there conflicts between accelerator commands? If so, is the most commonly used command given preference?

- If a common command is not given an accelerator shortcut, is a symbolic alternative offered (for example, Ctrl-X for Cut, and Ctrl-W for Close)?

- Is a quick-key or accelerator key (one-handed) interface possible?

COMMON UI CONVENTION FOR DIALOG BOX COMMANDS

- The X button in the top right corner of Windows means "close the current window" or "close the current window and cancel the current operation."

- Next means "go to the next dialog box and close the current dialog box."

- Back means "go to the previous dialog box and close the current dialog box."

- Cancel means "cancel the current operation and close the current dialog box."

- Resume means "resume the current application and close the current dialog box."

- Exit Setup means "exit the Setup program and close the current dialog box."

- Yes means "yes to the question being posed, and close the current dialog box."

- No means "I choose No to the question being posed, and close the current dialog box."

- Finish means "finish the installation and close the current dialog box."

COMMON ERRORS IN MISINTERPRETATION OF COLLECTED INFORMATION (WINDOWS-SPECIFIC)

- The installer misidentifies the existence (or nonexistence) of a certain application (e.g., a browser) or shared file (e.g., a DLL) because it refers to an unreliable source—for example, a wrong key in the registry database.

- The installer misidentifies the software platform and configuration (OS, drivers, browsers, etc.).

- The installer misidentifies the hardware configuration (CPU type, CPU clock speed, physical or virtual memory, audio or video player settings, etc.) because it misinterprets the return values of an API call.

COMMON INSTALLATION ERRORS RELATED TO OPERATING SYSTEM ISSUES (WINDOWS-SPECIFIC)

- The installer fails to register basic information (per Microsoft logo guidelines) such as company name, application name, or version in the registry.

- The installer copies files other than shared DLLs to \WINDOWS or \SYSTEM directories.

- The installer fails to register OLE objects in the registry.
- The installer places application fonts in a folder other than the Fonts folder.
- The installer fails to use a progress indicator.
- The installer fails to add shortcuts to the Start menu.
- The installer fails to register document types.
- The installer fails to support universal naming convention (UNC) paths.
- The installer does not autorun from a CD.
- The name of the installation program is not SETUP.EXE.
- The installer fails to configure the Context menu.
- The uninstaller fails to remove all information from the registry.
- The uninstaller fails to remove shortcuts from the desktop.
- NTFS compression: Some applications have problems and display erroneous I/0 error messages when they detect NTFS compression.

COMMON DLL-RELATED ERRORS (WINDOWS-SPECIFIC)

- The installer fails to copy required DLLs (perhaps the files are not even included in distributed media).
- The installer fails to install the correct versions of DLLs (MFC DLLs, IFC DLLs, and other shared DLLs).
- The installer fails to check for the existence of DLLs needed by the application.
- The installer fails to correctly reference count-shareable DLLs in the registry. Shared DLLs that are to be installed in the Windows\System or Program Files\Common Files directories (that are not part of a clean install of Windows 9x) need to register, increment, and decrement the reference count in the registry.
- The application fails to operate correctly due to the existence of several incompatible versions of DLLs that are shared by multiple applications.
- The application fails to operate properly due to the existence of several incompatible versions of DLLs that are produced or supported by a specific vendor.
- The installer fails to copy systemwide shared files (e.g., VBRUN40O. DLL) to the Windows\SYSTEM or WinNT\SYSTEM directories.
- The uninstaller fails to correctly reference count-shareable DLLs in the registry.

- After decrementing a DLL's usage count that results in a usage count of zero, the uninstaller fails to display a message offering to delete the DLL or save it in case it might be needed later.

- The uninstaller fails to completely remove files, including program folders (unless there is user data in them), LNK files, nonsystem-shared files (if no longer used), directories, and registry keys.

- The uninstaller mistakenly removes system DLLs.

Bibliography and Additional Resources

Bibliography

Agruss, Chris. "Automating Software Installation Testing." *Software Testing and Quality Engineering* (July/August 2000). (See www.stqemagazine.com.)

Chen, Weiying, and Wayne Berry. *Windows NT Registry Guide.* Menlo Park, CA: Addison-Wesley Developers Press, 1997.

Microsoft. *The Windows Interface Guidelines for Software Design.* Redmond, WA: Microsoft Press, 1996.

Wallace, Nathan. *Windows 2000 Registry: Little Black Book.* Scottsdale, AZ: Coriolis Technology Press, 2000.

Additional Resources

Jasnowski, M. "Installing Java with the Browser." *Java Developer's Journal* (March 2000).

(See www.sys-con.com/java.)

Microsoft Windows 9x/NT/2000 Logo Guidelines.

(See www.microsoft.com.)

InstallShield Resources:

(see www.installsite.org.)

CHAPTER

17

Configuration and Compatibility Tests

Why Read This Chapter?

One of the challenges in software development is to not only ensure that the product works as intended and handles error conditions reasonably well, but also that the product will continue to work as expected in all supported environments. In the PC stand-alone environment, this testing effort has proven to be a daunting task. Web application's client-server architecture further multiplies the testing complexity and demands. This chapter offers an analysis and guidance on configuration and compatibility testing. It discusses the needs of testing on both the server- and client-sides. It also offers examples of configuration- and compatibility-specific errors to suggest testing ideas that can be applied to your testing and bug analyzing.

Introduction

It's not possible to provide complete test coverage (see *Testing Computer Software*, Chapter 2, by Kaner, Falk and Nguyen, 1999), nor is it cost-effective. The goal of Web configuration and compatibility testing is to find errors in the application while it operates under the major real-world user environments. Performance and minimum system requirements—determined at the beginning of product development—are used as a baseline in the design of configuration and compatibility test cases.

The strategy in both configuration and compatibility testing is to run functional acceptance simple tests (FASTs), subsets of task-oriented functional tests (TOFTs), and modified sets of forced-error tests (FETs) to exercise the main set of features. These tests focus on data input and output, settings dependencies, and interactions on a wide range of software and hardware configurations in an effort to uncover potential problems.

These tests focus on problems that an application may have in running under a certain condition that is not covered under standard functional testing. Testing covers the expected user-installed base, in addition to other machines, configurations, connectivity, operating systems (OSs), browsers, and software that may be identified by the development or marketing team as problematic.

Configuration and compatibility testing are potentially more labor-intensive for Web systems, compared with the PC stand-alone system, due to both their component-based and distributed architectures. The configuration and compatibility testing of a Web system must take servers, databases, browsers, and connectivity devices into account.

Configuration and compatibility testing generally covers the following:

SERVER-SIDE

- Application server
- Web server
- Database server
- Firewall

- OS
- Hardware
- Concurrent applications

CLIENT-SIDE

- Browser type and version
- OS
- Minifirewall
- Childproof blocking
- Ad proofing
- Concurrent applications (instant messaging, virus checkers, etc.)
- Client-side hardware such as local printers, video, and storage
- Transmission Control Protocol/Internet Protocol (TCP/IP) stack
  - AOL stack
  - Microsoft Networking stack
  - Other third-party TCP/IP stacks

NETWORK DEVICES AND CONNECTIVITY

- Bridges, routers, gateways, and so forth
- Internet/intranet
- 10/100 Base-T, modems, T1, ISDN, DSL, and so forth

The Test Cases

The goal of configuration and compatibility test cases is to evaluate end-to-end functionality from a high level for most features and from a lower level for any feature that is expected to be problematic.

There is usually a time element involved in developing compatibility and configuration tests. It is not practical to execute the entire set of tests on every environment. Time considerations may allow only a very short testing time per environment. If you run four hours of tests on 20 OS, hardware, and browser combinations (not really that many), you have already spent two weeks just testing. This does not take into consideration time for bug submission, research, or system setups.

Choosing the right set of configuration and compatibility test cases requires experience and team input. The best approach is to target troublesome areas, as well as to ask developers about particularly vulnerable configuration or incompatibility scenarios. For example, if DHTML (Dynamic Hypertext Markup Language) is heavily used, incompatibility issues should be expected among browser types and versions.

Approaching Configuration and Compatibility Testing

Choose the test configurations and test cases wisely. Tests should focus on the types of things that can go wrong when you change from one configuration to another. A good strategy for configuration and compatibility test planning is to model it after the seven steps to good configuration testing outlined in *Testing Computer Software*, Chapter 8, (Kaner, Falk and Nguyen, 1999).

1. *Analyze the market share.* If you can only support four major releases of browsers or database servers, which ones do the majority of your target audience use? Focus the testing and fixing of configuration and incompatibility on those platforms.

2. *Analyze the software on both the client-side and the server-side.* For example, you need to fully understand how the browser works to come up with useful test cases, that is, to understand how the various settings on the browser will affect the application, how various releases of the browser will affect the application, how various releases of the Web servers will affect the application, and so on. How will various settings on server-side affect the behavior of the application or the security of the overall system? (These topics are discussed throughout this book.)

3. *Analyze the ways in which the server generates content and in which the browser interprets, then formats and displays the content.* For example, if the application is browser-based (supporting the major commercial releases of browsers such as Netscape Navigator and Internet Explorer), you might not have to worry about dealing with incompatibility among various printer, display, audio, and other input/output (I/O) devices. However, you will have to test with various releases of each major browser because the understanding is that there will be an incompatibility issue in interpreting HTML, style sheet information and scripts, executing Java applets or ActiveX control, and so on.

4. *Save time.* Work in equivalent classes and go for broad and then deep coverage. For example, start testing with the major release of each supported browser. Look for functionality and configuration-specific issues first. Have those issues resolved before moving on to testing various minor releases.

5. *Improve efficiency.* Always look for ways to automate repetitive tasks. Keep good records so that you won't have to waste time testing redundant test cases and configurations.

6. *Share your experience.* Archive configuration lists, test cases, and other test documentation for later reuse. Build a knowledge base of configuration and incompatibility issues to share with other testers or to use in the next project.

7. *How do software and hardware components interact with each other?* Chapter 5, "Web Application Components," discusses how the various components potentially interact with each other on both the client-side and the server-side. In this chapter, the section entitled "Distributed Server Configurations" also demonstrates an example of how a physical server configuration might affect the functionality of the application. Focus your thinking around those issues in deciding the configurations with which the application needs to be tested.

Although it is not feasible to test for every conceivable combination of hardware and software, compatibility testing can deliver reasonable risk assessment by testing a cross section of available hardware and software. Representative models from each class of hardware and software are tested in combination, thereby offering significant insight into major risk issues.

Equivalence class analysis requires experience, research, knowledge, and careful thought. To partition various operating environments, you must have knowledge of the technologies used in the Web site or application. This includes technologies like Java applet, ActiveX control, QuickTime, or Windows Media Player, along with an understanding of how these components work in various browsers. The general idea is to cluster like components into classes so that the testing of any one member of a class is representative of all other members of the class. Components that are under test should be grouped into a common class when it is expected that their testing will generate identical results.

For example, the browser-based application under test supports report printing. It relies on the browser to render the page and send it to the printer. We know that in this application most of the HyperText Markup Language (HTML) pages sent to the browsers are pure HTML. Only a few of them contain Java applets that are visible in the browser. Analyzing this application, we discover two classes of content in the Web pages: (1) pure HTML and (2) HTML mixed with visible Java applets. For the pure HTML class, we would not expect to find any errors in the outputs sent to the printer because pure HTML printing is well tested by the browser vendor. When we see a Java applet displayed in the browser, however, that applet might not show up when the page is sent to the printer. This is an incompatibility issue in the browser. Therefore, printing tests should be exercised for all pages with Java applets. This type of analysis helps determine the configurations to focus on as well as those configurations that can be excluded in the interest of time.

Before testing begins, it's recommended that the test team present the results of their equivalence class analysis to the project team. The results should be in the form of a test matrix that clearly details which equivalent classes have been identified and which hardware and software components represent the various classes. (For more information on equivalent class partitioning, read *Testing Computer Software*, by Kaner, Falk, and Nguyen, pp. 7–11, 126–133, 399–401. See the Bibliography at the end of this chapter.)

Considering Target Users

The system under test should be analyzed against the target-user installed base. For example, a company's internal Web-based application may be used almost exclusively with Netscape Navigator 4.73 on laptops of a particular brand or variety. In such a scenario, testing should focus primarily on the application's performance on laptops.

An example of this is an application that will be used by schools or graphic artists, including book publishers: it should be tested on Apple Macintosh computers. Demographics of the intended users for your application may show a large divergence from the "industry standards."

Remember to also test the less-common configurations. Testing that is limited to only the most popular or common configurations might miss important errors and may give you a false sense of security that you have covered your bases and know the risk.

User-installed base analysis may indicate that the application:

- Must run on certain current browsers.
- Must run on certain current hardware.
- Must run on certain types of Internet connections (with and without proxy servers, firewalls, modems, and direct connections of various bandwidths).

When to Run Compatibility and Configuration Testing

Compatibility and configuration testing should begin after the first round of functional tests has been completed and, ideally, after many functional errors have been discovered. Otherwise, it may be difficult and time-consuming to differentiate configuration errors from functionality errors. If there are suspected problem areas, limited configuration testing may be run during the functionality testing phase; this may also be done to validate functionality on specific devices.

While conformity of hardware and software may be a desire of the IT department, it is a good practice to test with a wide selection of computers, operating systems, browsers, e-mail clients, word processors, and other products. Often, being one or two versions behind on the latest revision of the system software will reveal problems the developers will miss, hence will represent more closely the average customer's configuration.

Potential Outsourcing

With the rapid advances in hardware manufacturing, OS development, software component development, and browser releases, it is not always feasible for software development organizations to maintain an array of system configurations preserved for in-house compatibility testing. Testing labs that can handle most configuration and compatibility testing needs are available.

Comparing Configuration Testing with Compatibility Testing

The line between configuration and compatibility testing is often misunderstood. *Configuration testing* is designed to uncover errors related to various software and hardware combinations, and *compatibility testing* determines if an application, under supported configurations, performs as expected with various combinations of hardware and software flavors and releases. For example, configuration testing might validate that a certain Web system installed on a dual-processor computer operates properly; compatibility testing would thereafter determine which manufacturers and server brands, under the same configuration, are compatible with the Web system.

Configuration testing of Web systems involves the testing of various supported server software and hardware setups, browser settings, network connections, TCP/IP stack setups, and so on. The goal is to ensure that the application is thoroughly exercised with as many configurations as possible. With each supported configuration, it is expected that the features will operate as a reasonable user would expect. Should there be an error condition, the error should be detected and gracefully handled by the application.

Due to the complexity of the client-server architecture, environmental-specific errors are more difficult to reproduce in client-server systems than they are in the single-PC model. In Web application environments, we often do not know the actual cause of failure conditions. When experiencing failures, a Web application might present an incorrect error message because it's not capable of recognizing the main causes of the failure. Test partitioning is effective in weeding out such elusive environment-specific errors—commonly caused by session time-outs, lack of disk space, downloading activities, or security settings that prevent ActiveX controls from being downloaded. (See Chapter 5, for more information regarding test partitioning.)

TESTING THE SAMPLE APPLICATION: CONFIGURATION ISSUES

This example illustrates the challenge of differentiating configuration issues from actual software errors. Figure 17.1 shows a failed login error message that has been generated by the sample application. By simply looking at this error message, it is impossible to determine whether this error is the result of a software bug, a server-side configuration issue, a compatibility issue, a browser configuration issue, or all of these. Possible conditions that might generate this error message include:

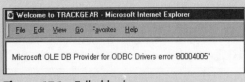

Figure 17.1 Failed login error message.

SERVER-SIDE CONFIGURATION ISSUES

IIS (Web server) virtual directory has not been set up properly.

- ◆ This is a server configuration issue. However, if the installation program failed to programmatically configure the Web server according to specification, then this is a software error. If the system administrator fails to properly configure the Web server according to specification, then this is a user error.

Application directory has not been configured properly to execute scripts.

- ◆ The issue is similar to that described previously.

Default Web page has not been set up properly.

- ◆ The issue is similar to that described previously.

SQL server is not running.

- ◆ The SQL server must be running for the application to work properly.

DLL/COM objects are missing or were unsuccessfully registered.

- ◆ This problem is often caused by software errors in the installation program. If the components must be manually registered, then this is a configuration issue.

CLIENT-SIDE CONFIGURATION ISSUES

JavaScript has been disabled.

◆ Because the application requires the browser to have JavaScript enabled, this is a client- or browser-side configuration issue.

JavaScript has been disabled.

◆ Because the application requires the browser to have JavaScript enabled, this is a client- or browser-side configuration issue.

High-security settings have been enabled.

◆ High-security settings prevent the application from downloading and running certain unsecured active contents (e.g., ActiveX controls, Java applets, etc.) required by the application.

Configuration/Compatibility Testing Issues

The following subsections explore some of the many issues that may be encountered during configuration and compatibility testing. Some error examples are also included.

COTS Products versus Hosted Systems

The testing of commercial-off-the-shelf (COTS) products is potentially more labor-intensive than the testing of hosted Web systems. With a hosted Web system, your development team has a lot more control over the server environment. Occasionally, your hosted system might be pulling some content (e.g., stock quotes information, news, weather information, etc.) from your partner, but for the most part, this system is considered a controlled environment. The system is overseen by an information services staff and system developers. The testing of this type of system is run on only those configurations specified by the system's designers and network administrators (specific server, specific amount of memory, specific connectivity, etc.). In contrast, COTS systems should be exercised with all configurations claimed to be supported by their product data sheets. Commercial-off-the-shelf products commonly have to integrate well with the buyers' environments, and certainly, you don't have much control over the server-side configurations of your customers.

TESTING THE SAMPLE APPLICATION: INCOMPATIBILITY ISSUES

Figures 10.20 and 10.21 in Chapter 10, "User Interface Tests," illustrate an incompatibility issue between two browsers. This example demonstrates that the same HTML page served by a Web server can be interpreted or formatted very differently by different browsers.

Distributed Server Configurations

On the macro level, a Web system may work correctly with some distributed server configurations while not working correctly with others. Figures 17.2 and 17.3 illustrate two possible distributed server configurations that comprise identical server software components. Any errors generated by altering server distribution should be classified as configuration errors.

A typical system under test might utilize any of the following:

- Application servers
- Database servers
- E-mail servers
- Web servers
- Proxy servers

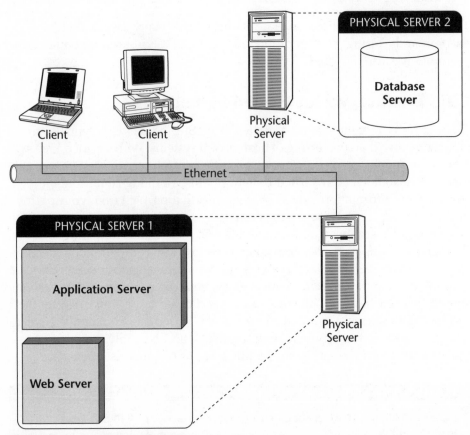

Figure 17.2   Two-box configuration.

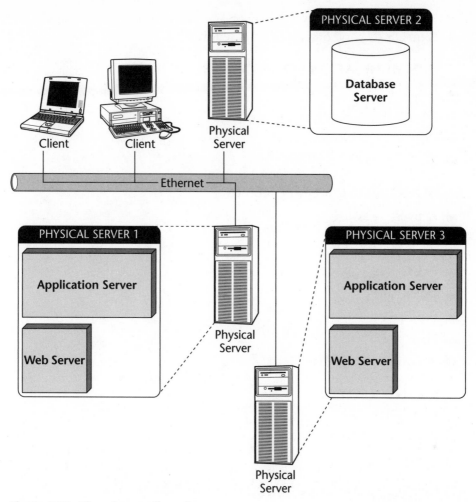

Figure 17.3   Three-box configuration.

Client-Side Issues

The client-side of Web systems may be responsible for numerous types of compatibility and configuration issues. To determine which client-side tests a Web application requires, identify the components that make up the client-side of the Web application.

The system under test may include the following client-side components:

POSSIBLE OPERATING SYSTEMS

- Windows (95, 98, 2000, NT)
- Various flavors of UNIX
- Macintosh

- Linux
- Palm OS, CE, and other mobile-based devices

COMMUNICATION COMPONENTS

- Browser
- E-mail
- Chat
- FTP

CLIENT-SIDE UI COMPONENTS

- ActiveX
- Java applets

PLUG-INS

- QuickTime
- RealPlayer
- Flash
- Windows Media Player

CONNECTIVITY

- Dial-up
- Leased line
- ISDN
- DSL

HARDWARE

- Manufacturer
- CPU
- RAM
- Graphic display card
- Video capture card
- Sound card
- CD-ROM drive
- Monitor
- Printer device
- Input device (mouse, tablet, joystick, etc.)
- Network card, modem card

Additionally, client-side compatibility differences may include the following:

- Input/output device drivers (mouse, sound, graphics display, video, memory manager)
- Extensions running in the background
- Applications that provide input to the application under test, such as a word processor that creates files or a graphics program that creates images that the application is expected to use
- Applications running concurrently
- Network software
- Online services

TESTING THE SAMPLE APPLICATION

Configuration may occur at any point within a Web system: client, server, or network. Here is an example that involves distributed server configurations. Figures 17.4 and 17.5 show two possible physical server configurations: *one-box* and *two-box* configuration.

The application under test has some charting capabilities that enable a user to generate metrics reports, such as bar charts and line charts. When a user requests a metrics report, the application server pseudocode runs as follows:

1. Connect to the database server and run the query.
2. Write the query result to a file name c:\temp\chart.val.
3. Execute the chart Java applet. Read from c:\temp\chart.val and use the data to draw a graph.
4. Send the Java applet to the browser.

During testing for this application, we discovered that the charting feature worked on one of the preceding configurations but not the other. After further investigation, we learned that the problem occurred only in the two-box configuration. After examining the code, we realized that the problem was in steps 2 and 3. In step 2, the query result is written to c:\temp\chart.val of the database server local drive. In step 3, the Chart Java applet is running on the application server that is not in the same box with the database server. When it attempts to open the file c:\temp\chart.val on the application server local drive, the file is not there. Does it mean that we read the code every time we come across an error? No, we can leave the debugging work for the developers. The key is to clearly identify which server configurations are problematic and include such information in bug reports. It's also recommended to have a cursory suite of test cases to be executed on all distributed configurations that are supported by the application server under test, to ensure that configuration-specific errors are uncovered.

(continued)

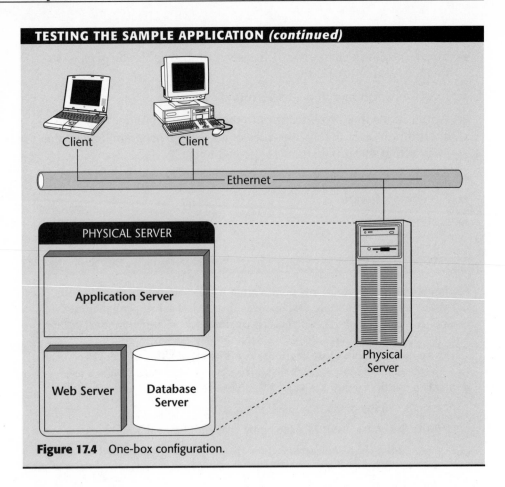

TESTING THE SAMPLE APPLICATION *(continued)*

Client

Client

Ethernet

PHYSICAL SERVER

Application Server

Web Server

Database Server

Physical Server

Figure 17.4 One-box configuration.

Web Browsers

Web browsers are the central client-side component of most Web applications. A browser acts as an application shell in which a Web application runs. The behavior of different browser brands can vary, as can their support for Java commands, implementation of security settings, and other features. Each browser (and its relative release versions) may also have one or more interpreters—which may not be compatible with one another.

One of the primary challenges of browser testing is that there are more browser versions in use today than can feasibly be managed in functionality testing. The myriad browser settings that are available within each browser complicate things further. It is a good idea to include browser and browser settings testing in the compatibility test phase, rather than in the functionality test phase.

The number of browsers that are available in the marketplace continues to increase at a rapid rate. (For a list of browsers and the technologies that they support, check out CNET.com⇨Software⇨Browsers.) It is a good idea for the test team to meet with project management and developers to determine which browsers and browser settings will be included in test matrices. If the versions of supported browsers are not identified, test for compatibility with at least the two most recent releases of all supported browsers.

As with all software, browser patches should be thoroughly tested. In Internet time, people are shipping now and patching later—*patches* are nothing more than bug fixes. Without current patches, software may include buggy components.

Create a Web compatibility matrix to test Web-based applications for compatibility issues related to scripting, Java applets, ActiveX controls, style sheets, HTML, and plug-ins. The goal of such tests is to hunt down browser configuration errors. Web application user interfaces (UIs) are heavily dependent on browser settings. The assigned size values of tables, cells, fonts, and other elements can potentially distort a UI and/or printed reports.

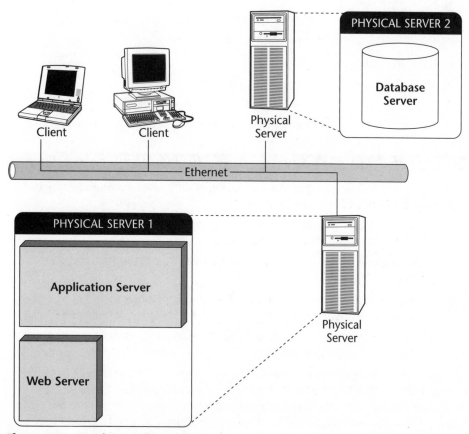

Figure 17.5 Two-box configuration.

TESTING THE SAMPLE APPLICATION: BROWSER SETTINGS

The sample application requires an ActiveX control to be downloaded for the charting feature to work. The browser security setting for ActiveX control is set to High. In this case, it means only signed ActiveX control (a control that comes from a traceable and trustworthy source) is allowed for downloading.

Testing with this security setting, we discover that the charting feature no longer works, because the ActiveX we use is unsigned. To support users who will require this particular security setting on High, we need to have the ActiveX control registered as a signed control. (For more information on getting control registered, see Chapter 18, "Web Security Testing.")

Web applications should be tested under a combination of various browser settings:

- General settings
- Connection settings
- Security settings (including ActiveX controls, plug-ins, Java, scripting, downloads, user authentication, etc.)
- Content settings
- Programs settings
- Other advanced settings (including browsing options, multimedia options, Java VM options, printing options, and HTTP options)

TESTING THE SAMPLE APPLICATION: BROWSER INCOMPATIBILITY

Let's look at another example of a compatibility difference between Microsoft Internet Explorer and Netscape Navigator.

◆ The home directory path for the Web server on the host myserver is mapped to: C:\INETPUB\WWWROOT\.

◆ A file name (mychart.jar) is stored at C:\INETPUB\WWWROOT\MYAPP\ BIN.

◆ The application session path (relative path) is pointing to C:\INETPUB\WWWROOT\MYAPP\BIN, and a file is requested from .\LIB.

◆ When a page is requested from http://myserver/, data will be pulled from C:\INETPUB\WWWROOT\.

Using Internet Explorer version 4.x, the Web server looks for the file in C:\INETPUB\WWWROOT\MYAPP\BIN\LIB because the browser relies on relative paths. This is the intended behavior, and the file will be found; this means that the application will work as expected using Internet Explorer 4.x.

Instead, if Netscape Navigator version 4.x (a browser that doesn't like .\) is used, the Web server defaults to C:\INETPUB\WWWROOT\LIB and tries to look for mychart.jar from there. This is a problem for this particular application because the file (mychart.jar) will not be found there—so the current implementation for this feature will not work with Netscape Navigator. This is not to say that Internet Explorer is better than Netscape Navigator; it simply means that there are incompatibility issues between browsers and that the code should not assume that relative paths work for all browsers. More important, it suggests that when you experience an error in one environment, the same error may *not* appear in a different environment.

UNIX file names are case-sensitive, which causes many potential problems using Netscape on different platforms.

Testing Considerations

It is essential that the system under test be analyzed against the target-user installed base.

- Which browsers will the users have?
- Which related applications will the users have?
- What hardware will the users have?
- What types of Internet connections will the users have?

Issues involved in server configuration testing fall into the following categories:

- Distributed server configuration
- Server administration and configuration
- Software compatibility
- Hardware compatibility
- Server software running on top of the OS (IIS, SQL)
- Differences between database types (SQL, Oracle, Informix, Sybase, etc.) and versions (Oracle 7.x versus Oracle 8.x)
- Proxy servers
- Server OSs (UNIX, Mac, PC)
- OS/browser combination
- Hubs
- Network cards
- TCP/IP stack

TESTING THE SAMPLE APPLICATION: MAC INCOMPATIBILITY

What are the issues involved with installing client software on a Mac? Macs are NOT compatible with ActiveX, so, if your site contains an ActiveX component, you're out of luck. Most of the applications resident on the Web would need to be in Java for them to be compatible with Macs.

The installation is similar to Windows in that the application residing in the Web page is downloaded and executed in a JVM, or virtual machine, since you need to create this environment for an OS running Java. Those applications are kept within the browser component/application "cache," or library, and used when the user frequents the Web site. In most cases, installation via a browser is no different from installing on a Windows machine.

UI PLUG-IN ISSUES PARTICULAR TO MACS

Most of the plug-ins you get in the Windows world you can get in the Mac world. In most cases, however, the versions that are being executed are not as current as they are in the Windows world.

Mac plug-ins generally are a generation behind. Plug-ins are usually developed first for the Windows market and then, if successful, are ported to the Mac. This means they often lag behind the current Windows version, so it's important to look for versioning issues when it comes to plug-ins on MacOS browsers. With OS X, this is getting better, since many more developers are adopting this operating system.

Commercial-off-the-shelf products, such as the sample application, require the following testing:

- Server-software configuration tests
- Hardware configuration tests
- Connection configuration tests
- Stack configuration tests

Compatibility testing considerations include the following:

- *Compatibility issues* involve the swapping of comparable elements within a properly configured system.
- Test only with supported configurations. Focus on how the application performs with alternate hardware and software components.
- Test multiple releases of supported components.

Software compatibility includes differences in the following:

- Operating system versions
- Input/output device drivers (mouse, sound, graphic display, video, memory manager)

- Extensions running in the background

- Applications running concurrently with tested application

- Network software supported by the tested application

- Online service supported by the tested application

- Firewall configuration

- Effects of the client living behind a proxy

Installation considerations include the following:

- *Server installation compatibility tests* look for system-specific problems that have not been uncovered during TOFT or installation functionality tests—not to confirm that the install functions as prescribed. (See Chapter 16, "Installation Tests," for more detail regarding installation testing.) The same is applicable to client installs, which should already have been functionality tested. Client installation compatibility tests evaluate the client installation over a variety of systems to see if there are any reboot problems or browser-specific issues.

- Server installation compatibility tests verify that the following installation functions operate correctly across all target OSs and possible system architectures:

  - Necessary directories are created in the proper locations.

  - System files—such as DLL files—are copied to the correct directories.

  - System files—such as registry keys—are modified as appropriate.

  - Error conditions are detected and handled gracefully.

  - Uninstall program removes all installed files and restores the operating environment to its original state.

Browser testing considerations include the following:

- The behavior of different browser brands can vary, as can their support for Java commands, implementation of security settings, and other features. Each browser (and its relative release versions) may also have one or more interpreters—which may not be compatible with one another. Browser testing should be thorough, and performed early in the functionality testing phase, so that as many browser-related bugs as possible can be identified early.

- Does the application under test utilize a media player? Does the player (for example, QuickTime) need to be preinstalled with the application?

- Are ActiveX controls, Java scripts, or other scripting downloaded by the application?

- Create a *Web compatibility matrix* to test your Web-based applications for incompatibility issues related to scripting, Java applets, ActiveX controls, style sheets, HTML, and plug-ins.

Following are some other browser testing issues that might require attention:

- *Active desktop*. Different versions of Internet Explorer should be tested both with and without the use of the active desktop.
- *Encryption*. 40- versus 128-bit.
- Instant messaging.
- *Style sheets*. Not all browsers support style sheets. Of those browsers that do support style sheets, many do not necessarily support full style sheet implementation. (For more information on cascading style sheets, visit the World Wide Web Consortium's site at www.w3.org/style/css/#browsers, or visit the following URL to access a style sheet compatibility chart: www.webreview.com/style/css1/charts/mastergrid.shtml.)

For browser statistics and information on which browsers support which technologies, visit www.browsers.com and http://websnapshot.mycomputer.com/browsers.html. Note that the functionality issues associated with browser technologies such as cascading style sheets, JavaScript, dynamic HTML, tables, links, and frames are discussed at length in Chapter 10, "User Interface Tests."

Bibliography

Kaner, Cem, Jack Falk, Hung Q. Nguyen. *Testing Computer Software*, 2nd ed. New York: John Wiley & Sons, Inc., 1999.

LogiGear Corporation. *QA Training Handbook: Testing Web Applications.* Foster City, CA: LogiGear Corporation, 2003.

——— *QA Training Handbook: Testing Windows Desktop and Server-Based Applications.* Foster City, CA: LogiGear Corporation, 2003.

——— *QA Training Handbook: Testing Computer Software.* Foster City, CA: LogiGear Corporation, 2003.

Additional Resources

www.compinfo-center.com/tpsw12-t.htm

CHAPTER 18

Web Security Testing

Why Read This Chapter?

Security issues are becoming the gravest concern of many companies. Despite this fact, security testing often remains the least understood and least well-defined testing activity. It is a broad effort that requires domains of expertise beyond traditional software testing. This chapter contains a discussion of security concepts and outlines the role of testing in the big picture of security testing. It also discusses the application of security-related testing ideas and techniques to Web-based applications, including suggestions for exposing common security vulnerabilities at the application level.

TOPICS COVERED IN THIS CHAPTER

- ◆ Introduction
- ◆ Security Goals
- ◆ Anatomy of an Attack
- ◆ Attacking Intents
- ◆ Security Solution Basics

(continued)

TOPICS COVERED IN THIS CHAPTER *(continued)*

- ◆ **Common Vulnerabilities and Attacks**
- ◆ **Testing Goals and Responsibilities**
- ◆ **Testing for Security**
- ◆ **Other Testing Considerations**
- ◆ **Bibliography and Additional Resources**

Introduction

For application producers and users to feel confident with a Web-based system, they must have a reasonable level of comfort with the system's security. Unfortunately, a 100 percent secure Web-based system does not exist. Web systems include far too many variables to enable the complete removal of all their vulnerabilities. Software, for example, one of the key components of the Web system, can never be bug-free because it's impossible to completely test a system. As a result, bugs in software components create vulnerabilities of the Web system. Additionally, every time a new security tool is released, many other tools follow with the sole purpose of defeating the original tool. So, is there a point in pursuing something that can't be done perfectly?

The effort of securing a system is an ongoing process of change, test, and improvement. Because it's impossible to have a perfectly secure system, the goal is to determine the level of protection that adequately meets the organization's needs.

Security trade-offs consist of compromises between security and functionality/ usability. If the security of the system is too rigid, it will be difficult to use the system or to get work done effectively. If the security is too primitive, the system is vulnerable and raises the potential for intrusions.

Web security testing, in the traditional sense, means testing the effectiveness of the overall Web system security defenses. It requires a combination of knowledge of security technologies, network technologies, programming, and often, real-world experience in penetrating the security of network systems. Most software testers do not have this level of knowledge. That said, however, we should understand the full range of security issues so that we understand which tasks we should do and which tasks should be done by other experts.

For the purposes of this discussion, it is assumed that software testers are responsible for testing the systems to uncover functionality, interoperability, configuration, and compatibility errors, as they relate to security implementation and potential problems introduced by security design flaws (primarily at the application level). It is further assumed that software testers are *not* responsible for the overall effectiveness of Web security defenses. With that in mind, this chapter introduces various types of system vulnerabilities and the intent of several types of attacks. It identifies security goals and responsibilities and offers an introduction to Web security technologies, followed by testing examples and considerations. Additional reference information is provided as a guide for those interested in further research and reading.

What Is Computer Security?

Computer security is a combination of many protective measures taken to ensure the safety of the data and resources of both the owners and the users of computer systems. Computer security is twofold: It involves keeping private information safe and preventing loss of resources. Computer security concerns include: active attacks from external sources, internal abuse, and inadvertent loss of information. If, for example, your application displays data from a particular account to a different client when that client did not request the data, your application contains at least one security failure.

In much of the following discussion, we speak of an "attack" as coming from a malicious outsider trying to wreak havoc or steal information. However, this is just one type of a security attack. Another type of security vulnerability is when the authorization level of the user is not enforced, granting him or her inappropriate access to the data. For example, not all internal employees need access to the same data; providing complete access to all employees' health information to the entire human resources staff constitutes a security risk. In this case, the application must provide various access levels to the data, based on the authorization level of the user. The system must also authenticate the users to verify their identity within the computer system.

Security Goals

"Good enough security," as narrowly defined, is achieved when the cost of additional security measures would be greater than the expected cost from security breaches not prevented by existing measures.

The expected cost of a specific breach is the product of the damage that breach would cause times the probability of that breach. At the same time, the ideal solutions are those that deter persistent intruders by making penetrating the system so difficult and time-consuming that it's not worthwhile even when their efforts succeed.

Security in the physical world is fundamentally different from security in the digital world. In the physical world, redundancy can increase security; for example, installing additional locks, posting security guards by the door, or installing a badge reader are all ways of improving physical security. In contrast, in the digital world, redundancy can increase complexity and create additional vulnerabilities; one small utility program, surrounded by many layers of protection, can open the security hole necessary to compromise an entire system.

From Which Threats Are We Protecting Ourselves?

Threats are the means or events that might damage or cause loss of data and resources from an information system through security violations. In the digital world, we protect ourselves from the common threats in the following ways:

- *Protecting data:*
  - *Integrity:* Ensuring that business transaction data is not altered or corrupted. If something has been changed or modified since it was created, verify that the changes are legitimate.
  - *Confidentiality:* Ensuring unauthorized access to information will be denied.
  - *Protecting the privacy of user data:* In general, Web sites and applications should have a privacy statement that defines how user information will be handled.
  - *Data as intellectual property:* Ensuring that business intelligence, the source code, and any data related to intellectual property are safeguarded.
  - *Availability:* Ensuring that data accessibility is as expected. A denial-of-service attack and a natural disaster are examples of data availability threats (see the "Common Vulnerabilities and Attacks" section later in this chapter for a description of a denial-of-service attack).
- *Protecting network computing resources:* Ensuring that unauthorized uses of network resources are denied.

Common Sources of Security Threats

Typically, security threats come from one or more of the following places:

- Software and hardware errors and failures
- Human errors and failures
- Environmental failures, such as poor security for the physical environment, loss of electric power, and natural disasters
- Ongoing changes to the systems

What Is the Potential Damage?

The consequences of a security breach can stem beyond financial loss, to include exposure of sensitive personal information or even personal injuries caused by failure of an attacked control system. Financial losses can result from loss of sales, property, and productivity, in addition to bad publicity and litigation.

The critical questions to ask are:

- What risks are we willing to take? That is, for each possible type of damage, how high a probability of that damage occurring are we willing to tolerate?

- How much funding are we willing to commit in order to reduce our risks?

- What is the objective of, and the budget allocated to, testing the Web site and Web application security?

Security goals depend significantly on how these questions are answered, primarily by management staff.

Common targets that need protection include:

- *Host-based:* Protecting data and the resources at the host level. These computers can be part of the private network, such as a LAN behind the firewall, which are protected from the outsiders; or they might reside in a public network such as the Internet, which exposes them to untrusted users.

- *Private network-based*: Protecting data and resources at the private network level.

- *Perimeter-based*: Protecting data and resources at the private network entrances. An example of a perimeter-based protection is the use of a firewall.

- *Public network-based*: Protecting the data transferred across the public network. Encryption technology is an example of safeguarding data from attackers on a public network.

- *Application-based*: Protecting the applications from threats caused by vulnerabilities in the applications. The common causes for these vulnerabilities are poor programming practices and software configuration errors. In the context of software testing, this is the most interesting topic. In fact, this is where we will focus our discussions on testing Web sites and applications for security vulnerabilities.

Anatomy of an Attack

In the Web environment, or network environment in general, a security hole is an exposure of the hardware or software that allows unauthorized users to gain increased access privilege without going through the normal authorization process. Attackers use numerous techniques to break into the Web system to exploit security holes or vulnerabilities in each component of the system. The attack strategy consists of three steps: *information gathering*, *scanning*, and *attacking*.

Information Gathering

This subsection describes an information-gathering process in which an attacker tries to understand the system. Knowledge about the system can come from many sources. By viewing public documents, an attacker can learn a great deal about the hardware and software. Viewing the source code of a public Web site will often show the path names, allowing the attacker to create maps of your system. Often the first step in learning about a Web site is to copy the entire site and search the source code for comments and to map out any links (anchors) to the target system.

For example, entering an invalid URL can provide useful information (see Figure 18.1). In this case, we learn which version of the Apache Web server the company is using and that the server is using port 80 (the default port for most Web servers.)

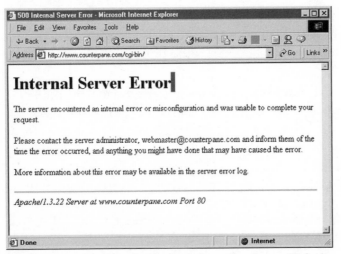

Figure 18.1   Example of gathering information from a Web site.

Other useful sources of information to an attacker are the names and/or e-mail addresses of programmers, testers, and support staff. Sometimes, this information is embedded in comments in the HTML pages and/or the JavaScript files that are downloaded. By using search engines, the attacker can also find all the external links to your site. Some of these links may be to personal Web pages belonging to company employees. Learning the names of employees might enable the attacker to contact individuals at work; and finding out, for example, the names of an employee's children and pets from personal Web pages can help the attacker launch a "social engineering" conversation or a "con game" (human interaction that involves tricking other people) to learn more about the system.

By carefully examining the information discovered, the attacker will develop a great deal of knowledge about the target company, its people, and software. The attacker will learn which operating system the company is using, how its system is configured, and which third-party applications are installed. From this knowledge, the attacker can then identify many weaknesses in the systems. Suppose, say, that your application runs on Solaris and uses an Oracle database. To break into your application, the attacker begins by determining common mistakes made by programmers using these products. The attacker's next step is to determine the common installation and configuration (or misconfiguration) mistakes made by organizations.

The attacker may also have copies of data files, CGIs, and applications (see Figure 18.2), enabling the attacker to figure out where vital information is located. For example:

- Your application is always installed at: ~myApp.
- The configuration file is unprotected and stored in: ~myApp/config.rc.
- The attacker may try www.yourCompany.com/~myApp/config.rc.
- The attacker will receive the entire configuration data for your application.

Often, the configuration file contains administrator names, e-mail addresses, and passwords. It may show where log files are written, and may contain the name and password for the Oracle database used by the application. By using your data and application, the attacker essentially has the keys to all of your organization's data.

It is remarkable how much information is accidentally given away. To test this yourself, we recommend you spend an evening trying to learn all you can about an organization—perhaps your own—from using just the Web site or application. We also suggest you refer to *"Attacking Exposed: Network Security Secrets and Solutions,"* by Stuart McClure, Joel Scambray, and George Kurtz (see the Bibliography at the end of this chapter). This is a source book of ideas that will help you generate strategies to gain information.

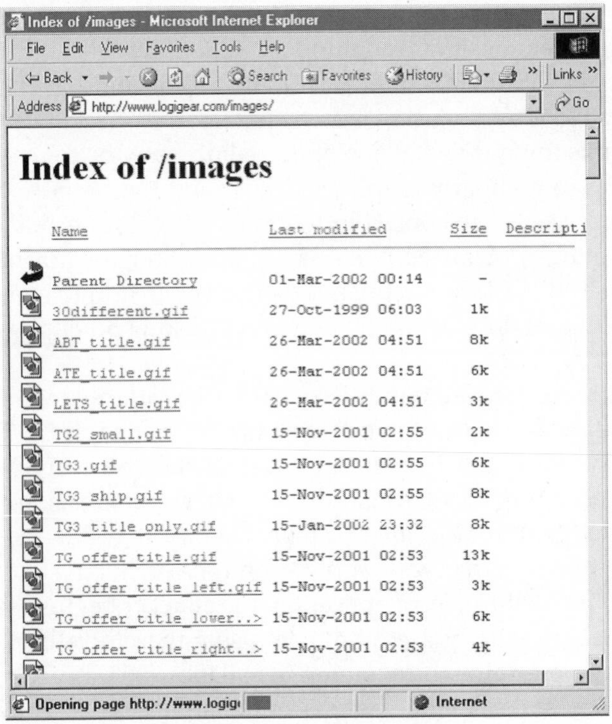

Figure 18.2   Example of browsing Web server directories and retrieving files.

Network Scanning

Scanning continues the information-gathering process. It involves testing your assumptions about the target systems. For example, did the installers change the default password for the database? Does your application protect the configuration files? This step often involves scanning the system to determine which servers are "alive" and reachable from the Internet by using a host of readily available tools and techniques, such as port scans for discovering open ports, and ping sweeps or ICMP (Internet Control Message Protocol), a simple network scanning technique used to determine which of a range of IP addresses map to live computers. Many advanced tools are available to professional and novice attackers alike for checking out thousands of potential IP addresses. Many of the tools, with user documentation, are available at www.insecure.org.

Once a useful hole is found, the attacker usually stops, as most are looking for a single way into your network and stop once it is found. In contrast, as a tester, you are interested in *all* the ways into your application. Moreover, you do not need to successfully complete the attack; proving that the hole is there is usually enough to report the problem and get it fixed.

Attacking

This step is an active process of intrusion, such as trying to connect to the reachable host through its open port, running queries on the system, or cracking the IDs and passwords. This is the step often dramatized in the movies: The lone attacker is seen sitting in front of a terminal trying different combinations to determine how best to crack the target application.

Attacking Intents

Depending on the magnitude of a security hole, it can open the target system varying degrees of exposure, resulting in anything from service disruption caused by a denial-of-service attack to unauthorized full access from a remote host. Depending on the attacker's motive, each attack is designed with a certain intent. Some of the common intents include the following:

TO STEAL

- *Stealing money*, by capturing credit card numbers, or spoofing certain users to conduct financial transactions such as money transfers.

- *Stealing confidential data*, such as proprietary information, business plan and financial information, or private e-mail communications.

- *Stealing information*, by capturing user data such as address information and computer configuration information, or by tracking purchasing patterns for marketing and sales purposes or other financial gains.

- *Stealing intellectual property*, including downloading software applications, source code, or product design information.

TO DISRUPT ACTIVITIES

- Attacks such as *denial of service or buffer overflow* are often designed to knock the victim's server(s) out of commission with the intent to disrupt or degrade the level of service and, perhaps, to cripple a competitor and to get media exposure in the process.

TO EMBARRASS

- *Through spoofing or other attack methods*, attackers may alter the content of a Web site with their own content. This type of vandalizing is normally designed to embarrass the owner or operator of the site.

- Often, the intent is also to *embarrass the software producers* whose buggy software is used by the site operator.

TO PLAY A GAME

- Attacks such as *disseminating a virus, destroying user data, or* vandalizing a Web site are sometimes done (by adults or children) for the sake of "playing" or "having fun."

Security Solution Basics

By studying the anatomy of an attack, we can devise a strategy to protect ourselves from the threat of attack. In developing a successful defensive strategy, three essential elements must be carefully studied: *education, prevention,* and *detection.* We must learn what attackers do and how they do it. We then build defenses that reduce risks by eliminating vulnerabilities that a attacker might take advantage of. Finally, we put mechanisms in place for detecting attacks so we can react before it's too late.

Typically, an organization will deploy many products and methods, each claiming to solve the security problems. As a tester, you must have a good understanding of these implementations. From there you will ask:

- How well will a given product actually protect against a given threat?

- What are the limitations of each implementation? For example, the firewall is designed to protect your network, but it does nothing to protect your Web application.

- What are the responsibility, focus, and limitation of each given implementation? For example, if your testing focuses on the application level, you will not be looking for network-level systems, such as the IDS (Intrusion Detection Systems).

The application you are testing is the innermost piece of code, surrounded by networks, operating systems, and other software. You will learn that an attempt to corrupt your system will be directed at many locations other than just your software. Many of these "wrapper" products or technologies provide only limited success in securing your application. For example, passwords may provide *authentication* of users, but this is much different from providing *authorization,* which is usually role-based and occurs after the user has properly logged on to the system. You will test your application with the assumption that these products may be present as well as absent. This is discussed further in the "Security Testing" section.

The following subsections describe a number of classic methods, technologies, and tools that can be used to protect an organization's virtual assets. Each of the tools offers vital protection for a specific portion of the security problem, and each has many strengths that would seem to be reason enough to purchase and deploy them. However as a security tester, you are interested only in their weaknesses and how they might fail to provide the expected protection. Keep in mind that even if you use all of these products correctly, you still will not be able to provide total security. In that context, then, think of your application as a *gateway* through which an attacker can slip past all these barriers to attack the organization.

Strategies, People, and Processes

Education

Understanding the basic security issues is imperative to secure your application, so providing education on security issues to everyone involved in the effort is the primary step in developing a successful security program. Programming, testing, and IT staff all should be educated, but education should not stop with them. The people involved in securing the application should constantly monitor information sources to learn about existing and new vulnerabilities in applications and servers used in the system. Good sources of security-related information include vendor Web sites, security portals, and security mailing lists. QACity.Com offers a good list of these sources for you to use.

Developers, of course, play an essential role in Web application security, so they, too, should be educated on the latest practices. They must familiarize themselves with the basics of the technologies and tools used to implement the defensive strategies, as well as those used by attackers to counter those technologies. Also, they need to be familiar with tools that can help to better design, implement, and test security. Plans, designs, implementations, monitoring procedures, and maintenance for security should all be part of the software development cycle. Developers and testers, working as a team, should communicate early during the development cycle about the tests that will be run. This can be done in a design walk-through process by asking pointed questions related to security design and implementation. An illustration of this walk-through process is described in the testing discussion in Chapter 5, "Web Applications Components."

Nonfunctional features are just as important as functional features when designing for security. Therefore, implement authentication routines early. Typical tactical mistakes include using the anonymous Web server account (even when the user will eventually need to be authenticated using an ID and password) and deferring addressing the authentication routines until the last stages of development. If there are flaws in the authentication routines due to lack of time for design and test, security vulnerabilities will be introduced. In addition, late bug discovery can cause delays in the launch of your application.

Corporate Security Policies

Although it does not happen as often as it should in the real world, effective security defense is accomplished through a security policy. The security policy sets the tone for the security requirements. Developing a security policy forces an organization to think about the risks raised by security vulnerabilities and threats, and what should be done to address them. The organization will determine which objectives must be met to protect business properties, and at what cost.

That said, even when an organization has a security policy, it does not automatically follow that the policy will be understood by everyone, or enforced and reinforced. For example, only portions of an organization's security policy may be enforced with software products. This enforcement is often incomplete due to poor design and coding practice, software bugs, and misconfiguration of the systems. Testing responsibilities should focus mainly on the implementation errors in software, poor programming practice, and misconfiguration. Other security-related challenges should be handled by the IT staff.

Although management will create the security policy, not QA/testing staff, we should take part in contributing to the development of this policy. To that end, follow these guidelines:

- Align the security policy with the company's business goal.
- Focus the security policy on guidelines and high-level procedures to be enforced, rather than on technologies and tools used to enforce the policies.
- Be sure the policy includes, but is not limited to, such things as logging off terminals, backing up data, virus checking and updating, file downloading, e-mail practice, and so on.
- Continually review, improve, communicate, and enforce the policy.
- Make sure that every member of the staff understands the risks and implications of a security breach.
- Verify that the security-related instructions are clear and enforceable.
- Continually review, monitor, audit, and update the policy and procedure documents.

Corporate Responses

A corporation will respond to security threats with many different tools and approaches. The IT department will invest in IDS, increase audit trails, and enforce a policy for changing passwords. The organization will institute security classes for all employees, as well as additional classes for IT and development teams.

Often it is difficult to obtain resources for security-related activities before a major break-in occurs. Everyone will complain about the draconian measures if an attack does not occur. To the application tester, these responses will have little impact on your testing. Again, your testing must assume that all these policies, tools, procedures, and education will fail. Education, for example, usually is offered only once; so if your company has, say, a 20 percent annual turnover rate, then you can expect that within a month of the class, untrained employees will be using the system. Intrusion detection only finds the problem (usually after it has been exploited by an attack); it doesn't remove defects from the design or implementation. Finally, if you are selling this Web application, then you will have no control over the corporate environment of your customers. You have to test your application for many possible configurations or environments.

Authentication and Authorization

Authentication is a validation method used to determine whether a person or a computer system is in fact who or what it claims to be. *Authorization* gives the authenticated person or computer permission to do something. *Cryptography* is the science of encoding messages so that they cannot be read by anyone other than their intended recipients.

Passwords

Authentication is commonly done through the use of passwords. Passwords are keys to open the locks on the virtual doors of your system. The system assumes the user is authentic if he or she knows the password. Once allowed into an application or system through password authentication, little can be done to prevent the user from snooping or destroying the application or system. Some of the weaknesses inherent to the use of passwords include:

- Many people find them a nuisance and therefore pick easy-to-guess passwords.
- People often are required to have many IDs and passwords, sometimes one for each place that requires authentication; therefore, they tend to choose the same password for everything so that they do not have to remember multiple passwords.
- People forget their passwords. Therefore, applications are forced to provide "backdoors," through which users who forget their passwords can enter.
- Passwords can be stolen or accidentally revealed.
- Many applications provide default passwords and users that, often, system administrators don't change.

Authentication between Software Applications or Components

To automatically access password-protected applications, the calling program must provide the password. The password must be stored, often "in the clear," on the system. This creates a few problems and is among the most interesting areas in testing to focus on for Web application security. Consider:

- If the location where the passwords are stored is discovered, the passwords can be stolen.

- A packet *sniffer* can capture unencrypted passwords sent from the calling application to the to-be-called application over the public network.

- Authentication can be introduced at several levels such as host-based, application-based, or file-based.

Finally, although authentication is a required step before authorization, and although these two methods are often combined, keep in mind they are *not* the same. Once you are authenticated, you will also be authorized, or given permission, to do many things to the system. UNIX systems are examples of the separation between authentication and authorization. In these systems, passwords (a host-based password, for example) provide only authentication; that is, they identify who is trying to use the system, but they provide no authorization. All authorization is done through permission attributes set on the files and directories in the file system.

Cryptography

Encryption makes it possible to transfer and store information while preventing examination by outside parties. Encryption is most useful for securely moving data. It does not provide any authorization or authentication of the persons requesting the data. In order to use encryption, each party must have and maintain keys to encrypt and decrypt the messages. If the system must share data with a large number of users, it becomes vulnerable to information loss because someone might not follow the security policy. In sum, encryption supports:

- *Privacy and confidentiality.* It ensures that confidential textual information transmitted over the Internet (user IDs, passwords, credit card numbers, etc.) is protected (from sniffing devices, for example). Encryption does not prevent the theft of information; it simply ensures that information cannot be read by anyone other than its intended recipient.

- *Integrity.* It is not possible to modify an encrypted file and then retrieve the message. The message can be protected from modification by first encrypting the message with the private key.

Public Key Cryptography Basics

Public key cryptography, as illustrated in Figure 18.3, is a method of securely transmitting messages between parties by using two types of keys, which are strings of numbers used to decode encrypted messages. As the names imply, *public keys* are published freely, whereas *private keys* are protected from public access. For example, Party A might send one of many public keys to Party B in anticipation of Party B transmitting a confidential message. Party B could use the public key sent by Party A to encrypt a message that is sent back to Party A. In theory, no one intercepting the message could decrypt the message because they would not have access to Party A's private key.

Digital Certificates

Digital certificates support authentication; they are used to verify the identity of people and organizations for the purpose of public key encryption and decryption. In this case, Party A can encrypt the entire message using A's private key, or, more often, create a "signature" that is an encryption using A's private key. On receipt of the message, Party B uses A's public key to check the "signature." Checking involves computing the function on the plain text message, decrypting the digital signature, and checking that the two strings match. If they do, B knows that the message was not changed since it was sent. B also knows that it was encrypted using A's private key, which is grounds for believing that A sent the message.

Pretty Good Privacy

Pretty good privacy (PGP), which uses a variation of the public key system, is a program that allows files and e-mail messages, or any data needing public key encryption, to be encrypted and decrypted. Originally developed by Philip R. Zimmermann, PGP today is available both as freeware and commercially; it has become a widely accepted standard for e-mail security by individuals as well as corporations. For more information, or to download or purchase a commercial version, visit www.pgpi.com and www.nai.com.

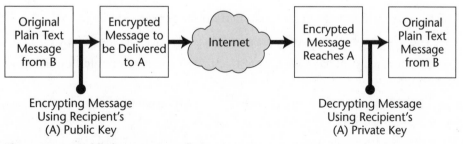

Figure 18.3   Public key cryptography.

Secure Multipurpose Internet Mail Extensions (S/MIME)

Secure Multipurpose Internet Mail Extensions (S/MIME), using the RSA (RSA Security, Inc.) encryption system, is a method that allows users to send secured e-mail messages over the Internet. At the writing of this book, the latest versions of both Microsoft's and Netscape's Web browsers include S/MIME. RSA has proposed S/MIME as a standard to the Internet Engineering Task Force (IETF). For more information, go to www.rsasecurity.com/standards/smime/faq.html.

Other Web Security Technologies

Three other commonly supported security technologies, itemized in Figure 18.4, are:

- *Secure-enhanced Hypertext Transport Protocol (S-HTTP)*. S-HTTP operates at the application layer. For more information on S-HTTP, see the S-HTTP Request for Comments (RFC) draft that has been submitted to the Internet Engineering Task Force for consideration as a standard. RFC Internet draft 2660 describes S-HTTP in detail: www.ietf.org/rfc/rfc2660.txt.

- *IP Security (IPSec)*. IPSec operates at the network or IP layer and is usually implemented in routers and switches.

- *Secure Sockets Layer (SSL)*. SSL operates at the session layer and is most commonly supported by commercial Web browsers and servers. It offers:

  - Private client-server communication using encryption.

  - Data integrity for client-server communication via verification of contents within exchanged messages, to ensure that messages have not been altered or tampered with during transmission.

  - Client-server authentication via the exchange of digital certificate.

SSL security support is a two-sided operation; that is, both client and server sides must be configured to use SSL:

- A certificate is created and installed on the server-side.

- The Web server must support security protocols such as SSL or PCT.

- Support for protocols such as SSL and PCT must be enabled on the client-side.

- HTTPS must be properly encoded in HTML links to enable secure communication.

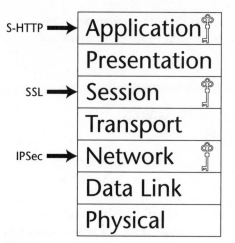

Figure 18.4   Security technologies.

If the application under test will support HTTPS, then certificates will be required for the server, as will proper setup for HTTPS communication on both the server- and client-sides. If the HTTPS server is behind the firewall, port 443 should also be open for HTTPS traffic between client and server (see Figure 18.5).

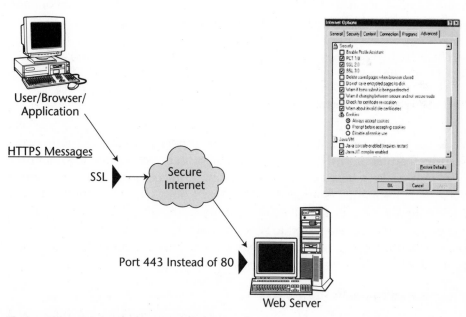

Figure 18.5   Secure Sockets Layer (SSL).

NOTE Other Web transaction security supports that are comparable to SSL include Transport Layer Security (TLS) and Microsoft Private Communication Technology (PCT).

Perimeter-Based Security: Firewalls, DMZs, and Intrusion Detection Systems

Firewalls and DMZs (a DMZ or demilitarized zone is a computer or small network situated between a private network and the outside public network) protect the internal network by isolating it from the outside world. Data must travel through the firewall before it is made available to the inside applications. To be useful, the firewall must have "holes" through which data can enter the organization. Unfortunately, these same holes can be used to attack the system.

Firewalls

Firewalls are shields that protect private networks from the Internet. They prevent unauthorized users from accessing confidential information, using network resources, and damaging system hardware, while allowing authorized users access to the resources they require. Firewalls are combinations of hardware and software; they make use of routers, servers, and software to shield networks from exposure to the Internet.

There are two types of firewalls: *packet-filtering* firewalls (routers) and *proxy-based* firewalls (gateways). See Figure 18.6 for an example.

Packet-Screening Firewalls (Routers)

The simplest firewalls block information by screening incoming packets. Packet filtering, typically implemented in routers, provides basic network security features at the IP level. Router tables can be configured to either drop or permit packets, based on communication protocols, application port numbers, and destination/source IP addresses. Routers inspect the headers of packets to determine where they are coming from, where they are going, and the protocol that is being used to send the data; routers can then block certain packets based on this information. Network administrators determine which types of information are allowed to pass through firewalls.

Proxy-Based Firewalls (Gateways)

A proxy server is a more secure firewall technique than packet filtering. A proxy server is software that runs on host computers around the perimeter of a network. Because proxy servers are located on the perimeter of a network, they are not part of corporate network themselves. Proxy servers are designed to be a private network's only connection to the Internet. Because it is only the proxy server that interacts with the Internet—as opposed to many client computers and servers—security is easier to maintain. Proxy servers are also useful for logging traffic that passes between a private network and the Internet.

As shown in Figure 18.7, routers can be used in combination with proxy servers to add another level of network protection; a router can take over in the event that a proxy server fails.

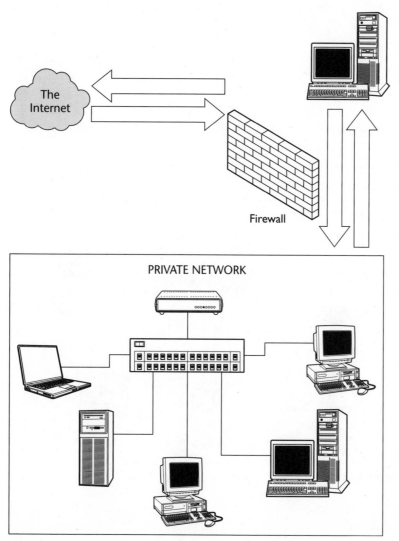

Figure 18.6 Firewall.

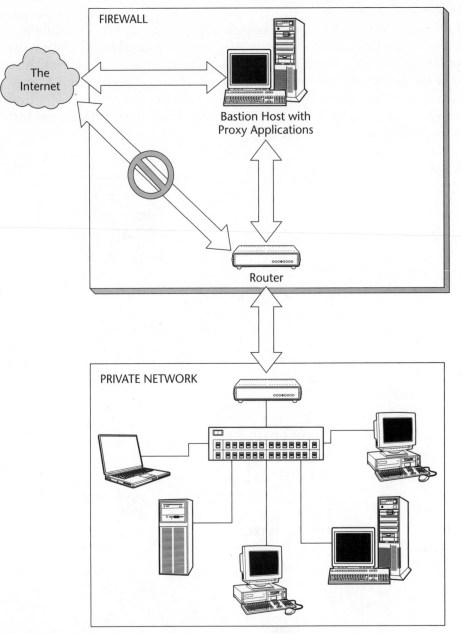

Figure 18.7   Proxy server.

Setting Up a DMZ

A *DMZ* prevents outside users from gaining direct access to any server or host
on a private company network. Normally, a DMZ host receives requests from
users within the private network for access to Web sites or other data on the

Internet. It then creates sessions for these requests on the Internet. However, the DMZ host is not able to initiate a session back in the private network.

Outside users on the Internet can access only a DMZ host or network. The DMZ host, typically, also contains the company's Web servers and FTP servers so the data can be "served" to the outside world. However, the DMZ does not provide access to any hosts within the private network because it cannot initiate any inward connections. In the event that the DMZ network is compromised, the data in those servers is compromised. Nevertheless, the private network will not be exposed.

Intrusion Detection Systems (IDS)

An IDS collects and analyzes external and internal activities on the system to detect possible malicious activities such as footprinting activities, abuses of access privilege, irregular uses of the system, and so on. Based on some publicly known vulnerabilities, the IDS collects and analyzes several sources, including user and system activities, system configurations and vulnerabilities, and system integrity and data integrity. Most important, an IDS should be capable of detecting typical attack patterns in order to timely detect intrusions. An IDS also indirectly supports privacy and confidentiality by notifying the system's owners when privacy violations have occurred. Similarly, it can indirectly enforce authorization by reporting attempts to bypass authorization procedures.

Common Vulnerabilities and Attacks

Vulnerabilities are weaknesses in the design and implementation of information and security systems. There are many causes that lead to these vulnerabilities, including failures in the hardware, software, cryptographic system, security-related protocols and procedures, and human error.

Using many well-known techniques to exploit the vulnerabilities, attackers (unauthorized users) can gain access to Web system resources and, if they wish, block authorized users from accessing data and computing resources. Many other attacks are designed to cause inconvenience and service degradation or to destroy data. Several of the attacks and common vulnerabilities exploited by intruders are described in the upcoming subsections. Once you understand these vulnerabilities and forms of attacks, your problem-finding and analyzing skills will quickly improve.

NOTE Many of the vulnerabilities described here are more the responsibility of a network or system administration staff, rather than testers. We discuss them here to present you with an overview and framework from which to work with security issues.

Software Bugs, Poor Design, and Programming Practice

Many security vulnerabilities are the result of bugs in programs such as Web browsers and Web servers. These bugs, unfortunately, either were undetected during the testing process or were side-effects of fixes, which in turn opened up security holes. Some are easier to exploit than others.

Buffer Overflows

One of the more commonly mentioned bugs is *buffer overflow*, which allows malicious code to be executed on the unauthorized machine. These errors might exist in production code, test and debug code, or third-party code. For example, entering a URL that is much longer than the buffer size allocated for it will cause a memory overwrite (buffer overflow) error if the browser and/or the Web server does not have error-detection code to validate the length of the input URL. A seasoned attacker can cleverly exploit this bug by writing a too-long URL with code to be executed that can cause a browser or server to crash, to alter its security settings, or, in the worst-case scenario, to corrupt user data or grant the attacker full control of the system.

Because buffer overflow is one of the most common attacks used on the Web, let's walk through a rudimentary memory overwrite, or buffer overflow, example to clarify it. By examining the source code in Listing 18.1, you'll find that the string buffer size for the function show_string is 5 bytes; but when show_string is called, it will potentially get a str1 buffer that is larger than 5 bytes.

```
#include <stdio.h>
void show_string(char* str2)
{
        char buffer[5];
        strcpy(buffer, str2);
        printf("Your string is: %s\n", buffer);
}
main()
{
        char str1[10];
        gets(str1);
        show_string(str1);
        exit(0);
}
```

Listing 18.1   Source code in C of a simple program.

When an application asks the operating system to allocate a buffer of 5 bytes, but actually writes more than 5 bytes, we then have a buffer overflow error (see Figure 18.8). Keep in mind that a buffer overflow is not only a security-specific bug but also a functionality bug. When was the last time that you came across a nonreproducible bug, or intermittently reproducible bug? One of the explanations for this is that you didn't have the right conditions to expose the failure caused by the buffer overflow error (see the dynamic operating environments discussion in Chapter 3, "Software Testing Basics," for more information). When we do black-box testing, we don't see the error. We only see the failure; that is the symptom of the error.

For example, when you compile and execute the program in show in Listing 18.1, what will you discover? Will it be an application crash, data corruption, or nothing? The failure you will experience will be nondeterministic because it will depend on the conditions in memory. You will potentially see a different result every time you execute the program. We can explain this by asking what was overwritten in memory (Figure 18.8).

If the overwritten memory space is unused, then you will not see any failure (see Figure 18.9). If the overwritten memory has been allocated for application data (it might be yours or a different application's data), then it causes a data correction. The failure in this case further depends on what's in the data. If the overwritten memory space has been allocated and currently has code in it, then one of the applications or processes will be affected by this error. All of these possible scenarios describe functional bugs caused by buffer overflow.

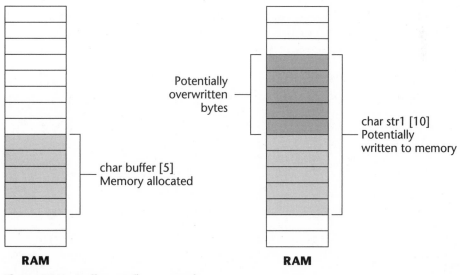

Figure 18.8   Buffer overflow example.

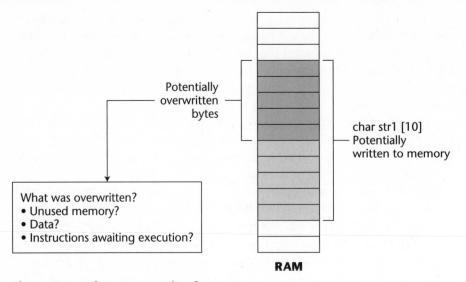

Figure 18.9 What was overwritten?

Attackers understand how the buffer overflow works. They capitalize on it by "pushing" well-crafted instructions to the space where other coded instructions are waiting for execution. If the corrupted program is operating with privileges, the attackers can control their own code execution with the same privileges. From there, the potential damages are up to the attackers' creativity.

Fortunately, as mentioned earlier, because we understand how buffer overflows work, we know how to fix or prevent (better strategy) them. Listing 18.2 elaborates that point by adding a piece of code to do *bounds-checking*, which will prevent the potential error.

```
#include <stdio.h>
void show_string(char* str2)
{
    char buffer[5];
    if(strlen(str2) >= 5)
        }
        printf("Don't do this to me!\n");
        exit(1);
        }
    strcpy(buffer, str2);
    printf("Your string is: %s\n", buffer);
}
main()
{
    char str1[10];
```

Listing 18.2 What can a developer do?

```
    gets(str1);
    show_string(str1);
    exit(0);
}
```

Listing 18.2 *(continued)*

Finally, if you are a good tester, you will notice that there is still a buffer overflow error in the program shown in Listing 18.2. Ask yourself what will happen when the function gets(str1) receives a string that is bigger than 10 bytes? Of course, it will be a buffer overflow error.

After software vendors introduce their products on the market, and as these bugs are discovered, they quickly design and apply fixes. However, as fixes are applied, many more bugs are discovered, creating new vulnerabilities.

Malicious Input Data

Invalid input data are designed to capitalize on such errors as buffer overflows to compromise the security of the system or to corrupt the application services and data.

Command-Line (Shell) Execution

Commonly, in both installation and application code, your programmer constructs scripts that consist of command-line sequences that can be executed in a command window, such as command.com shell in Microsoft Windows. By going to the shell and by executing them, your programmer can take advantage of the many utilities often included with the operating system. For example, using the function system to execute a DOS command-line sequence such as system ("del c:*.*") makes it possible to execute a DOS shell command to delete all files under C:\ root directory. Attackers often attempt to do two things to exploit the potential vulnerabilities:

- Attackers interrupt the execution of the command-line sequence, then use the interrupted shell with the privilege of the calling program and run their own command lines with malicious intent.

- With a command-line sequence that accepts parameters, attackers can try to replace the passed-in parameters with ones of their own, causing the unauthorized and unintended commands to be executed.

Backdoors

Programmers often put *backdoors* into programs as a means to get inside the program by avoiding the normal security checks. Sometimes these backdoors are part of the design, but often developers include backdoors without telling anyone of their existence. Backdoors are usually "protected" by the mistaken idea that no one will ever discover them (i.e., security by obscurity).

JavaScript

JavaScript security holes often compromise a user's privacy or enable the capture of a user's data. For example, a malicious script can be attached to a request you send to a Web server, such as a URL or a database query, while you are navigating to a link in a Web page from an untrusted site. When the Web server responds to your request, the unwanted script tags along. The malicious script then begins executing in your browser. It is possible that confidential information such as your user ID and password will be captured and sent to someplace (a server on the Internet) without your knowing it.

CGI Programs

Badly written and virtually untested CGI programs are a major source of security break-ins. Remember, CGI is not a programming language; it is a standard. Many compile languages such C/C++ as well as scripting languages such as Perl can be used to write CGI programs. These scripts are usually found in a subdirectory on a Web server named /cgi-bin. CGI scripts are used to handle many routine tasks on a Web server. Many times a new application will use previously written scripts. These scripts supposedly perform the functions required; however, the documentation is incomplete and former test cases are often unavailable.

Java

Although the Java security model is to restrict the behavior of applets or applications to a set of safe actions, it is possible to have malicious instruction sets in Java code embedded in HyperText Markup Language (HTML) pages. For example, a Java application can contain instructions to delete files or reformat a local drive. (In theory, a Java applet which runs in a Web browser "sandbox" cannot operate outside of the browser environment.) If a Java application can be downloaded and executed, the user is exposed to this type of attack. This illustrates one of several security holes caused by bugs in Java implementations. Certainly, many of the bugs have been detected and fixed, but undoubtedly many others are still unexposed, and new ones keep appearing that can potentially compromise security.

ActiveX

The key issue with ActiveX controls is that they are distributed as executable binaries and allowed to have functionality similar to an application that is run on a local drive. This means that a malicious control can easily delete files on a local drive or transmit the user's confidential information to an unknown server on the Internet.

The ActiveX security model is very different from Java. ActiveX has no restriction on what a control can do. Instead, each ActiveX control can be digitally signed by its author. This model relies on the user to control security by configuring the browser settings. For example, a browser can be configured to allow only downloading of signed ActiveX controls. One potential problem is that a signed ActiveX control is certified by an untrustworthy certifying authority. In such a case, how comfortable are you executing that control on your system?

Cookies

A *cookie* is data that is created and left in the client browser memory or hard drive to provide certain information (e.g., state information, user's identity, etc.) about the client or user every time the Web server receives a request from the client. In this model, the user is the target and only the Web server that sends or creates the cookie can understand the cookie information. Cookies allow a client to maintain information about itself between HyperText Transfer Protocol (HTTP) requests. The information might be something simple such as display preferences and last visited page, but it might also be personal information such as user ID and password, snail mail, or e-mail address information. That means that if your cookie information is exposed to other Web applications or Web sites, others can use the information to, for example, access your Web-based email account.

In May 2000, a security alert from Peacefire.Org reported that cookies that had been set in Internet Explorer could be read by any third-party Web site outside of the domain that set the cookie. Though Microsoft fixed this bug, the incident has several lasting implications. For one, by intercepting a cookie set by a free Web-based e-mail site that uses cookies for authentication, the operator of a malicious Web site could break into a visitor's free mail account, such as a HotMail or YahooMail account, and read the contents of his or her Inbox. (For more information on this particular security alert, go to www.peacefire .org/security/iecookies/. For more information on cookies, go to www.cookie central.com.)

From the user's perspective, there are two classes of concern regarding using cookies: (1) Malicious Web sites can capture cookie information and use it in a way that may harm the user, and (2) there are privacy concerns regarding the tracking of user behavior on the Web.

Spoofing

Spoofing is an act of deceit perpetrated by assuming a different identity for the purpose of stealing information (such as intercepting a buyer-merchant transaction and pretending to be a merchant to steal a credit card number) or gaining access to unauthorized resources. There are many forms of spoofing: e-mail spoofing, to pretend that an e-mail is sent from someone else; Internet Protocol (IP) spoofing, to pretend that data are coming from a trusted machine; Web page spoofing, to pretend that the page is coming from a trusted source; and others.

Malicious Programs

Virus and Worm

A *virus*, as most of us know by now, is a computer program that is designed to cause unexpected and uninvited events or activities to occur, from the merely annoying, such as displaying playful messages, to the dangerous, such as erasing data on your hard disk. A computer transmits or receives a virus by interacting with other computers, usually through e-mail messages, attachments in e-mail messages, and moving or downloading files. When an infected program or the virus itself (as a program) is executed, the virus code is loaded and run, often with two primary objectives: (1) to do whatever it's designed to do (e.g., erase your hard disk), and (2) affect other programs by appending itself to those programs so it can then be propagated.

A *worm* is similar to a virus, with one difference: a worm can self-propagate by sending a copy of itself to other machines (via e-mail, for example).

Trojan Horses

A Trojan horse is a program that is installed because it does something the user wants it to do; however, the program has other functions which are unknown and not desired by the user. Many attacker utilities contain undocumented "features" of seemingly handy and helpful programs that are given away and widely distributed.

Misuse Access Privilege Attacks

Misuse access privilege attacks are inside attacks, often carried out by authorized users taking advantage of the privileges granted to them, coupled with internal knowledge about the systems, with the intent to access unauthorized services and data.

Password Cracking

There are many password-cracking programs available that can be used by an attacker to systematically uncover a password to log in and gain access to the system.

Denial-of-Service Attacks

Denial-of-service (DoS) attacks involve bombarding servers with so many requests or e-mail messages that the servers are not able to process any legitimate requests that it receives. DoS attacks commonly involve attackers secretly placing on servers software agents that are not related to the target server. A master command activates the agents and identifies the target; the full-bandwidth capacity of the servers hosting the agents is then unleashed upon the target server.

Denial-of-service agents are a challenge to find because they are placed via backdoor methods. For example, an attack could be initiated from a cheap computer connected through a pay telephone—in which case the attacker might never be tracked down. The attacks might also be initiated from foreign countries where prosecution might be more difficult or impossible.

A high-profile example that illustrates the need for better security measures across the Internet is the three-day assault that was waged against a number of prominent Web sites beginning February 7, 2000. Some of the Internet's biggest sites (Yahoo!, Amazon.com, E*Trade, buy.com, CNN, eBay, and ZDNet) were either temporarily shut down or seriously impaired by a series of denial-of-service attacks. Yahoo!, for example, was bombarded with server requests from about 50 different IP addresses (at rates of up to 1 gigabyte per second!). It was a surprise to many that Yahoo!'s servers proved to be vulnerable to attack. Many experts speculated that the attacks were intended to demonstrate the lack of security measures at most content and e-commerce Web sites. It does not appear that the attacks resulted in their instigators gaining access to confidential user information or financial gain, but they did receive a good amount of media exposure.

Some of the common forms of DoS attacks include: ping and smurf attacks, bombarding the servers with pings or ICMP (Internet Control Message Protocol) pings to consume the available bandwidth and resources; mail bomb attacks, clogging up the mail server with excessive volumes of mails, in quantity as well as size; SYN attacks, filling up the available TCP connection; and UDP (User Datagram Protocol) attacks, generating massive network traffic by bouncing bogus UDP packets between the hosts.

For more information, read the article, "Managing the Threat of Denial-of-Service Attack," written by the folks at the CERT Coordination Center: www .cert.org/archive/pdf/Managing_DoS.pdf.

Physical Attacks

Physical attacks include breaking into a facility to steal a computer to get to the data on the hard disk, or simply sitting in front of an already-logged-in computer while the owner is on a break to access unauthorized resources. Computer theft is also a possibility, now that computers are much smaller and are not bolted to the floor. Many of these handheld or laptop computers may contain passwords for accessing much bigger systems.

Exploiting the Trust Computational Base

Attackers exploit the trust relationship of computer systems, access privileges, and data to accomplish malicious tasks. Here's how this works: Inside a secure system is a community of components (hardware, operating systems, utility programs, and applications) that "trust" each other and that are protected by a boundary to untrusted programs. Attackers often attempt to cross the boundary to get into the trusted circle. Once that task is accomplished, malicious activities can be carried out.

Information Leaks

Information about organizations, networks, and applications is always made available to external sources. Often, groups within the organization provide information to clients as part of their jobs. For example, both marketing and customer support work to supply helpful information to clients. In addition, because it is considered good development practice to accurately comment code, and because Web-visible directories may contain readme files, all this information can become tools for the attacker.

   Information leaks can be uncontrollable as well as controllable. An example of an uncontrollable leak is information that is made available to the public, such as company and executive staff information. Another example is when a user registers for a domain name: the contact information provided during the registration process becomes available to the public. Controllable leaks consist of information made known to the public unintentionally, often due to lack of security awareness or poor practices. Some examples of this type of leak are described in the following subsections.

Social Engineering

Social engineering is the practice of capturing mistakenly revealed information that can be useful to attackers who are planning an attack. For example, assume your IS engineer posts a message on a forum that reads, "I just installed a [COTS] firewall to our network; can anyone help me configure it?" Essentially, it is an invitation to attackers to pay a visit.

Keystroke Capturing

Device software can be planted on a host to capture keystrokes generated through a normal user session. The captured information can reveal what the user has typed, including user ID, password, and other sensitive information.

Garbage Rummaging

Low-tech intruders can always attack by rummaging through physical or virtual "garbage cans" to look for confidential information, such as a list of user IDs and passwords, a network map, and employee contact information.

Packet Sniffing

Using a sniffing program, an attacker can collect information transfer over the public network. System-specific information such as the sending/receiving server IP address, ports, and protocols used can be gathered. Sensitive data such as user IDs, passwords, and credit card account numbers sent in cleartext also can be easily captured.

Scanning and Probing

Scanning is the practice of looking for open ports on the hosts connected to the network, then attempting to connect to hosts with the intention of illegally gathering information.

Network Mapping

Using a combination of trace-route, scanning, and probing, an attacker can piece together a logical map of your network systems. From there, the attacker can analyze the map to identify vulnerabilities of the systems and devise the best method to break in. In the physical world, network mapping would be analogous to roaming around a building to capture the floor plan and determine the location of exit doors before breaking into a vault within the building.

Network Attacks

Using all the methods described in this section, intruders may direct their attacks at various targets in the network hardware and software services, such as the firewall, the DNS server, the RAS server, the DHCP server, the router, Web server, database server, mail server, and so on.

Testing Goals and Responsibilities

Often, there are numerous people within an organization who influence the security concerns and operational infrastructure; these individuals make up an organization's *security team*. A security team may include the following:

- *Policymakers*, who define security requirements that enhance user and producer confidence in system security defenses.

- *Network administrators*, who design and implement security measures to provide security at the operational level.

- *Software developers*, who design and implement security defenses at the application level (to meet security requirements).

- *Software testers*, who are responsible for testing the systems to uncover functionality, interoperability, configuration, and compatibility errors as they are related to security implementation (primarily at the application level and perhaps at the operational level as well), and discovering potential problems introduced by security design flaws.

- *Security experts and consultants*, who help test and maintain your security programs as well as handle security breaches. Often, this group of people consists of reformed attackers-for-hire. Former attackers, who developed their domain of expertise through practice over the years, are responsible for conducting penetration tests (designed to evaluate the effectiveness of Web system defenses through the use of a combination of attack tools, security and attacking expertise, and IT knowledge) prior to the deployment of a system as well as on an ongoing basis. Unless your organization does not have an expert to handle penetration testing, it's often not expected that a typical software tester or developer would have this responsibility.

The main focus of our goals as testers should be testing the Web site and Web application security at the application level. It means that we should seek out vulnerabilities and information leaks caused primarily by programming practice and, to a certain extent, by misconfiguration of Web servers and other application-specific servers. We should test for the security side effects or vulnerabilities caused by the functionality implementation. At the same time, we should also test for functional side effects caused by security implementation (see Figures 18.10 and 18.11).

Functionality Side Effect: An Error-Handling Bug Example

Applications often are not aware of the actual causes of failure conditions they experience. Errors may be due to session time-outs, absence of available disk space, incomplete downloads, or browser security settings that prevent the downloading of active content (Java applets, ActiveX controls, etc.). An application might misinterpret an error condition and, in turn, display a misleading error message for all such error conditions.

Figure 18.10 shows the Internet Explorer safety-level screen. Note that Medium has been selected as the active content security setting, which means (among other things) that ActiveX controls cannot be downloaded. This application is a Web-based e-mail reader. It requires an ActiveX control to be downloaded before it can download attachments. Because the security level is set to medium, the ActiveX control cannot be downloaded. However, the application presents an erroneous error message in this scenario, such as that shown in Figure 18.11. Based on the advice given in the message, the user has two choices: (1) continue to wait or (2) click on the Reload button to reload the control; but either choice will fail to download the ActiveX control because, in reality, the browser's security setting is the cause of this error condition.

Specifically, the following areas should be considered as our testing responsibilities:

- Test the security prevention implementation. Seek out vulnerabilities and various means to exploit them so they can be fixed.

- Test the security detection implementation. Help determine the information that should be logged and mechanisms to track; alert and trap suspicious activities.

- Test the requirements and designs.

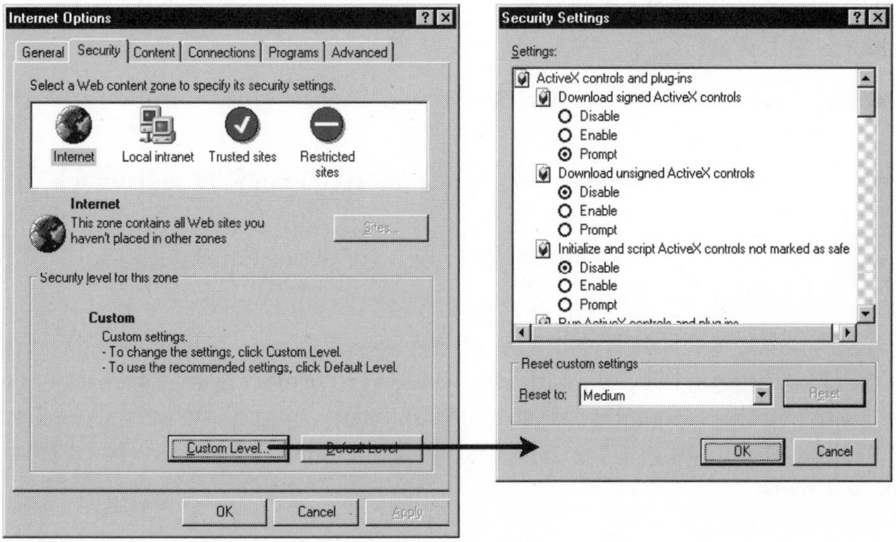

Figure 18.10   Internet Explorer safety-level settings.

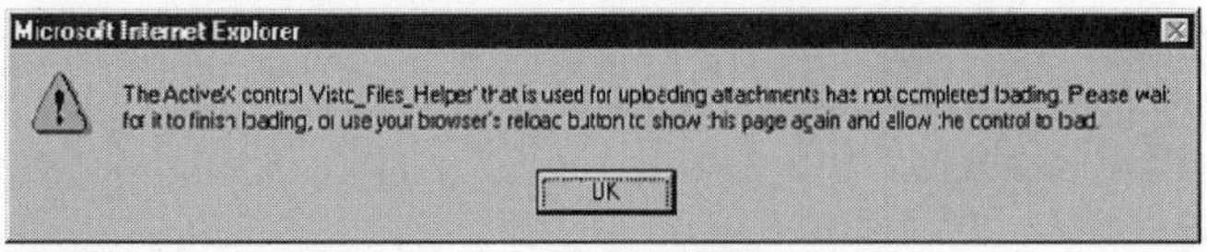

Figure 18.11 Inaccurate error message.

- Test the code and programming practices.
- Test interoperability with third-party components with specific focus on known vulnerabilities.
- Test for misconfiguration.
- Test the deployment.
- To a certain extent, do penetration testing.

Other common goals of Web system security measures—and, therefore, their associated testing considerations—follow.

These goals are particularly appropriate for e-commerce systems:

- Interactions and transactions between buyers and your company's system should be confidential.
- Data integrity should be preserved.
- Buyers and your company's system should be able to verify each other's identities (at least, electronically).
- Transaction records should be in a form that can withstand scrutiny in a court of law.

As a producer of Web-based systems, your company should be protected from the following:

- Exposing private network access to unauthorized external and internal intruders.
- Losing confidential data and proprietary technology through attack activities.
- Losing data due to hardware and software errors, natural disasters, and theft.

As a side issue, although many of the security protection measures via browser settings on the client-side are designed to protect users, users do have the responsibility of protecting themselves from vulnerabilities by properly controlling these settings. Users of Web-based systems can be protected from the following:

- Exposure to virus attacks via active contents, plug-ins, cabinet files (.CAB), executables (.EXEs), DLLs, ActiveX controls, and other components

- Exposure to offensive contents

- Exposure of private information to third parties, either in violation of the Web site's stated policy or as an unauthorized data capture by a third party that is independent of the intent of the Web site owner

Testing for Security

Though much of the security responsibility is at the corporate IT level, the application tester is also involved. As explained earlier in the chapter, the most prevalent security weakness is the buffer overflow bug, which, you'll recall, is solely a coding problem within a program. The problem exists regardless of design considerations, operating systems, or implementation language. It is, simply put, a coding oversight, and it plays a part in over half of all reported problems. That said, it is possible to uncover and rectify buffer overflow bugs if you use the proper security testing strategy, so we'll begin this discussion on security testing to see how to accomplish this.

In testing the security of Web-based applications, it is best to assume that attackers have skill, luck, and time on their side, and to recognize that the attacker might be one lone "script kiddy" or a major international espionage organization. Another aspect of the testing management's risk assessment is to determine how much value will be lost if the application is attacked. The more valuable the assets maintained by the application, the more likely that someone will spend a significant amount of time and effort to break in.

Testing the Requirements and Design

Requirements Are Key

Every system is built using a set of requirements. Sometimes these requirements are written clearly, but often they are vague statements only partially defined. The product manager may state, for example, "The application must be secure." But what does "secure" mean and just how much should be spent making it secure? Security has been defined as a trade-off between risk and reward. Deciding how much risk is a question for management to answer. For example, a very large Web site hosted on hardware that is not connected to the corporate intranet, and consisting of hundreds of pages and welcoming thousands of external visitors every day, might require little security because all of the available data is public knowledge. In this case, there is little reason for anyone to deface the Web site. The Gutenberg Project's Web site is just such a place. In contrast, a very small Web application that tracks company sales and is restricted to only the sales staff of a single company could be a major target. How many attackers would like this information on IBM or Microsoft?

The point is, in order to provide "just enough" testing, the test team must understand how much the system is worth, both to the organization using the application and to the possible attackers of the application.

Trusted Computational Base (TCB)

As noted previously in the subsection titled "Exploiting the Trust Computational Base," inside a secure system is a "community" of components (hardware, operating systems, utility programs, and applications) that trust each other. The members of this community all have established boundaries for untrusted programs. In order to test your application, you will need to determine where those boundaries lie and what data can be transferred across those boundaries. This is the *Trusted Computational Base (TCB)*. For example, a client's browser is almost always untrusted. The user can easily control data sent from a browser to the application. The application can rarely maintain control of the browser software.

Trust is also often extended to disk files residing on the server. However, other users can modify these files. Understanding what is inside and what is outside your TCB enables you to build power scenarios for the application.

Be aware that the TCB can change over time. Network configurations change. Data files that were once secure can become insecure. Passwords expire. On some systems, once a person logs on to the system, he or she may never log off. We all know people who have gone on vacation and have left their system logged on, and have not even set a screensaver to prevent unauthorized users from accessing their system.

Access Control

Important questions to ask in terms of access control are: Who can access the program? Are there different classes of users? Does each class of user have the correct functionality? Can a user of one class obtain additional privileges? Most programs will have different classes of users, as well as categories of people who should not have any access to the program. Networked-based programs will most certainly need to consider access controls for system administrators, back-up utilities, the owners of the application, and users of the application.

Testing must also determine if the target application has the correct access rights to the server it uses. While a program may require access to servers such as databases, access rights should be limited to the minimum rights required, and only for the duration that access is necessary. Granting a target application "superuser" (unrestricted) access rights forever (unlimited) is an expensive mistake.

Which Resources Need to Be Protected?

The first thing that may come to mind in regard to protecting resources is the denial-of-service (DoS) attack. Remember, in a DoS attack, an outside attacker does not try to steal or destroy information, but instead shuts down your system by making repeated requests, thus overloading your system. Several other types of denial attacks are possible and other resources need to be protected. Shutting down or rebooting the computer is a simple attack. Overloading the printer, writing very larges file to disk, and filling the system monitor (standard out) with garbage are other effective attacks that can use an application as the source of the problem.

Client Privacy Issues: What Information Needs to Be Private?

There are many laws concerning record keeping and how data must be stored, particularly financial, work history, legal, and medical data. A company's confidential information will have user-based read and/or write access to the information.

Furthermore, such information is often screen-dependent. It will require us as testers to build a matrix, of which specific screens are available to each class of user. Does the user of one screen have a right to access all the data? Can users accidentally gain access to additional screens? A common problem occurs when a screen has a link to additional screens. Some of the questions we should consider asking include:

- How well and securely do your Web applications or does your Web site handle client data?
- Does the Web site have a privacy policy readily available and accessible from every Web page?
- Does your Web site tell users how their information will be collected and used? Have you tested your Web site or application to ensure it delivers what is promised?

Testing the Application Code

A common attack is to replace libraries or utilities required by the application with modified versions of these products. Your application then calls these products and inadvertently aids in the attack. As mentioned earlier, your application must carefully check every piece of software outside your TCB.

Backdoors

To reiterate from the earlier discussion, backdoors are created by the developers to facilitate debugging and troubleshooting. Unfortunately, it is not uncommon for backdoors to be left in the production code, thereby introducing security risks. For example, a backdoor that allows the user to go directly to the application without any form of authentication can be a dangerous problem. Check to make sure that all backdoors are closed in the production release.

Exception Handling and Failure Notification

Programs often contain *exception-handling* code to deal with unexpected events or errors. What is the correct way to handle these exceptions?

- Sometimes the program should fail silently; for example, the program may be able to ignore extra data sent to a buffer.

- Other times, the condition causing the exception needs to be reported so that the user can decide on an appropriate action to take, such as failure finding a DNS entry for a Web site.

- Sometimes, the error also needs to be logged so that the system administration can later determine the cause of problems.

The error might be minor and routine, or caused by performance problems; or it might be the result of other attacks on the system. For example, a function handles the buffer overflow correctly by ignoring all data larger than the buffer can contain. However, though silently handling this failure beats the attacks, it also causes the unusual requests to not be reported.

Reports must have the right flag of priority. Some error-handling messages may be sent to a log file and never be viewed unless there is a problem. Other types of errors may need to be summarized and distributed as performance reports. Some failures may require immediate notification to the owners of the application. As a tester, you need to understand which response is correct for each condition. Then you can build test cases to make sure the logic is implemented correctly.

ID and Password Testing

When it comes to ID and password testing, follow these guidelines:

- *Check for the misuse of superuser accounts.* For the sake of convenience, your developers might inadvertently use this account to procrastinate in completing a thorough design and implementation for dealing with access rights and permissions. A major principle of security design is to give users (including your application as a user) the minimum amount of access such that they can perform required tasks but are prevented from performing illegal operations. With superuser access, the end user can create, delete, alter, or write to data tables. An end user with superuser privilege can alter URLs with SQL code to do many malicious tasks.

- *Look for IDs and passwords "in the clear" when connecting to and accessing servers, directories, databases, and other resources.* These are potentially hard-coded in Active Server Pages (ASP), Java Server Pages (JSP), or a configuration data file stored in an insecure location. If an ASP, JSP, or configuration file that stores the hard-coded ID and password can be retrieved, danger is eminent. Retrieving these files can be done in several ways. For example, not too long ago, the IIS3 bug enabled Web users to retrieve the APS source by placing a dot at the end of the URL (e.g., www.mtesting.com/mycode/login.asp.) or, due to server misconfiguration, allowed directory browsing.

Testing for Information Leaks

To test for information leaks, follow these guidelines:

- Test for comments in the HTML code that might reveal user ID and password information, code paths, or directory and executable file names.

- Test for error messages that reveal server name, root directory name, or other pertinent information about the servers.

- Check to make sure that the directory browsing option on the Web server is turned off (see Figure 18.12).

- Check to ensure that Access to Source configuration on the Web server is turned off.

- Check to ensure that the Write privilege to local path is blocked.

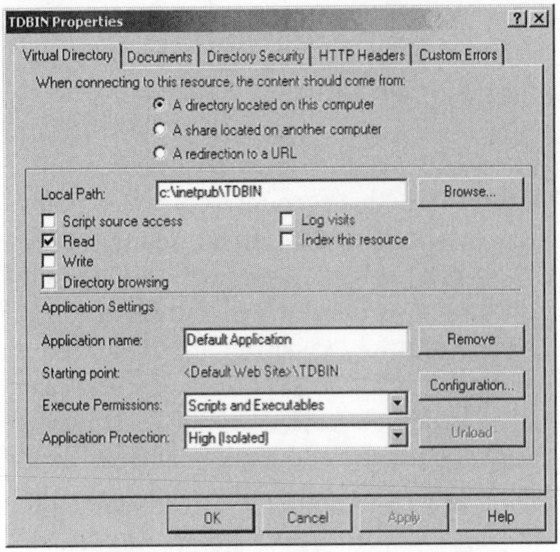

Figure 18.12 Server configuration example.

Random Numbers versus Unique Numbers

Many times, programmers will use a *random number* when what they really want is a *unique number*. It is important to distinguish between these two concepts. In randomness, the same number may come up several times. A word of caution: When the program actually requires random numbers, make sure it is getting random numbers, as most random number generators are not that random.

For testing purposes, it is often useful to replace a random number generator with a list of known numbers. By having such a list, you can repeat tests and expect that it should give the same results. Using a list of generated numbers also allows you to test edge cases for randomness; that is, what happens when numbers are repeated, possibly several times? You should also test boundary conditions such as zero.

Finally, run at least one test using truly random numbers to test the behavior that the developers intended to achieve.

Testing the Use of GET and POST

Two common methods used by HTTP are GET and POST. When information is transferred using the GET method, information, in the form of parameters, is passed via the URL after a question mark (?). For example, www.mtesting .com/userdata.htm?credit=visa&card_number-111222233334444.

- GET requests can be logged by the Web server in cleartext format. If sensitive data such as user ID and password or credit card information is transmitted using the GET method, even when used with HTTPS, data can be logged in cleartext in the server log. If an attacker can download a log file from the server, he or she will have access to sensitive data.

- When a user clicks on a link in the page to go to an externally linked Web site, the browser will send the URL information to the linked site as part of the REFERRER information. Hence, sensitive information is leaked.

- Finally, the GET requests are often tracked by the user's browser in the history file.

The POST method sends data in a similar way except that POST commands use the HTTP body to handle information. Therefore, the information is hidden from view and will not be logged on the server-side. However, keep in mind that the information is still sent in cleartext unless HTTPS is used.

- Whenever possible, check for the preferred use of POST instead of GET for transferring data.

- Check the information in URLs to make sure that they don't show sensitive information.

- Try to access the file or directory shown in the URL to look for information leaks.

- Given the URL in the earlier example, if the browser collects information using the POST method, such as `<form METHOD="POST" action="/userdata.htm">`, you might want to try accessing `www.mtesting.com/userdata.htm`, `www.mtesting.com/data/userdata.htm`, or `www.mtesting.com/userdata/userdata.htm`.

Parameter-Tampering Attacks

Try to manipulate the URL strings to retrieve sensitive information.

- For example, SQL calls are often made to access data on the back-end database. By playing with the name of an SQL stored procedure or the parameters, a malicious user potentially can obtain a user ID and password list. (See "SQL Injection Attacks" in the next subsection for more information.)

- As another example, suppose that by going to `www.mtesting.com/saving_acct001.pdf`, you can retrieve a report on your savings account activities. What happens if you replace `saving_acct001` `.pdf` by `saving_acct002.pdf`? Will you be able to get a report for another savings account for which you do not have authorization?

■ Hidden fields. Hidden fields are not hidden because the data can be viewed by selecting view source option provided by a browser. Hidden fields often carry sensitive data, including pricing information. Try to View Source, change the price of an item, and then save the HTML on the client-side to see if the server will use that value to calculate the actual bill. The good programming practice here is not to trust client-side inputs, and always double-check reference values on the server-side.

SQL Injection Attacks

As an example of an SQL injection attack, consider an application that uses the following SQL command to authenticate a user signing in:

```
SELECT * FROM bank WHERE LOGIN='$id' AND PASSWORD='$password'
```

If an attacker signs in, using an ID of:
ADMIN
and a password of:
no ' OR 1 #,
this can cause the database to use the following SQL command:

```
SELECT * FROM bank WHERE LOGIN='ADMIN' AND PASSWORD='no' OR 1 #'
```

The pound (#) sign can cause the database to ignore the trailing single quote, interpreting 1 as true.

Since anything OR 1 is true, the application will think that the attacker has authenticated as administrator, and will return the records. In testing for SQL injection attacks, you want to manipulate input data used as SQL commands or stored procedure input parameters to look for application failures in sanitizing malicious data.

Cookie Attacks

By changing the values in cookies, attackers might be able to gain access to accounts that they don't own. Stealing a user's cookie might enable the attacker to access an account without having to use an ID and password. Corrupting a cookie chain may cause data corruption.

What's in a cookie? Listing 18.3 shows an example, and Listing 18.4 shows the code that created this cookie.

```
BigFood
a%20very%20big%20cookie
www.evil-spirit.com/
0
1334000384
31689671
678306528
29486907
*
```

Listing 18.3   An example of cookie data.

```
<script>
    //
    //  Cookie Functions - Second Helping  (21-Jan-96)
    //  Written by:  Bill Dortch, Idaho Design <bdortch@netw.com>
    //  The following functions are released to the public domain.
    //
    //  Please refer to the official cookie spec, at:
    //
    //        http://www.netscape.com/newsref/std/cookie_spec.html
    //
    //        SetCookie (myCookieVar, cookieValueVar, null, "/myPath",
null, true);
    //
    function SetCookie (name, value) {
      var argv = SetCookie.arguments;
      var argc = SetCookie.arguments.length;
      var expires = (argc > 2) ? argv[2] : null;
      var path = (argc > 3) ? argv[3] : null;
      var domain = (argc > 4) ? argv[4] : null;
      var secure = (argc > 5) ? argv[5] : false;
      document.cookie = name + "=" + escape (value) +
        ((expires == null) ? "" : ("; expires=" +
expires.toGMTString())) +
        ((path == null) ? "" : ("; path=" + path)) +
        ((domain == null) ? "" : ("; domain=" + domain)) +
        ((secure == true) ? "; secure" : "");
    }
</script>
```

Listing 18.4   The source code for the cookie in Listing 18.3.

Because cookies are simple to create, and provide a means to create session states or to be used however the designer intends, they are found everywhere. And because they are found everywhere, it is easy for an attacker to modify cookies on his or her computer and then reconnect to the victim's application.

An attacker can also steal cookies from other users and manipulate the information in them to masquerade as those users. This type of attack allows the intruder to gain all the access rights of the stolen identity.

Another potential problem exists if cookies are used to allow traveling employees to connect to the system using their laptop computers. What happens when a laptop is stolen? (By the way, if you have not seen the movie, *Enemy of the State*, check it out. In addition to being entertaining, a segment of the story illustrates the problem described here.)

Testing for Buffer Overflows

Testing for buffer overflows requires testing everywhere a buffer is used. Most commonly, buffers are used to store inputs before they are processed by your application. Each of these inputs may have a buffer to hold data, and not all buffers are immediately obvious. For example, data returned from a database inquiry may be buffered.

The goal of testing for a buffer overflow is to show that sending too much data to the program will cause the program to behave in an unexpected manner. As discussed earlier, common problems with a buffer overflow include the application failing to leave the program running while still consuming additional resources, or causing the application to consider the additional data as program instructions and executing this new code.

How do you test for buffer overflow? You send very large amounts of data to the buffer. Using cut-and-paste is one way to generate large amounts of data. Another common method is to use a record and playback automation tool, then edit the script with additional input data. For large amounts of data, first try several kilobytes, then megabytes of data.

Besides very large amounts of data, there are other interesting boundary conditions to test. Sending data that is exactly the size of the buffer, as well as data that is one byte more or less than the buffer's size, may cause problems. When determining the size of the data you are sending to a buffer, you must also include any "hidden" characters, such as linefeeds and carriage returns.

Finally, keep in mind these two points: (1) Input data cannot be trusted, and (2) applications can receive data from interfaces (such as API, protocol, file, etc.) other than the UI. Think of all the worst data conditions that you can pass on to the program, as well as many different ways that you can send data to the program beyond the UI method.

Testing for Bad Data

Entering bad data can have either immediate or long-term effects on the system. The most famous immediate effect is seen from the use of the character combination <Ctrl>-C, which can terminate execution of the program. Several other character combinations may cause unexpected system intervention with the program; and, remember, developers put backdoors into programs to allow debugging or to test different data sets. If these "features" are not removed, they can be used to change the program's behavior after release.

In terms of long-term effects, bad data may not present a problem when first entered. For example, entering </body></html> into an application as your name may work fine, and this name is stored into the database. As a result, later, when the database produces reports that are to be viewed with a browser, these reports are broken.

Data entered into an application often gets passed to additional applications. For example, if you are requesting data from a database and send an asterisk (*) instead of the person's last name, the database may return data for all entries with this last name. This could result in an invasion of privacy if the unauthorized data is returned to the user. Also, this problem may cause a buffer overflow since the application wasn't expecting a large amount of data to be returned from the database.

The general rule is: Never trust incoming data. We can't control end-users' applications or end-users' data because we don't have control over them. Therefore, we should be comfortable only with what we can control. Developers should implement routines to sanitize or control the inputs to ensure that the data conforms to the server-side application's expectation. Here are some guidelines to follow:

- Ask: "How effective is the coverage, design, and implementation of the server-side input validation?"

- Sanitize input at the server-side. For example, strip and encode the less-than sign (<) such as in <scripts>. A conventional practice is to substitute "<" with &lt, and > by &gt.

- Add two-way data filtering procedures to help reduce security risks as well as functionality errors (e.g., the double quote and single quote characters are notorious for causing trouble for SQL databases).

- Regarding files and data sent to server, ask: "Should the user be allowed to post executable scripts or file to the server?"

Reliance on Client-Side Scripting

To test reliance on client-side scripting, follow these guidelines:

- Check that the application does not rely solely on the client-side scripting for error checking.

- Check that the application does not rely solely on the client-side scripting for authentication because users can bypass the routine by authoring or modifying the Web page.

- Try to bypass authentication by going to the URL directly.

- After a valid login, try to capture the URL. Launch a new browser and use the captured URL to go to the page that supposedly you must go through proper authentication. Can you get in?

When Input Becomes Output

Data can easily pass though various programs and then become valid statements for a different interpreted language program. As an example, and a test case to try, when prompted to fill in your name, try this name:

```
<B><I>Bob</I></B>
```

Using this name you may find that, when redisplayed, HTML directives (i.e. tags) have been sent to the browser.

Have you ever used the name:

</BODY></HTML>

Doing so, many applications could break in strange places. If names are stored in a database, and later those names are part of status reports sent to administrators via Web pages, the reports would end abruptly. This name could be much more destructive, too. For example, a semicolon ends one SQL statement and begins the next statement. So your attack could have started a new request to delete or modify different records in the database, as shown here:

```
Bob; delete * from all;
```

Filtering an application to protect from malicious user input requires a lot of complex error-handling code and requires that you understand how the data moves through the components of the application. Then you must determine what would constitute a malicious command in each of those components.

Data that is passing through the system must be checked and rechecked several times. It is good practice to check data when it is entered. For example, a Web browser can validate inputs on the client's machine. This prevents unnecessary communication with the server and allows fast checking that the data is correct before being sent. However, a malicious user can easily bypass these checks. The most important checks of an application's inputs must be done under total control of the application.

- Implement a code walk-through to ensure that the code is thoroughly reviewed.

- Take advantage of the tools available to facilitate script scanning, to detect common vulnerabilities.

    - CGI scripts can be scanned with Rain Forest Puppy's whisker .pl scripts. The tool is free for download at `www.wiretrip.net/rfp`.

    - NuMega has tools to facilitate code reviews, at www.numega.com.

    - L0pht offers tools at `www.I0pht.com`.

    - Cigital's ITS4 is a source scanning tool for C and C++ that can be found at `www.cigital.com/its4`.

    - WebInspect, produced by SPI Dynamics at `www.spidynamics.com`, can scan Web pages, scripts, code cookies, and application components for commonly known vulnerabilities.

Testing Third-Party Code

Known Vulnerabilities

To ensure that known vulnerabilities in third-party software used in the Web applications are patched requires an ongoing effort; you must monitor security information and alerts and take timely actions. The application should check that third-party software meets the configuration required during application initialization. This will prevent the application from executing with known incompatible components.

During application development, identify all third-party software that will be used by your application. Research the security related problems that exist with each third-party software product. Use Bugtraq and general Web searches to find information on problems of interest. Determine if patches or workarounds are available for each reported problem. Work with the developers to determine if your application might be susceptible to any of these problems.

Race Conditions

Applications can use multiple threads to achieve concurrent processing. As a result, tasks do not always take the same amount of time to execute and database queries may return in a different order. Likewise, publicly declared variables may change value between two apparently contiguous code statements and files may be rewritten in different order (last write wins) causing changes to be lost.

Race condition errors depend on many environmentally changing attributes of the network; hence, they are very hard to find and often impossible to duplicate. Any time you discover a failure, especially when it is not reproducible, it must be reported. Often, it is only after a long period of time, during which several problems are reported, that a pattern will emerge.

Testing the Deployment

Installation Defaults

Most programs are installed with the default settings, and it is usually not clear what the security implications of these default settings are. When testing the program's installation, you need to check that the defaults provide the maximum amount of security. If less security is desired at a customer's installation, the customer should be fully informed as to the risks they are assuming.

When testing the installation, you must check that files have the correct permissions. Making all files, particularly program and configuration files, writeable is a dangerous idea. Typically, install programs copy the files and all the attributes directly as they are set in the installation media.

Default Passwords

Applications should never have passwords preset, because many users will accept the defaults and not change them. Attackers know this and try the default passwords first and are often successful.

Internationalization

Where will the application be deployed? In which countries will the company sell the application? International laws are very different. Reporting rules for private data collected by your application are different on a country-by-country basis. Export laws on encryption products also are different. Some of the third-party products you have licensed may not be licensed for distribution to all countries. Many countries have limits on the content and the wording of certain notices and may require legal review.

The application may be free to travel the World Wide Web. Organizations using the application will need to inquire locally about "road" conditions.

Program Forensics

Leave a trail. This is important should the application (or system) be compromised. Using log files can provide information to those trying to determine what happened. Log files are also an important resource for the tester. Understanding which events generate a log entry allows you to build test cases to cover those exceptions and to verify that the test actually ran and produced the expected results. (See Chapter 12, "Server-Side Testing," for more uses of log files during testing.)

Expect log files to get large, and don't be afraid to request additional information to be logged. In production, log files can be purged regularly. While testing, you can create filters using grep, awk, and other text processing programs, to reduce the log data to the records you are interested in viewing. Log files should make liberal use of timestamps, user IDs, and IP addresses to help identify the data.

Ask: Can the program provide additional information? The default installation should copy (in UNIX use the "tee" utility) the messages to "standard error" and "standard out" to a log file. This allows a review of the messages that were displayed during normal operation of the application.

Working with Customer Support Folks

After the application has been deployed and is being used by customers, your support team will learn a lot of tricks about the program. They will find numerous undocumented ways the application can be used to provide diagnostic clues. These clues will also provide a means for attackers to gain more information about other installations. Consequently, technical support has to be extremely careful in handling this information.

Penetration Testing

Penetration testing evaluates the effectiveness of network system defenses. It involves a series of tests that require a combination of attack tools, security expertise, and information technology (IT) knowledge. Penetration testing is a technically involved process that often exceeds the skills and resources of many organizations. Therefore, this type of testing is *not* normally done by software testers. Unless there is an in-house expert, it's common practice to bring in external expertise to help with this testing effort. Some issues to consider during penetration testing include the following:

- Penetration testing should be conducted before systems go live.

- Penetration testing must continue on a live system, particularly when any part of the system changes.

- Penetration testing activities often mimic the actions of real-life attackers.

- Penetration testing should consider the vulnerabilities of delivered data and intellectual property. For example, how easily might attackers be able to decrypt encrypted data, such as e-commerce transactions? Or how easily might attackers be able to reverse-engineer a COTS application, and thereby steal proprietary source code?

- Have penetration testing requirements been established?

- Given the scope and knowledge that is required for penetration testing of a system, how can effective testing be implemented?

- Is there a penetration test plan with identified resources?

- Does the testing staff have the required time and skill to effectively run penetration testing? Can others within the organization help? If not, who will be responsible? Can the testing be outsourced?

- How effective are system router and firewall defenses?

- How easily might intruders be able to gain access to server or client hosts on a network?

- What are the open and closed ports on a server? If an intruder connects to the open ports, how far in the network system could he or she go? Given these vulnerabilities, what are the worst possible risks the system could face?

- Testing should be done from outside the network perimeter as well as from inside the perimeter (through limited-privilege accounts within the network).

- How effective are the system's security defenses as far as the delivery of data and applications goes?

- Define objectives, scope, roles, and responsibilities for penetration testing.

- Develop a strategic test-planning process.

- Define simple test metrics to evaluate severity and risk (e.g., a database can be corrupted via a break-in).

- Consider evaluating and acquiring COTS testing tools to assist your organization in penetration testing.

For more information on currently available security tools, go to the CERT/CC site, at www.cert.org/tech_tips/security_tools.html, and the Microsoft site, at www.microsoft.com/technet/security/tools.asp.

Testing with User Protection via Browser Settings

Browser settings that limit exposure to harmful Internet content can be set within browsers such as Netscape Navigator and Microsoft Internet Explorer. It's expected that the user will alter some of these settings. Furthermore, there is a major shift on the user-side in terms of controlling these settings. Web users are gradually becoming more educated on using various settings to protect themselves. As a Web site or a Web application development team, you cannot force users to accept default settings. Therefore, you need to test with various combinations of the settings.

- For example, in Internet Explorer (IE) you can configure the browser to use one of the predefined zones. More important, the browser can also be configured to the security level for each zone. In some corporations, the IT department might specify the zone and security-level settings on the users' browser. How do you think your application will be affected by a browser security setting of high? Make sure that you test with all browser security settings. For example, if the user has set a weak browser security setting, and the server can handle only strong encryption, errors will result.

- As part of each security level, the behavior of active contents will vary accordingly. You can customarily set the behavior of each type of active content (Java, ActiveX, scripting, cookies, etc.). How would the setting of type of content affect your application? For example, if cookies handling is disabled, will your application still work? If it will not, is it a software error, design error (unnecessary reliance on cookies), or is it a technical support issue?

- Is the third-party Java applet used in your application marked safe for your users to use?

- Is the third-party ActiveX control used in your application marked safe for your users to use?

- Note that most users never change these settings. Those who do restrict what they allow in and out of the browser.

  - Internet zone security settings on Internet Explorer are as follows:

    High. Active content that could potentially damage a user's computer is restricted.

    Medium. Users are warned before potentially damaging active content is run.

    Low. Users are not warned before potentially damaging active content is run.

Custom security settings for active content. Enable users to define support options for specific active content types, including the following:

- ActiveX controls
- Java applets and Java scripting
- File types
- Fonts
- Active content downloading and printing
- Installation and launching of desktop applications
- Submission of nonencrypted form data
- Downloading and installation options for software that comes from software distribution channels

Whether you use Netscape Navigator or Microsoft Internet Explorer, you need to test your Web application with various security configurations of various active content settings (Java, scripting, cookies, etc.). As discussed earlier, these settings enable users to protect themselves on the client-site, because we have also established that the higher the security measurements, the lower the functionality and usability. How would these browser side settings affect the behavior of your application?

Additional browser security settings include the following:

Do not save encrypted pages to disk. In a shared server environment, this will prevent intruders from seeing the user's secure information.

Warn if submitted forms are being redirected. Enables the browser to warn the user when information on a Web-based form is being sent to a location other than that of the Web page.

Warn if changing between secure and nonsecure model. Enables the browser to warn users when they are switching from a secure site to a nonsecure site. This is useful when testing an application in a supposedly secure mode.

Check for certificate revocation. Prevents users from accepting invalid certificates that have been revoked.

Warn about invalid site certificates. Enables the browser to warn a user when a URL in a certificate is invalid.

NOTE Should your application use certificates, such as Site Certificate or Code Signing, to allow users to identify active content such as Java applets and ActiveX controls before accepting, test the installation of these certificates accordingly.

Accepting cookies: | Always | Prompt | Disable |. Enables users to specify whether cookies will be allowed to be stored on their system (with or without first alerting them) or disallowed altogether. Again, a cookie is a file that is sent by an Internet site and stored on a user's machine. In theory, cookie files track information about user identity and preferences for a particular Web site. In regard to cookies, ask:

- Does your application require the use of cookies? If yes, can the use of cookies be avoided?

- If your application requires the use of cookies, is your team prepared to lose sales to the population of users who will adamantly disallow their browser to accept cookies?

- If cookies are used, ask:

  - What information is set in a cookie and how is the information used by the application?

  - Is the information in the cookie sensitive (such as ID, password, etc.)?

  - Is the information in the cookie personal (potentially violating the user's privacy)?

- If the information in the cookie is sensitive and personal in nature, is it encrypted?

- Does your application tell the user why it wants to use cookies— exactly what information your application collects, why, and how long it intends to keep the information?

- If the user chooses not to accept cookies, does your application still work?

- When do cookies expire? What happens when a cookie expires?

Enable and disable HTTP 1.1 support. Many old Web servers still support only HTTP 1.0. This feature enables users to specify which protocols their browser will use.

Certificate settings. Enables the user to specify how certificates will be used to identify them, certificate authorities, and publishers.

Content settings. Enables users to specify whether inappropriate content will be restricted. If it is, users can specify which rating service to use for blocking the restricted content (for example, RSACi, the Recreational Software Advisory Council). Users can also set restriction levels on categories of objectionable content: offensive language, sex, and violence.

Testing with Firewalls

Recall that the software testing team often is not responsible for testing the effectiveness of the firewalls and their configurations. The general focus of testing with firewalls is to identify the functionality side effects created by traversing data across different networks. Some are private and others are public networks. Following is an example of testing with firewalls.

Figure 18.13 tracks a typical e-commerce transaction from the client to the vendor's servers to the bank and back to the client. Along the way, numerous databases, firewalls, and open Internet transmissions transpire. Note that steps 7 through 12 (detailed in the following list) occur beyond the bank's firewalls, and are therefore not accessible for testing.

1. User browses an e-commerce site and purchases a product by entering personal information and credit card data. Transaction is submitted.

2. User-submitted data are sent from the client to an e-commerce company Web server via the Internet (the public network).

3. When the submitted data hit the company firewall, the firewall examines the packet headers to determine the type of protocol used (e.g., HTTP, HTTPS, FTP, etc.). Depending on the firewall's configuration, the firewall might only allow packets that meet its security criteria (e.g., allowing only packets using HTTP and HTTPS, and disallowing FINGER and FTP).

4. The company Web server receives, examines, and disassembles the packets into the appropriate data forms. Based on the information (data, function calls, redirection, etc.), the Web server will pass data to other processes such as ISAPI DLL, CGI, ASP programs, Java servlets, SQL stored procedures, and so forth. The verification server is called by the Web server, receives user data for verification, and responds to the bank server with results. The Web server then redirects the data to the bank Web server for authorization.

5. Redirected data hit the company firewall. The firewall examines the packet header to determine if it should allow the data to pass through (e.g., the destination URL is a trusted URL and therefore the data are allowed to pass through).

6. Company-submitted data are sent to the bank via the Internet.

7. (Bank network) The bank's firewall examines the packet headers to determine the type of protocol used. Depending on the firewall's configuration, the firewall may or may not allow the packets to proceed.

8. (Bank network) The bank's Web server receives, examines, and disassembles the packets into appropriate data form. Based on the information (data, function calls, redirection, etc.), the Web server passes data to other processes such as ISAPI DLL, CGI, ASP programs, Java servlets, SQL stored procedures, and so on.

9. (Bank network) The authorization server gets called by the Web server, receives user data for authorizing the transaction (e.g., determining whether the account is valid by checking the address and user account name or determining whether the transaction amount is within the balance limit).

10. (Bank network) Assuming that the transaction is authorized, the user and merchant account databases are updated with appropriate debit and credit information.

11. (Bank network) Authorization information is sent from the bank Web server back to the company Web server.

12. (Bank network) The bank's firewall examines the packet headers to determine if they should be allowed to pass through.

13. Bank-submitted data are sent to the company Web server via the Internet.

14. The company firewall again examines the packet headers to determine the type of protocol used and whether the packets should be allowed to pass through.

15. The company Web server receives, examines, and disassembles the packets into the appropriate data forms. Based on the information, the Web server may pass data to other processes.

16. The Web server calls the company accounting database server. The accounting database is updated.

17. The company customer-support database is updated.

18a. Data hit the company firewall. The firewall examines the packet headers to determine if the packets should be allowed to pass through.

18b. Customer support/fulfillment staff access the database for order-processing information.

19. Confirmation data are delivered to the user via the Internet.

20. User receives confirmation of purchase transaction.

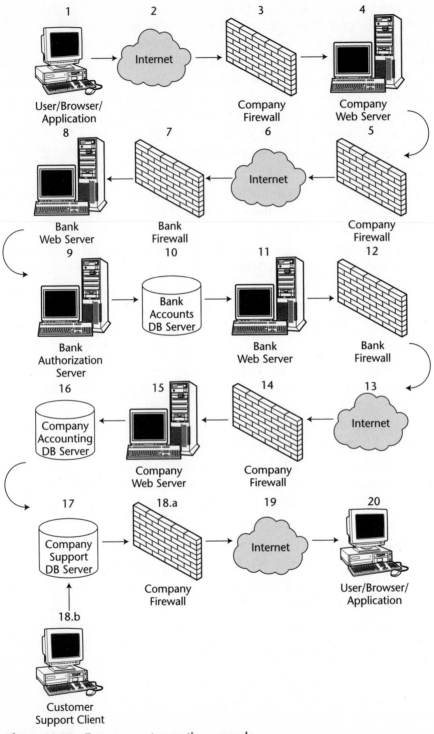

Figure 18.13 E-commerce transaction example.

First, we will use the diagram illustrated in Figure 18.13 to highlight all areas of the software that will be tested at each point and areas over which we won't have control. In this scenario, initially, testing should focus on points 3 and 5 and then advance to the testing of points 14 and 18.a (assuming that points 7 through 12 are processes that happen at the bank and are treated as black-box activities that are beyond the reach of testing).

Testing should begin with a no-firewall environment, so that functionality-specific issues can be ironed out before firewall issues are explored. Issues to look for include application-specific errors that result from firewall software, configuration, and security defenses that cause packet dropping or splitting. For example, suppose your application will rely on port 25 to talk to the SMTP server using SMTP protocol to support an e-mail notification feature. If your firewall is blocking out port 25, then the e-mail notification feature will fail. As another example, suppose your application will be deployed within an environment that uses a DMZ. Your system is designed to have Web and application servers separated from the database server. If you want the Web servers in DMZ but the database server inside the private network, the system will fail because the Web server cannot initiate requests to the database server that lives behind the private network.

The Challenges Testers Face

Now that you understand the complexity of security design and implementation, you can begin to take the first step in planning for the security-testing program. However, first consider these challenges that you will be facing in testing for security:

- Collaboratively defining a clear division of responsibilities with the IT and software development staff. One simple technique to accomplish this is to use a table format to collect requirements, prioritize tasks, and assign responsibilities. See Figure 18.14 for an example.

- Getting adequate resource and support to carry out the testing tasks.

- Keeping up with new technologies and the vulnerabilities they introduce.

- Developing a knowledge base of common test techniques and maintaining it on an ongoing basis.

- Keeping up with the available tools and their applicability and usefulness in supporting the software security testing effort.

Activities	Protection			Primary Target					Security Policies/Implementation					Testing Issues			
	User	Producer	Type	Client/Server Application	Database	Physical Server	Physical Client	The Network	Perimeter Security with Firewall[1]	Encryption[2]	Authentication[3]	Access Control[4]	Data Protection[5]	Requirement Testing[6]	Policy Implementation Testing[7]	Application Functional Testing[8]	System Functional Testing[9]
Offensive contents	x	x	a	x		x	x										
Anti-virus	x	x	b	x		x	x		x			x		x	x	x	x
Blocking database from unwanted access		x	b		x						x	x		x		x	
Data loss due to disaster		x	b			x							x	x			
Data loss due to hacking activities		x	b					x		x	x			x	x	x	x
Personnel security clearance		x	b			x						x		x	x		
Sabotage or theft of data		x	b			x						x		x	x		
Sabotage or theft of hardware		x	b			x						x		x	x		
Theft of credit card numbers	x	x	b	x	x	x		x					x	x	x	x	x
Unauthorized access to private network data		x	b	x	x	x		x	x		x	x		x	x	x	x
Unauthorized release of personal information	x	x	b	x	x	x											
Intellectual property loss due to hacking activities		x	c	x	x	x				x				x		x	x
Spamming		x	d	x			x										
Unauthorized access to private network resources	x	x	e	x				x	x		x			x			

1 Perimeter security plan; firewall products used and their configurations; tasks and tools required for maintaining security.
2 Encryption security plan and encryption technologies supported.
3 Authentication security plan; authentication mechanism; tasks and tools required for implementation.
4 Access control security plan; access implementation used for various platforms; access control configuration; task and tools required.
5 Data backup and recovery plan.
6 Examine the requirements to determine if they adequately meet the security objectives.
7 Test the security policy implementation to find security holes in the plan.
8 Test the application for security-enforced type of errors as well as application functional errors (side-effects).
9 Test the Web system as a whole for functional errors that are specific to configuration, compatibility and performance issues.

a Children
b Data
c Intellectual property
d Privacy
e Network resource

Figure 18.14   Security test table example.

Other Testing Considerations

Ten useful things to remember in Web security testing:

1. Security testing is active, not passive, testing.

2. Unhandled exceptions are gold mines in which to look for security vulnerabilities.

3. Input interfaces are gold mines for fault injection in which to look for security bugs.

   - Consider every conceivable invalid input on the client-side
   - Consider every conceivable invalid input on the server-side

4. Focus on input conditions where data is moved from untrusted to trusted domains.

5. Design test cases with special emphasis on the boundary between trusted and untrusted domains.

6. Look for bugs that allow users to execute a program onto the host.

7. Look for bugs that allow users to upload a program onto the host.

8. Look for bugs that allow users to elevate access privilege.

9. Be aware that the application often will mishandle some bad data coming from the untrusted client-side.

10. Look for input data that will potentially become executable (e.g., when input becomes output).

General testing considerations include the following:

- Every component in a Web system has its own security weaknesses. A security system is only as strong as its weakest link. The four usual places security defenses are violated are:

   - The client system (Web browser, other applications, and components)
   - The server (Web, database, and other servers)
   - The network
   - Online transactions

- An organization's security team, not the software testing team, determines policy on all security-related issues: user access, time-outs, content availability, database viewing, system protection, security tools, and more. Whether a company's security defense is secure enough is not determined by the testing group. The role of a testing group is to test the existing system in order to uncover errors in security implementation primarily at the application level.

- Usually, the IT team holds most of the responsibility for network security. Staff members other than the software testing team generally perform firewall testing, packet counting, traffic monitoring, virus protection, and server break-in testing.

- The IT team, not the software testing team, is responsible for installing IP address screening policies.

- In addition to looking for deficiencies in application-error detection and handling, testing objectives should be to gather configuration-related issues for the technical support knowledge base.

In terms of user-account password, login procedure testing considerations include:

- Does the Web system have an auto logoff feature (such as session time-out)? If so, does it work properly?

- Does the Web system implement and enforce frequent password changing? If so, does it work properly?

- If security is controlled at the application server level, rather than at the database server level, has the application's security logic been tested to determine whether user access is properly enforced? For example, to connect to a database server, a Web server must have an ID and password for such a database. It is possible for a Web server to use the same ID and password to log in to a database, regardless who the end user is. The authorization process can then be done at the application level. Alternatively, authorization can be done at the database level; that is, each end user would have an ID and password for the database account. Depending on who the end user is, the appropriate ID and password will be used.

- Have you tested the login logic enforced at the application level? Have you tested the login logic enforced at the database level? Have you tested the login logic enforced at both levels?

- Has any security-related testing been performed on third-party applications or components integrated with the Web system?

- How many consecutive failed logins are allowed (e.g., 3 times, 10 times, or an unlimited number of times)? Is this feature configurable by a user in a configuration file or a registry key? If yes, who has the privilege to make the change? Can the change be easily attacked?

- When the number of failed logins is exceeded, how does the application respond (e.g., by disallowing logins from that IP address until the security issue is reviewed or the security alert timer expires)?

- Which logics are applied to user names and passwords? Are they case-sensitive? Is there a minimum-number-of-characters rule? Is there a mixed rule that requires letter and number characters to be in combination? Does the implementation of these logics work?

- Are user names and passwords stored in the encrypted format (in user's registry database or configuration files, such as .INI files)?

- Have you tried to cut and paste user name and password?

- Have you tried to bypass the login procedure by using a bookmark, a history entry, or a captured URL? (For example, after you have logged in to a system successfully, try to capture the URL. Launch a new instance of the browser, then paste in the captured URL to see if you can get to the system.)

- Have you tested logging in using HTTP as well as HTTPS (assuming that your system supports HTTPS)?

- Are the user names and passwords encrypted at the application level? If yes, has the feature been tested?

In terms of authorization procedure, testing considerations include:

- Are all authorized users able to access the system?

- Are unauthorized users blocked from the system? If an unauthorized login is attempted, how easily can it be done?

- When a new password is created for first-time login, is the default password deactivated if a new unique password is chosen?

- Do chosen passwords meet specified requirements (e.g., length, letters/numbers)? What happens if the requirements are not met?

- When the user must periodically change passwords, are old passwords deactivated after new ones are chosen?

- When there is a time restriction for logins, is the transition between authorized and unauthorized periods handled correctly?

- Are outdated user account features removed and deactivated completely and correctly?

- Do expiration-based user accounts expire as expected?

In terms of database server security, testing considerations include:

- Are users granted excessive database privileges? In most database systems, users are given permission to access specific data that relate to their responsibilities. Additionally, certain users can often grant special access privileges to other users. Ensure that users are able to access appropriate data and that they are denied access to all other data. Can special access privileges be granted?

- Can special access privileges be granted to unauthorized users?

- Can special access privileges be limited to specific items?

- Can special access privileges be terminated?

- Do users in each group have appropriate access that meets, but does not exceed, their needs? Do all users get group assignments? Users are generally divided into groups of individuals who share the same access needs.

- Views are restricted tables that display portions of an entire table. Users can only access and edit fields that are visible to them within the view. Test to ensure that appropriate and intended information is accessible through individual views and that all other data is blocked. Also, test to ensure that views are protected from modification by unauthorized users, via both Graphical User Interface (GUI) management tools and SQL statements.

- Is the permission required to execute appropriate stored procedures granted to users?

- Do users have more access to the stored procedures than is necessary to perform their work? They should have access to only those stored procedures needed to perform their jobs.

- Can users other than the database administrator create, modify, or delete stored procedures? Ideally, only database administrators should have this type of privilege.

Bibliography and Additional Resources

Bibliography

Howard, M., and David LeBlanc. *Writing Secure Code*. Redmond, WA: Microsoft Press, 2002. Larson, E., and Stephens, B. *Web Server, Security, and Maintenance*. Upper Saddle River, NJ: Prentice-Hall PTR, 2000.

McClure, S., Joel Scambray, and George Kurtz. *Attacking Exposed: Network Security Secrets and Solutions*, 3rd ed. New York: McGraw Hill, 2001.

Orfali, R., Dan Harkey, and Jeri Edwards. *Client/Server Survival Guide*, 3rd ed. New York: John Wiley & Sons, Inc., 1999. Schneier, B. *Applied Cryptography: Protocols, Algorithms and Source Code in C*, 2nd ed. New York: John Wiley & Sons, Inc., 1996.

"Security of the Internet," in *The Froehlich/Kent Encyclopedia of Telecommunications*, vol. 15. New York: Marcel Dekker, 1997, pp. 231(255. www.cert.org/encyc_article/tocencyc.html.

Viega J., and G. McGraw. *Building Secure Software: How to Avoid Security Problems the Right Way*. Boston, MA: Addison-Wesley, 2002.

Additional Resources

Computer System Security: An Overview, SEI STR

   www.sei.cmu.edu/str.descriptions/security.html

Firewalls and Proxies, SEI STR

   www.sei.cmu.edu/str.descriptions/firewalls.html

Cross Site Scripting Explained

   www.microsoft.com/technet.treeview/default.asp?url=/technet/
   security/topics/csoverv.asp

"Malicious HTML Tags Embedded in Client Web Requests"

   www.cert.org/advisories/CA-2000-02.html

User Input in SQL Statement: AdCycle SQL Command Insertion
Vulnerability

   www.qdefense.com/Advisories/QDAV-2001-7-2.html

The OWASP Guide to Building Secure Web Applications and Web Services

   www.cgisecurity.com/owasp/OWASPBuildingSecureWebApplicationsAnd
   WebServices-V1.0.pdf

Useful Net Resources

Bugtraq

   http://online.securityfocus.com/archive/1

CERT/CC Web site

   www.cert.org

Cookie Central

   www.cookiecentral.com

Cookie Managers Utilities: *PC Magazine* download page

   www.zdnet.com/pcmag/features/utilities98/internetsecurity/
   cookie01.html

The Hacker Quarterly Magazine

   www.2600.com

Microsoft Web site on security

www.microsoft.com/security

The Open Web Security Project

www.owasp.org

QACity

www.qacity.com

RAS Security Web site

www.rsasecurity.com

Security Focus Online

http://online.securityfocus.com

Tools

Application scanning tools

- Cenzic Hailstorm at www.cenzic.com
- Sanctum AppScan at www.sanctuminc.com
- WebInspect, produced by SPI Dynamics can scan Web pages, scripts, code, cookies, and application components for commonly known vulnerabilities. It is available from www.spidynamics.com

Script scanning tools to detect common vulnerabilities

- CGI scripts can be scanned with Rain Forest Puppy's whisker.pl scripts. The tool is free at www.wiretrip.net/rfp .
- NuMega has tools to facilitate code reviews at www.numega.com.
- Cigital's ITS4, a source scanning tool for C and C++ at http://www.cigital.com/its4/.

Other tools resources

- Insecure.org Top 50 Security Tools at http://www.insecure.org/tools.html
- Rick Hower's Web Testing Tools page (including Web security testing tools) at http://www.softwareqatest.com/qatweb1.html
- L0pht tools at: www.10pht.com

Performance Testing

Why Read This Chapter?

When a user clicks on the Buy button, how confident are you that they are not being subjected to long waits and error-laden transaction processing, especially when the system is serving hundreds (or thousands) of other users at the same time? Conducting performance and load testing on your system is one of the best ways to ensure that your system can endure the actual load or projected business demand and, simultaneously, can serve multiple users in a reliable and timely manner. This chapter provides an introduction to fundamental performance and load testing concepts, to include defining system performance and load requirements—often from incomplete or vague objectives—creating and executing performance and load test plans, and, finally, interpreting your test results to determine likely bottlenecks and possible resolutions.

TOPICS COVERED IN THIS CHAPTER

- ◆ Introduction
- ◆ Performance Testing Concepts
- ◆ Performance Testing Key Factors

(continued)

Introduction

One of the key benefits of Web applications is that they enable multiple users to access the application simultaneously. Multiple users may request different services and gain access to varying features at the same time. Because multi-user support is central to the success of almost every Web application, we must evaluate the system's capability to perform critical functions during periods of normal and peak usage. Performance testing is done to answer the following questions:

- Can the system handle the expected load while maintaining acceptable response time?
- If not, at what point does system performance begin to deteriorate? Which components cause the degradation?
- Is the current system scalable, to accommodate future growth?
- When performance fails to meet acceptable customer-experience levels, what effect will this have on business objectives such as company sales and technical support costs?

Performance Testing Concepts

In the effort of evaluating multiuser support capabilities, three types of tests are commonly conducted: (1) performance, (2) load, and (3) stress tests. Although these terms are often used interchangeably, each represents a test that is designed to address a different objective. One of the key objectives in performance testing is to enhance the ability to predict when future load levels will exhaust the Web system so that effective enhancement strategies can be developed to maintain *acceptable user experience*.

Two important dimensions for acceptable user experience are *correctness* and *timeliness*. An example of correctness is when a customer orders a cappuccino at a coffee shop and, regardless how busy the shop is at the time, gets the cappuccino, not, say, a glass of orange juice. Continuing with the same example, if the average time that it takes to deliver the cappuccino to the customer is three minutes, then timeliness in this case is no more than three minutes. In the rest of this chapter, we will focus primarily on timeliness as the primary attribute for acceptable user experience.

A key measurement used to evaluate timeliness is *response time*. (See the "Determining Acceptable Response Time or Acceptable User Experience" section for more information on various definitions of response time.) In essence, response time is the time it takes for a system to serve a request or an order. Most important, from the user perspective, it is the amount of time that he or she must wait to be served. Obviously, the shorter the response time, the more satisfied the user; conversely, the longer the response time, the less satisfied the user. When the response time is too long, it becomes unacceptable to the user, which may lead to customer loss, sales loss, or bad publicity, and, ultimately, financial loss. As a result, we do performance testing so that we can provide management with the necessary information to make intelligent decisions about improvement and risk.

Determining Acceptable Response Time or Acceptable User Experience

What is an acceptable response time or acceptable user experience? The answer depends on two factors: the value of the product and service that the business offers, and the customer's value system expectation. For example, some people may consider that it's unacceptable to wait for more than five minutes at the checkout register in a grocery store, yet are willing to wait 45 minutes to get on a roller coaster ride. Some of us may not even have the patience to wait more than five minutes for anything.

Figure 19.1 diagrams a theoretical model to illustrate that as the load on the system increases, the response time increases accordingly. Suppose that customers consider that waiting for up to 8 seconds (on a 56 Kbps modem) for a particular request to be served is acceptable; that means that a response time between 0 to 8 seconds is within the acceptable user experience zone. When the response time (a.k.a. the wait) is more than 8 seconds (between 8 and 16 seconds in this example), the customers will deem their user experience as negative. Some of the customers may decide to leave and do business elsewhere, while other more patient customers may wait even though they are unhappy. This means that if the load is sizable enough to slow down the system response time, the system may begin to introduce notable business losses. If the system load is subjected to additional increases, the performance will continue to degrade, pushing the response time into the unacceptable zone (about 16 seconds in this example). Unless you have very interesting products or services to offer, and customers who believe that these products or services are valuable and cannot be acquired anywhere else, you will be losing most if not all your business. As the load continues to increase, it will push the system to the point at which it will stop responding. At this point, the system will produce no business.

Response Time Definition

As just noted, one of the most commonly used performance measurements is *response time*, which is defined in the International Organization for Standardization's *Information Technology Vocabulary* as:

> *The elapsed time between the end of an inquiry or demand on a computer system and the beginning of a response; for example, the length of time between an indication of the end of an inquiry and the display of the first character of the response at the user terminal.*

In the realm of Web applications, response time could be measured as the time between when the user clicks a button or a link and when the browser starts to display the resulting page. Most important, from the business perspective:

Shorter Response Time => Less Waiting => Better User Experience

Another common performance measurement is *transaction time*. Transaction time is the total amount of time required by the client, network, and server to complete a transaction. In a Web application, transaction time could be measured as the time between when the user clicks a button or a link and when the browser has finished displaying the resulting page (including the execution of any client-side scripts, Java applets, etc.).

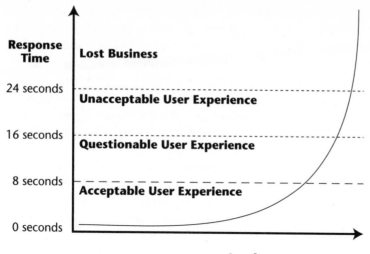

Figure 19.1 What's your system's acceptable response time?

Latency is the time required to complete a request. When referring to the time spent for data to travel from one computer to another computer, it's considered *network latency*. When referring to the time spent at a particular server to complete the processing of a request, it is considered *server latency*.

Latency can also represent a special hardware-specific delay. For example, a router is capable of processing a limited number of packets per second. If the data packet arrival rate exceeds the router's processing capability, the unprocessed packets will be queued and processed as soon as the router can handle them.

NOTE The terms *response time*, *transaction time*, and *latency* are sometimes used interchangeably. It is not important to decide which terminology or definition is correct; what is important is to know which one is being used to mean what in any discussion using these terms.

Performance and Load Stress Testing Definitions

Performance testing is an information-gathering and analysis process in which measured data are collected to predict when load levels will exhaust system resources. It is during this process that you will collect your benchmark values. These numbers are used to establish various load-testing and stress-testing scenarios. The benchmark metrics are also used on an ongoing basis as baselines that help you to detect when system performance either improves or begins to deteriorate.

Load testing evaluates system performance with a predefined load level. Load testing also measures how long it takes a system to perform various program tasks and functions under normal, or predefined, conditions. Bug reports are filed when tasks cannot be executed within the time limits (preferably defined by the product management or the marketing group). Because the objective of load testing is to determine whether a system performance satisfies its load requirements, it is pertinent that minimum configuration and maximum activity levels be determined before testing begins. Load tests can be for both volume and longevity.

The terms *performance* and *load* are often used interchangeably, but they are not the same: A load test is done to determine if the system performance is acceptable at the predefined load level; a performance test is done to determine the system performance at various load levels. The similarities between performance and load tests lie in their execution strategies. Typically, these tests involve the simulation of hundreds, or even thousands, of users accessing a system simultaneously over a certain period. Due to the time, effort, and money involved, it is often impractical to have people execute such testing without the aid of automated testing tools.

Stress testing evaluates the behavior of systems that are pushed beyond their specified operational limits (this may be well beyond the requirements); it evaluates responses to bursts of peak activity that exceed system limitations. Determining whether a system crashes and, if it does, whether it recovers gracefully from such conditions is a primary goal of stress testing. Stress tests should be designed to push system resource limits to the point at which their weak links are exposed.

Unlike performance and load tests, stress tests push systems past their breaking points. System components that break are subsequently investigated and reinforced. Performance and load tests simulate regular user activity. The results of these tests give developers insight into system performance and response time under real-world conditions.

Searching for Answers

Performance testing involves extensive planning for the definition and simulation of the workloads you want to test. It also involves the analysis of collected data throughout the execution phase. Performance testing considers such key concerns as:

- Will the system be able to handle increases in Web traffic without compromising system response time, security, reliability, and accuracy?
- At what point will the performance degrade, and which components will be responsible for the degradation?
- What impact will performance degradation have on company sales and technical support costs?

Each of these concerns requires that measurements be applied to a usage model (how the system resources are used based on the activities or workload generated by the users) of the system under test. System attributes, such as response time, can be evaluated as various workload scenarios are applied to the usage model. Ultimately, we can draw conclusions and initiate corrective actions based on the collected data. (For example, when the number of concurrent users reaches X, response time equals Y. Therefore, the system cannot support more than X number of concurrent users.)

A Simple Example

Consider the following simplistic example to understand how increased traffic load—and, consequently, increased response time—can result in lost company revenue. (Refer to Figure 19.2 for detailed analysis of the traffic, percentage, and dollar amounts described in the following example.)

Suppose your site currently handles 300,000 transactions per day: 300,000 transactions divided by the amount of seconds in a day equates to about 3.47 transactions per second:

$300,000/(24 * 60 * 60) = \tilde{\ }3.47$ transactions per second

This means that if the system can handle approximately four transactions per second while maintaining acceptable response time, your site can stay in business.

NOTE For simplification, the formula used to compute the average transactions per second assumes that the workload will be spread evenly over a 24-hour period. In reality, we need to take into account the irregularity of the workload or traffic over the period of the time. There will be a peak time as well as downtime, just like morning and evening rush-hour traffic or lunch and dinner hours at a restaurant. Peak load normally can be several times greater than the normal load.

Suppose a marketing survey is conducted and the findings show that, for the typical user:

- The *transaction response time* is of an acceptable level as long as it does not exceed four seconds.

- If the transaction response time is between 4 to 8 seconds, 30 percent of users cancel their transactions.

- If the transaction response time is between 8 to 10 seconds, 60 percent of users cancel their transactions.

- If the transaction response time increases to over 10 seconds, over 90 percent of users cancel their transactions.

Suppose in the next six months, the number of transactions is expected to rise between 25 and 75 percent from the current level and that the potential revenue for each transaction is $1. Management would like to learn how the performance would impact company revenue as the number of transactions per day increases.

A performance test is conducted and the findings show that the system cannot handle such increases in traffic without increasing response time. Consequently, user transaction cancellations and/or failures will result. If the number of transactions increases as expected, the company will face a potential revenue loss of between $112,500 and $472,500 per day (see Figure 19.2).

If we apply a similar theoretical model as the one shown in Figure 19.1, we can plot the test results of this simple marketing example in a chart, like the one shown in Figure 19.3.

It takes time, effort, and commitment to plan for and execute performance testing. The process involves individuals from many different departments. A well-planned testing program requires the coordinated efforts of members of the product team, upper management, marketing, development, information technology (IT), and testing. Management's main objective in performance testing should be to avoid financial losses due to lost sales, increased expenditure on technical support issues, and customer dissatisfaction.

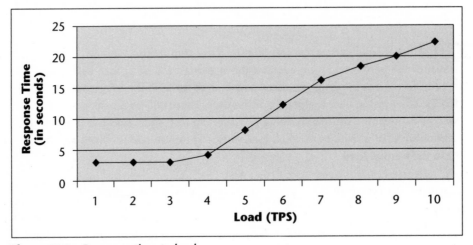

Figure 19.2 Response time to load.

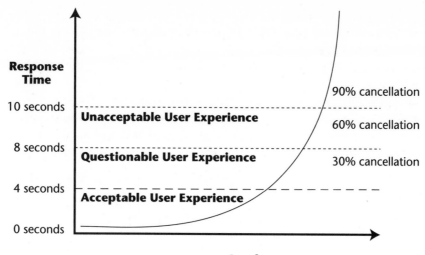

Figure 19.3   Potential business loss due to poor response time.

Performance Testing Key Factors

Performance testing involves the evaluation of three primary elements:

- Workload
- System environment and available resources
- System response time

Workload as the projected number of users. It can be challenging to estimate the number of users that a system will likely support because user activities can vary, as can access time and activity frequency. Representing the projected number of users in a workload model requires careful thought, as does the simulation of real-world users. To produce the list of possible activities you want to test, you can apply the user scenario technique discussed in Chapter 3, "Software Testing Basics." Also refer to the "Sizing the Workload" section later in this chapter for a discussion of user-based profiling.

Response time as acceptable performance. Determining the level of performance that is acceptable for a system requires input from marketing and product management. How performance will be measured, what it will cost, the tools that will be used, and the metrics that will be employed are all factors that must be considered. Understanding which components affect system performance is also important. Though it is possible to test on the actual system that will be used in production, most often you will be testing on smaller systems and will have to extrapolate your results to determine the system's performance.

Let's walk through an example of a typical Web transaction to illustrate how these three elements fit in the picture.

EXAMPLE OF A TYPICAL WEB TRANSACTION ON THE WEB CLIENT-SIDE

- The user enters a URL or clicks a link within a browser to request a file from a server.
- The Domain Name Server (DNS) converts the server's host name into the appropriate Internet Protocol (IP) address.
- The client connects to Web server.
- The client sends a HyperText Transfer Protocol (HTTP) request (such as GET or POST) to the server.

ON THE INTERNET (NETWORK)

- The network delivers data from the client to the server.

ON THE SERVER-SIDE

- Once the request reaches the server, data are disassembled based on the appropriate communication protocol (such as HTTP).
- The server responds to the request.
- The server processes the request by retrieving data or writing to a database. Once the process is complete, the server returns the requested file or resultant information back to the client.

BACK ON THE INTERNET (NETWORK)

- The network delivers data from the server to the client.

BACK ON THE CLIENT-SIDE

- The browser receives the requested data, displays HTML contents, and executes any active content.

Workload

Workload is the amount of processing and traffic management that is demanded of a system. To evaluate system workload, three elements must be considered: (1) users, (2) the application, and (3) resources. With an understanding of the number of users (along with their common activities), the demands that will be required of the application to process user activities (such as HTTP requests) and the system's resource requirements, you can calculate a system's workload. The users of a system can be divided into groups, such as administrators, data entry clerks, managers, and so on. Each group of user performs different activities, thereby producing a different load on the system. (In the "Defining the Workload" section later in this chapter, we will go into greater detail on the subject of workload.)

System Environment and Available Resources

There are three primary elements that represent the resources involved in any online transaction: (1) a browser on the client-side, (2) a network, and (3) the server-side (see Figure 19.4).

Since Web applications typically consist of many interacting hardware and software components, and a failure or deficiency in any of these components can affect performance drastically, it is important to clearly define the environment and resources to be tested. The environment and resources involved in a Web application (as well as in the performance testing of an application) include some or all of the following:

- *Network access variables*. For example, 28.8 Kbps, DSL, T1, and so on.

- *Demographic variables*. For example, a site with a predominance of power users may use the search function more frequently than novice users, resulting in lower overall page views.

- *Geographic variables*. For example, if the server is in California, and user requests are coming from London, the request arrival rate may be longer even though the data requested is identical.

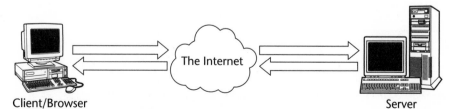

Client/Browser   The Internet   Server

Figure 19.4   Three primary transaction components.

- *ISP infrastructure variables.* For example, the data transfer rate available for each ISP.

- *Client configurations.* For example, OS, browser, and so on.

- *Server configurations.* For example, CPU speed, memory, OS, software, and so on.

Figure 19.5 illustrates the typical resources that cause performance bottlenecks, along with the activities that are associated with the three primary components of online transactions.

Response Time

Web applications may consist of both static and dynamic content, in pages of varying sizes. When a user submits a form or clicks a link, the resulting page might be a simple static HTML file containing a few lines of text, or it might be an order confirmation page that is displayed after a purchase transaction is processed and a credit card number is verified through a third-party service. Each of these types of content will have different acceptable response times. For example, an acceptable response time for the static HTML page might be two seconds, whereas the acceptable response time for the purchase transaction might be eight seconds.

Browser	Network	Server
Typical Resource Bottlenecks	Typical Resource Bottlenecks	Typical Resource Bottlenecks
CPU Time	Latency–Delays introduced by network devices & data queuing.	CPU Time
	Throughput or bandwidth.	I/O access time: I/O bus, disk controller and disk access.
Typical Activities	Typical Activities	Typical Activities
Receiving/Sending data	Packets routing from clients to servers.	Receives hits.
Formatting data	Packets routing from servers to servers.	Run scripts, library-functions, stored-procedures, executables, etc.
Displaying data	Packets routing from servers to clients.	
Executing scripts and active contents		

Transaction Time		
Client Processing Time	Connection Time + Send Time + Receive Time	Response Time

Figure 19.5 Activities and resources associated with performance bottlenecks.

As explained earlier, it is essential to define the acceptable response time for the various areas of a Web application so that appropriate action can be taken once the application has been tested. Not defining acceptable response times could result in a lack of action to improve the performance, or an unnecessary expenditure of time, resources, and money to improve performance that was already acceptable.

Figures 19.6 and 19.7 contrast how a naive view of expected workload and performance, respectively, might differ from real-world results. Figure 19.6 illustrates a naive expectation of the relationship between traffic load and *aggregate response time* (i.e., the sum of server, network, and browser response times). Note that the server, network, and browser response times in Figure 19.6 increase in a predictable and regular manner as transactions per second increase. Figure 19.7, in contrast, depicts a more likely system response scenario: note that system, network, and browser response times increase in a nonlinear manner. As the number of transactions rises, the transaction round-trip time (from the time the user submits a request to the time the first byte is received on the browser-side) increases. Ultimately, the number of transactions per second becomes saturated. The server response time eventually increases to such a point that the entire system stops responding to requests.

Bottlenecks are those system components that limit total improvement, no matter now much you improve the rest of the system. Often, your system will have built-in bottlenecks, such as network bandwidth.

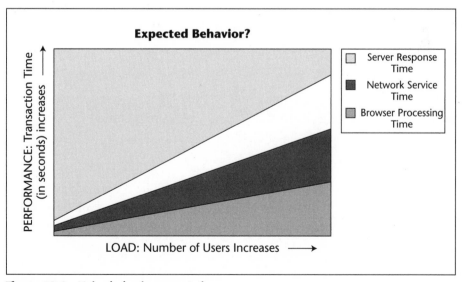

Figure 19.6 Naive behavior expectation.

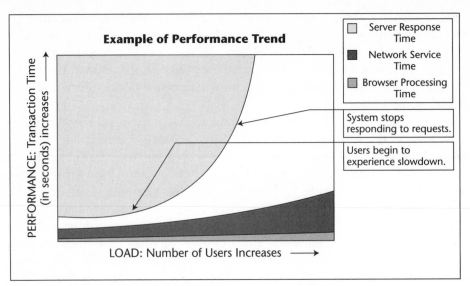

Figure 19.7   Actual workload versus response time analysis.

Key Factors Affecting Response Time or Performance

There are numerous workload, resource, and design- and implementation-related factors that can affect the performance of a Web application. These factors can be found both within the boundaries of the system (hardware/software) and outside the boundaries of the system (users):

- Users
  - Number of users
  - User types
- Objective types (e.g., browse, buy, and check order status)
  - User activities (tasks they perform)
- Frequency of activities
  - User behaviors (read/think/data-input time)
  - User/activity arrival rates (description of traffic-per-unit time and the arrival rate of the traffic)
- Sessions
  - Number of user sessions
  - Number of page views per session
  - Type of pages requested per session (e.g., static page versus credit card transaction authorization)

- Concurrency issues
  - Cache swapping
  - Priority needs of some tasks
- Size of data associated with each request—throughput
- Number of hits associated with each request—turns (i.e., number of trips the client has to take to the server to retrieve files such as graphics) and latency
- Processing required by each request—computation
- Application architecture and design—coding practices
- Client speed: CPU and memory
- Browser (software) rendering speed
- Client-side local network speed or throughput
- Public network latency
- Public network speed or throughput
- Server-side response time
  - Server speed: CPU, memory, I/O throughput, and so on
  - Server-side local network speed or throughput
  - Server-side distributed architecture
  - Software performance
  - System configuration
  - Security-related configuration

Three Phases of Performance Testing

The process of performance testing can be broken down into three phases: planning, testing, and analysis.

PLANNING PHASE

- Define the objectives and deliverables and set expectations.
- Gather system and testing requirements.
- Define workload.
- Select performance metrics to collect.
- Identify tests to run and decide when to run them.
- Decide on a tool option and generating loads.
- Write a test plan; design user-scenarios and create test scripts.

TESTING PHASE

- Get ready (e.g., set up the test bed and performance monitors on the network and servers).
- Run tests.
- Collect data.

ANALYSIS PHASE

- Analyze results.
- Change the system to optimize performance.
- Design new tests.

You should consider repeating this process on an ongoing basis. During development, the project team members will be making many assumptions during planning for the performance test. As the development nears completion, a review of the performance test plan will improve the test case selections. After the application is in production, the team will observe actual user activities, some of which will be unexpected; users always use products in new and unpredictable ways. The environment will also change constantly because hardware, operating systems, and third-party products undergo "improvement" on a regular basis.

Setting Goals and Expectations and Defining Deliverables

From the management perspective, the common issues and considerations before, during, and after planning for and execution of performance testing include:

- Will the Web application be capable of supporting the projected number of users while preserving acceptable performance, and at what cost?
- At which point will the Web application load-handling capability begin to degrade?
- What will be the financial implications of the degradation?
- What can be done to increase the Web application load-handling capability, and at what cost?
- How can the system be monitored after deployment so that appropriate actions can be taken before system resources are saturated?

While management has to set the goals, as a tester, you will be tasked with actually producing and executing the tests and reporting bugs found. Many of the performance-related problems are complex and difficult to repair. It is essential for the success of the testing process to adequately prepare for the expectations of the organization and its management. You must understand the test requirements and scope of what you are being asked to test. To that end, define, or at least answer:

- What are the objectives of the performance tests?
- Who cares (especially folks from the business side) enough to grant you the budget to plan for and run performance tests?
- Why measure? Have you budgeted adequate time and resources to enable the development teams to address performance problems, and to enable you to retest the system?

You must communicate:

- Your service capabilities and limitations
- Where you need help and how you can get help
- That upon completion of your test plan, you seek review and buy-in from the stakeholders

There can be numerous deliverables involved in a performance test. A test plan is important for providing visibility to the various stakeholders involved in the project. The test plan should include some or all of the following:

- Performance testing goals
- Workload definitions
- User scenario designs
- Performance test designs
- Test procedures
- System-under-test configurations
- Metrics to collect

In addition to the test plan, some or all of the following deliverables should be produced during the course of the testing:

- Tool evaluation and selection reports (first time, or as needed)
- Test scripts/suites
- Test run results
- Analysis reports against the collected data
- Performance-related error reports (e.g., failed transactions)
- Functional bug reports (e.g., data integrity problems)
- Periodic status reports
- Final report

Gathering Requirements

The requirements for a performance test can be broken into three groups:

- The *environment and resources* of the system under test must be defined in order to execute a test that successfully simulates the performance of the application in a production environment.

- The *workload* that will be applied to the system should be defined, based on marketing estimates and/or past experience.

- The acceptable *response time* for various parts of the application should be defined so that appropriate actions can be taken based on the results of the tests.

What Are You Up Against?

In an ideal testing situation, marketing and the system architects would agree on the expected workload and the acceptable response time long before test planning begins. The tester's job is to then execute the performance and stress tests and report bugs against the established requirements. Unfortunately, often this is not the case.

Sometimes the testing staff is the first to determine benchmark values for the application. This will mean creating the tests and executing them to produce values that the entire project team can evaluate. It may also mean determining anticipated usage and running similar tests against competitors' products to provide "industry benchmarks." Reading the business plan or talking with marketing and sales can help you find answers to these questions. For example, if the sales manager believes that the company must sell 100,000 units per month to break even, then you can estimate the number of database entries required and number of customers visiting the site per hour. These numbers, however, represent averages only; peak loads will be much higher.

What If Written Requirements Don't Exist?

You may not be given any written requirements, in which case you must begin testing before you can formalize the requirements. Nevertheless, you can still effectively test the system by constantly communicating with the stakeholders about what you are doing as the testing process progresses. The stakeholders will have the opportunity to provide you with feedback that reflects their objectives for the performance testing. While this may result in some backtracking as a result of misunderstood expectations, it allows all the stakeholders to communicate their objectives; likewise, it allows you to successfully execute a performance test that meets expectations. In the next section, "Defining the Workload," and later in the section "Which Tests to Run and When to Start," you'll get some ideas for testing without requirements. For now, just keep in mind that conveying your performance test plans to other stakeholders is as important as the actual testing: it can be an effective action you take to ensure your software has the performance level it needs.

Defining the Workload

The workload placed on a system can be defined in terms of *user-specific load* and *application-specific load*.

The numbers of users accessing a system, as well as the types of activities they perform, affect the overall workload on the system. Since different users perform different activities while using the application, they should be grouped into *types*, such as administrators, managers, data entry clerks, and so on. Each type of user will perform different activities with varying frequencies and at different speeds. For example, an administrator might use all the functionality in an application, and will perform tasks very quickly, but might not use the application very often. This can be deceiving since an administrator's activity, such as rebuilding the database, may be much more resource-intensive.

Consider the following when calculating workload:

USERS

- Total number of each type of users

- Maximum number of each type of concurrent users

- Ratio of (how many) concurrent users of each type within a certain period of time

- Length of user sessions in each type

- Number of each type of unique activity carried out by the users. (While the number of concurrent users does not change, the response time varies depending on different user activities.)

For example, whereas 1,000 concurrent users requesting a 2K static HTML page will result in a limited range of response times, response times may vary dramatically if the same 1,000 concurrent users simultaneously submit purchase transactions that require significant server-side processing. Designing a valid workload model that accurately reflects such real-world usage is no simple task. Designing workloads for stress testing is equally difficult. For stress testing you are not concerned so much with the typical or average workload; rather, you ask, "What is the worst possible case?"

APPLICATION

- Activities can be expressed in terms of service rates, such as transactions per second (TPS) or throughput, or the data transfer rate, often expressed in kilobits per second (Kbps).
- Ratios of specific pages requested by users.
- Specific transactions requested by users.
- Any other specific demands on the systems or applications in response to user-specific requests.

Sizing the Workload

There are four steps that you should take to determine workload size:

1. Before the system is deployed, consult any available performance requirement documents.
2. Assemble a small group of users who can act as a cross section of real-world users, for the purpose of simulating different personnel types and performing associated activities. Configure the server and use a log analysis tool to log user activity. Use the collected data to estimate workload.
3. Estimate the number of concurrent users that the system will handle; group the users into types; estimate the ratio of each type of user, the length of their sessions, their activities, and activity frequency (as described in the previous section).
4. After system deployment, use log analysis tools or a proxy server to collect workload data.

There are two different approaches you can take to determine the workload: Using the logs of the Web server hosting the application, you can create a *server-based profile*; or you can create a *user-based profile* by defining user scenarios.

Server-Based Profile

Server-based profile refers to the technique of using Web server logs to size your workload. Web server logs provide a wealth of information about how a Web application is being used. This information can be used to accurately simulate typical usage of the application. Since Web server logs are typically in a standardized format, there are a number of log analysis tools available that can produce metrics to assist you in sizing your workload.

Log data can be grouped into two categories: *general measurements* convey information about the overall load and performance of the system; *application-specific measurements* provide information in the context of specific user activities or requests, such as requests of certain pages.

Some of the useful general metrics include:

- Number of user sessions over a period of time
- Number of pages viewed over a period of time
- Page views per visitor
- Ratio of new users versus returning users
- Maximum (peak hour), minimum (least active hour), and average number of visitors to the site during 24-hour periods
- Average length of a user session
- Average number of pages viewed per user session

Analyzing the data collected from a Web server log can help you to understand the workload and to estimate the various workload ratios. For example, if the log shows that the maximum number of users during the peak hour is 300, and the average number of users hourly is 100, you can estimate that the peak traffic is three times the average traffic. Therefore, the system should be able to handle the traffic of about three times the average traffic while maintaining the acceptable response time.

You can make similar estimates for the number of page views. For example, if the log shows that the maximum number of page views during the peak hour is 600, and the average number of page views hourly is 150, you can estimate that the peak page views load is four times the average load. Therefore, the system should be able to handle the page views workload of about four times the average traffic while maintaining the acceptable response time.

As indicated earlier, many factors affect system performance. These factors include user activities and the translation of those activities into the workload, such as the number of specific files requested, the sizes of data files, and processing demands on the system that come with each request.

However, though the user-specific data collected here is useful to understand the nature of the traffic, it does not provide application-specific information, such as which file is most frequently requested or the average time the user spends on each page before requesting the next one. Some of the useful application- specific metrics include:

- Most requested pages
- Average time spent on pages

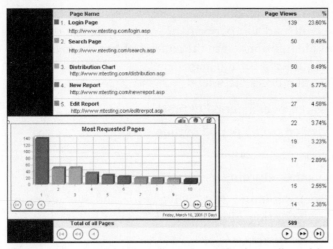

Figure 19.8 Example of application-specific data collected from a server log.

In the example shown in Figure 19.8, you can see that the Login Page was the most frequently requested page. Therefore, you might want to look to that page as a prime candidate for performance and load testing and optimization.

The Average Time Spent on Pages metric, shown in Figure 19.9, can help you extrapolate such information as read/think/data-input time. For example, if the average time that a user spent on a registration page is 29 seconds, you may interpret that it takes the user 29 seconds on average to read, digest the information, and fill out the form.

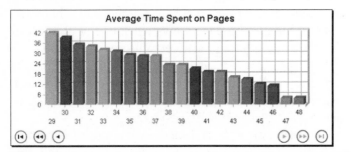

Figure 19.9 Example of average time (in seconds) spent on each page metric.

User-Based Profile

Another method of sizing your workload is through a *user-based profile*. With this approach, workload can be derived from the number of concurrent users, the ratio of different types of users, and the behavior of different types of users. Different types of users will have varying effects on the workload. Each type will use different features of the system at different speeds and varying frequencies.

When using the user-based profile method, it is important to take human behavior into account. For example, when determining the read/think/data-input time, you must consider how long a user might be expected to stay on a certain page. Returning users are likely to navigate more quickly than new users, as they will be more familiar with the application. Similarly, users have different levels of patience, which affects how quickly they will cancel a request if they do not get a response.

TESTING THE SAMPLE APPLICATION

The following tables offer a detailed example of how you might analyze the workload of the sample application (a Web-based bug-tracking application) in a hypothetical scenario where 10,000 concurrent users are using the system to report news bugs, work with existing bug reports, and generate charts.

Requirements documents (if you are lucky enough to get them) should detail the workload that Web applications are designed to support. For systems that are already employed, the network administration group might be able to provide information regarding system traffic. This can normally be done by using log analysis tools such as WebTrends Log Analyzer (www.webtrends.com) or Analog (www.statslab.cam.ac.uk/~sret1?analog/). Whichever log analysis tool you choose to use, use it consistently because each tool will produce slightly different statistics for the same amount of network traffic.

The three types of users that are factored into the following calculations are *testing, development,* and *project management.* Note that, normally, there would be more types of users. However, the sample application is a defect-tracking system and these are its primary users. The percentage of user type is also detailed (i.e., the testing group makes up 60 percent of the system's 10,0000 users, equating to 6,000 users), as is the average session length of each user type. From there, user activities and the frequency at which each activity is performed per session are detailed. Finally, the activities that are requested of the application and the transactions per second are covered.

Using the first row of Table 19.1 as an example, transactions-per-second calculations are arrived at using the following formula:

$$\frac{\text{User Type \% (0.60)} \times \text{total users (10,000)} \times \text{Frequency per Session (1)}}{\text{(60 minutes x 60 seconds)}}$$

(continued)

TESTING THE SAMPLE APPLICATION *(continued)*

Table 19.1   Calculating Transactions per Second

USER TYPE	USER TYPE %	SESSION LENGTH	USER ACTIVITY	USER SUB-ACTIVITY	FREQUENCY PER SESSION	APPLICATION ACTIVITY	TRANSACTIONS PER SECOND
Testing	60%	60 min.	Reporting	Reporting	1	Respond to a report submission by displaying the next blank report form.	1.7
	60%		Working with existing reports	Simple query	2	Respond by displaying the result in a single-report view	3.3
	60%			Complex query	1	Respond by displaying the result in a single-report view.	1.7
	60%			Navigate from one report to another.	8	Respond by displaying the result in a single-report view.	13.3
	60%			Submit an updated report.	0.5	Respond by displaying the updated information in the current report.	0.8
	60%		Obtaining metrics	First time	0.5	Respond by displaying a chart in a Java applet	0.8
	60%			Subsequent times	0.5	Respond by displaying a chart in a Java applet	0.8
Development	30%	30 min.	Working with existing reports	Simple query	2	Respond by displaying the result in a single-report view	3.3
	30%			Complex query	1	Respond by displaying the result in a single-report view	1.7
	30%			Navigate from one report to another	8	Respond by displaying the result in a single-report view	13.3
	30%			Submit an updated report	0.5	Respond by displaying the updated information in the current report	0.8
Project mgmt.	10%	90 min.	Working with existing reports	Simple query	2	Respond by displaying the result in a single-report view	0.4
	10%			Complex query	1	Respond by displaying the result in a single-report view	0.2
	10%			Navigate from one report to another	8	Respond by displaying the result in a single-report view	1.5
	10%			Submit an updated report	0.5	Respond by displaying the updated information in the current report	0.1
	10%		Obtaining metrics	The first time	0.5	Respond by displaying a chart in a Java applet	0.1
	10%			Subsequent times	0.5	Respond by displaying a chart in a Java applet	0.1

User activity data that is detailed in Table 19.1 should be analyzed to determine how often each transaction type is executed per second—regardless of which user type requests the transaction. Subsequently, each activity type (reporting, obtaining metrics, etc.) performed by all user types (testing, development, product management) is aggregated in Table 19.2, and an aggregate TPS rate is thereby calculated. The aggregate TPS rate is juxtaposed against the "acceptable" response time that has been established by management and the marketing group.

Table 19.2   Evaluating Transactions per Second

User Activity	User Subactivity	Frequency per Session	Application Activity	Frequency per Second (TPS)	Aggregate TPS	Acceptable Response Time (sec)
Reporting	Reporting	1	Respond to a report submission by displaying the next blank report form.	1.7	1.7	2
Obtaining metrics	Subsequent times	0.5	Respond by displaying a chart in a Java applet.	0.8		
	Subsequent times	0.5	Respond by displaying a chart in a Java applet.	0.1	0.9	5
Obtaining metrics	The first time	0.5	Respond by displaying a chart in a Java applet.	0.8		
	The first time	0.5	Respond by displaying a chart in a Java applet.	0.1	0.9	30
Working with existing reports	Complex query	1	Respond by displaying the result in a single-report view.	1.7		
	Complex query	1	Respond by displaying the result in a single-report view.	1.7		
	Complex query	1	Respond by displaying the result in a single-report view.	0.2	3.5	5
Working with existing reports	Navigate from one report to another.	8	Respond by displaying the result in a single-report view.	13.3		
	Navigate from one report to another.	8	Respond by displaying the result in a single-report view.	13.3		
	Navigate from one report to another.	8	Respond by displaying the result in a single-report view.	1.5	28.1	2
Working with existing reports	Simple query	2	Respond by displaying the result in a single-report view.	3.3		
	Simple query	2	Respond by displaying the result in a single-report view.	3.3		
	Simple query	2	Respond by displaying the result in a single-report view.	0.4	7.0	2
Working with existing reports	Submit an updated report.	0.5	Respond by displaying the updated information in the current report.	0.8		
	Submit an updated report.	0.5	Respond by displaying the updated information in the current report.	0.8		
	Submit an updated report.	0.5	Respond by displaying the updated information in the current report.	0.1	1.8	2

(continued)

TESTING THE SAMPLE APPLICATION *(continued)*

DETERMINING HOW MANY VIRTUAL USERS TO SIMULATE

The two factors to keep in mind when determining the appropriate number of virtual users are *response time* and *throughput*. Five transactions happening simultaneously, for example, may have an effect on response time, but should have little effect on throughput. Five hundred transactions spaced evenly apart, on the other hand, may not have an effect on response time, but may present a throughput issue.

The appropriate number of virtual users required by load and performance testing depends on the focus of testing. Considering the sample application, there are a few different ways that an appropriate number of virtual users can be calculated.

- ♦ To test only the performance of the application and database servers in terms of response time and throughput, 40 (the aggregate number of transactions per second) is a good number of virtual users to consider.

- ♦ To test the performance handling of concurrent open sessions on each server, as well as response time and throughput, 10,000 (the actual number of concurrent users) is a good number of virtual users to consider.

- ♦ Perhaps an arbitrary number of users *between* 40 and 10,000 should be considered to test certain performance scaling models that must be validated.

It is useful to group the users of the system into different categories when sizing the workload. Likewise, it is important to have a good mix of simulated users if you are to accurately test your application. As the response time increases, it is also important to simulate user cancellations. Some of the groupings that might be useful include:

- Percentage of users by group
- Percentage of users by human speed
- Percentage of users by patience
- Percentage of users by domain expertise
- Percentage of users by familiarity
- Percentage of users by connection speed

Problems Concerning Workloads

It is essential, although not always easy, to make accurate workload estimates during the planning stage and to revise these estimates as you gain more information about the system and users. Misunderstanding performance data can be extremely expensive to the organization. Some common problems are:

- Unrealistic load (simulated load does not closely represent real-world load):
  - Inaccurate modeling of the user load.
  - Mistranslating user load into system load.
- Inaccurate measurements:
  - A one-second difference between eight and seven seconds of response time may cost you 30 percent of your business.
  - A performance improvement of one second on a current response time of nine seconds is much more significant than on a current response time of 24 seconds.
- Misinterpreting results:
  - What's the difference between transaction time and response time? Know which variable and definition is being used.

Selecting Performance Metrics

Between the metrics collected by load generating tools and those collected by the performance monitors on the servers being tested, it is possible to collect a huge amount of data during the course of a load test. With this in mind, it is important to select metrics that are relevant to your testing goals. When selecting the metrics to monitor, consider what are the performance requirements of your application. Select metrics that will indicate whether these performance requirements are being met.

The most common metrics to collect are:

- *Transactions per second (TPS).* The number of transactions handled by the server per second.
- *Hits per second.* Typically, the number of hits per second the Web server receives from users. (Keep in mind that a transaction requesting a single HTML page can trigger multiple hits to the server.) As the number of transactions rises and the number of hits per second reaches saturation point, transaction-round-trip time (latency) becomes longer.
- *Concurrent connections.* The number of concurrent open connections.
- *Throughput.* The amount of data that the server processes (measured in KB/Sec).

Throughput Calculation Example

The objective of throughput calculation is to determine the level of bandwidth required to support system workload. For example, consider a Web server that supports 10,000 concurrent users who request documents from a pool of 10 different HTML documents (with an average size of 2K each) every 3.5 minutes. To calculate the bandwidth requirement for handling this throughput, use the following calculation:

$$\text{Throughput} = \frac{10,000 = (2 \times 1024 \times 8)}{(3.5 \times 60)} = 780,190 \text{ bps}$$

Or use:

$$10,000 \text{ concurrent users} \bullet \frac{(2 \text{ Kbytes} \times 1024 \text{ bytes/Kbytes} \times 8 \text{ bits/byte})}{(3.5 \text{ min} \times \text{s/min})} = 780,190 \text{ bps}$$

To handle this throughput load, the network connection should be at least a T1 line (1,544,000 bps). Use the time, data size, and bandwidth conversion tables (Tables 19.3 through 19.5) to perform other workload assessments.

Table 19.3 Time Conversion

Week	Day	Hour	Minute	Second	Millisecond
1	7	168	10,080	604,800	604,800,000
	1	24	1,440	86,400	86,400,000
		1	60	3,600	3,600,000
			1	60	60,000
				1	1,000
					1

Table 19.4 Data-Size Conversion

Gigabyte	Megabyte	Kilobyte	Byte	Bit
1	1,024	1,048,576	1,073,741,824	8,589,934,592
	1	1,024	1,048,576	8,388,608
		1	1,024	8,192
			1	8
				1

Table 19.5   Bandwidth Conversion

Line	Mbps	Kbps	bps
28K Dial-up	0.028	28	28,000
56K Dial-up	0.056	56	56,000
ISDN Single	0.064	64	64,000
ISDN Double	0.128	128	128,000
T1	1.544	1,544	1,544,000
Token Ring	4.00	4,000	4,000,00
10-BaseT	10.00	10,000	10,000,000
Token Ring	16.00	16,000	16,000,000
T3	45.00	45,000	45,000,000
100-BaseT	100.00	100,000	100,000,000
FDDI (Fiber Distribution Data Interface)	100.00	100,000	100,000,000
Gigabit Ethernet	1,000.00	1,000,000	1,000,000,000
ATM	155.52	155,520	155,520,000
ATM	622.08	622,080	622,080,000

Other metrics commonly collected include:

- Connect time
- Send time
- Receive time
- Process time
- Transaction time
- Failed transactions per second
- Requests per second
- Failed requests per second

Performance testing often requires the aid of automated testing tools to simulate workload, collect measurement data, and present data in a format that can be used for performance analysis. Each tool vendor uses slightly different terms to describe similar concepts. Table 19.6 lists a sampling that includes many of the commonly used response and performance testing terms. It is not important to concern yourself with which definition is correct; it is essential to know which definitions are used in the reports generated by the tools.

Which Tests to Run and When to Start

As with other forms of testing, performance testing should be started as early as possible, and should be repeated as often as possible. It is easier and less costly to address performance issues and fix errors early in the development cycle. The earlier a performance issue is uncovered, the more time the developers will have to find a solution and verify that it solves the problem.

If the tests are ready early in the development cycle, they can be run as part of a regression suite against each new build. The effects of changes made in each build on the overall performance can then be measured by running a load or performance test. (The tests should have the same number of virtual users across runs in order to make them comparable.) New performance issues can be correlated to changes made in the build and addressed appropriately. (By the way, performance is especially vulnerable to regression in an unstable feature setting; that is, when a lot of functionality is added or changed, it can easily compromise performance without anyone noticing until the system is deployed.)

Load tests are also useful for finding rare and often nonreproducible problems. Timing problems, race conditions, and deadlock conditions may only rarely cause a detectable bug, but by repeatedly executing the load tests, you increase your chances of finding these problems.

Some tips to make performance testing successful:

- Specify which tests you will run.
- Estimate how many cycles of each test you will run.
- Schedule your tests ahead of time.
- Specify by which criteria you will consider the system under test (SUT) to be ready to test.
- Do "forward thinking": Determine and communicate the planned tests and how the tests will be scheduled.

Certain requirements must be met before load testing can begin:

- Hardware must be installed and operational.
- The network should be fully functional.
- Any server software required by the application should be installed and operational.
- The functionality of the application being tested should be complete. (That said, depending on the tool being used and the parts of the application being tested, it may be possible to begin load testing before the application is fully functional.)
- The tests themselves, tools, and/or scripts must be fully developed or incorporated into current test scripts. (Previously developed test scripts can often be used as-is.)

Table 19.6   Performance Testing Terms

Attribute	Typical Definition	Comments
Connect Time	The time (typically in seconds) required for the client and the server to establish a connection.	Time spent at network.
Send Time	The time (typically in seconds) required to send data from the client to the server.	Time spent at network.
Receive Time	The time (typically in seconds) required to send the response data from the server to the client.	Time spent at network.
Process Time	The time (typically in seconds) required for the server to respond to a client request.	Time spent at server.
Response Time	The time (typically in seconds) required to complete a particular transaction.	Time spent at server.
Transaction Time	The time (typically in seconds) required for the client to process the data received.	The total amount of time spent at network, client, and server to complete a transaction. This is an interesting measurement because it represents the end-to-end performance of the system.
Transaction per Second	The total number of transactions—such as Head, Get, or Post per second—that the system received.	As the number of virtual users increases, but the number of transactions per second decreases or is saturated, it will cause transactions to fail.
Failed Transactions per Second	The total number of transactions per second that the system failed to complete.	The failed transactions metric is one of the primary sources of technical support or sales loss problems.
Requests per Second	The number of hits the Web servers received.	This details the interaction intensity between browsers and Web servers. When the number of requests per second is saturated, it will cause transactions with multiple requests to fail.
Failed Requests per Second	The total number of failed requests.	The number of hits the Web server failed to serve.
Concurrent Connections	The total number of concurrent connections over the elapsed time.	A Web server connection is opened when a request is generated from a browser. If the number of concurrent connections increases, but the number requests per second does not increase, it means that the request demands cause the connections to stay open longer to complete the service. This trend will eventually saturate the maximum number of open connections on a Web server, hence introduce a performance bottleneck.
Throughput—Kilobytes per Second	The amount of data transmitted during client-server interactions.	When the number of virtual users or transactions increases but the amount of data transmitted is saturated, data throughput has become a performance bottleneck.

In addition to the basic performance, load, and stress tests, you should also consider executing one or more of the following:

- *Acceptance test (10 to 100 users with simple scripts).* It is a good idea to plan for the acceptance test. We have seen numerous products deemed ready for performance testing when they can barely handle more than five concurrent users.

- *Baseline test.* This test is designed to determine at what size workload the response time will begin to deteriorate. When you gradually apply load to the system under test, at first you will find that the response time does not change proportionally to the load size. But when the load size approaches a particular threshold, the workload will begin to have an impact on the response time (see Figure 19.10). At that point, you can record the threshold load size and the response time. These values represent the current baseline of your system performance. One reason it is useful to collect the baseline data is that when you want to improve the performance of the system under test, you can optimize software and hardware so that either the baseline response time will be lower, the baseline workload size will be higher, or both. When you are simulating a load, you need to consider that the actual load may not show the same baseline, depending on how realistic your simulated load is.

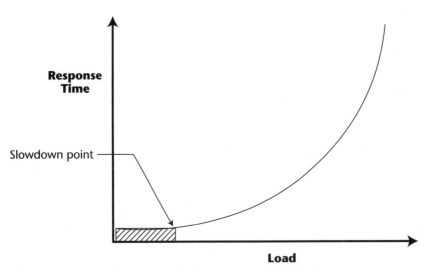

Figure 19.10 Discovering the slowdown point in baseline test.

- *2x/3x/4x baseline tests.* After you have determined the baseline, you increase the workload size using the baseline workload as the increment unit. The baseline test 2x/3x/4x/and so on tests are useful especially when you do not have the performance requirements before the planning and execution of the performance test (see Figure 19.11). This method enables you to present a known set of data, use it as a reference point to educate others, and establish concrete test requirements.

- *Goal-reaching test.* In this test, you want to set a load objective such that when the threshold is reached, you stop the test, collect, and analyze the results. An example of a goal-reaching test could be one that stops when the workload size is four times the size of the baseline workload, or when response time exceeds 10 seconds.

- *A longevity or endurance test.* This tests how well a system handles a predefined load over a long period of time. The idea is to determine whether system performance degrades over time (due to resource leaks) under a load that would be expected in the production environment. If performance does degrade, determine when it becomes unacceptable and which hardware/software components cause the degradation.

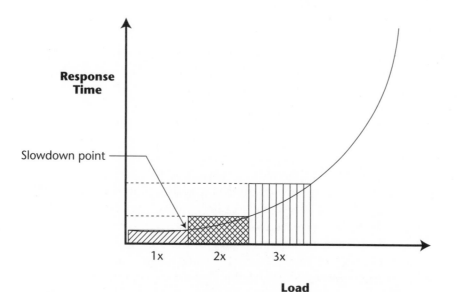

Figure 19.11   Apply 2x and 3x the load and collect the response time data.

- *Peak test.* This tests the performance at peak load. For example, a stock exchange board's peak load during opening and closing periods could be four times the normal load.

- Stress test. This test checks the error handling capability of the system.

- *Scalability test.* Refer back to Chapter 3, "Software Testing Basics," for a definition of this type of test.

- *Availability and reliability test.* Refer back to Chapter 3 for a definition of this type of test.

Tool Options and Generating Loads

Tool Options

To decide which testing tools would best assist the testing effort, you must identify the *operating environment* that the testing tool must support. This includes: operating system, hardware platform, network infrastructure (WAN or LAN), network protocols, and so forth. And be aware that the tool might have to work on multiple platforms. Also consider the *number of users* that must be simulated; make sure that the tool can simulate enough users to produce an adequate test.

As far as test-script generation and execution is concerned, determine whether a tool that provides *script recording* (as opposed to manual scripting) will be needed. Make sure that the tool can log all discrepancies. The tool should also be able to simulate multiple versions of browsers and network connections. Make sure that the tool also supports user *think time.* Finally, look for support of HTTPS, Java, ActiveX, scripts, and cookies.

Off-the-shelf (OTS) tools, such as those listed in Chapter 21, "Web Testing Tools," can be expensive. Additionally, it takes time to learn these tools and become proficient at the scripting languages they use. Furthermore, off-the-shelf tools may not meet the needs of the project; hence, you may end up paying for features that the test project does not require.

Homegrown tools can also be expensive due to the in-house costs related to their development. The maintenance and testing costs associated with the development of homegrown tools can be significant. Internal engineering resources may be limited, as well, making it challenging to develop tools in a reasonable time frame and maintain them over time.

The best solution may be a combination of off-the-shelf and homegrown tools. As with most decisions related to software testing, the earlier that you assess testing needs, the better. Evaluate the tools that are available and assess the needs of the system under test as early in the testing effort as possible. (For a list of available testing tools, see Chapter 21, or visit the Software QA/Test Resources Web site at www.softwareqatest.com/qatweb1.html#LOAD.)

Analyzing and Reporting Collected Data

When evaluating tools used to gather and analyze data, consider whether a tool provides the result analysis and publishing features that will be needed. Without such features, manual collection, analysis, and report tabulation of test results will be necessary. Also consider what type of data analysis the tool will need to perform: Will specific Structured Query Language (SQL) statements need to be captured? Should the tool monitor system resource usage and network communication activity?

Generating Loads

There are two different approaches you can take to generating load. The *hardware-intensive approach* involves multiple users at multiple workstations generating load against the application. Each user executes specific steps to simulate a typical user of the system.

The hardware-intensive approach has some advantages: It allows the generation of load from different types of machines and browsers that would typically be used to access the system. These sorts of tests are very fast to set up and execute, as the only real requirements are available machines and available users to generate the load. Compared to the software-intensive approach, the disadvantage of the hardware-intensive approach is that it is not very scalable, hence it can quickly become expensive if the test requires numerous human users and must be run several times. For each simultaneous user accessing the system, you must have a computer and a person available to generate load. Typically, there is no centralized mechanism for gathering metrics such as response time and transaction time.

The *software-intensive approach* involves the use of a tool to simulate many users accessing the system simultaneously. Typically this tool runs on one machine, but some tools are designed to use multiple machines to generate load. These tools typically generate load either by simulating a user interacting with the browser or by directly sending HTTP requests to the Web server.

There are many different tools that can be used to generate load. OTS tools are common choices. These tools typically provide some or all of the following features:

- Support for the Document Object Model (DOM) to parse HTML pages
- Functional validation features
- Simulation of different browsers
- Support for Web-related technologies such as cookies, session state, Java, ActiveX, and so on
- Powerful reporting features
- Integration with server performance monitors

There are several load-generating tools available free of charge, but they typically do not support scripting and offer limited reporting capabilities. Still, they may be sufficient for your needs and, if so, will reduce the costs of your project significantly.

Another option for load-generating tools is to use an *application service provider* (ASP). Several companies are now providing hosted load generation as a service. There are several advantages to this model. One of the most significant advantages is that you don't need to devote resources (computers and bandwidth) to generating load. This allows you to increase the load applied to the system under test without worrying about whether you will have enough computing power and network bandwidth. An ASP will typically allow you to generate load from various locations around the world, and at different speeds. This allows you to closely simulate the expected demographics of the users of the application. Using an ASP to generate load typically requires less setup time before load can be generated, and can also be more cost-effective than the OTS approach.

The disadvantage to the ASP approach is lack of flexibility. Typically, these tools do not offer the same advance ID scripting support as OTS tools, making it difficult to execute load tests that simulate complicated scenarios.

Yet another option for generating load is to build the load-generating tool yourself. This is typically done using a language that supports TCP/IP, such as Perl, Python, or Java. By building your own tool, you get exactly what you want (if it's built right). But building your own tool can turn out to be quite expensive, as you must allocate development resources to work on the tool and you must functionally test it before it can be used to generate loads. Typically, homegrown tools do not have the same powerful reporting capabilities as OTS tools, but often you will not need the additional flexibility found in the OTS tools.

There are several factors you should consider when choosing a tool for generating load. The decision of which tool to use should be made as early as possible in the testing process, to allow time to determine exactly what needs to be done to get ready for the test. Points to consider when choosing a tool include:

- Can the tool generate the workload required for your test? If so, how much hardware does it require to generate the workload?
- Can the tool generate the type of load needed for your test? Can the tool simulate the scenarios that you want to use in your test? Can the tool generate the metrics reports needed?
- How much time will it take to learn how to use the tool?
- How much does the tool cost, and is it worth it?
- What other costs does the tool have?
- On which platform(s) must the tool run?

- What are the licensing costs associated with generating the necessary workload?

- Does the tool support record and playback of scenarios? How much scripting is required before a test can be run?

See Chapter 21 for more information on commercial load and performance testing tools and services.

Writing the Test Plan

As discussed in Chapter 7, "Test Planning Fundamentals," the test plan should document test objectives, test requirements, test designs, test procedures, and other project management information. All development and testing deliverables should be documented in the test plan.

NOTE For your convenience, at QACity.com/Test+Types/Load+Performance/ you will find a performance test plan template that you can use as a framework for planning and documenting your performance testing project.

With the objectives of performance, load, and stress testing in mind, you can begin to develop an effective test planning process. In addition to the software testing team, the testing effort requires the involvement of the IT as well as the software engineering team. Many of the following test planning activities are typical of all test planning projects.

Identifying Baseline Configuration and Performance Requirements

In defining baseline configuration and performance requirements for the system under test, it is important to identify system requirements for the client, server, and network. Consider hardware and software configurations, network bandwidth, memory requirements, disk space, connectivity technologies, and so on. To determine system workload, you will also have to evaluate the system's users and their respective activities.

Determining the Workload

Please see the section "Defining the Workload," earlier in this chapter.

Determining When to Begin Testing

Testing should be performed as early in the product development process as possible. It is far cheaper, easier, and more feasible to correct errors early in the development process than it is to fix them late in the development process. Additionally, the earlier that testing begins, the more tests you can repeat; and the more often that tests are repeated, the more opportunity the development team will have to improve product performance, which increases the value of the effort invested in building the tests.

Performance, load, and stress tests can be a part of the regression testing suite that is performed with each build. Regression testing determines whether new errors have been introduced into previously tested code. Early detection of performance requirement failures can be critically important because it offers developers the maximum amount of time to address errors.

Determine Whether the Testing Process Will Be Hardware-Intensive or Software-Intensive

The *hardware-intensive approach* involves the use of multiple client workstations in the simulation of real-world activity. The advantage of this approach is that you can perform load and stress testing on a wide variety of machines simultaneously, thereby closely simulating real-world use. The disadvantage is that you must acquire and dedicate a large number of workstations to perform such testing.

The *software-intensive approach* involves the virtual simulation of numerous workstations over multiple connection types. The advantage of the software-intensive approach is that only a few physical systems are required to perform testing. The disadvantage is that some hardware-, software-, or network-specific errors may be missed.

Developing Test Cases

Generated loads may be designed to interact with servers via a Web browser user interface (UI), or via HTTP requests such as GET and POST (thereby bypassing the browser). Consideration must be given to the types of requests that are sent to the server under test by the load generator (hence, the amount of data per transaction that the server processes) and the resources available to the load generator.

Testing Phase

Once you have completed the planning phase, you are ready to begin running your tests. Typically, the testing phase of your project will consist of the following activities:

- Generating test data.
- Setting up a test bed of data.

- Setting up the test suite parameters.
- Running the tests.
- Tuning the tests.
- Rerunning the tests.

Generating Test Data

Most performance tests will require some data in order to be run. For example, you might need a set of user names and passwords to log in to an application, and then some data to enter into a form. There are several different options for generating test data. The first is to create the data manually, but this can be time-consuming and might result in data that is not necessarily representative of the data that will be used in a real-world scenario; however this is sometimes the only option.

Rather than generate the data manually, you may want to do it programmatically. For example, you can create a script that generates a user name and password for each of the simulated users in your load test. One advantage of this approach is that you will be able to use the same test data for several runs of the test. While there is some initial cost to develop the script, typically you will save quite a bit of time during future runs of the test.

Another option is to use existing data from the system under test. This can typically be done if the system has already been put into production. This approach allows you to perform your testing using data that has been generated by real-world users. With most load-generating tools, it is fairly simple to convert data from the production environment into a format that the testing tool can use. For example, you might run a query against the production database to get a set of test data, then save the query results into a file that will be used by the load tool.

Setting Up the Test Bed

Once the test data is prepared, you should make some final preparations for the test. These preparations may consist of some or all of the following:

- Configuration of the system under test environment
- Configuration of the test environment
- Preparation of the network resources
- Configuration of performance monitors
- Determination of the metrics to monitor and collect

Setting Up the Test Suite Parameters

Most load-generating tools have a number of parameters that can be configured. You may need to configure some or all of the following:

- Number of threads and sockets used to simulate users
- Test-run schedules and duration
- Demographic and geographic segmentation of simulated users
- Request delay factors
- Ramp-up speed
- Cool-down speed
- Special handling such as cookies and sessions
- Server metrics to collect
- Distribution/ratios of scripts
- Bandwidth throttling and ratios
- Load targets such as failed transaction threshold, response time threshold, and so on

Performance Test Run Example

During the beta testing phase, the objective of this performance test is to determine if the system can handle 100 users logging in concurrently within a reasonably acceptable response time and without any transaction failure.

The process of setting up this test is something like the following:

1. Record a login script.

2. Modify the recorded script in such a way that it can rerun the same login procedure just by reading from an external text file a line at a time. Each line has two fields, holding the user ID and password respectively. Here's the modified script:

```
// This is an example of load testing on the sample
// application, TRACKGEAR
function InitAgenda() {
CopyFile("c:\\login.txt", "c:\\login.txt")
}
//Set up the array
login = GetLine("c:\\login.txt" ,",")
//Synchronize the Data points
```

```
SynchronizationPoint(3000)
//Go to the Web site
wlHttp.Get("http://engservices.logigear.com/trackgear/default.asp")
wlHttp.FormData["company"] = "trackgear"
wlHttp.Get("http://engservices.logigear.com/bts/bin/login.asp")
//Post Username & Password
Sleep(8840)
wlHttp.FormData["user_name"] = login[1]
wlHttp.FormData["password"] = login[2]
wlHttp.FormData["Login"] = "Login"
wlHttp.FormData["PageNumber"] = "2"
wlHttp.FormData["company"] = "y"
wlHttp.Post("http://engservices.logigear.com/bts/bin/login.asp")
if (login.LineNum = 100) InfoMessage("done with read")
//Time the Login Process, and return that value
SetTimer("LoginTime")
wlHttp.Get("http://engservices.logigear.com/bts/bin/usercont.asp")
wlHttp.Get("http://engservices.logigear.com/bts/bin/title.asp")
wlHttp.Get("http://engservices.logigear.com/bts/bin/mainuser.asp")
wlHttp.Get("http://engservices.logigear.com/bts/bin/refresh.asp")
SendTimer("loginTime")
```

Next is the content of the text file, named user.txt (100 users' IDs and passwords) that the performance test script reads in when it begins to execute the test.

```
beno, beno
chrisv, chrisv
.., ..
ursulap, john
```

3. Prepare the controlling and the monitoring consoles, as well as a computer to use as a load generator to spawn threads to simulate.

4. Set up the test script to be run with the tool. (The performance test tool used in this example is RadView's WebLoad.)

In this particular test, we discover the response time is within expected limits, less than a half of a second, but that transaction failures are occurring at the Web server. As shown in Figure 19.12, three of the 100 transactions failed to respond.

When examining the metrics data, in addition to time-specific metrics, we also need to pay attention to errors. (See the Online Purchases study, reported in 1999, in the accompanying sidebar.)

ONE IN FOUR ONLINE PURCHASES THWARTED, STUDY FINDS

Andrea Orr
December 20, 1999

PALO ALTO, Calif. (Reuters)—The problem with the explosion of online stores is that more than a quarter of all the purchases attempted over the Internet never go through, according to a study. Andersen Consulting went shopping at 100 of the biggest and best-known online stores. Out of 480 gifts it tried to buy, it was able to complete only 350 purchases. The study found that more than one-quarter of the top Web sites either could not take orders, crashed in the process, were under construction, had entry blocked, or were otherwise inaccessible.

"It was pretty eye-opening," said Robert Mann of Andersen's Supply Chain practice. He said he was stunned by the results of the survey, which had initially been designed to study only the time it took to complete and fulfill orders.

Mann said he found instead that "speed is not really the issue. The issue is reliability." Although Andersen did not single out the best and the worst of these online stores, Mann said that none of them was problem-free. In general, though, the study found that the traditional retailers had a worse track record than the pure-play Internet stores, known as e-tailers. "The e-tailers who depend on this as their bread and butter have generally invested more on back-end systems. Many retailers have not invested as well," said Mann.

Another big problem was orders not arriving on time. The traditional retailers were once again the big offenders, according to the study, which found they delivered the order when promised only about 20 percent of the time. E-tailers, by comparison, were on time about 80 percent of the time. Curiously, some items took much longer to deliver. The average time for an electronics gift to arrive was 3.9 days, while music deliveries typically took 7.4 days.

Andersen plans to next study online merchants' ability to handle returns — which Mann said could be their next big challenge if consumers sent back all those gifts that did not arrive by Christmas Day.

Analysis Phase

Once performance testing results have been gathered, corrective measures for improving performance must be considered. For example, should additional system resources be added? Should network architecture be adjusted? Can programming improvements be made? Is more load testing necessary? Are there bottlenecks that should be addressed? The results of your test should provide answers to these questions.

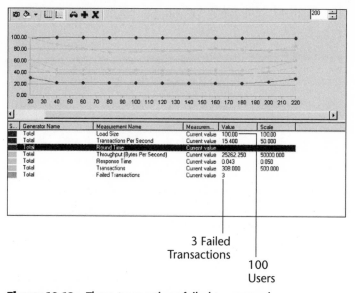

S...	Generator Name	Measurement Name	Measurem...	Value	Scale
■	Total	Load Size	Current value	100.00	100.00
	Total	Transactions Per Second	Current value	15.400	50.000
	Total	Round Time	Current value		
	Total	Throughput (Bytes Per Second)	Current value	25262.250	50000.000
	Total	Response Time	Current value	0.043	0.050
	Total	Transactions	Current value	308.000	500.000
■	Total	Failed Transactions	Current value	3	

3 Failed
Transactions

100
Users

Figure 19.12   Three transactions failed to respond.

The examination of test results can be described as a three-stage process. The first step is to *characterize* the system: organize the performance data you have gathered.

The next step is to *analyze* the results and look for the sources of performance problems. Typically, the source of a performance problem can be found by examining the performance monitors on the servers receiving the load. For example, if the amount of memory being used by the server is greater than the physical memory installed, then physical memory might be the bottleneck.

Today's Web-based applications can be extremely complex, involving the interactions of many different hardware and software systems. A failure or deficiency in any of these systems can affect the performance of the entire Web application. Some of the common hardware-related problems that can lead to poor performance include:

- Memory (physical, virtual, and storage, plus heap and stack space)
- Central processing unit (CPU) time
- Transmission Control Protocol/Internet Protocol TCP/IP addresses
- Network bandwidth
- File handles

Some of the common software-related problems (including operating systems) include:

- Software failures caused by hardware interrupts
- Memory runtime errors (such as leakage, overwrite, and pointer errors)
- Database problems (deadlocks, number of connections)
- Multithreading problems
- File system problems (naming conventions, files per directory, number of file handles allowed)

The final step is to *optimize* the system under test by addressing the problems found in your analysis. (Note: Although optimization is not done by testing, we present the information here for completeness.) These optimizations can be made to both hardware and software. For example, if your analysis revealed that there was a memory bottleneck, then a possible solution might be to add more memory to the server. The memory bottleneck might also be due to inefficient memory management in the applications on the server, in which case the application code can be optimized. In general, consider the following when optimizing the system:

- Add processing power.
- Add RAM.
- Add storage.
- Add bandwidth.
- Add load/balancing capability to improve performance through scalability.
- Create smaller pages to improve download speed.
- If the problem is the data size such as a single, large graphic file, try to break the file into a set of smaller graphics to improve download speed.
- If the problem is too many round-trips (to retrieve several smaller graphics), try larger graphics.
- Investigate whether the performance of third-party banner ads affect the performance of your site.
- Increase cache size on the Web server to improve performance.
- Build a "light" version of your Web site/pages as a text-only version for use when the response time exceeds the preset threshold (due to heavy load, for example).

The final test report should cover how the test requirements are addressed. It should also contain a summary of the relevant findings from the tests.

Other Testing Considerations

- It takes time, effort, and commitment to plan and execute performance, load, and stress tests. Performance testing involves more people in an organization than just testers. A well-planned testing program requires a joint effort between all members of the product team, including upper management, marketing, development, IT, and testing.

- Aggregate response time is a sum of browser processing time, network service time, and server response time. Performance analysis takes all of these factors into consideration.

- Server-side analysis of *performance bottlenecks* often includes examination of the Web server, the application server, and the database server. Bottlenecks at any of these servers may result in server-side performance problems, which may ultimately affect overall response time.

- Begin performance testing as early in the development process as possible to allow time for the analysis of data and the resolution of performance issues.

- Repeat performance tests as many times as possible prior to deployment so that performance degradation issues can be identified early. Allow plenty of time to isolate and troubleshoot performance issues.

- Determining a *projected number of users* can be complex. Consider the following issues:

    - User activities vary.

    - User-access behavior and activity frequencies vary from one time period to the next.

    - Projected numbers of users must be considered within an appropriate *workload model.*

    - Virtual users do not necessarily behave in the same ways that real users do.

    - Consider what will happen if the product is wildly successful. That is, what will happen if you have grossly underestimated the number of users?

    - The number of users or the volume of transactions is predictable for an intranet (controlled environment) but is unpredictable for a Web site, such as an e-commerce site on the Internet (uncontrolled environment).

- Determining *acceptable performance* can be challenging. Consider the following issues:
    - There are different means of measuring performance (metrics); each has different associated costs.
    - Which factors affect performance in the system under test?
    - Many different tools are available on the market; each offers unique benefits and drawbacks.
- Regarding *data analysis* and *corrective action planning,* consider how performance degradation can be resolved:
    - By adding system resources.
    - By adjusting network system architecture.
    - Through programming.
    - How can user workload be monitored so that appropriate actions can be taken to avoid saturation?
    - Continue monitoring system performance after deployment so that scalability issues can be addressed in a timely manner.
    - Performance testing is a capability planning process, not pass/fail testing.
    - Systems often have multiple performance bottlenecks.
    - Test script creation often requires programming skills. Prepare to train your testing staff.
    - Does the system's performance meet user expectations during standard operation (when the load is within specified limits)? If the answer is yes, how is performance affected when the load exceeds specified limits?
    - When the system is overloaded (i.e., when user demand exceeds system resource availability) and forced into an error condition, does the system accurately detect, handle, and recover gracefully from the condition? Does the system crash or begin to behave erratically?
    - How scalable is the system? Can the system be upgraded easily and quickly (server memory, disk space, software, etc.) to accommodate increased load demand?
    - Focus testing on individual objects, rather than on entire systems, to yield more detailed and, consequently, more practical information regarding load limitations.

- Determining workload involves the following issues:
  - How many groups of users will be involved in a load test?
  - How frequently will each user in each group access and interact with the application during a load test?
  - What will be the typical activities performed by each group of users?
- Performance testing is a server-capacity planning process that involves three fundamental steps:
  1. Establishing a baseline.
  2. Gathering and analyzing data.
  3. Predicting future server capacity based on gathered data.
- In defining baseline configuration and performance requirements, you should identify system requirements for the client, server, and network. Consider hardware and software configurations, network bandwidth, memory requirements, disk space, and connectivity technologies.
- In determining which tools are most appropriate for your test project, you should consider the following:
  - What are the operating systems, hardware platforms, network infrastructure types (WANs and LANs), and network protocols that the tool must support? Must the tool work on multiple platforms?
  - How many users must the tool simulate to produce an effective test?
  - Must the tool provide script-recording functionality, in addition to manual scripting?
  - Look for a tool that can run unattended and accurately log all discrepancies.
  - Does the script support user think time, to more realistically simulate real-world conditions?

Bibliography

Anderson, M.D. "13 Mistakes in Load Testing Applications." *Software Testing and Quality Engineering,* September/October, 1999.

Killelea, P. *Web Performance Tuning*, 2nd ed. Sebastopol: CA: O'Reilly & Associates, 2002.

Menasce, D.A., and V.A.F. Almeida. *Capacity Planning for Web Performance.* Upper Saddle River, NJ: Prentice-Hall, 1998.

—— *Scaling for E-Business.* Upper Saddle River, NJ: Prentice-Hall, 2000.

Nguyen, H.Q. "Testing Web Applications." *LogiGear Corporation Training Handbook,* 2003.

Radview Software, Inc. "The Web Load User's Guide." Lexington, MA: Radview, 1998.

Savoia, A. "The Science and Art of Web Site Load Testing." *STQE STAREAST,* 2000.

———— "Web Load Test Planning." *STQE Magazine,* March/April 2001.

———— "Trade Secrets from a Web Testing Expert." *STQE Magazine,* May/June 2001.

———— "Web Page Response Time 101." STQE Magazine, July/August 2001.

Schelstrate, M. "Stress Testing Data Access Components in Windows DNA Applications." *MSDN News,* March/April, 2000, http://msdn.microsoft.com/voices/news.

CHAPTER

20

Testing Mobile Web Applications

Why Read This Chapter?

In this chapter, we go beyond the concept of mobile Web applications presented in Chapter 6, "Mobile Web Application Platform." The objective here is to offer you the experience-based information that you can use in the development of test strategies, test plans, and test cases for mobile Web applications.

TOPICS COVERED IN THIS CHAPTER

- ◆ Introduction
- ◆ Testing Mobile versus Desktop Web Applications
- ◆ Various Types of Tests
- ◆ Survey of Mobile Testing Support Tools
- ◆ Other Testing Considerations
- ◆ Bibliography and Additional Resources

Introduction

The problems discovered and the strategies used in testing Web-based and client-server applications will continue to apply in testing mobile Web applications. In addition, there will be a series of new issues and strategies for you to take into consideration due to the fact that the mobile platform is a different environment, especially on the client-side. In this chapter, we will contrast testing mobile with desktop applications, pointing out many restrictions on a typical mobile client that cause a new host of problems. We will discuss the various types of tests in the context of mobile application testing, testing with emulators, a survey of testing support tools, and a few lessons learned.

Testing Mobile versus Desktop Web Applications

As discussed in Chapter 6, the main difference between a mobile and desktop client is that, in the mobile case, the Web content is interpreted by a Web browser that runs on a client computer. This type of browser has many restrictions that a typical desktop client does not have, because it runs on a mobile device and often uses a wireless network with low bandwidth. Overcoming these restrictions, listing according to category here, requires creative designing and programming solutions. These solutions, however, will be the source of new errors for which we should seek out.

DEVICE LIMITATIONS

- *Small screen size.* Due to the size restriction, it is not enough to just convert the standard HTML Web content so that a handheld microbrowser can correctly parse the data. A redesign of the Web site or Web application is needed to take into account the limited real estate available on the mobile device. Our tests need to make sure the redesign accomplishes its objectives.

- *Limited CPU power (mobile phone).* Given limited computing power, the client is more efficient as a thin client, often working with a text-only microbrowser. It takes work to convert an existing workstation thick-client Web application to a thin-client mobile Web application.

- *Limited RAM.* This limitation prohibits running serious applications on the device.

- *Limited secondary storage.* This means no or limited client-side data storage capability.

- *Power management dependencies.* What happens if the user is in the middle of filling out a form and the device "goes to sleep?" Will the session be lost?

- *Limited battery life dependencies.* An out-of-battery condition might result in data loss. A client device with built-in connectivity will consume power while it is connecting to the server to execute transactions, which will quickly drain the battery. How does this affect the use of mobile Web applications with extensive feature offerings?

- *Cumbersome input UI.* So-called thumb typing and graffiti writing with a stylus, rather than traditional typing and use of a mouse, can also be problematic.

NOTE Many of these restrictions may be more severe for a mobile phone than for a PDA or a handheld PC.

WIRELESS NETWORK AND CARRIER ISSUES

- *Poor network bandwidth.* Requires "light" version of the Web content to reduce the size of data transferred across the network.

- *Third-party support infrastructure-dependent.* This is especially challenging due to a number of different infrastructures deployed by carriers in the United States and worldwide, such as Nokia, Ericsson, Nortel, and Lucent. Furthermore, there are different gateway implementations and different combinations of data traffic optimization servers in use by different carriers. It is common for one application in a mobile Web application to work well with one combination of carrier/ infrastructure/ gateway but fail or function incorrectly on another carrier's network.

- *Character handling.* Each carrier might have special handling for certain characters. Using these characters in the input data might cause problems.

- *Message size limitation.* If the input data is larger than the maximum size allowed to be transmitted across the wireless network each time, the excess data might be truncated or dropped by the carrier.

- *User storage and data size limitation.* When a user subscribes to a wireless account, often there is a set limitation on the storage size and data size allocated each month. If the user has used up all of allotted space, excess data might be undelivered. This condition might cause problems to the mobile Web application under test.

OTHER DEPENDENCIES

- *Data synchronization dependency.* Mobile devices and mobile applications use the data synchronization process to move the data between the client and the server, and vice versa (see Chapter 6 for an explanation).

■ *Web content format dependency.* Table 20.1 lists the browsers available for each type of operating system, and whether each supports these Web browser features: SSL, HTML, HDML, WML, XML, cHTML, cookies, ActiveX, Java applet, tables, and images. This information makes it clear just how different these browsers are. The point is, you will want to gather all the pertinent information you need to understand what you will be facing when a device or device OS company wants to support x, y, and z browser; then you will be able to adequately test that support. Furthermore, as discussed in Chapter 17, "Configuration and Compatibility Tests," you should be aware that even when a given browser promises support for certain features, it does not mean that it will be compatible with your server contents, such as scripts, CSS, and Java applet.

NOTE The information contained in Table 20.1 is not meant to be comprehensive. Also, by the time of publication of this book, some of the information may no longer be accurate or up to date.

The example shown in Figure 20.1a, 20.1b, and 20.1c illustrates the issues that you might face in testing mobile Web applications.

The Web page has a drop-down menu from which the user can select an item. It then relies on an onChange="jumpTo" command to execute the script to displaying the Audio-Visual selection.

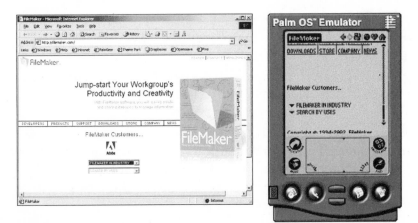

Figure 20.1a   The drop-down lists available on the Web page displayed in a desktop browser and Palm OS browser, respectively.

OS	Device	Browser	Browsing Comments	SSL	HTML	WAP (HDML/WML)	XML	IMODE (cHTML)	Cookies	Scripts	ActiveX	Java Applet	Proxy Server	Tables	Images
Palm	Palm 05 and Compatible	AvantGo	OnLine, Offline channels	Yes	Yes	No	No	No	Yes	No	No	No	Optional	Yes	Yes
		EndoraWeb	Online	Yes	Yes	No	No	No	Yes	No	No	No	Yes	Optional	No
		PocketLink	Online, cached contents for offline viewing	N/A	Yes	N/A	No	Yes	Yes	No	No	No	Yes	No	Yes
		Xlino (PalmScape)	OnLine, Offline	Yes	Yes	No	No	Yes	Yes	No	No	Yes	Yes	Yes	Yes
		Blazer	Online	Yes	Yes	Yes	No	Yes	Yes	No	No	No	Optional	Yes	Yes
		Wapaka	Online	No	No	Yes	No	N/A	N/A	Yes	No	No	Optional	No	No
		Go.web	Online, Web Clipping	N/A	Yes	Yes	No	N/A	Yes	No	No	No	Optional	Yes	Yes
Windows CE	PocketPC and Compatible	IE 2002	OnLine, Offline channels	Yes	Yes	Yes	Yes	Yes	Yes	Yes	Yes	Yes	Optional	Yes	Yes
		AvantGo	OnLine, Offline channels	Yes	Yes	No	No	N/A	Yes	No	N/A	N/A	Yes	Yes	Yes
		Go.Web	Portal	Yes	Yes	N/A	No	No	Yes	N/A	N/A	N/A	Yes	Yes	Yes
Blackberry	Blackberry series	Blackberry series	Online, Offline, Push alerts	Yes	Yes	No	No	No	Yes	Yes	No	No	Yes	Yes	Yes
		Blackberry series	Online, Offline, Push alerts	Yes	Yes	Yes	No	No	Yes	N/A	No	No	Yes	Yes	Yes
Symbian	Psion Revo Plus	Psion Ravo Plus	Online	Yes	Yes	No	N/A	N/A	Yes	Yes	N/A	Yes	N/A	Yes	Yes

N/A: Data was not available

Table 20.1 Example of PDA Browsers

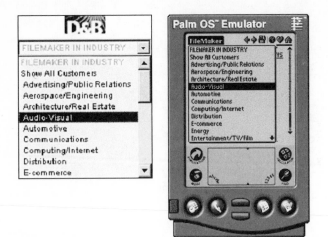

Figure 20.1b Audio-Visual selected from the list.

This example shows that using the same sequence on a browser running on Palm OS, will not work since it does not support the onChange-"jumpTo" command; hence, the user will not be able to navigate to a different page using the drop-list menu interface as designed.

Note that this example is not meant to show specifically whether the Web browser, Web site, or Web page is working correctly or incorrectly; it's merely intended to point out potential incompatibility that might exist. This type of incompatibility does not discriminate against browsers or Web sites.

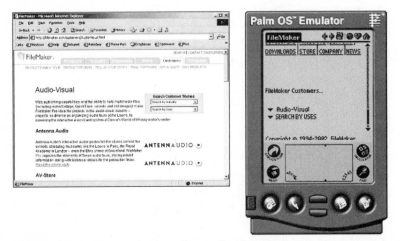

Figure 20.1c Upon selection, the Audio-Visual page displays properly in the desktop browser but not in the Palm OS browser.

Figures 20.2a, 20.2b, 20.2c, and 20.2d show another example of how various Web browsers display the same Web page differently. Although the Web page is functional in all cases, notice that the browsers format the images differently: Palmscape scales the Hot Jobs GIF (Graphics Interchange Format) while the others do not; the banner ad GIF is displayed in some but not in all.

Figure 20.2a   Yahoo.com in EudoraWeb 2.1(text-only browser).

Figure 20.2b   Yahoo.com in Palmscape 3.1.6E.

Figure 20.2c Yahoo.com in Blazer 2.0.

Figure 20.2d Yahoo.com in AvantGo 4.0.

Figures 20.3a, 20.3b, and 20.3c illustrate problems in the display of a Web page using three different browsers. In all cases, the browsers are capable of parsing the content. In the case of the desktop browser and the Palm-based browser that support HTML and WML, respectively, the content not only is parsed correctly but it is also useful. In the case of a Palm-based browser that does not support WML, it parsed the HTML content correctly but the display and format is not useful. Again, the point here is not to say that the Web site is at fault or that the browser is at fault. Perhaps, they all work as intended, or the operator and application producer don't support certain modes. The main idea here is to show you the potential problems you might encounter, or should look for, in testing your mobile Web applications.

Figure 20.3a   Lycos Home page in HTML displayed in Microsoft IE 6.0.

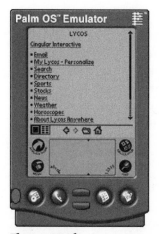

Figure 20.3b   Lycos Home page in WML displayed in a Palm-based browser that has support for WML.

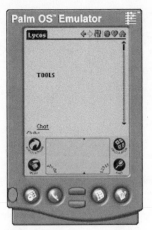

Figure 20.3c   Lycos Home page in WML displayed in a Palm-based browser that does not have support for WML.

Various Types of Tests

Add-on Installation Tests

Thick-client mobile devices such as PDAs and smart phones, offer secondary storage and the capability to install add-on software including the browser itself, other client-side components, and templates (such as the Web Clipping Applications for Palm OS-based devices). You need to consider the implications of the installation of these elements and design test cases to cover various installation scenarios, including cross operating systems, cross devices, cross releases of browsers, and so on. (See Chapter 16, "Installation Tests," for more information on this subject.)

Data Synchronization-Related Tests

Due to the fact that wireless bandwidth is limited, one of the common design solutions is to download Web content for offline browsing. This synchronization process can be done in two ways:

- The method for downloading data onto the mobile device that does not have a connection to the Internet or network is to synchronize with the desktop application. In this case, the desktop already has a connection to the Internet. In turn, Web content on the desktop can be transferred over to the device via a data synchronization process.

■ Synchronization can also be done wirelessly. The user synchronizes the device with a proxy server via a wireless modem connection. Preformatted Web pages stored on Web servers connected to the proxy server will be transferred to the device during the synchronization process. The user can browse the transferred Web pages, now stored on the device.

For example, AvantGo provides access to preformatted HTML pages that are loaded onto mobile devices for offline viewing in the AvantGo browser. Specifically designed HTML pages formatted for viewing on mobile devices can be organized into *channels*. AvantGo provides guidelines on creating compatible pages to developers. The finished pages reside on the Web server and are synchronized to the user's device via the AvantGo proxy server. Then the users can browse the stored pages as they would in any other Web browser. They can complete forms, add and delete pages, and refresh content on subsequent synchronization.

Conversely, the user can do real-time, online browsing during which Web pages can be retrieved via a direct wired or wireless connection between the device and the Web server. The browsed Web pages might be synchronized with the desktop at a later time. Although the Web application under test has little control over the synching mechanism, there are potential side effects of the behavior of the application that are related to data synchronization. For example, if you get a cookie by browsing a particular Web site, when you connect directly to that Web site, the cookie will be sent to the mobile client (assuming that it supports cookies). Later, when you go to the same site for offline content via the synchronization process with the desktop, the desktop version of the cookies for that Web site might be overwriting the version on the device, which is not desirable.

All of these scenarios should be considered in the test planning and test case design process.

UI Implementation and Limited Usability Tests

Some of the factors that affect the usability judgments include the target audience to which you market and the limitation of the devices, such as screen size, bandwidth, device-specific and Web site-specific technologies. Therefore, in testing for UI implementation and usability errors, questions you should consider asking include:

■ How do the data input methods on supported platforms affect usability?

■ How does the Web site under test appear in the browser with default settings for attributes such as page size, images, text size, and so on?

- How does the Web site under test appear in the browser with alternate settings (other than default) for attributes such as page size, images, text size, and so on?

- How does the network latency affect the functionality of the Web application under test? For example, while doing a transaction with a banking application over a slow connection, will the server time-out in the middle of the transaction? When that event occurs, what happens to the transaction?

- Is it useful to take advantage of tools to do testing for invalid WML and WMLScript syntax, missing links, missing images, unsupported contents, and the like?

- Does text-wrapping work properly?

- Is the navigation intuitive?

- Are the input interfaces consistent and friendly?

- Is there consistency among menu, button, and error-handling implementations?

- Are the graphics well fit and positioned in the display?

UI Guideline References

It is handy to have guidelines to follow during UI design and implementation. Your developers might use them to establish certain design principles for the application. This is not to say that such guidelines should be followed religiously; rather that you use the information as a *reference* to prevent your developers from having to "reinvent the wheel" for every UI design and implementation. Three online UI guideline resources worth checking out include:

Palm OS User Interface Guidelines. This document provides guidelines on user interface design for Palm OS applications. Go to: www.palmos.com/dev/support/ docs/ui.

MSDN Library User Interface Design and Development page. This page provides a lot of information on user interface design for Microsoft applications. Go to: http://msdn.microsoft.com/ui.

BREW User Interface Guideline. This document provides guidelines on user interface design for BREW applications. Go to: www.qualcomm .com/frew/developer/ developing/docs/90-D4231 A.pdf.

Browser-Specific Tests

All issues surrounding Web application testing on a desktop PC client are applicable to mobile Web application testing. Some of the browser-specific issues that are worth reiterating here, and for which you should develop test cases to seek out problems, include:

- *The side effects introduced by the application under test*, due to lack of support or incompatible support for cookies, scripts, plug-ins (e.g., Macromedia Flash), Java applet, ActiveX, Cascading Style Sheet (CSS), and secure connection using Secure Sockets Layer (SSL).

- *Incompatibility or lack of support for one or more markup languages*, such as HDML, WML, cHTML, xHTML, HTML, or XML.

- *Support for PQA or Web Clipping-based applications*, versus channel-based applications.

- *Legacy support issues*. For example, consider the previous version of your application's support for HDML. Now it supports WML but it must also carry users with browsers that understand DHTML only; therefore, dual-mode support must be in place.

- *Caching issue*. Cache memory stores Web content temporarily, on the browser-side, server-side, or both. For example, with cache turned on (you can usually vary the size of your cache) on the client- or browser-side, when you go to a Web page, that page will be stored on your hard disk, in a cache file. Later, when you go to that Web page again, the browser will look in cache memory. If it finds that page there, it will get the page from the cache rather than from the original Web server, saving time and reducing network traffic. Sometimes it affects the testing or the functionality of a Web application in this way: the browser will not get the latest code or content from the original server timely, leading to undesirable results.

Platform-Specific Tests

When your company develops an application for a particular platform, such as Windows, UNIX, MacOS, Palm Computing, or Windows PocketPC, you need to execute these tests to seek out bugs that are platform-specific rather than functionality-specific. For example, on the Windows platform, incorrectly removing a DLL or updating a registry key can cause a platform-specific error. When your application behaves as expected on a target platform, it is considered to be compatible with that platform.

Although the scope and depth of platform-specific testing will be dictated by the test requirements or objectives, this type of test is often standardized, and several vendor-driven standards for mobile applications are available today. Samples of these standards are described in the following subsections.

Platform or Logo Compliance Tests

When a hardware producer licenses an operating system or platform software to be embedded in a mobile device, the licensers often ask the producers or licensees to conduct platform compliance tests to make sure that the device software implementation follows the licenser's standard, meaning it will be compatible with other OS-related components and software applications. The same process may also apply to a software producer that releases its application for a target device or platform. Most operating system and platform vendors have public test plans that document these standard tests, and make them available on their Web sites for downloading. The Microsoft Logo Certification standard test plan for various Windows platforms is an example of platform compliance tests. You may download the test plans by going to: http://msdn .microsoft.com/ certification/download.asp#plans.

In some cases, your company might have a contractual obligation to run these certification tests; but more often than not, running the tests is optional. In fact, the Web application under test only uses the facilities provided by the client device, in this case, the browser. Regardless, studying these standard tests might give you useful ideas for creating test cases, to exercise areas of the application that might be subject to platform-specific errors.

Configuration and Compatibility Tests

Using an emulator (see the "Device and Browser Emulators" section for more information), you can cover the basic functional testing. Others might have to be conducted on the physical device. It means that on the client-side you will be dealing with:

- Cross devices
- Cross operating systems including standards and OEMs
- Cross browsers
- Cross versions
- Cross languages (if required)
- Graphic formats
- Sound formats

To familiarize yourself with compatibility issues, go to www.nttdocomo .co/jp/englishy/i/tag/imodetag.html, where you will find a document titled "Outline of i-Mode compatible HTML." It describes compatibility issues as they present in HTML: content- and device-specific issues, such as special characters, number of characters per page, image file compatibility, screen size, color resolution, cache size, and so on.

Connectivity Tests

Connectivity tests involve seeking out errors related to how the device and the network can be connected to each other; and while being connected, how interference during data transmissions can cause functionality, as well as data integrity, failures. Aspects to consider are described in the following subsections.

Devices with Peripheral Network Connections

These devices, which include 802.11b, Bluetooth, and IR, examine the following:

- How does the device deal with initiating a network connection?
- How often does it time-out?
- Is the time-out setting configurable? How do the connection settings (for example, disconnect every five minutes) affect the behavior of the mobile Web application under test?
- How do time-out conditions affect the application functionality or data in transit?

Latency

Messages transmitted across the network take time to reach their destinations. Depending on the size of the message, the data transfer rate, the reliability and the coverage of the wireless network, there will be delays in the transmission process. The question is, how well does the application keep track and inform the users of these delays?

In addition, it is possible that the messages will be delivered some time after they were sent due to long delays caused by interference, such as network congestion or by the device going to sleep. Therefore, consider checking whether the application keeps track of the state of the transmission, to ensure that users are aware when the information (such as a stock quote) is outdated, due to delay, and when it is current.

Transmission Errors

As indicated earlier, data transferred over the wireless network are subject to interference. Therefore, content transmitted by the client device and the server might be altered due to the interference or latency. Wireless network protocols often will be able to detect and correct many errors; however, at the application level, your developer will need to come up with an error-handling scheme to address various types of transmission errors.

For example, different network carriers handle data transmission errors differently. Certain carriers are designed to continually resend at different times until the message reaches the client application. Some will alert the users about the failure and leave it to them to decide whether to resend the message. Others might just drop the message altogether without any notification to the users. Differences in the implementation might have an effect on the data transmitted by your mobile Web application under test.

Transitions from Coverage to No-Coverage Areas

While connected to the server, the device might be transporting from an area with good coverage to one that has no coverage. The mobile Web application should treat this condition similarly to other conditions that cause transmission errors, as discussed earlier.

For example, say that on the server-side, the application is checking the status of the connection every 30 seconds, and 10 seconds into the last check, the device is transported from a good-coverage area to a no-coverage area and 15 seconds later, it is back to the good-coverage area. At the next check, the application determines that the connection is still good, without knowing that there is a 15-second gap in which the connection was lost. This gap might put the application into an unknown state that causes functionality failures or data integrity problems.

Transitions between Data and Voice

How does the device handle incoming data while on a voice call, and vice versa? On many carrier networks and mobile phones, you cannot have a voice conversation and access the Web via TCP/IP at the same time. Interruptions during data transmissions by incoming calls might introduce erroneous conditions that the mobile Web application under test does not know how to handle.

Data or Message Race Condition

Different network carriers have different methods of sending a series of messages between the client and the server. Don't rely on the carrier to send messages in the same order that was sent from the mobile Web client. Check to make sure the application under test has its own implementation, to protect data integrity.

Performance Tests

Many performance testing issues discussed in Chapter 19, "Performance Testing," are applicable to testing mobile Web applications.

When testing your gateway, such as a WAP gateway, which translates protocols from HTTP to WSP (Wireless Session Protocol in WAP), or SSL and WTLS (Wireless Transport Layer Security), and vice versa, make sure that the test tool has support for those protocols.

Figure 20.4 shows an example of a Web request and response via a WAP gateway. It also illustrates the additional activities that occurred at the WAP gateway:

1. When the mobile user makes a request, a WSP request is sent to the WAP gateway.

2. The WAP gateway, in turn, converts the encoded WSP request into an HTTP request.

3. From there, the HTTP (or HTTPS, if SSL is used) request is sent to the Web/App server, just as in the standard Web architecture.

4. When the Web server responds with Web contents, such as HTML, WML, or WMLScript, the WAP gateway performs HTTP-to-WSP header conversion, HTML-to-WML conversion, graphics formats conversions (e.g., GIF to WBMP), WML encoding, WMLScript compilation, and so on.

5. The WAP gateway then sends a WSP response with encoded content to the mobile client.

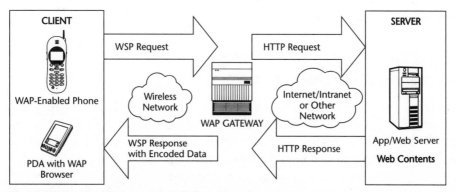

Figure 20.4   The WAP model of Web request/response.

Other considerations include the tool's capability to emulate limited bandwidth in the 2G/3G network environments, and additional features for handling scripts, cookies, and other features.

Security Tests

Refer to Chapter 18, "Web Security Testing," for discussions of many testing issues to consider at the application level, for many of the vulnerabilities in Web sites, Web applications, and software applications also exist in mobile Web applications. Furthermore, a host of new security issues inherent to the mobile environment involve both the client mobile device and the wireless network.

Mobile devices such as PDAs were originally designed for managing personal information; they were not meant to be communication devices that would use a network to connect with other servers. Consequently, in the early days, there was little focus put on security for these devices. It's also known that mobile devices inherently have limited processing power for strong encryption handling and solid password security. Wireless LAN, such as the 802.11b standard, is still in its infancy; therefore, data is transmitted with insufficient encryption. Of course, these issues are being addressed as this book goes to press. The problem is that we continue to push the use of the mobile device and wireless infrastructure to deliver more data and applications beyond its normal capabilities and resources. This raises the question: Will new functionality development slow down long enough to enable security to catch up? It remains to be seen. In the meantime, the best practice is to make sure that we understand the security implications and raise them in an appropriate and timely fashion so that decisions can be made according to the risk-based analysis with the data provided.

For example, we should make sure that the mobile Web browser and gateway (if any) perform SSL certificate realm and expiration validation correctly before connecting to the secure Web server. This problem is known to exist in production WAP systems.

Testing Web Applications Using an Emulation Environment

When your mobile Web application is ready, a good way to start testing the application is to use a mobile device emulator. Fortunately, with emulators, many basic types of tests, including acceptance testing and functionality-specific testing, can be conducted without many physical devices. An added benefit is that there will be no charge for connect time during testing. For information on the various types of mobile device emulators available, and how to get them, refer to the section "Survey of Mobile Testing Support Tools" later in this chapter.

Testing Web Applications Using the Physical Environment

Unfortunately, because there are many classes of errors that emulators fail to catch, it is also necessary to test using the physical devices themselves, to ensure that the mobile Web application under test works correctly. Emulators typically can't emulate: actual network speed and availability, actual device-specific content-rendering speed, memory limitation, cache size, CPU speed, and stack size.

Especially for phone-based devices such as WAP-phones, it is only by testing with the actual device and with the network upon which the device relies to access the Web servers and WAP servers directly or via a WAP gateway that you can verify that the application will work properly within the production environment. This is often known as *integration testing*. Another benefit of working with the device is that it enables you to test for usability-related issues such as data entry or UI navigation using the device keypad.

Phone-based devices also raise additional issues, beyond those of a typical PDA or smart phone. For one, unlike PDAs and smart phones, the mobile screen is typically a lot smaller, hence imposes greater restriction on the display size. Therefore, the same Web content might display properly on one phone but not on another. Also, network latency will introduce long response times; and the keyboard or keypad on a phone is cumbersome and slow to use for navigation and data entry. That said, a T9-enabled ("text on 9 keys" input technology) phone does improve the process of entering text via the mobile phone keypad. (For more information on AOL's T9 Text Input, go to: www .t9.com.)

Other testing considerations for WAP-based microbrowsers in the phone include:

- Compatibility across handsets or devices, browsers, WAP gateways and WAP servers, HDML, WML, and WMLScript versions. Table 20.2 lists a sample of the differences in support between HDML and WML that can lead to incompatibility issues.

- Script compatibility with many other devices, since WAP-based clients are hardware-dependent.

- Usability of WML pages displayed in a rather small screen.

- Backward compatibility with different WAP specifications (WAP specifications can be found at the WAP Forum: www.wapforum.org/what/ technical.htm.)

- Unsupported graphic formats. For example, the device might support WBMP (Wireless Bitmap) but not others.

- Device-specific screen resolutions, maximum graphic sizes, unsupported code and extensions on certain phones.

Table 20.2   Example of Differences between HDML and WML

Attributes/Supports	HDML	WML
XML-based	No	Yes
Document Type Definition (DTD)	No	Yes
Scripting	No	WMLScript
Timers	No	Yes
Multiple Selection Lists	No	Yes
Bookmarks	Yes	No[1]
Nested Activities	Yes	No[2]
Images in Labels/Selections	Yes	No[2]
Key Accelerators for Links	Yes	No[2]

[1]UP.Browser supports this feature via WML meta tag.
[2]UP.Browser 4.0 supports this via WML extended tag.

Source: www.allnetdevices.com

NOTE Additional examples of differences among WAP phones can be found at www.cellular.co.za/wap_browser_spec.htm.

Just as emulator-based testing has limitations, there are downsides to testing with the physical devices. Primarily, it can be expensive, especially in compatibility testing, for which you need to test with many different models of the devices that your mobile Web application supports.

Survey of Mobile Testing Support Tools

Chapter 21, "Web Testing Tools," discusses testing support tools, most of which are applicable for testing mobile Web applications. In addition, due to the unique nature of mobile Web application testing, which depends greatly on the client hardware, it is useful to have emulators to help test the application prior to the actual deployment on the physical device. Two useful types of emulators are *device emulators* and *browser emulators*.

Device and Browser Emulators

Most vendors that license their operating systems or development platforms offer a device emulator. Since the devices are OS-based, given the same operating system, you might be able to emulate different types of devices by changing the *skin*. The term *skin* (most commonly used in the mobile phone world) is used to describe the capability to change the outside (the "skin") of a device, while leaving the inside (the operating system) the same, to give you a different device. As discussed in the "Testing Web Applications Using an Emulation Environment" section, you can see the benefits of having the various emulators available.

Palm Computing

Palm Computing offers POSE, Palm OS Emulator software that emulates the hardware of the various models of Palm-powered handhelds. This is a useful tool for developing, testing, and debugging Palm OS-based applications. POSE itself does not do anything; to make use of it, you must install a device-specific ROM to emulate a specific handheld. Think of POSE as a mobile device or a computer with no operating system. The ROM that you pick to install is the specific operating system the emulated device will use. In addition, you may also use a specific skin with the emulator. POSE, like other emulators, uses so-called skin files to present the image of a handheld. Originally, the skin is simply a graphic. It does not change the ROM or the handheld being emulated; it simply changes the appearance of the Emulator window. (Note that the default skin for POSE is the PalmPilot version 1.0.). If you need to have POSE emulate the look of the actual device under test, you will also need to obtain the device-specific skin. Increasingly, the skin selection also determines the specifics of the target hardware features being emulated (not just the look of the device).

Another very useful part of POSE is called "Gremlins," an automated testing tool. It performs extra integrity checks of the applications and the OS, such as memory access, stack overflow, and so on, that cannot be performed on the real hardware.

For more information, and to download POSE and the various device-specific ROMs, go to www.palmos.com/dev/tools/emulator.

OpenWave

OpenWave offers the UP.SDK, which includes the phone emulator that you can use to test phone-specific compatibility with WML and legacy HDML; you can test your application with the generic emulator UI, as well as with a specific skin of a specific phone that supports the UP.Browser.

To get more information and to download UP.SDK, go to: http://developer.openwave.com/download/.

Nokia

Like OpenWave, Nokia offers SDKs and emulators to help develop and test applications, including mobile Web browser-based applications for the company's wireless phones.

To get more information, and to download emulators, go to the Nokia Forum at www.forum.nokia.com/.

YoSpace

YoSpace delivers WAP emulators, as well as J2EE MIDP (Mobile Information Device Profile) emulators, that can be used to support the testing of mobile Web applications. One of the nice features of WAP emulators is their capability to emulate multiple WAP-based devices simultaneously, making it possible to both test and compare the rendering and formatting of the same content over different emulators. The SmartPhone Emulator Developer Edition also supports a scripting system called SPEScript, which enables programmatic control of the WAP emulator. You can write scripts to simulate user events or user interaction with the emulator. This is essential for automating the testing mobile Web applications through the use of the WAP emulator.

To get more information, and to download, go to the YoSpace Web site at www.yospace.com/.

Microsoft

Microsoft offers its version of emulators as part of the Pocket PC 2002 SDK. Pocket PC 2002 SDK Device Emulator Images are also available. These are Emulator language-specific files that enable basic testing for applications developed to be distributed internationally.

For more information, and to download, go to Microsoft's Web site at www .microsoft.com/mobile/developer/downloads.

Web-Based Mobile Phone Emulators and WML Validators

For Web-based mobile phone emulators and WML validators, visit these sites:

- *www.gelon.net/*. Offers Wapalizer, which enables you to do syntax and other checking and Web browser testing for your WML pages. It provides several WAP phone emulators that you can use to do basic testing for your WML content.

- *WAPman*. Similar to Gelon.net, Wapsilon offers a Web-based browser for WML content.

Desktop WAP Browsers

Several microbrowser emulators are available, including WAP browsers that can be used to test your mobile Web applications for WAP specific issues.

- *WinWAP*. A WAP browser that runs on various versions of the Microsoft Windows operating systems, including 9x, NT, 2000, and XP. It is available at www.winwap.org.

- *WAPman*. A WAP browser available for several platforms, including Palm OS and various versions of the Windows OS. For more information and downloading, go to www.edgematrix.com.

Other Testing Considerations

- How do the test devices manage their cache? Is it user-configurable? Are the parameters known? Specific instructions may need to be presented somewhere in the test plan for each device concerning these issues.

- How do you determine the expected results for the way content is displayed across platforms and browsers? What are the guidelines, if any?

- External links: How are they handled in offline browsing?

- "E-mail to" and "Phone-dial" links: Are they supported on the test platforms? Is error handling on unsupported browsers being checked?

- Memory-full testing or stress testing: How do you execute memory-full and near-full test cases on the test platforms?

- How do you write generic test scripts that will apply to the various platforms?

- How do you write reusable test cases for different devices?

- What do you need to know about the way the different test platforms are accessing the Web content (Palm device accesses HTML directly, phone A goes through WAP gateway, phone B goes through cHTML proxy, etc.)? How will it affect your testing?

- HTTP or WAP protocols allow files in different formats to download onto the client device. What happens when a device attempts to download an unsupported file format?

- If your Web site supports multiple formats, including WML, i-Mode, and HTML, which rules does a browser use to determine which content to load?

- Does the browser properly interpret tables, frames, lists, checkboxes, drop-downs, scripts, and so on?

- Some sites recognize the browser version to determine compatibility. Are you checking for compatibility?

Bibliography and Additional Resources

Bibliography

Arehart, Charles, et al. *Professional WAP*. Birmingham, UK: Wrox Press Inc., 2000.

Collins, Daniel, and Clint Smith. *3G Wireless Networks*. New York: McGraw-Hill Professional, 2001.

Garg, Vijay Kumar. *Wireless Network Evolution: 2G to 3G*. Upper Saddle River, NJ: Prentice-Hall PTR, 2001.

Lin, Yi-Bing, and Imrich Chlamtac. *Wireless and Mobile Network Architectures*. New York: John Wiley & Sons, Inc., 2000.

Rhodes, Neil, and Julie McKeehan. *Palm OS Programming: The Developer's Guide*, 2nd ed. Sebastopol, CA: O'Reilly & Associates, 2001.

Additional Resources

QACity.Com | Mobile

www.qacity.com/Technology/Mobile

i-Mode Tools

www.devx.com/wireless/articles/I-Mode/I-ModeTools.asp

Mobile Information Device Profile (MIDP)

http://java.sun.com/products/midp/

WAP Tutorials

www.palowireless.com/wap/tutorials.asp

WAP Devices Metrics

www.wapuseek.com/wapdevs.cfm

WAP FAQs

www.wapuseek.com/wapfaq.cfm

WAP Testing Papers

   www.nccglobal.com/testing/mi/whitepapers/index.htm

WAP Testing Tools

   http://palowireless.com/wap/testtools.asp

Online WAP Testing Tool

   www.wapuseek.com/checkwap.cfm

i-Mode FAQ

   www.eurotechnology.com/imode/faq.html

i-Mode FAQ for Developers

   www.mobilemediajapan.com/imodefaq

i-Mode-Compatible HTML

   www.nttdocomo.co.jp/English/i/tag/imodetag.html

Compact HTML for Small Information Appliances

   www.w3.org/TR/1998/NOTE-compactHTML-19980209/

Mobile Software Resources (for i-Mode/HTML development)

   www.mobilemediajapan.com/resources/software

Mobile Technology Resources

   www.mobilemediajapan.com/resources/technology

Mobile Computing Magazine (news magazine for mobile computing)

   www.mobilecomputing.com

Pen Computing Magazine

   www.pencomputing.com

mBusiness Magazine (wireless technology magazine and books)

   www.mbusinessdaily.com

Internet.Com Wireless Page

   www.internet.com/sections/wireless.html

GSM, TDMA, CDMA, and GPRS.

www.wirelessdevnet.com/newswire-less/feb012002.html

Developer Resources Page on pencomputing.com

www.pencomputing.com/developer/

mpulse-nooper.com (an article: "Application Testing in the Mobile Space")

http://cooltown.hp.com/mpulse/0701-developer.asp

Nokia Forum

www.forum.nokia.com

YoSpaces's Emulator

www.yospace.com

WinWAP (mobile Internet browser for Windows)

www.winwap.org/index.html

Web-based WAP Emulator: TTemulator

www.winwap.org

HDML or WML

www.allnetdevices.com/developer/tutorials/2000/06/09/
hdml_or.html

CHAPTER

21

Web Testing Tools

Why Read This Chapter?

Web applications operate in dynamic environments. Occasionally, testing tools are required to complement manual testing efforts. Some test types (e.g., load and performance testing) would be impractical to perform without the help of tools to simulate the actions of thousands of users. The value of various tools varies according to the specific testing needs, budget, and staffing constraints associated with the system under test.

TOPICS COVERED IN THIS CHAPTER

- ◆ Introduction
- ◆ Types of Tools
- ◆ Additional Resources

Introduction

This chapter describes various types of Web testing tools, how the tools are used, and where the tools can be acquired. Many of the software vendors listed in this chapter offer evaluation copies of their products. Return-on-investment calculations (both short-term and long-term) can help you decide which tool makes the most sense for your particular project.

Types of Tools

Following are lists of various Web testing tools and descriptions of each.

Rule-Based Analyzers

Type: Static analyzer (Note: The notion of *static analyzer* means that the code does not have to be compiled and executed.)

Input: Source (code)

Output: Various analytical and error reports

Primary user: Developer

Secondary user: Tester

Technology principle. This type of tool reads the input source and compares the written code with the coding standards or language-specific rules in an effort to uncover inconsistencies and potential errors. They are, in some ways, comparable with grammar and spell checkers found in word processors.

In some cases, the tool also includes an agent or a *bot* (short for *robot*) that simulates human activities, accessing commands such as hyperlinks in HTML pages. On the content side of Web development, the two common rule-based analyzers are HTML validators and link checkers. Often they are fully integrated into commercial-off-the-shelf products.

Sample List of Link Checkers and HTML Validators

These tools check for bad links and HTML tags, browser compatibility (to a certain extent), dead links, popular links, load time, page design, spelling errors, and so on.

WATCHFIRE LINKBOT PRO

Description: Link checker and HTML validator incorporated into an enterprise solution that manages complex and dynamic enterprise Web sites.

Source: Watchfire

Platform: Windows

Evaluation copy: Yes

Address: www.watchfire.com

PARASOFT WEB KING

Description: Link checker, HTML validator in a complete development and testing management tool.

Source: ParaSoft

Platform: Windows, Linux, and Sun Solaris

Evaluation copy: No, but free demo scan using Web King: available

Address: www.parasoft.com

MACROMEDIA HOMESITE

Description: A code-only editor for Web development that includes a link checker and HTML validator (HTML Editor).

Source: Homesite 5

Platform: Windows

Evaluation copy: Yes

Address: www.macromedia.com/software/homesite/

XENU'S LINK SLEUTH

Description: This is an excellent link checker and it's free. The QACity team uses this utility every day to test this site. The authors have done the work for you and have provided a comparison of link checkers to help you select the utility that works best for you.

Source: N/A

Platform: Windows

Evaluation copy: N/A

Address: home.snafu.de/tilman/xenulink.html

DR. WATSON

Description: Dr. Watson is a free service you can use to analyze your Web page on the Internet. You give it the URL of your page and Dr. Watson will get a copy of it directly from the Web server. Watson can also check out many other aspects of your site, including link validity, download speed, search engine compatibility, and link popularity. (Note: This service has nothing to do with the Dr. Watson that comes with Microsoft Windows products.)

Source: Addy & Associates

Platform: N/A

Evaluation copy: N/A

Address: watson.addy.com

Sample List of Rule-Based Analyzers for C/C++, Java, Visual Basic, and Other Programming and Scripting Languages

These tools generally check for bad syntax, logic, and other language-specific programming errors at the source level. This level of testing is often referred to as *unit testing* and *server component testing.* The developer executes this testing.

REASONING ILLUMA

Description: Code inspection service for high-reliability C and C++ code.

Source: Reasoning

Platform: N/A

Evaluation copy: N/A

Address: www.reasoning.com

TEST CENTER

Description: Source code analysis for C and C++.

Source: Center Line

Platform: Sun-4/SPARC stations, UltraSPARC HP 700 Series, HP 800 (PA 1.1), IBM RS600 workstations

Evaluation copy: No

Address: www.centerline.com/productline.html

PARASOFT CODEWIZARD

Description: Source code analysis, C/C++.

Source: ParaSoft

Platform: UNIX and Windows

Evaluation copy: Yes

Address: www.parasoft.com

PARASOFT JTEST

Description: Source code analyzer with automation features for test case design and test execution, Java.

Source: ParaSoft

Platform: Windows

Evaluation copy: Yes

Address: www.parasoft.com

Load/Performance Testing Tools

Type: Web-load simulator and performance analysis

Input: Simulated user requests

Output: Various performance and analytical reports

Primary user: Tester

Secondary user: Developer

Technology principle. This type of tool enables you to simulate thousands of users accessing the Web site/application, requesting data, and submitting transactions, in addition to other e-commerce and e-business activities. Virtual load can also simulate various versions of Web browsers and network bandwidth. While the simulated load is applied to the server, performance data is collected and plotted in several useful report formats for further analysis. (See Chapter 19, "Performance Testing," for more information on this type of test.)

Web Load and Performance Testing Tools

These tools generate test scripts by recording user activities and combining them with scripting languages. They can spawn multiple threads, each thread running a specific test script or scenario to simulate real-world requests being sent to the servers. Performance metrics such as response time and data throughput can be tracked and reported in tabular as well as graphical formats for performance analysis.

EMPIRIX ELOAD

Description: Load, performance, and scalability testing.

Source: Empirix

Platform: Windows

Evaluation copy: Yes

Address: www.rswsoftware.com

COMPUWARE QACENTER PERFORMANCE EDITION

Description: Load, performance, and scalability testing.

Source: Compuware

Platform: PC/Windows; IBM mainframe/OS/390/MVS/VM

Evaluation copy: Yes

Address: www.compuware.com/products/qacenter/performance/

XML LOAD TESTING

Description: ANTS Load testing and code profiling .NET appsSource: Red-gate

Platform: Windows

Evaluation copy: Yes

Address: www.red-gate.com/advanced_dotnet_testing_system.htm

MERCURY INTERACTIVE APPLICATION PERFORMANCE MANAGEMENT

Description: Load, performance, and scalability testing.

Source: Mercury Interactive

Platform: Windows

Evaluation copy: Yes

Address: www.mercuryinteractive.com

SEGUE SILKPERFORMERS

Description: Load, performance, and scalability testing.

Source: Segue

Platform: Windows

Evaluation copy: Yes

Address: www.segue.com

LOADTESTING.COM PORTENT

Description: Load, performance, and scalability testing.

Source: LoadTesting.Com

Platform: Java (Tested with Windows 9x, NT, 2000, Linux, and Solaris x86)

Evaluation copy: Yes

Address: www.loadtesting.com

WEBPARTNER STRESS TESTING

Description: Load, performance, and scalability testing

Source: WebPartner

Platform: Web-based

Evaluation copy: Yes

Address: www.webpartner.com/st_main.html

GUI Capture (Recording/Scripting) and Playback Tools

Description: Captured user activities are played back, enabling unattended functionality and regression testing.

Input: Recorded/scripted events or messages applied on GUI controls

Output: Error logs indicating discrepancies discovered during playback

Primary user: Tester

Secondary user: Developer

Technology principle. This type of tool enables you to consistently rerun repetitive test cases with little to no human interaction. These tools have the capability to recognize GUI controls such as form buttons, tables, links, Java applets, and so on, in Web browser pages. During the capturing phase, these tools track input events (generally from keyboard and mouse) as they are applied to specific GUI control objects. The events represent user activities and are converted into scripts that, at a later time, the playback engine will use as input to replay the prerecorded activities. The event-capturing process can also be done via scripting. During playback, the program-state information, as well as output results (whether data or user interface settings), are compared with the original results. If there is any discrepancy, the tool makes the condition known. Keep in mind that to fully utilize the capability of this type of tool, a significant amount of training and planning is required. Otherwise, the return on investment (or lack thereof) may be disappointing.

Sample List of Automated GUI Functional and Regression Testing Tools

These tools generate test scripts by recording user activities and combining them with scripting languages. The recorded or scripted events can then be played back repeatedly. This type of tool is also commonly used for acceptance tests and functionality-regression tests, because the test cases are so well defined.

MERCURY INTERACTIVE WINRUNER

Description: Automated GUI functional and regression testing tool.

Source: Mercury Interactive

Platform: Windows

Evaluation copy: Yes

Address: www.mercuryinteractive.com

SEGUE SILKTEST

Description: Automated GUI functional and regression testing tool.

Source: Segue

Platform: Windows

Evaluation copy: Yes

Address: www.segue.com

RATIONAL (IBM) VISUALTEST

Description: Load, performance, and scalability testing.

Source: Rational

Platform: Windows

Evaluation copy: Yes

Address: www.rational.com

MANUFACTURER'S CORBA INTERFACE TESTING TOOLKIT

Description: Automatic Testing of Interfaces.

Source: NIST

Platform: Solaris, NT; adaptable to any

Evaluation copy: Yes

Address: www.mel.nist.gov/msidstaff/flater/mcitt/

COMPUWARE QACENTER ENTERPRISE EDITION

Description: Automated GUI functional and regression testing.

Source: Compuware

Platform: PC/DOS/OS/390/MVS/VM /PC/Win95/98/NT/AS400/
IBM mainframe

Evaluation copy: Yes

Address: www.compuware.com/products/qacenter/qarun/

EMPIRIX ETESTER

Description: Automated GUI functional and regression testing.

Source: RSW Software

Platform: Windows

Evaluation copy: Yes

Address: www.rswsoftware.com

Runtime Error Detectors

Type: Dynamic analyzer (Note: Code needs to be compiled and executed before dynamic analyzers can catch errors.)

Input: Execution of test cases

Output: Trap and track runtime errors

Primary user: Developer

Secondary user: Tester

Technology principle. This type of tool either inserts its code into the production code prior to compilation and execution or it tracks memory read/write activities between the program (and its components) and the operating system. During the execution of the program, it looks for invalid and erroneous operations that are requested by the application so that the errors can be trapped and reported. This type of tool catches errors like memory overwrites, memory leaks, read errors, and memory double-freezes. Without a way of tracking such errors, memory-related bugs are difficult to reproduce.

Memory is a dynamic environment condition. When there is an error such as a memory overwrite problem, the symptoms from the black-box testing perspective may vary from nothing happening at all to a total system crash. This is due to the fact that the environment required for the error symptom to expose itself varies. This type of tool helps detect errors at the source level rather than at the symptomatic level.

Sample List of Runtime Error-Detection Tools

These tools check memory and operating system API-specific errors.

RATIONAL (IBM) PURIFY

Description: Detecting memory-related and other errors at runtime.

Source: Rational

Platform: Windows NT and UNIX

Evaluation copy: Yes

Address: www.rational.com

PARASOFT INSURE PLUSPLUS

Description: Detecting memory-related and other errors at runtime.

Source: ParaSoft

Platform: UNIX and Windows

Evaluation copy: Yes

Address: www.parasoft.com

ONYX Q

Description: Memory runtime error detection and stress testing.

Source: Onyx Technology

Platform: Macintosh

Evaluation copy: Yes

Address: www.onyx-tech.com

MICROQUILL HEAP AGENT

Description: Detecting memory-related and other errors at runtime.

Source: MicroQuill

Platform: Windows

Evaluation copy: Yes

Address: www.microquill.com

COMPUWARE BOUNDSCHECKER

Description: Detecting memory-related and other errors at runtime.

Source: Compuware

Platform: Windows

Evaluation copy: Yes

Address: www.compuware.com

Sample List of Web Security Testing Tools

These tools can be used to detect and analyze potential security issues in a network or Web application.

SURFINGATE FIREWALLS

Description: Personal firewall detects malicious VBScript, Java, JavaScript, and ActiveX applications. SurfinGate provides proactive security for active Web content and can block new or known attacks.

Source: Finjan Software

Platform: Windows

Evaluation copy: Yes

Address: www.finjan.com

NETSCAN TOOLS

Description: Traditional UNIX network tools ported for use on Windows systems.

Source: Northwest Performance Software, Inc.

Platform: Windows

Evaluation copy: No

Address: www.nwpsw.com

WINDOWS TASK LOCK

Description: Controls access to applications.

Source: Posum Software Security Technologies

Platform: Windows

Evaluation copy: Yes

Address: www.posum.com

WEBTRENDS SECURITY ANALYZER

Description: Analyzes Internet and intranet for security problems.

Source: Webtrends

Platform: Windows, Solaris, Linux

Evaluation copy: Yes

Address: www.webtrends.com/products/wsa/

NETWORK TOOLBOX

Description: Suite of tools for analyzing security weaknesses on Windows systems.

Source: J. River

Platform: Windows

Evaluation copy: Yes

Address: www.jriver.com/products/network-toolbox.html

Java-Specific Testing Tools

These tools are used for testing Java applications only.

COMPUWARE QACENTER ENTERPRISE EDITION

Description: Enables testing teams to define their own support for customized Java controls.

Source: Compuware

Platform: PC/DOS/OS/390/MVS/VM/PC/Win95/98/NT/AS400/ IBM mainframe

Evaluation copy: Yes

Address: www.compuware.com/products/qacenter/qarun/

JPROBE SUITE

Description: The JProbe Suite contains a profiler, memory debugger, thread analyzer, and coverage tool.

Source: Quest Software

Evaluation copy: Yes

Address: java.quest.com/jprobe/jprobe.shtml

JUNIT

Description: JUnit is a Java-based regression testing framework designed for developers.

Source: Open Source

Evaluation copy: Yes

Address: www.junit.org

Other Types of Useful Tools

- Development/test management tools
- Code-based performance and profiling tools
- Code-based coverage analyzers

Database Testing Tools

These comprise tools and utilities for testing databases.

PRINCETON SOFTECH'S RELATIONAL TOOLS

Description: Princeton Softech's Relational Tools enable you to extract, edit, and compare comprehensive subsets of related data. By improving test data management with RT, you can produce quality applications, on time and within budget.

Source: Princeton Softech

Platform: MVS, OS/390, Windows 95/98/NT/2000

Evaluation copy: Yes

Address: princetonsoftech.com/products/relationaltools.htm

DATATECH

Description: A software program used for generating and outputting a variety of test data to ASCII flat files or directly to RDBMS, including Oracle, Sybase, SQL Server, and Informix.

Source: Banner Software

Platform: Windows

Evaluation copy: Yes

Address: www.datatect.com

Defect Management Tool Vendors

Tools offered by these vendors allow software development teams (testing, project management, development, marketing, and others) to effectively communicate and manage defect-related issues.

LOGIGEAR CORPORATION

Description: Defect Management.

Source: LogiGear Corporation

Platform: Windows/Web-based

Evaluation copy: Yes

Address: www.logigear.com/products/trackgear.html

QACity.Com Comprehensive List of DEFECT TRACKING Tool Vendors

Address: www.qacity.com/Other+Resources/Tools+Utilities/
Defect+ Management+Tool+Vendors/Links.htm

Additional Resources

On the Internet

xProgramming.com

An Extreme Programming resource with link to xUnit test framework Web site and links: www.xprogramming.com/software.htm

DBMS Online Buyer's Guide Testing and Software Quality

A compilation of various software testing tools, including Web and load testing tools: www.dbmsmag.com/pctest.html

Rick Hower's Software QA/Test Resource Center—The Software QA Software Testing Tool Page

This page offers links to information on various software engineering and testing tools: www.softwareqatest.com/qattls1.html

The Original Brian Marick's Testing Tool Suppliers List

This list was originally compiled by Brian Marick, but is now maintained by Danny Faught. The information comes directly from vendors' e-mail submissions: www.testingfaqs.org/tools.htm

LogiGear Corporation

The producer of TRACKGEAR, the Web-based issue-tracking and resolution management solution, offers information on testing tools, software testing training, and outsourced testing services: www .logigear.com or www.qacity.com.

Development and Testing Tool Mail-Order Catalogs

These catalogs supply development and testing tools:

Programmer's Paradise, Internet Paradise, and Components Paradise

www.pparadise.com

The Programmer's Supershop Buyer's Guide

www.supershops.com

VBxtras

www.vbxtras.com

CHAPTER

22

Finding Additional Information

Why Read This Chapter?

Web technologies (and the testing methods that are appropriate for them) are evolving at a rapid rate. Inevitably, new technologies will become available after this book goes to print. This chapter will help you gain access to the most up-to-date information regarding Web-application testing.

TOPICS COVERED IN THIS CHAPTER

- ◆ Introduction
- ◆ Textbooks
- ◆ Web Resources
- ◆ Professional Societies

Introduction

This chapter lists textbooks, Web sites, and professional societies that are great sources of information for test-case design and Web-application test planning.

Textbooks

3G Wireless Networks, by D. Collins and C. Smith, McGraw-Hill Professional, 2001; ISBN: 0071363815.

About Face: The Essentials of User Interface Design, by A. Cooper, IDG Books Worldwide, 1995; ISBN: 1568843224.

Administrating Web Servers, Security, and Maintenance, by E. Larson and B. Stephens, Prentice-Hall, 1999; ISBN: 0130225347.

Beginning Active Server Pages 3.0, by D. Buser, et al., Wrox Press, 2000; ISBN: 1861003382.

Building Secure Software: How to Avoid Security Problems the Right Way, by J. Viega and G. McGraw, Addison Wesley, 2001; ISBN: 020172152X.

The Craft of Software Testing: Subsystems Testing Including Object-Based and Object-Oriented Testing, by B. Marick, Prentice-Hall, 1997; ISBN: 0131774115.

Designing Microsoft ASP.NET Applications, by D.J. Reilly, Microsoft Press, 2001; ISBN: 0735613486.

Designing Web Usability, by J. Nielsen, New Riders, 1999; ISBN: 156205810X.

Dynamic HTML: The Definitive Reference, by D. Goodman, O'Reilly and Associates, Inc., 1998; ISBN: 1565924940.

Exploring Expect, by D. Libes, : O'Reilly & Associates, 1994, ISBN: 1565920902.

Hacking Exposed: Network Security Secrets & Solutions, 3rd ed., by Stuart McClure, Joel Scambray and George Kurtz, McGraw-Hill, 2001, ISBN: 0072193816.

Information Architecture for the World Wide Web: Designing Large-Scale Web Sites, by L. Rosenfeld and P. Morville,: O'Reilly & Associates, 1998; ISBN: 1565922824.

Inside Server-Based Applications, by D. J. Reilly, Microsoft Press, 2000; ISBN: 1572318171.

Integrated Test Design and Automation, by Hans Buwalda, et al., Addison-Wesley, 2001, ISBN: 0201737256

Internetworking with TCP/IP: Client-Server Programming and Applications: Windows Sockets Version, Volume 3, by D. Comer and D. Stevens, Prentice-Hall, 1997, ISBN: 0138487146.

Internetworking with TCP/IP: Design, Implementation, and Internals, Volume 2, 2nd edition, by D. Comer and D. Stevens, Douglas, Prentice-Hall, 1994; ISBN: 0131255274.

Internetworking with TCP/IP: Principles, Protocols, and Architecture, Volume 1, by D. Comer, Prentice Hall, 1991; ISBN: 0134685059.

JavaScript Bible, by D. Goodman and B. Eich, IDG Books Worldwide, 1998; ISBN: 0764531883.

Learning Perl on Win32 Systems, by R. Schwartz et al., O'Reilly & Associates, ISBN: 1-56592-324-3.

Microsoft SQL Server 2000 Resource Kit, by Microsoft Corporation, Microsoft Press, 2001; ISBN: 0735612668.

Palm OS Programming: The Developer's Guide, 2nd ed., by N. Rhodes and J. McKeehan, O'Reilly & Associates, 2001; ISBN: 1565928563.

Palmpilot: The Ultimate Guide, 2nd ed., by D. Pogue and J. Hawkins, O'Reilly & Associates, 1999, ISBN: 1565926005.

Professional WAP, by C. Arehart, et al., Wrox Press Inc., 2000; ISBN: 1861004109.

Scaling for E-Business: Technologies, Models, Performance, and Capacity Planning, by D. Menasce and V. Almeida, Prentice-Hall, 2000, ISBN: 0130863289.

Software Test Automation: Effective Use of Test Execution Tools, by M. Fewster and D. Graham, ACM Press, 1999; ISBN: 0201331403.

SQL Server 7 Beginner's Guide, by D. Petkovic, McGraw-Hill, 1999, ISBN: 0072118911.

Testing Computer Software, 2nd ed., by C. Kaner, Jack Falk and Hung Nguyen, John Wiley & Sons, Inc., 1999. ISBN: 1850328471.

Tcl and the Tk Toolkit, by J. Ousterhouse, Addison-Wesley, 1994; ISBN: 020163337X.

The World of Scripting Languages, by D. Barron, John Wiley & Sons, Inc., 2002; ISBN: 0471998869.

UNIX C Shell Field Guide, by Gail Anderson and Paul Anderson, Prentice Hall, 1992; ISBN: 013937468X.

Wireless Network Evolution: 2G to 3G., Vijay Kumar Garg, Prentice-Hall PTR, 2001. ISBN: 0130280771.

Wireless and Mobile Network Architectures, by Y. Lin and I. Chlamtac,: John Wiley & Sons, Inc., 2000, ISBN: 0471394920.

Writing Secure Code, by M. Howard and D. LeBlanc, Microsoft, 2002; ISBN: 0735617228.

Web Resources

Useful Links

QACITY

An online resource on Web testing and other testing-related subjects, hosted by Hung Q. Nguyen and LogiGear Corporation. www.qacity.com.

Amjad Alhait's BetaSoft Inc.

Hosts QA discussion forums, many QA links, and download directories for automated testing. www.betasoft.com.

Bret Pettichord's Software Testing Hotlist

A well-organized page offering links to several interesting papers on test automation, testing-related white papers, and other useful information. www.io.com/~wazmo/qa.html.

Brian Marick's Testing Foundations

A thorough site with lists and descriptions of tools, contractors, training courses, papers, and essays from Brian Marick, the author of *The Craft of Software Testing*. www.testing.com.

Cem Kaner's Web Site

Kaner's site has information on software testing, software quality, and his own work. It includes several of Cem's papers on quality, software testing, outsourcing, technical support, and contracts. www.kaner.com.

Elisabeth Hendrickson's Quality Tree Web Site

Offers various papers on automated testing and useful QA-related links. www.qualitytree.com.

James Bach's Web Site

Offers various useful presentations and articles on software testing. www.satisfice.com.

Kerry Zallar's Software Testing Resources

Includes numerous links and information about test automation. www.testingstuff.com.

Rick Hower's Software QA/Test Resource Center

A software-testing and QA-related site that offers a collection of QA FAQs, plus useful links to QA/testing organizations and tool vendors. www.softwareqatest.com.

Software-Engineer.org

A community of software engineers dedicated to free information sharing between software engineers (i.e., industrials, faculty members, and students). This is a very useful site. www.software-engineer.org.

STORM

Software Testing Online Resources, STORM, is hosted by Middle Tennessee State University. A well-organized site with links to many software testing and QA sites, including directories of software testers, consultants, and software testing consulting companies. www.mtsu.edu/~storm/.

Center for Software Development

Established in 1993, the Center for Software Development provides the key resources that software developers need to start and grow the next generation of successful technology companies. www.center.org/.

Software Productivity Center

Methodology, training, and research center that supports software development in the Vancouver, British Columbia, area. The SPC is a member-driven technical resource center that caters to day-to-day problems faced by software development companies. www.spc.ca/.

Centre for Software Engineering

The Centre for Software Engineering is committed to raising the standards of quality and productivity within the software development community, both in Ireland and internationally. www.cse.dcu.ie/.

European Software Institute

An industry organization founded by leading European companies to improve the competitiveness of the European software industry. Particularly interesting for information about the Euromethod contracted-software life cycle and related documents. www.esi.es/.

Software Testing Institute

A membership-funded institute that promotes professionalism in the software test industry. Includes links to industry resources, including quality publications, industry research, and online services (Online STI Resource Guide). www.softwaretestinginstitute.com.

Software QA/Test Resource Center, Rick Hower

This page offers a good collection of links to various software engineering and Web testing tools. www.softwareqatest.com/qatweb1.html.

StickyMinds.Com—Software Testing Area | Web Testing Zone, Software Quality Engineering

This is my favorite place to go for my Web testing online research. This site contains several dozen good articles on topics related to testing Web applications. www.stickyminds.com.

Anybrowser.org

Organization that advocates a nonbrowser-specific World Wide Web. www.anybrowser.org.

Carnegie Mellon University's SEI Software Technology Review

Contains papers on many Web-related software technologies. www.sei.cmu.edu/str/.

Counterpane Internet Security, Inc.

Information on Web security and other security-related issues. www.counterpane.com/about.html.

Cookie Central

A site dedicated to information about cookies. www.cookiecentral.com.

CNET's "BROWSERS.COM"

Information, resources, and download page for browsers. www.browsers.com.

E-Business Testing—Parts 1 and 2, Paul Gerrard

Two well-written papers that thoroughly discuss testing issues and strategies, including techniques for testing Web-based applications. www.evolutif.co.uk/articles/EBTestingPart1.pdf and www.evolutif .co.uk/articles/EBTestingPart2.pdf.

Find Out How Stuff Works

This site contains a wide range of useful explanation of technical concepts that may help you better understand the technology employed by the product you are testing. www.howstuffworks.com.

HTML Goodies Browser List

A comprehensive site that lists the entire gamut of Web browser information. The site also features primers and tutorials for HTML, CGI/Perl,

XML, ASP, and more. www.htmlgoodies.com/directories/dir.html
.tools.browser.html.

InfoSysSec

A comprehensive computer and network security resource that includes
the latest on security alerts. www.infosyssec.com.

InstallSite.Org

Created for InstallShield developers, this site is an excellent resource for
staying current with installation technology, testing issues, tips, and
tools. www.installsite.org.

Internet.com's Internet Technology Channel

A portal page that offers links to other information portals on Internet
technologies, including browsers, servers, database, hardware, and
software. www.internet.com/sections/it.html.

Microsoft USA Presentations

Microsoft-specific presentation materials associated with its past technical events, offering great overviews on various topics, including Windows
platform, security, performance, and scalability. www.microsoft.com/
usa/presentations/ms.asp.

MSDN

Microsoft's online resource for developers. msdn.microsoft.com.

Tech Encyclopedia

A database that offers definitions for computer-related jargon.
www.techweb.com/encyclopedia.

Whatis.com

A very cool search engine that offers definitions for, and links to,
various technological terms. www.whatis.com.

ZD Net's Browser Help and How-To Page

Information regarding browser plug-ins, settings, and more.
www.zdnet.com/zdhelp/filters/subfilter/0,7212,6002396,00.html.

Web Apps Are Trojan Horses for Hackers, Mandy Andress

The author provides an overview and a thorough list defining the "holes" in a typical Web site, and where to look for them. iwsun4 .infoworld.com/articles/tc/xml/01/04/09/010409tcwebsec.xml.

webmonkey Home Page-Resource for Web Developers

Extensive how-to resource for Web technologies. hotwired.lycos.com/webmonkey/.

webmonkey Brower Reference Chart

Details on which features are supported by which versions of various browsers. hotwired.lycos.com/webmonkey/reference/ browser_chart/index.html.

Useful Magazines and Newsletters

Software Testing and Quality Engineering

www.stqemagazine.com

SD Times

www.sdtimes.com

Software Development

www.sdmagazine.com

Java Developer's Journal

www.javadevelopersjournal.com

MSDN News

msdn.microsoft.com/voices/news

Miscellaneous Papers on the Web from Carnegie Mellon University's Software Engineering Institute

Client/Server Software Architecture—An Overview

www.sei.cmu.edu/str/descriptions/clientserver.html.

Common Object Request Broker Architecture (CORBA)
   www.sei.cmu.edu/str/descriptions/corba.html.

Component Object Model (COM), DCOM, and Related Capabilities
   www.sei.cmu.edu/str/descriptions/com.html.

Computer System Security—An Overview
   www.sei.cmu.edu/str/descriptions/security.html.

Firewalls and Proxies
   www.sei.cmu.edu/str/descriptions/firewalls.html.

Java
   www.sei.cmu.edu/str/descriptions/java.html.

MiddleWare
   www.sei.cmu.edu/str/descriptions/middleware.html.

Multi-Level Secure Database Management Schemes
   www.sei.cmu.edu/str/descriptions/mlsdms.html.

Object-Request Broker
   www.sei.cmu.edu/str/descriptions/orb.html.

Software Inspections
   www.sei.cmu.edu/str/descriptions/inspections.html.

Three-Tier Software Architecture
   www.sei.cmu.edu/str/descriptions/threetier.html.

Two-Tier Software Architecture
   www.sei.cmu.edu/str/descriptions/twotier.html.

COTS and Open Systems—An Overview
   Explains the decisions involved in choosing off-the-shelf software
   products.
   www.sei.cmu.edu/str/descriptions/cots.html#110707.

Professional Societies

American Society for Quality (ASQ)

The ASQ is a society of both individual and organizational members that is dedicated to the ongoing development of quality concepts, principles, and techniques. The ASQ was founded in 1946 to enable local quality societies in the United States to share information about statistical quality control, in an effort to improve the quality of defense materials. The ASQ has since grown to more than 130,000 individual and 1,000 organizational members. Most of the quality methods now used throughout the world—including statistical process control, quality cost measurement, total quality management, and zero defects—were initiated by ASQ members.

This site describes the organization and its activities. It offers information on quality standards, certification programs (including Certified Software Quality Engineer and Certified Quality Engineers), and a useful ASQuality Glossary of Terms search engine. www.asq.org.

Special Interest Group in Software Testing (SIGIST)

Testing branch of the British Computer Society (BCS). www.bcs.org.uk/sigist/index.html.

American National Standards Institute (ANSI)

A voluntary, nonprofit organization of U.S. business and industry groups formed in 1918 for the development of trade and communications standards. ANSI is the American representative of the International Standards Organization. It has developed recommendations for the use of programming languages, including FORTRAN, C, and COBOL. www.ansi.org.

The Institute of Electrical and Electronics Engineers (IEEE)

The Institute of Electrical and Electronics Engineers (IEEE) is the world's largest technical professional society. Founded in 1884 by a handful of practitioners of the new electrical engineering discipline, today's institute comprises more than 320,000 members who conduct and participate in activities around the world. www.ieee.org.

International Organization for Standardization (ISO)

Describes the International Organization for Standardization (ISO), with links to other standards organizations. www.iso.ch/.

National Standards Systems Network (NSSN)

Describes the National Standards Systems Network, with lots of links to standards providers, developers, and sellers. www.nssn.org.

Society for Technical Communication (STC)

The STC's diverse membership includes writers, editors, illustrators, printers, publishers, educators, students, engineers, and scientists who are employed in a variety of technological fields. STC is the largest professional organization serving the technical communication profession. This site (www.stc.org) provides many links to research materials on documentation process and quality, including:

- Links to technical communication conferences
- Links to STC special-interest groups
- Links to technical communication seminars
- Links to educational technical communication-related resources, from indexing to online help to usability

APPENDIX

A

LogiGear Test Plan Template

LG-WI-TPT-HQN-0-01-080500

Date

Copyright © 2003, LogiGear Corporation

All Rights Reserved

W.650.572.1400

F.650.572.2822

E-mail: info@logigear.com

www.logigear.com

Contents

Product Name

Test Plan

Author Name Version 1.0

I. Overview

1. Test Plan Identifier

[LG]-[client's init]-[project's init]-[author's init]-[phase#][serial#]-[dist. date]

  Example:

LG-WI-TPT-HQN-0-01-080500

LG	LogiGear Corporation
WI	Widget Inc.
TPT	Test Plan Template project
HQN	Hung Q. Nguyen
0	0 = Development Phase; 1 = Final Phase
01	The first distributed draft
080500	Distributed date: August 5, 2002

2. Introduction

An introduction of the overall project.

3. Objective

What we strive to accomplish, taking the following factors into account: quality, schedule, and cost.

4. Approach

The overall testing strategy to satisfy the testing objectives.

II. Testing Synopsis

1. Test Items

Deliverable products or applications to be tested.

1.1. Software Application Items

1.1.1. Main Application Executables

1.1.2. Installer/Uninstaller

1.1.3. Utilities/Tool Kits

1.1.4. Online Help

1.2. Software Collateral Items

1.2.1. Font

1.2.2. Clip Art

1.2.3. Related Multimedia Items

1.2.4. Sample/Tutorial

1.2.5. Readme

1.2.6. Others

1.3. Publishing Items

1.3.1. Reference/User Guide

1.3.2. CD/Disk Label

1.3.3. Packaging

1.3.4. Marketing/Product Fact Sheet/Advertising Blurb

2. Features to Be Tested

List of features to be tested. The list may include the environment to be tested under.

3. Features Not to Be Tested

List of features that will not be covered in this test plan.

4. System Requirements

SERVER HARDWARE AND SOFTWARE CONFIGURATION REQUIREMENTS

- Pentium PC (Pentium II or higher recommended)
- 128 Mb RAM
- 100 Mb of free disk space

- Windows 2000 Server
- Microsoft Internet Information Server 4.0 or higher
- Microsoft SQL Server 7.0 with Service Pack

CLIENT REQUIREMENTS

- An active LAN or Internet connection
- Microsoft Internet Explorer 4.x or higher
- Netscape Navigator 4.x

MICROSOFT INTERNET INFORMATION SERVER

- Microsoft IIS 5 is bundled as part of the Windows 2000 Server and Windows 2000 Advanced Server Operating Systems.
- Microsoft IIS 4 is available, free of charge, as part of the Windows NT 4.0 Option Pack.

DATABASE SUPPORT

- Microsoft SQL Server 7.0

SUPPORTED BROWSERS

- Supports clients using Microsoft Internet Explorer 4.x or higher, or Netscape Navigator 4.x on any hardware platform.

  [The software and hardware requirements to run the application. Normally, this information is found in the product specification or user manual. See the preceding example.]

5. Product Entrance/Exit

Describe the milestone/acceptance criteria.

6. Standard/Reference

- IEEE Standard for Software Test Documentation (ANSI/IEEE std 829-1983)
- Cem Kaner et al. *Testing Computer Software*, 2nd ed. New York: John Wiley, & Sons, Inc., 1993
- LogiGear Corporation Test Plan Template
- XXXX 3.0 Test Matrix

  [List of any standards, references used in the creation of this test plan. See the preceding example.]

7. Test Deliverables

List of test materials developed by the test group during the test cycle to be delivered upon the completion of this project.

7.1. Test Plan

7.1.1. The Original Approved Development Test Plan

Essentially, this complete document with appropriate approvals.

7.1.2. The Executed Development Test Plan

Test-case tables, matrices, and other test-related materials (as part of this test plan) with appropriate check-marking as verification of test completion.

7.1.3. The Original Approved Final Test Plan

Usually, the final test plan is a scaled-down version of the development test plan. This plan is produced and used in the final testing cycle. Appropriate approvals should also be included.

7.1.4. The Executed Final Test Plan

Test-case tables, matrices, and other test-related materials (as part of the final test plan) with appropriate check-marking as verification of test completion.

7.2. Bug-Tracking System

7.2.1. Bug Reports

- Summary list of all bugs found
- Full description copies of all bugs found

7.2.2. Bug Database

A soft copy of the bugbase containing all bugs found during the testing cycles, including paper-form reports.

7.3. Final Release Report

The Final Release Report should be submitted prior to the release of this project. This report is a quality assessment document that describes the scope of the testing project, testing completeness, test results focused primarily on the areas of concern, and release recommendation (for or against).

III. Testing Project Management

1. The Product Team

List of product team members and their roles.

2. Testing Responsibilities

Who will lead up the testing efforts? Other people resources and responsibilities.

3. Testing Tasks

- Develop test plans, including test cases, matrices, schedule, and so on.
- Conduct test-plan reviews and obtain appropriate approvals.
- Procure hardware/software/tools required.
- Create bug database.
- Perform tests.
- Report bugs.
- Conduct bug deferral meeting.
- Produce weekly status report.
- Produce final release report.

4. Development Plan and Schedule

What is to be delivered for testing? Schedule: when the preceding items will be delivered.

5. Milestone Entrance/Exit Criteria

Milestone definitions, descriptions, and measurable criteria.

6. Test Schedule and Resource

6.1. Schedule

Testing task grouping: list of task groups and their descriptions. Preliminary schedule matched with resource needs and test tasks.

6.2. Resource Estimate

Estimates of people resources required for completing the project.

7. Training Needs

Identify training needs.

8. Environmental Needs

8.1. Test Components

List of all software and hardware resources needed to complete the project. Resources availability and strategies to acquire them.

- Hardware
- Software
- Online account

8.2. Test Tools

- Off-the-shelf tools
- In-house tools
- Tools to be developed

8.3. Facilities

All testing will be done at [Company Name's] lab. If there is need to outsource some of the testing tasks, we'll update this plan accordingly.

9. Integration Plan

Is there an integration plan? If yes, how it would fit in the testing strategy?

10. Test Suspension and Resumption

When should testing be suspended? When should a suspended testing process be resumed?

11. Test Completion Criteria

When should testing stop?

12. The Problem-Tracking Process

12.1. The Process

Describe the bug-tracking process.

12.2. The Bug-Tracking Tool (database)

Describe the bug-tracking tool.

12.3. Definition of Bug Severity

Bug severity is a subjective method used by reporters to grade the severity level of each report. Following are guidelines for grading bug severity.

12.3.1. 1—Critical

Severity 1—*Critical* (show-stopper) *bugs* are those that result in loss of key functionality, usability, and performance of a product in normal operation; there is no workaround solution available. These also include nonprogrammatic bugs such as an obviously embarrassing misspelling of a product or company name in the splash screen, wrong video clip in the intro screen, erroneous instructions for a frequently used feature, and so on. Following are a few sample categories:

- Crash or core dump
- Data loss or corruption
- Failure of key feature

12.3.2. 2–Serious

Severity 2—*Serious bugs* include key features that don't function under certain conditions or nonkey features that don't function at all, degradation of functionality or performance in normal operation, difficult-to-use key features, and so on. Usually, these bugs should be fixed during the normal development cycles. Only during the final testing phase, these bugs might be carefully assessed and perhaps considered defer as appropriate.

12.3.3. 3–Noncritical

Severity 3—*Noncritical bugs* are those that represent some inconvenience to the user but perhaps don't happen frequently. These include minor display/redraw problems, poorly worded error messages, minor design issues, and the like. Usually, these bugs should be fixed provided time permitting or minimum efforts required by the programming team. Keep in mind that if many Severity 3 noncritical bugs get deferred; there will be a definite quality-degradation effect to the product.

13. Status Tracking and Reporting

- In what form will the status be reported?
- What is the reporting frequency?
- What types of information will be reported?

14. Risks and Contingencies

Risks and possible adjustments to the plan.

15. The Approval Process

15.1. Test Plan Approval

How is the test plan approved?

15.2. Final Release Approval

What is the approval process for releasing the tested product?

Appendix 1: Setup/Installation Test Case

Table A1.1 Functional Test: The Installer Executable

ID	CAT.	TEST PROCEDURE	EXPECTED RESULT	P/F	COMMENTS
	N				
	P				
	N				
	P				
	P				
	P				
	S				
	N				
	P				
	N				

Table A1.2 Functional Test: XXX

ID	CAT.	TEST PROCEDURE	EXPECTED RESULT	P/F	COMMENTS
	P				
	P				
	P				
	P				
	P				
	N				
	P				
	P				
	P				

Appendix 2: Test Case for Application Shell

Table A2.1   Fast: XXX

ID	CAT.	TEST PROCEDURE	EXPECTED RESULT	P/F	COMMENTS
	P				
	N				
	P				
	N				
	P				
	P				
	P				
	P				
	P				

Table A2.2   Fast:

ID	CAT.	TEST PROCEDURE	EXPECTED RESULT	P/F	COMMENTS
	P				
	P				
	P				
	P				
	P				
	P				
	P				
	P				
	P				

(continued)

Table A2.2   *(continued)*

ID	CAT.	TEST PROCEDURE	EXPECTED RESULT	P/F	COMMENTS
	P				
	P				
	P				
	P				
	P				
	P				
	P				
	P				
	P				

Appendix 3: Test Matrix for XXXXX

Table A3.1   Task-Oriented Functional Test

ID	CAT.	TEST PROCEDURE	EXPECTED RESULT	P/F	COMMENTS
	P				
	P				
	P				
	P				
	P				
	P				
	P				
	P				
	P				
	P				
	P				
	P				

Table A3.1   *(continued)*

ID	CAT.	TEST PROCEDURE	EXPECTED RESULT	P/F	COMMENTS
	P				
	P				
	P				
	P				
	P				
	P				

Appendix 4: Compatibility Test Systems

- Acer Altos 330 Intel Pentium II Processor, 300MHz, 512KB, 4.3GB Ultra-wide 64MB ECC SDRAM 32X

- Compaq Proliant 1600R Intel Pentium III Processor, 550MHz, 128MB RAM

- Hewlett-Packard 9780C Minitower, AMD Athlon Processor 900MHz, 128MB RAM, 60 GIG Hard Drive, DVD, CD-ROM

- Hewlett-Packard Netserver LH4 Intel Pentium III Processor, 550MHz, 512K

- IBM 300GL P3 733, 128MB, 20.4GB, 48X, SDRAM, 32MB, AGP4 256KB NT

- IBM 300PL P3 733, 20.4GB, 128MB, 48X, 16MB ENET SND 98 256KB

Weekly Status Report Template

Product Name Status Report
Report No. 23
Week Ending Month XX, 200X

Author
Month XX, 200X

I. Testing Project Management

1. Project Schedule*

DEVELOPMENT MILESTONE	DATE	TESTING MILESTONE*	DATE
Prealpha	xx/xx/xx	Test plan first draft delivered	xx/xx/xx
		Test plan second draft delivered	xx/xx/xx
		Test plan completed/ approved	xx/xx/xx
Alpha	xx/xx/xx	Begin alpha test phase	xx/xx/xx
Beta	xx/xx/xx	Begin beta test phase	xx/xx/xx
Release candidate	xx/xx/xx	Begin final test phase**	xx/xx/xx
Golden master	xx/xx/xx	Testing Completed	xx/xx/xx

Italicized milestones are completed milestones.
*Also see the detail test schedule in the test plan.
**Assuming the release candidate is accepted.

2. Progress and Changes Since Last Week

- Completed install/uninstall tests.
- Completed configuration/compatibility tests.
- Regressed all outstanding fixed bugs.
- Completed testing the online help system.
- Reported 16 new bugs.

3. Urgent Items

- LogiGear Testing group still has not received the xxxxx and xxxxx to be included with the product. The missing items might cause a schedule delay of the release candidate.
- It has been three weeks and the majority of memory bugs are still unfixed. This is a very high-risk issue. This might cause a delay in the shipping schedule.

4. Issue Bin

Nonurgent issues to be addressed in the next week or so park here.

5. To-do Tasks by Next Report

- Complete regressing all fixed bugs.
- Deliver final test plan for review and approval.
- Review executed test plans to verify testing completeness.
- Complete all procedures in preparation of final testing phase.
- Perform acceptance test for the release candidate.

II. Problem Report Status

1. Bug Report Tabulation

	LAST WEEK	THIS WEEK
Bugs found and reported	15	9

Bugs found this week = Total bugs this week – Total bugs last week

STATUS	LAST WEEK	THIS WEEK
New	15	9
Open	183	149
Total new and open	198	158
Resolved	65	98
Closed	252	275
Total resolved and closed	317	373
Grand Total	515	531

2. Summary List of Open Bugs

Summary lines of open bug reports.

III. Trend Analysis Report

Stability Trend Chart

This line chart Figure B.1 shows the curves of the total number of bug reports and its breakdowns in term of [open + new] and [closed + resolved] status. As the [closed + resolved] curve rises and the [open + new] curve drops, they will eventually intersect. This intersection indicates the beginning of the *maturity phase*. Ultimately, at the time the product is ready for release, the [closed + resolved] curve will meet the Total Bug Reports curve and the [open + new] curve will drop to zero. Observing the progressing trend from the beginning of the *maturity point* onward will give you reasonable predictability of the schedule.

For definitions of *open, new, closed,* and *resolved,* see the section entitled "Problem Report Status."

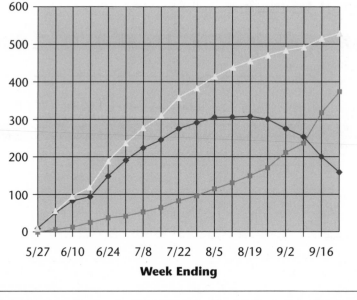

Figure B.1   Stability Trend Chart.

Quality Trend Chart

Valid bugs may be resolved by either fixing or deferring them. A high number of closed (fixed) bugs and a low number of deferred bugs indicate that the quality level is high. The Quality Trend Chart (shown in Figure B.2) includes the cumulative curves of Total Bug Reports, [closed + resolved] bugs, closed (fixed), and deferred bugs. Similar to the Stability Trend Chart, [closed + resolved] and Total Bug Reports curves in this chart will eventually intersect when the product is ready for release. Observing the progressive trend of the fixed and deferred curves relative to the closed curve will give you reasonable quality interpretation of the tested product.

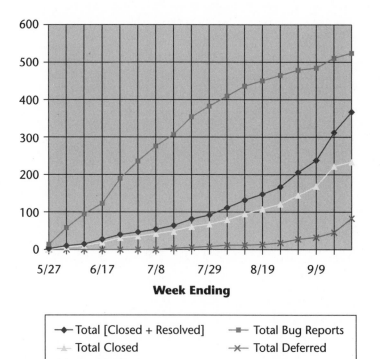

Figure B.2   Quality Trend Chart.

APPENDIX

C

Error Analysis Checklist: Web Error Examples

Check for the Existence of DNS Entry

Symptoms

No response when clicking on certain links. This only happens when you are outside of the intranet.

Possible Problems

This symptom may be caused by a number of problems. The most common is that the server cannot be found due to a missing DNS entry rather than coding error.

Examples

When you are outside of the intranet and click on the QA Training or TRACK-GEAR button in the page illustrated in Figure C.1, the browser appears to hang or you don't get any response from the server. However, when you report the problem, your developer who accesses the same links could not reproduce it.

One of the possible problems is the DNS entry for the server in the links is only available in the DNS server on the intranet and is not known to the outside world.

Tips

1. Use the View Source menu command to inspect the HTML source.

2. Look for the information that's relevant to the links.

In this example, you will find that clicking on the QA Training and the TRACKGEAR button will result in requests to the server named "authorize" in the qacity.com domain.

```
...
<td>
<map name=01b238de91a99ed9>
<area shape=rect coords="0,0,88,20"
href=https://authorize.qacity.com/training-login.asp?>
<area shape=rect coords="0,20,88,40"
href=https://authorize.qacity.com/trackgear-login.asp?>
...
...
</td>
...
```

3. Try to ping authorize.qacity.com to see if it can be pinged.

4. If the server cannot be pinged, tell your developer or IS staff so the problem can be resolved.

Figure C.1   Nonresponding browser window.

Check for Proper Configuration of the Client Machine and Browser Settings

Symptoms

Cannot get response from a server after entering a URL.

Possible Problems

This symptom may be caused by a number of problems. The two most common problems are:

1. The client machine is not properly configured to connect to the network.

2. One or more browser settings are not properly configured.

Examples

- Your machine is not connected to the network. Therefore, there is no TCP/IP connection for your browser to be served.

- Your browser is configured to use proxy server. However, the address of the proxy server in your browser settings is invalid (see Figure C.2) or the proxy server is not accessible. Therefore, the browser can't be served.

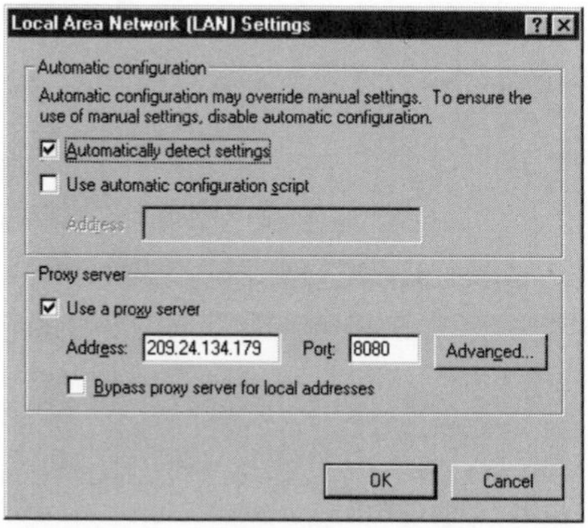

Figure C.2   Configure LAN window.

Tips

To check your network connection on a Windows machine:

- Run IPCONFIG or WINIPCFG to obtain the default gateway IP and the default DNS IP address.

- Ping the default gateway machine to ensure that your machine is properly connected with it.

- Ping the DNS server to see if it can be found from your machine.

- Ping one of the known servers on the Internet to ensure that your machine can access a server outside of your LAN.

To check your browser settings to ensure accessibility:

- Pick a couple of intranet pages on a remote server and try to access those pages to test your browser accessibility within the LAN.

- Pick a couple of popular nonrestricted Web sites and go there when you need to test your browser accessibility. Two you can try are www.cnn.com and www.cnet.com.

- Identify if the proxy server is used. If yes, try to ping the proxy server to ensure it can be found.

- Check the security settings to ensure that the site you are trying to get to is not part of the restricted sites.

Check the HTTP Settings on the Browser

Symptoms

Cannot connect to certain Web servers.

Possible Problems

This symptom may be caused by a number of problems. One possible issue is the browser is having difficulties connecting to a server that can only support HTTP 1.0 through proxy server.

Examples

If your Web server only supports HTTP 1.0 by using proxy server, and your browser is configured to only use HTTP 1.1, the communication between the browser and the Web server will not work. See Figure C.3.

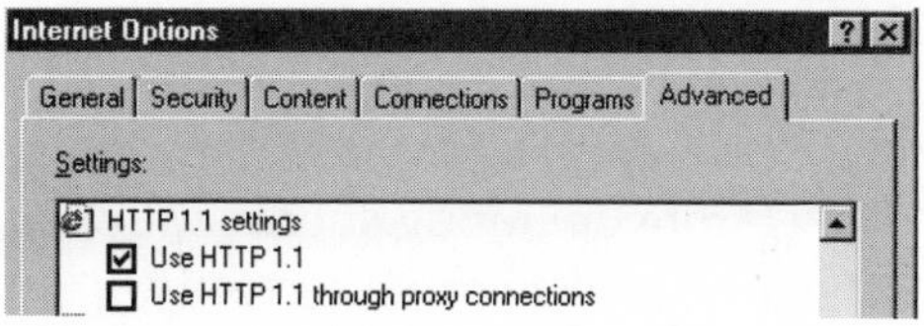

Figure C.3   Configure HTTP settings tab.

Tips

- Try to connect to the server with the HTTP 1.1 boxes cleared to see if the problem reoccurs.
- Verify that server can support HTTP 1.1.

Check the JIT Compiler-Enabled Setting on the Browser

Symptoms

Java applet works properly on one browser but not on another, although both browsers are on the same platform, produced by the same vendor, and their release versions are identical.

Possible Problems

This symptom may be caused by a number of problems. One possible issue is that the Java JIT (Just-in-Time) compiler enable option is checked. See Figure C.4.

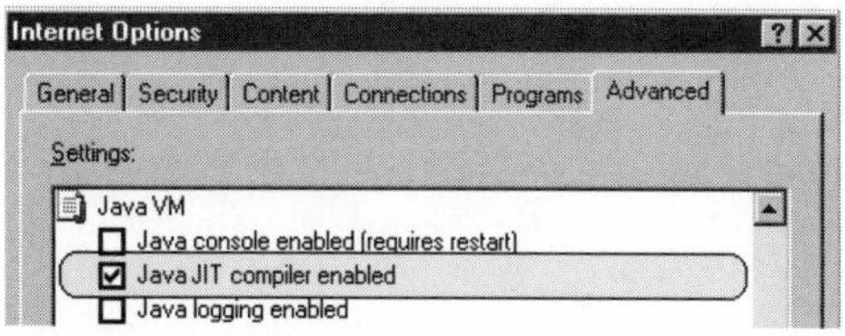

Figure C.4   Configure Java VM settings tab.

Examples

If a Java JIT compiler is incompatible with a Java applet, having the compiler setting turned on may prevent the Java applet from operating successfully. On the browser that has this option cleared, the Java applet works correctly.

Tip

Before reporting an error, check the Java JIT compiler setting on both browsers to see if they are different.

Check the Multimedia Settings on the Browser

Symptoms

Unable to play animations, sounds, and videos, or display pictures properly on one browser, but able to do so on another, although both browsers are on the same platform, produced by the same vendor, and their release versions are identical.

Possible Problems

This symptom may be caused by a number of problems. The most common problem is that the multimedia options are not checked to enable multimedia contents to be played in the browser.

Examples

If the "Show pictures" check box is cleared, as illustrated in Figure C.5, the graphics will not display in the browser as shown in the next screenshot.

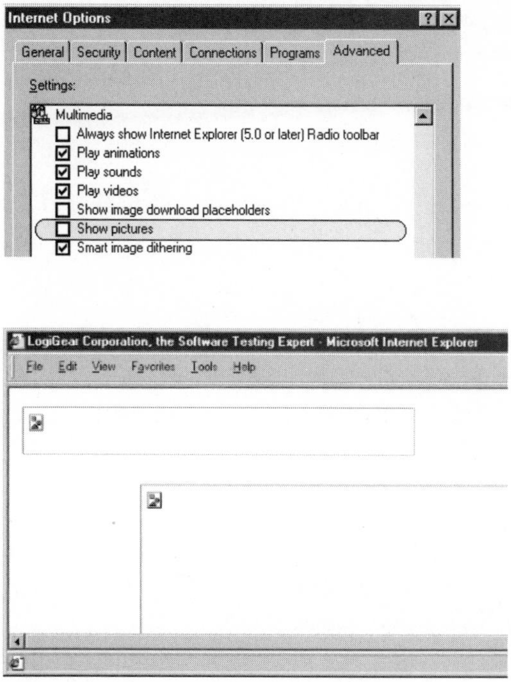

Figure C.5   Web page display error due to Multimedia settings.

Tip

Before filing a bug report related to the execution or display of multimedia contents, check the multimedia settings to see if they are properly enabled.

Check the Security Settings on the Browser

Symptoms

Unable to process purchase transactions or connect in secured mode (HTTPS).

Possible Problems

This symptom may be caused by a number of problems. One common issue is that the supported version of the security protocol by the server is not enabled on the server-side.

Examples

If your server only supports encryption through SSL 2.0 protocol, but the SSL 2.0 security on the browser-side is cleared, the browser will not be able to connect to the Web server through HTTPS. See Figure C.6.

Tip

Before filing a bug report related to public/private encryption, check the security options to ensure that they are configured properly.

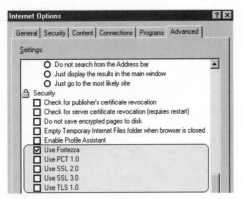

Figure C.6   Configure Security settings tab.

Check for a Slow Connection

Symptoms

Login fails to authenticate with certain types of connection.

Possible Problems

This symptom may be caused by a number of problems. One common issue is that you might have a slow connection that causes a time-out in the login or authentication process.

Examples

With certain types of connections, such as dial-up, it may take too long (longer than the script time-out value) for the client-server to send/receive packets of data, the script will eventually time-out, causing the login or authentication process to fail. The problem could not be reproduced when your developer tries to do so on an intranet or a LAN connection.

Tips

- Use an alternate dial-up configuration (RAS, a different ISP, or a different modem) with the same bandwidth to see if the problem is reproducible. This process helps you eliminate the configuration dependency (other than a slow connection) theory.

- Connect with a slower connection to see if the problem reproduces. If yes, then the slow connection theory can be further validated.

- Connect with a faster connection to see if the problem reproduces. If not, then the slow connection theory can be further validated.

Check for Proper Configuration on the Web Server

Symptoms

Unable to access certain pages (on certain servers).

Possible Problems

This symptom may be caused by a number of reasons. One of the possible issues is the application server has not been configured to allow running scripts or executables.

Examples

When you click on certain links or buttons on a Web page from your "TEST" server, you get the error message shown in Figure C.7. When your developer tries the same links or buttons on another server, such as the "DEVELOP-MENT" server, the problem does not reproduce. On an IIS server, this may mean that the "TEST" server is not configured to allow running scripts or executables. For example, the screenshot in Figure C.8a shows the Execute Permissions setting on the "TEST" server for myApp configured to None, and the next screenshot (Figure C.8b) shows the Execute Permissions setting on the "DEVELOPMENT" server configured to Scripts and Executables.

Tips

- Identify the server names by examining the URL or the HTML source.
- Once the servers are identified, examine the settings on both servers to identify any discrepancies.

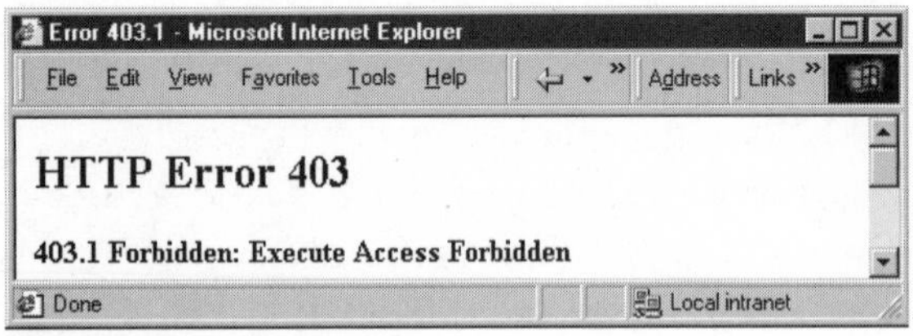

Figure C.7   Browser Error.

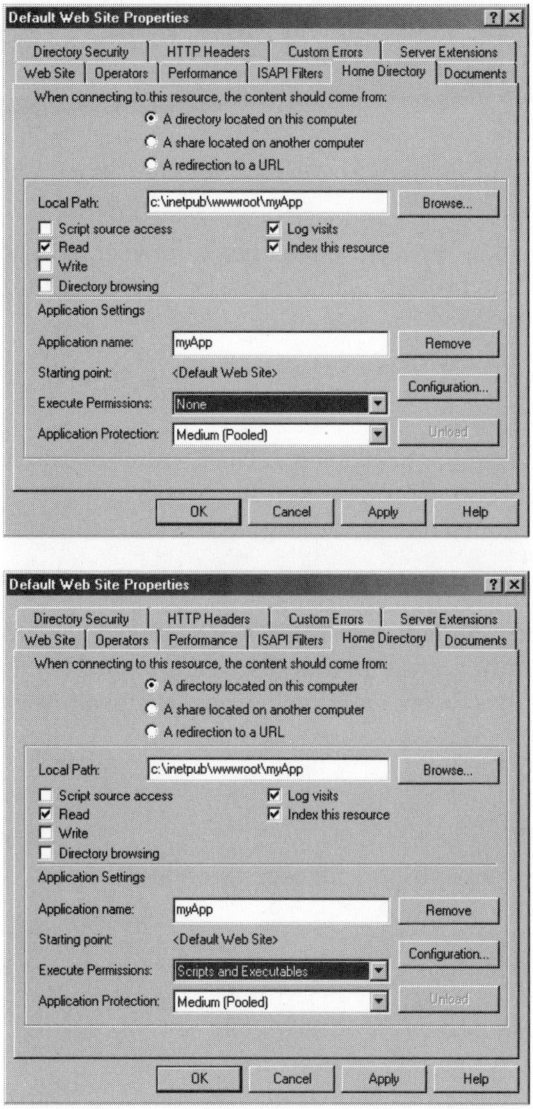

Figure C.8   (a,b) Web Site Properties settings.

NOTE Is this a software error? It depends. If the documentation instructs the system administrator to configure the Web server properly but it was not done, then it's a user error, not a software error. On the other hand, if the installer is supposed to configure the Web server programmatically but failed to do so, then it's a software error.

Check for the Deletion of Your Browser Cache (Temporary Internet Files)

Symptoms

The recent fixed bug appears to be fixed on your developer's browser but not on yours, although both browsers are from the same publisher with identical release versions.

Possible Problems

This symptom may be caused by a number of problems. The possible reason is that the data is still cached memory on the browser-side.

Examples

You report a bug. Your developer immediately fixed it and asked you to regression-test the fix. You execute the test script and discover the problem is still not fixed, although the fix has been validated on your developer's browser.

Tip

Delete your browser cache and try reexecuting your regression test.

APPENDIX

D

UI Test-Case Design Guideline: Common Keyboard Navigation and Shortcut Matrix

UI Test-Case Design Guideline: Common Keyboard Navigation and Shortcut Matrix

Modifier Key	Left Arrow	Right Arrow	Up Arrow	Down Arrow	Home	End	Page Up	Page Down	Tab	Tab	Tab	Left Arrow	Right Arrow	Up Arrow	Down Arrow	Home	End	Page Up	Page Down	C	O	P	S	V	X	Z	ESC	ESC	ESC
None	◆	◆	◆	◆	◆	◆	◆	◆	◆																		◆		
Shift										◆		◆	◆	◆	◆	◆	◆	◆	◆										
Ctrl											◆									◆	◆	◆	◆	◆	◆	◆		◆	
Alt												◆																	◆

Page/Dialog/
Java applet/
ActiveX/
UI elements

(remaining rows of matrix are blank for test-case entry)

UI Test-Case Design Guideline:
Mouse Action Matrix

UI Test-Case Design Guideline: Mouse Action Matrix

Mouse Actions	Pointing	Pressing (mouse-over)	Dragging	Clicking	Double-clicking	Pressing	Dragging	Clicking	Double-clicking	Pointing	Pressing	Dragging	Clicking	Double-clicking	Pressing	Dragging	Clicking	Double-clicking	Pointing	Pressing	Dragging	Clicking	Double-clicking	Pressing	Dragging	Clicking	Double-clicking	Mouse Action Invalid Cases	Mouse Action Invalid Cases	Mouse Action Invalid Cases
Mouse Button 1	◆	◆	◆	◆	◆					◆	◆	◆	◆	◆					◆	◆	◆	◆	◆							
Mouse Button 2						◆	◆	◆	◆						◆	◆	◆	◆						◆	◆	◆	◆			
SHIFT										◆	◆	◆	◆	◆	◆	◆	◆	◆												
CTRL																			◆	◆	◆	◆	◆	◆	◆	◆	◆			
Page/Dialog/ Java applet/ ActiveX/ UI elements																														

APPENDIX

F

Web Test-Case Design Guideline: Input Boundary and Validation Matrix I

Additional Instructions:

	Type in each of the entry fields, one at a time	Illegal characters for SQL	\ Back slash	/ Slash	: Colon	* Asterisk	? Question mark	> Greater	< Less Than		Pipe	Other interesting characters	!~"'.#$%&;'()+-=`@[]^	Additional invalid cases										
Web Page Text Fields																						
Text boxes																						
Rich-Text boxes																						
Combo box																						
Drop-down Combo box																						
Spin box																						
Static text																						
Shortcut Key Input control																						
Examples																						
Save As dialog																						
File name																						
Schedule an activity dialog																						
Date																						
Time																						
Enter "My Record" Information																						
Company																						
Name																						
Address 1																						
Address 2																						
Address 3																						
City																						
State																						
Zip																						
Phone																						
Extension																						

Additional Instructions:

	Type in each of the entry fields, one at a time	Nothing	Valid value	At LB of value	At UB of value	At LB of value - 1	At UB of value + 1	Outside of LB of value	Outside of UB of value	0	Negative	At LB number of digits or chars	At UB number of digits or chars	Empty field (clear the default value)	Outside of UB number of digits or chars	Nondigits	Space	Nonprinting char (e.g., Ctrl+char)	Upper ASCII (128-254)	Uppercase chars	Lowercase chars	Modifiers (e.g., Ctrl, Alt, Shift-Ctrl, etc.)	Function Key (F2, F3, F4, etc.)
Web Page Text Fields																							
Text boxes																							
Rich-Text boxes																							
Combo box																							
Drop-down Combo box																							
Spin box																							
Static text																							
Shortcut Key Input control																							
Examples																							
Save As dialog																							
File name																							
Schedule an activity dialog																							
Date																							
Time																							
Enter "My Record" Information																							
Company																							
Name																							
Address 1																							
Address 2																							
Address 3																							
City																							
State																							
Zip																							
Phone																							
Extension																							

G

Display Compatibility Test Matrix

DISPLAY COMPATIBILITY TEST MATRIX
Logigear Premium Compatibility Test Lab

Client: _____
Project: _____
Version: _____

Tester: _____
Date: _____
Config ID: _____

Color Depth

Resolution	Font Size	4-bit	8-bit	16-bit	24-bit	32-bit
640x480	Small					
	Large					
	Custom					
800x600	Small					
	Large					
	Custom					
1024x768	Small					
	Large					
	Custom					
1280x1024	Small					
	Large					
	Custom					

OS

Release	95	98	ME	NT 4.0	2000	XP
Original						
Upgrade A						
OSR2 B						
OSR2.5 C						
SE						
SP1						
SP2						
SP3						
SP4						
SP5						
SP6						
SP6a						

Browsers

Navigator 3.02	IE 3.0
Navigator 3.04	IE 3.02
Communicator 4.01	IE 3.04
Communicator 4.02	IE 4.0 *
Communicator 4.04	IE 4.01 *
Communicator 4.06	IE 4.01 SP1 *
Communicator 4.07	IE 4.01 SP1a *
Communicator 4.08	IE 4.01 SP2 *
Communicator 4.5	IE 5.0 *
Communicator 4.51	IE 5.0a *
Communicator 4.6	IE 5.01 *
Communicator 4.61	IE 5.5 *
Communicator 4.72	IE 5.5 SP1 *
Communicator 4.73	IE 5.5 SP2 *
Communicator 4.75	IE 6.0 *
Communicator 6.0	IE 6.0 SP1 *
Communicator 7.0	
Netscape 4.75 MAC	IE 4.5 MAC
Netscape 6.0 MAC	IE 5.0 MAC
Netscape 7.0 MAC	IE 5.2 MAC

* Active Desktop

APPENDIX H

Browser OS Configuration Matrix

BROWSER/OS CONFIGURATION MATRIX			20020913	
BROWSERS				
Internet Explorer			Netscape	America Online
IE 3.02			NS 3.01	AOL 3.0
IE 4.0 =	ver. 4.71.1712.6		NS 3.02	AOL 4.0
IE 4.01 =	ver. 4.72.2106.8		NS 3.03	AOL 5.0
IE 4.01 SP1 :	ver. 4.72.3110		NS 3.04	AOL 6.0
IE 4.01 SP1a :	ver. 4.72.3110.8		NS 4.04	AOL 7.0
IE 4.01 SP2 =	ver. 4.72.3612.1713		NS 4.05	
IE 5.0 =	ver. 5.00.0910.1309		NS 4.06	
IE 5.0 =	ver. 5.00.2014.0216		NS 4.07	
IE 5.0 =	ver. 5.00.2014.0216IC		NS 4.08	
IE 5.0a =	ver 5.00.2314.1003		NS 4.5	
IE 5.01 =	ver. 5.00.2516.1900 (W98 SE)	56 bit	NS 4.51	
IE 5.5 Beta =	ver. 5.55.3825.1300	56 bit	NS 4.6	
IE 5.5 =	ver. 5.50.4134.0600	128 bit	NS 4.61	
IE 5.5 sp1 =	ver. 5.50.4522.1800	128 bit	NS 4.72	
IE 5.5 sp2 =	ver 5.50.4807.2300	128 bit	NS 4.73	
IE 6.0 =	ver 6.00.2426.0000	128 bit	NS 4.75	
IE 6.0 SP1 =	ver. 6.00.2800.1106	128 bit	NS 6.0	
			NS 7.0	

OS					
	day 1	day 2	day 3	day 4	day 5
W95					
W95a					
W95b					
W95c					
W98					
W98 SE					
W ME					
W NT					
W NT SP 3					
W NT SP 4					
W NT SP 5					
W NT SP 6					
W NT SP6a					
W 2000					
W 2000 sp1					
W 2000 sp2					
W XP					
W XP sp1					
MAC OS 7.6.1					
MAC OS 8.1					
MAC OS 8.5.1					
MAC OS 8.6					
MAC OS 8.6.1					
MAC OS 9.1					
MAC OS 9.2					
MAC OS 10.0.4					
MAC OS 10.1					
MAC OS 10.2					

Index